HOUSE OF M

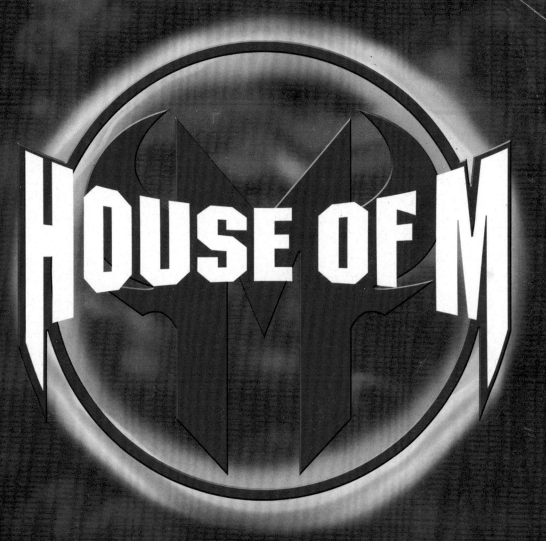

HOUSE OF M

Writer: BRIAN MICHAEL BENDIS
Penciler: OLIVIER COIPEL
Inkers: TIM TOWNSEND
with RICK MAGYAR,
SCOTT HANNA & JOHN DELL
Colorist: FRANK D'ARMATA
Letterer: CHRIS ELIOPOULOS
Cover Artist: ESAD RIBIĆ
Assistant Editors: STEPHANIE MOORE,
MOLLY LAZER & AUBREY SITTERSON
Associate Editor: ANDY SCHMIDT
Editor: TOM BREVOORT

THE PULSE:
HOUSE OF M SPECIAL EDITION

Writers: BRIAN MICHAEL BENDIS,
ED BRUBAKER,
CHRIS CLAREMONT, PETER DAVID,
NUNZIO DEFILIPPIS, DAVID HINE,
REGINALD HUDLIN,
JOHN LAYMAN, FABIAN NICIEZA,
GREG PAK, TOM PEYER,
DANIEL WAY & CHRISTINA WEIR
Art: MIKE MAYHEW
Colors: AVALON STUDIOS
Designer: PATRICK MCGRATH
Creative Director: TOM MARVELLI
Assistant Editor: AUBREY SITTERSON
Editor: ANDY SCHMIDT

Collection Editor: JENNIFER GRÜNWALD
Assistant Editor: DANIEL KIRCHHOFFER
Assistant Managing Editor: MAIA LOY
Assistant Managing Editor: LISA MONTALBANO
VP Production & Special Projects: JEFF YOUNGQUIST
Book Designer: MEGHAN KERNS
SVP Print, Sales & Marketing: DAVID GABRIEL
Editor in Chief: C.B. CEBULSKI

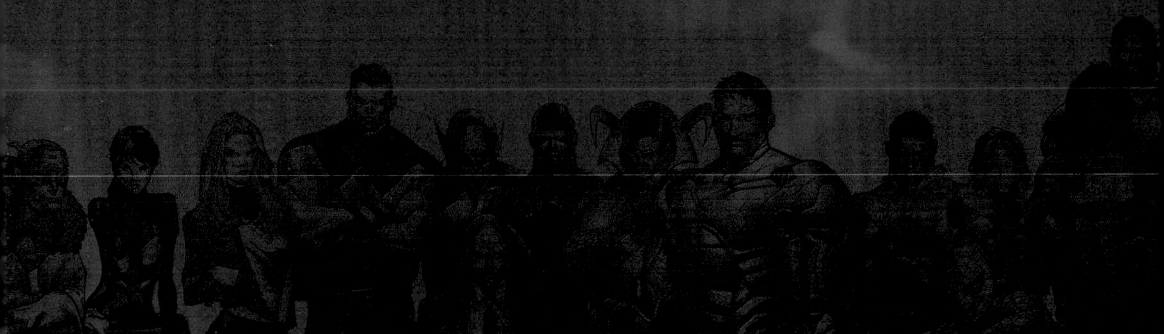

HOUSE OF M. Contains material originally published in magazine form as HOUSE OF M #1-8 and THE PULSE: HOUSE OF M SPECIAL EDITION. Eleventh printing 2021. ISBN 978-0-7851-1721-6. Published by MARVEL WORLDWIDE, INC., a subsidiary of MARVEL ENTERTAINMENT, LLC. OFFICE OF PUBLICATION: 1290 Avenue of the Americas, New York, NY 10104. © 2006 MARVEL No similarity between any of the names, character persons, and/or institutions in this magazine with those of any living or dead person or institution is intended, and any such similarity which may exist is purely coincidental. **Printed in Canada.** KEVIN FEIGE, Chi Creative Officer; DAN BUCKLEY, President, Marvel Entertainment; JOE QUESADA, EVP & Creative Director; DAVID BOGART, Associate Publisher & SVP of Talent Affairs; TOM BREVOORT, VP, Executive Editor; NICK LOW Executive Editor, VP of Content, Digital Publishing; DAVID GABRIEL, VP of Print & Digital Publishing; JEFF YOUNGQUIST, VP of Production & Special Projects; ALEX MORALES, Director of Publishing Operations; DA EDINGTON, Managing Editor; RICKEY PURDIN, Director of Talent Relations; JENNIFER GRÜNWALD, Senior Editor, Special Projects; SUSAN CRESPI, Production Manager; STAN LEE, Chairman Emeritus. For informatio regarding advertising in Marvel Comics or on Marvel.com, please contact Vit DeBellis, Custom Solutions & Integrated Advertising Manager, at vdebellis@marvel.com. For Marvel subscription inquiries, please ca 888-511-5480. **Manufactured between 2/26/2021 and 3/30/2021 by SOLISCO PRINTERS, SCOTT, QC, CANADA.**

20 19 18 17 16 15 14 13 12 11

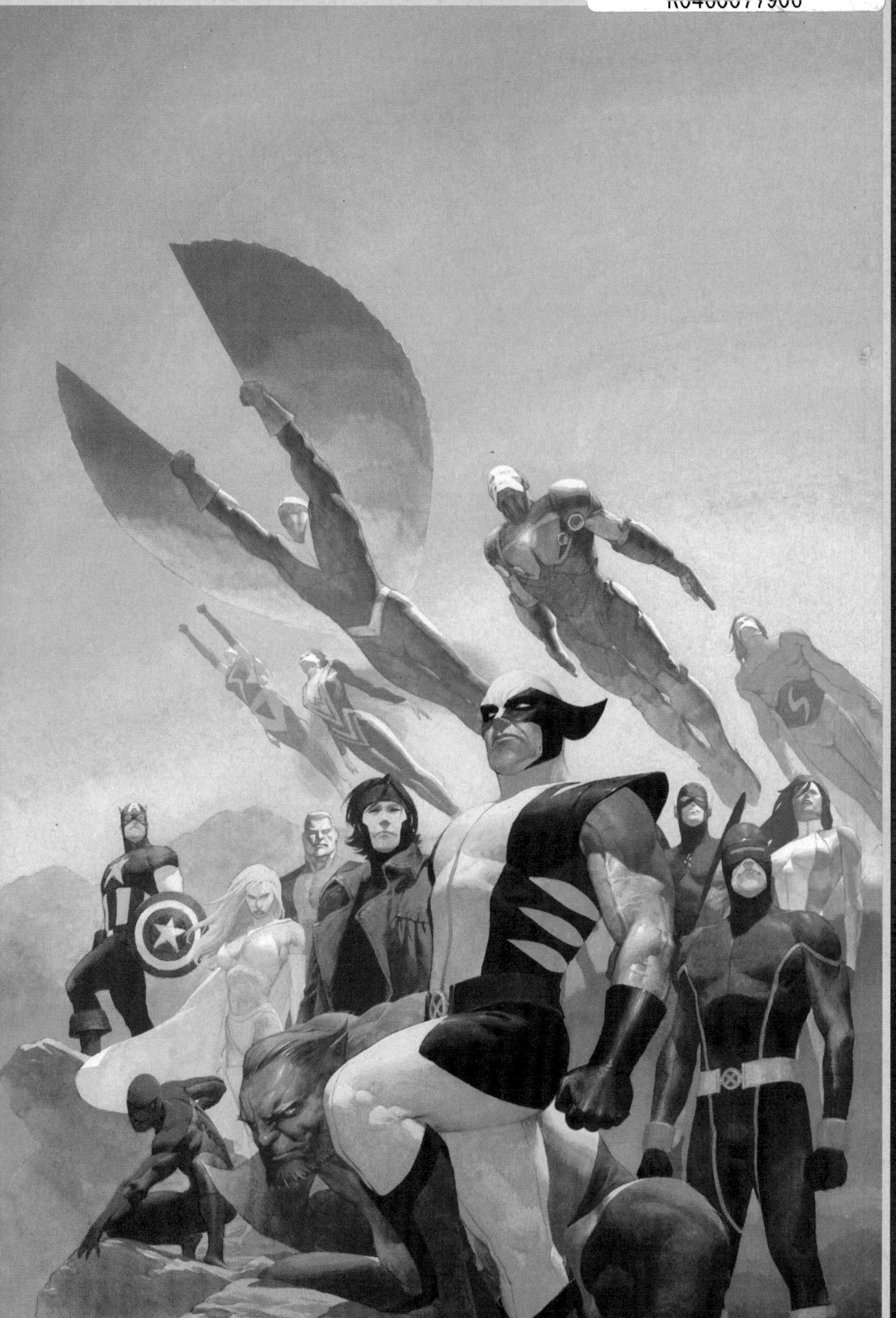

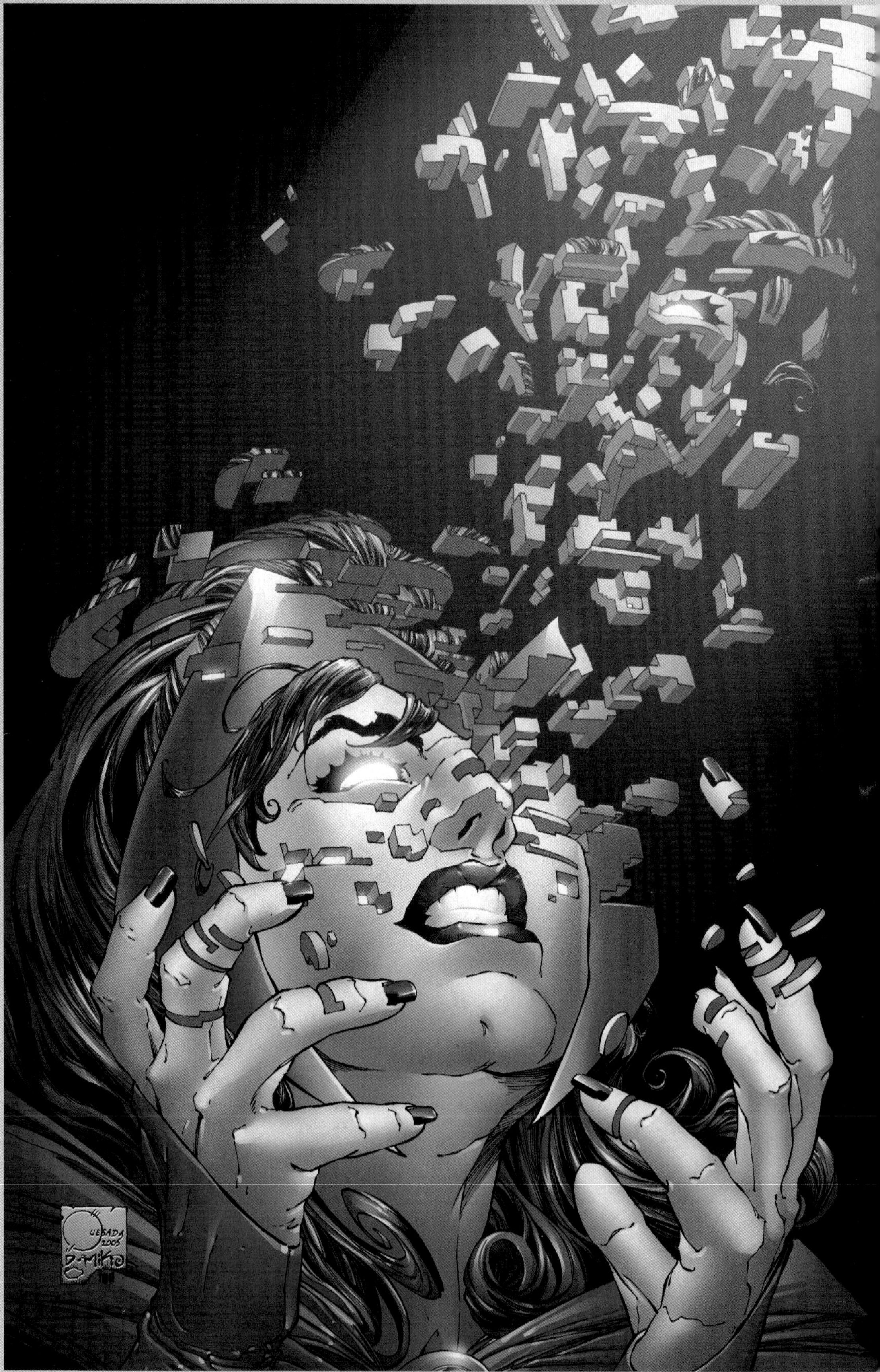

QUESADA 2005
D-MIKI

HOUSE OF M #1

Variant cover by Joe Quesada, Danny Miki & Frank D'Armata

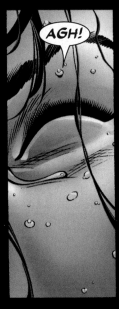

AGH!

NNN...

AARRGGH!

ALMOST THERE...

OH GOD!!!

HERE THEY COME! HERE THEY COME!!

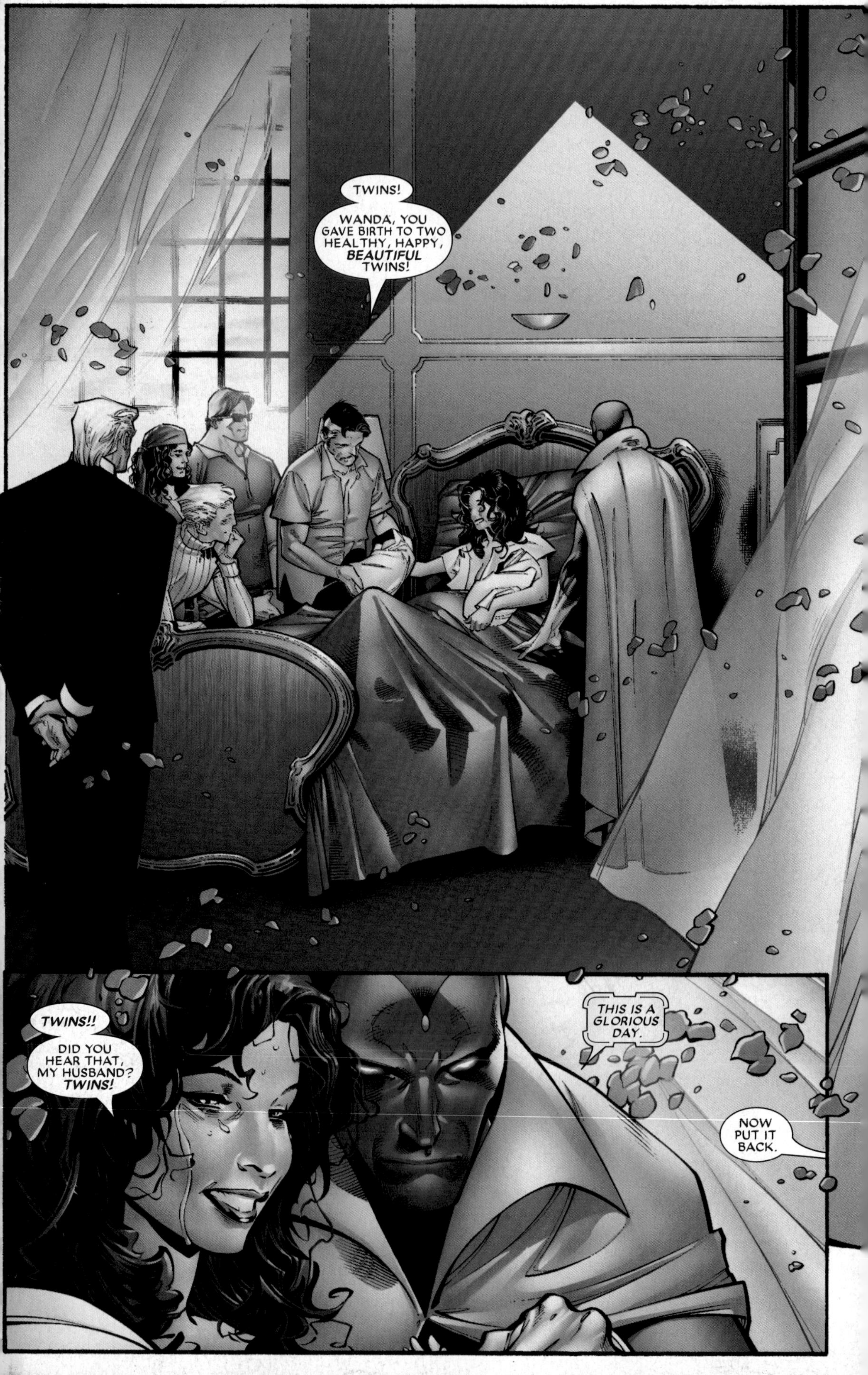
TWINS!
WANDA, YOU GAVE BIRTH TO TWO HEALTHY, HAPPY, BEAUTIFUL TWINS!
TWINS!!
DID YOU HEAR THAT, MY HUSBAND? TWINS!
THIS IS A GLORIOUS DAY.
NOW PUT IT BACK.

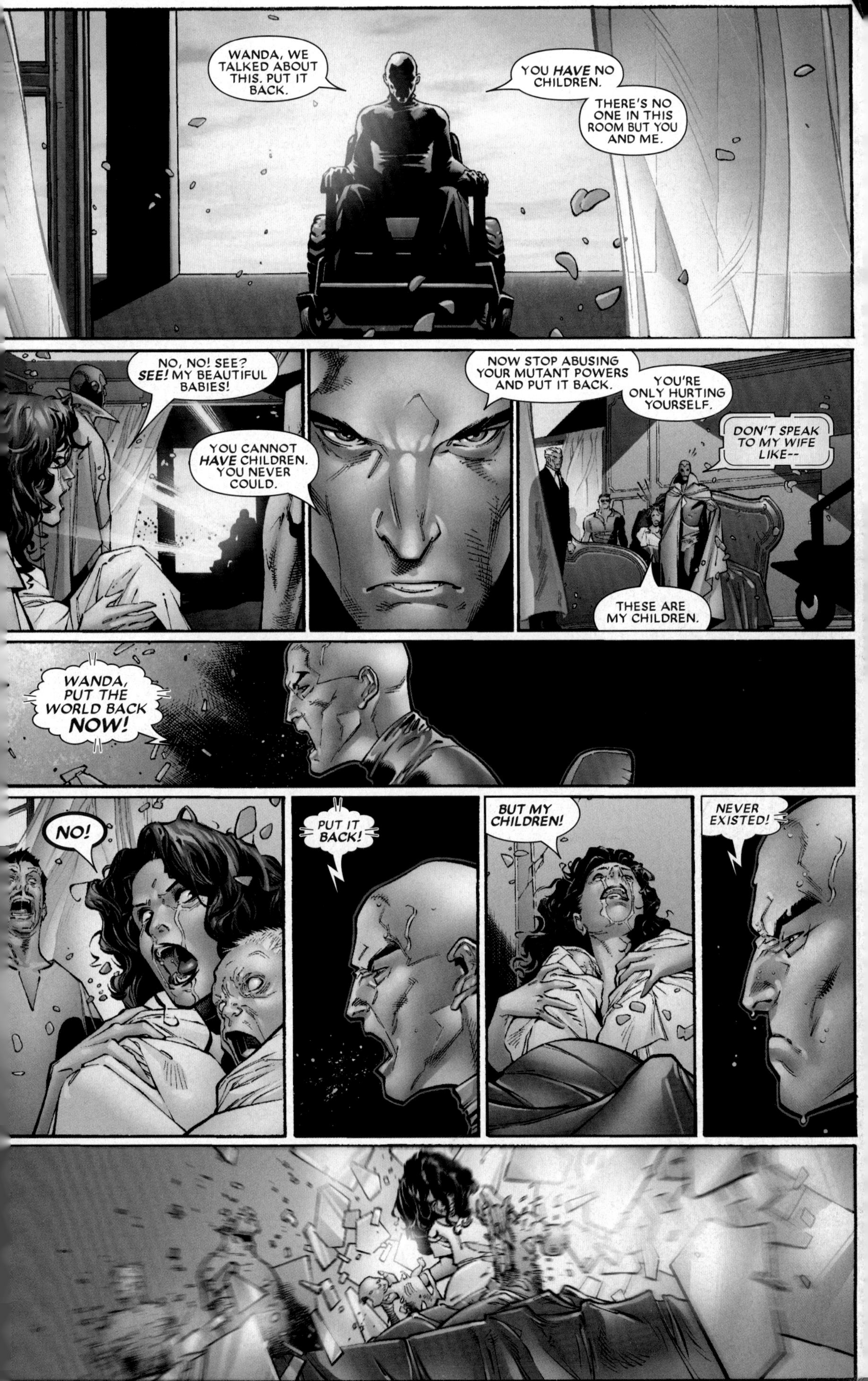
WANDA, WE TALKED ABOUT THIS. PUT IT BACK.
YOU HAVE NO CHILDREN.
THERE'S NO ONE IN THIS ROOM BUT YOU AND ME.
NO, NO! SEE? SEE! MY BEAUTIFUL BABIES!
YOU CANNOT HAVE CHILDREN. YOU NEVER COULD.
NOW STOP ABUSING YOUR MUTANT POWERS AND PUT IT BACK.
YOU'RE ONLY HURTING YOURSELF.
DON'T SPEAK TO MY WIFE LIKE--
THESE ARE MY CHILDREN.
WANDA, PUT THE WORLD BACK NOW!
NO!
PUT IT BACK!
BUT MY CHILDREN!
NEVER EXISTED!

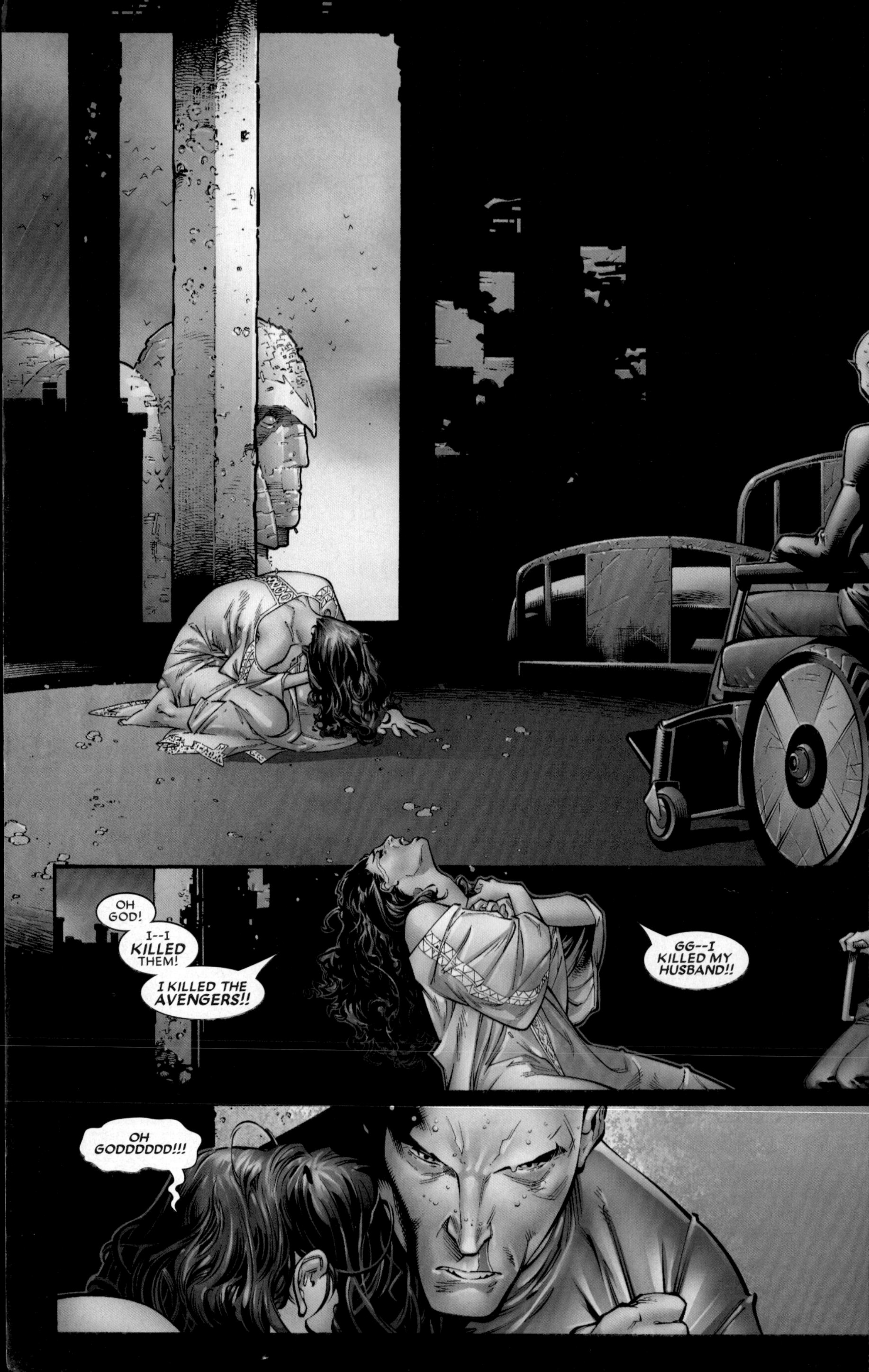
OH GOD! I--I KILLED THEM!
I KILLED THE AVENGERS!!
GG--I KILLED MY HUSBAND!!
OH GODDDDDD!!!

And there came a day, a day unlike any other, when Earth's mightiest heroes found themselves united against a common threat! On that day, the Avengers were born--to fight the foes no single super hero could withstand!

Born with strange powers, the mutants known as the X-MEN use their awesome abilities to protect a world that hates and fears them!

Professor Charles Xavier--legendary founder of the X-Men who dreams of a peaceful coexistence between humans and mutants--has come to Genosha with one intention: to rebuild a mutant nation from its devastated ashes.

It was the worst day in Avengers history. The Scarlet Witch suffered a total nervous breakdown after losing control of her reality-altering powers. In the chaos created around the breakdown, beloved Avengers Hawkeye, Ant-Man and the Vision lost their lives. Many of the other Avengers were hurt, both emotionally and physically.

That was six months ago.

HOUSE OF M

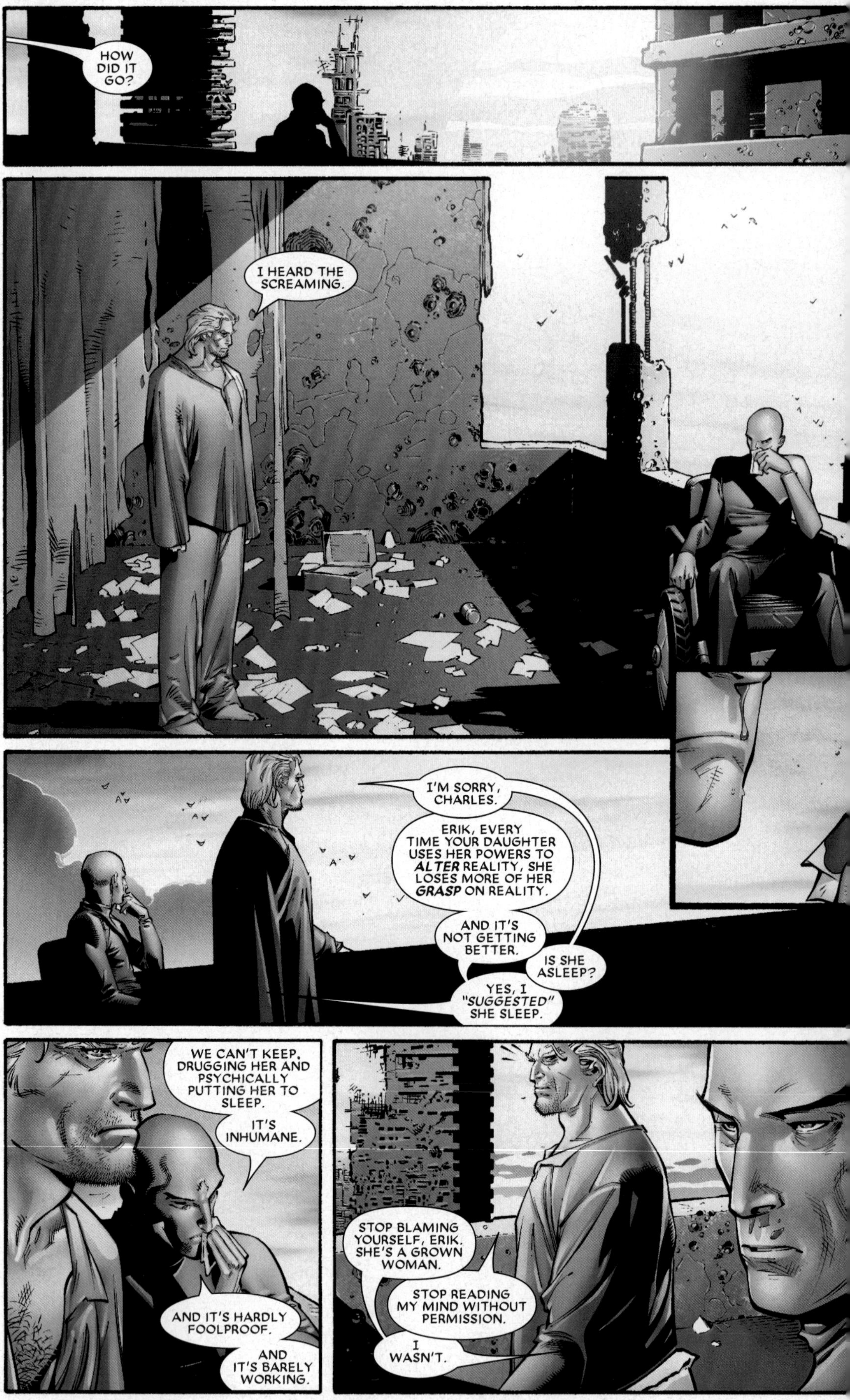
HOW DID IT GO?
I HEARD THE SCREAMING.
I'M SORRY, CHARLES.
ERIK, EVERY TIME YOUR DAUGHTER USES HER POWERS TO *ALTER* REALITY, SHE LOSES MORE OF HER *GRASP* ON REALITY.
AND IT'S NOT GETTING BETTER.
IS SHE ASLEEP?
YES, I "*SUGGESTED*" SHE SLEEP.
WE CAN'T KEEP, DRUGGING HER AND PSYCHICALLY PUTTING HER TO SLEEP.
IT'S INHUMANE.
AND IT'S HARDLY FOOLPROOF.
AND IT'S BARELY WORKING.
STOP BLAMING YOURSELF, ERIK. SHE'S A GROWN WOMAN.
STOP READING MY MIND WITHOUT PERMISSION.
I WASN'T.

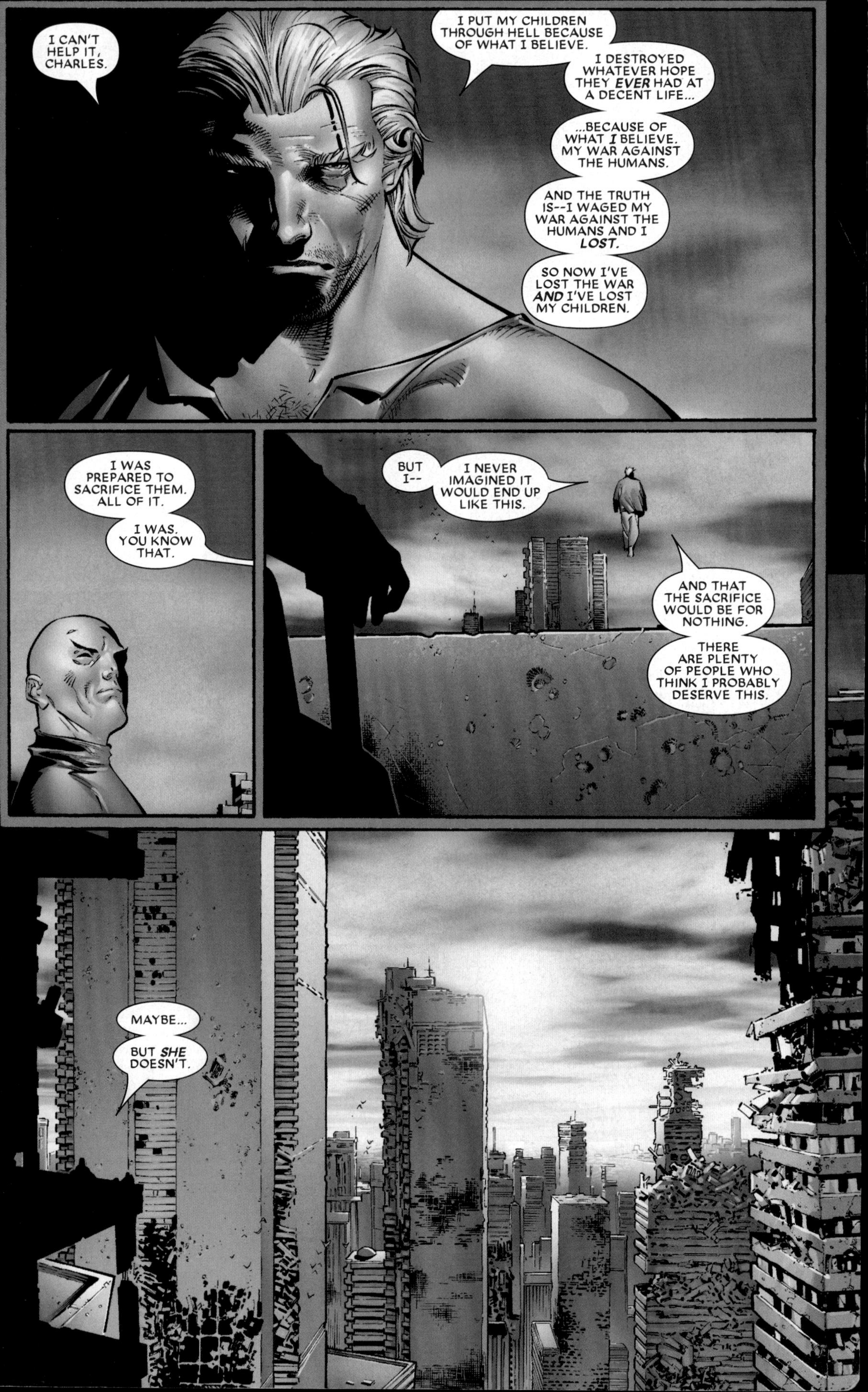
I CAN'T HELP IT, CHARLES.
I PUT MY CHILDREN THROUGH HELL BECAUSE OF WHAT I BELIEVE.
I DESTROYED WHATEVER HOPE THEY EVER HAD AT A DECENT LIFE...
...BECAUSE OF WHAT I BELIEVE. MY WAR AGAINST THE HUMANS.
AND THE TRUTH IS--I WAGED MY WAR AGAINST THE HUMANS AND I LOST.
SO NOW I'VE LOST THE WAR AND I'VE LOST MY CHILDREN.
I WAS PREPARED TO SACRIFICE THEM. ALL OF IT.
I WAS. YOU KNOW THAT.
BUT I--
I NEVER IMAGINED IT WOULD END UP LIKE THIS.
AND THAT THE SACRIFICE WOULD BE FOR NOTHING.
THERE ARE PLENTY OF PEOPLE WHO THINK I PROBABLY DESERVE THIS.
MAYBE...
BUT SHE DOESN'T.

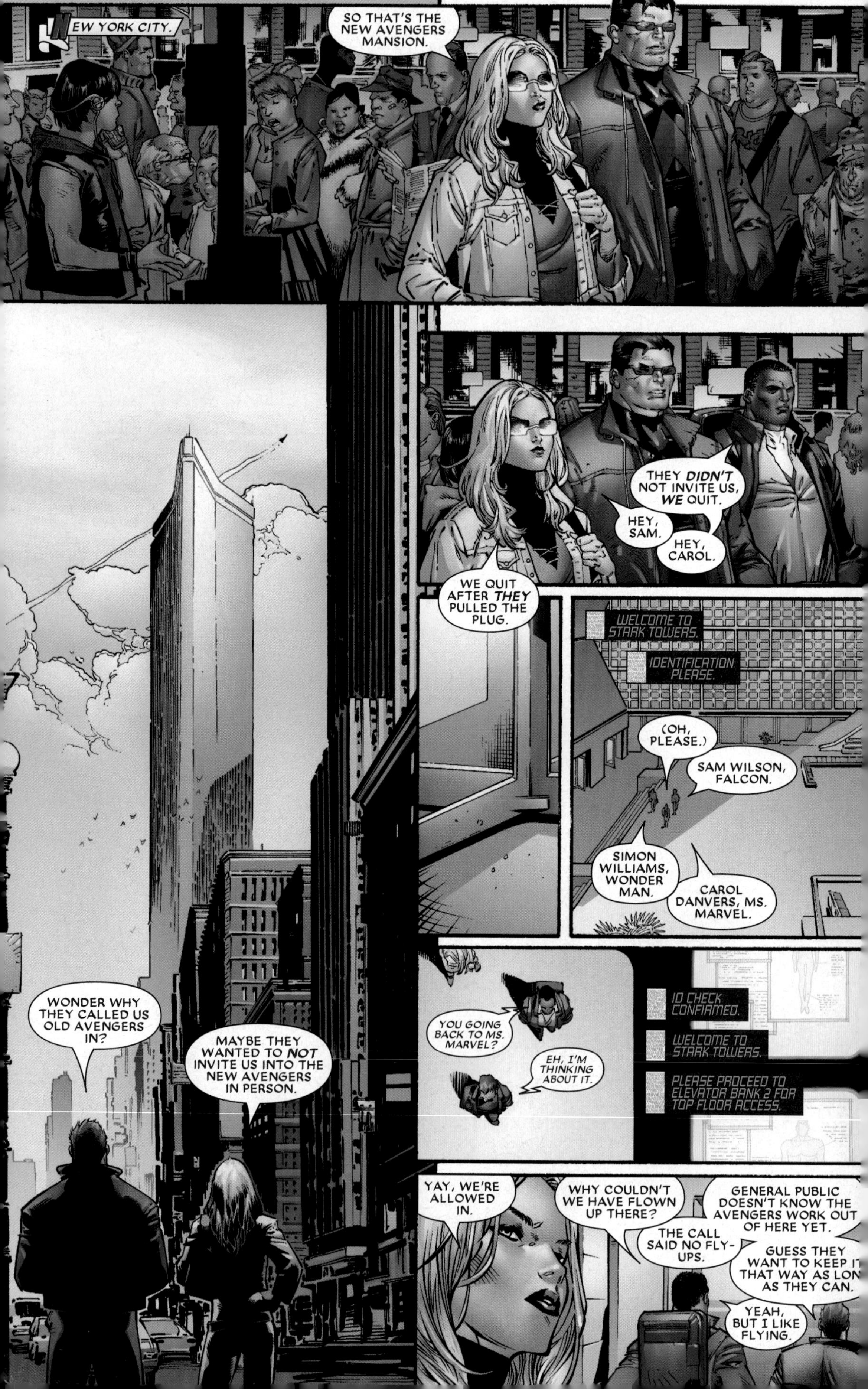

NEW YORK CITY.
SO THAT'S THE NEW AVENGERS MANSION.
THEY DIDN'T NOT INVITE US, WE QUIT.
HEY, SAM.
HEY, CAROL.
WE QUIT AFTER THEY PULLED THE PLUG.
WELCOME TO STARK TOWERS.
IDENTIFICATION PLEASE.
(OH, PLEASE.)
SAM WILSON, FALCON.
SIMON WILLIAMS, WONDER MAN.
CAROL DANVERS, MS. MARVEL.
WONDER WHY THEY CALLED US OLD AVENGERS IN?
MAYBE THEY WANTED TO NOT INVITE US INTO THE NEW AVENGERS IN PERSON.
YOU GOING BACK TO MS. MARVEL?
EH, I'M THINKING ABOUT IT.
ID CHECK CONFIRMED.
WELCOME TO STARK TOWERS.
PLEASE PROCEED TO ELEVATOR BANK 2 FOR TOP FLOOR ACCESS.
YAY, WE'RE ALLOWED IN.
WHY COULDN'T WE HAVE FLOWN UP THERE?
THE CALL SAID NO FLY-UPS.
GENERAL PUBLIC DOESN'T KNOW THE AVENGERS WORK OUT OF HERE YET.
GUESS THEY WANT TO KEEP IT THAT WAY AS LON AS THEY CAN.
YEAH, BUT I LIKE FLYING.

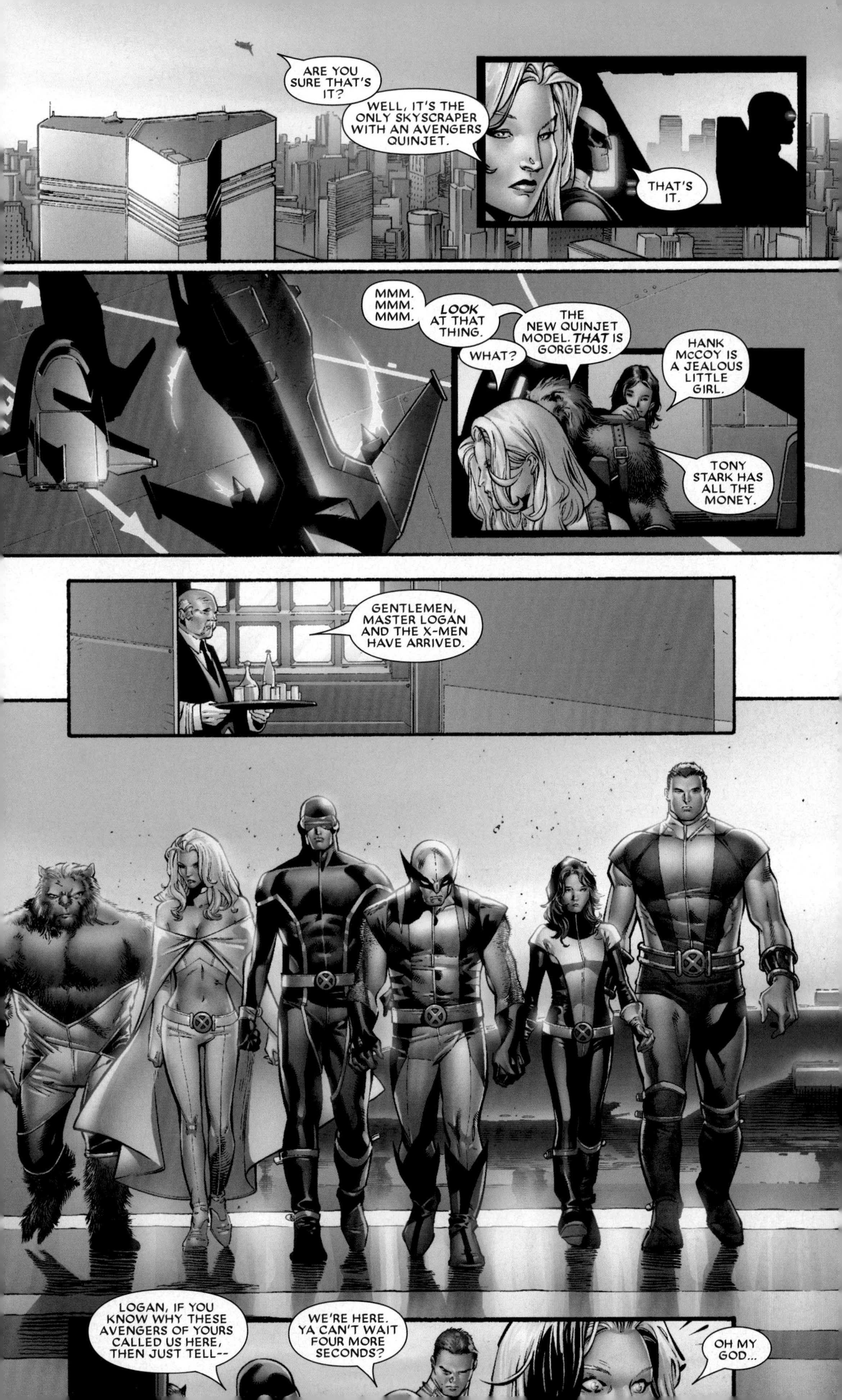

ARE YOU SURE THAT'S IT?
WELL, IT'S THE ONLY SKYSCRAPER WITH AN AVENGERS QUINJET.
THAT'S IT.
MMM. MMM. MMM.
LOOK AT THAT THING.
THE NEW QUINJET MODEL. THAT IS GORGEOUS.
WHAT?
HANK McCOY IS A JEALOUS LITTLE GIRL.
TONY STARK HAS ALL THE MONEY.
GENTLEMEN, MASTER LOGAN AND THE X-MEN HAVE ARRIVED.
LOGAN, IF YOU KNOW WHY THESE AVENGERS OF YOURS CALLED US HERE, THEN JUST TELL--
WE'RE HERE. YA CAN'T WAIT FOUR MORE SECONDS?
OH MY GOD...

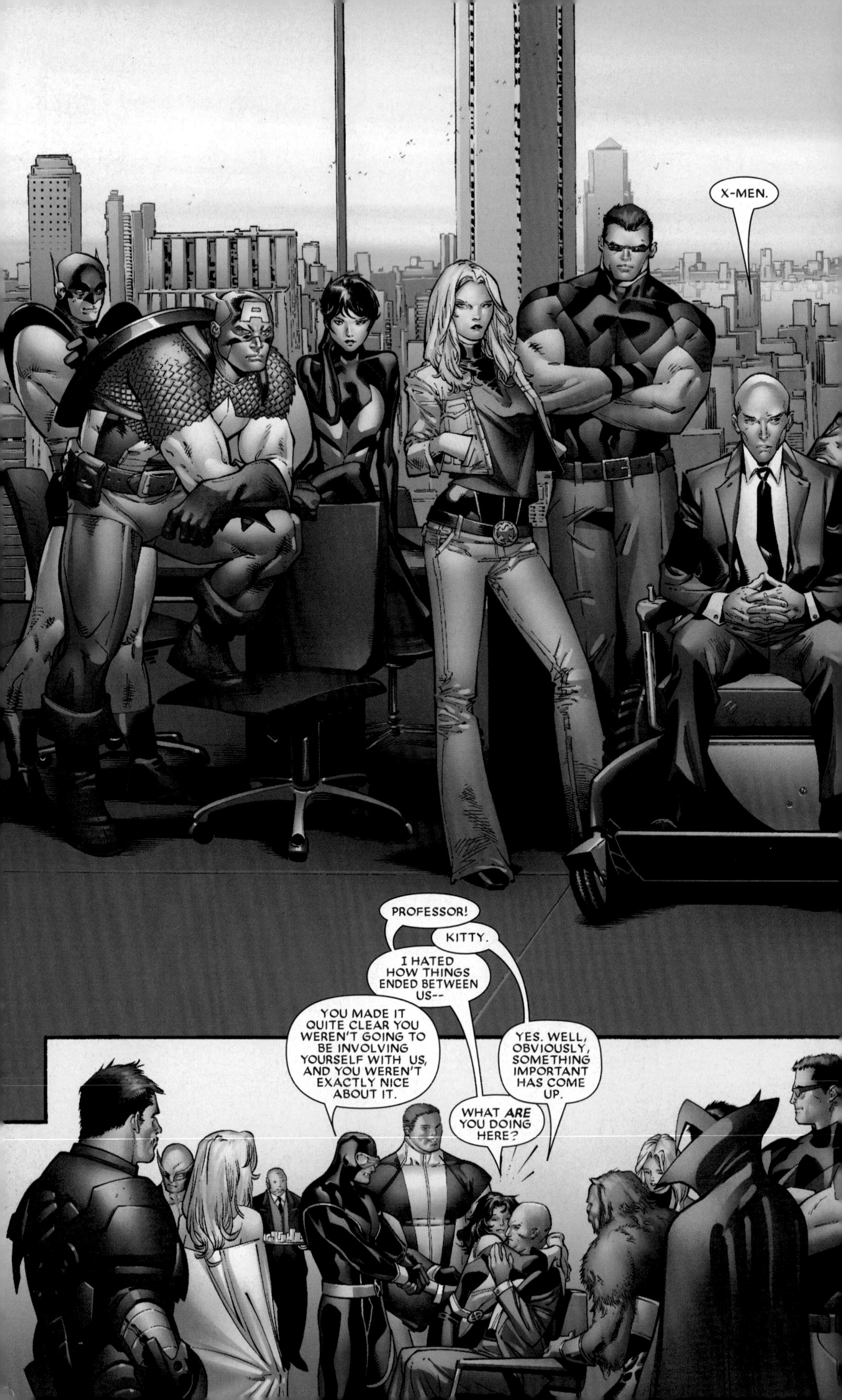
X-MEN.
PROFESSOR!
KITTY.
I HATED HOW THINGS ENDED BETWEEN US--
YOU MADE IT QUITE CLEAR YOU WEREN'T GOING TO BE INVOLVING YOURSELF WITH US, AND YOU WEREN'T EXACTLY NICE ABOUT IT.
YES. WELL, OBVIOUSLY, SOMETHING IMPORTANT HAS COME UP.
WHAT ARE YOU DOING HERE?

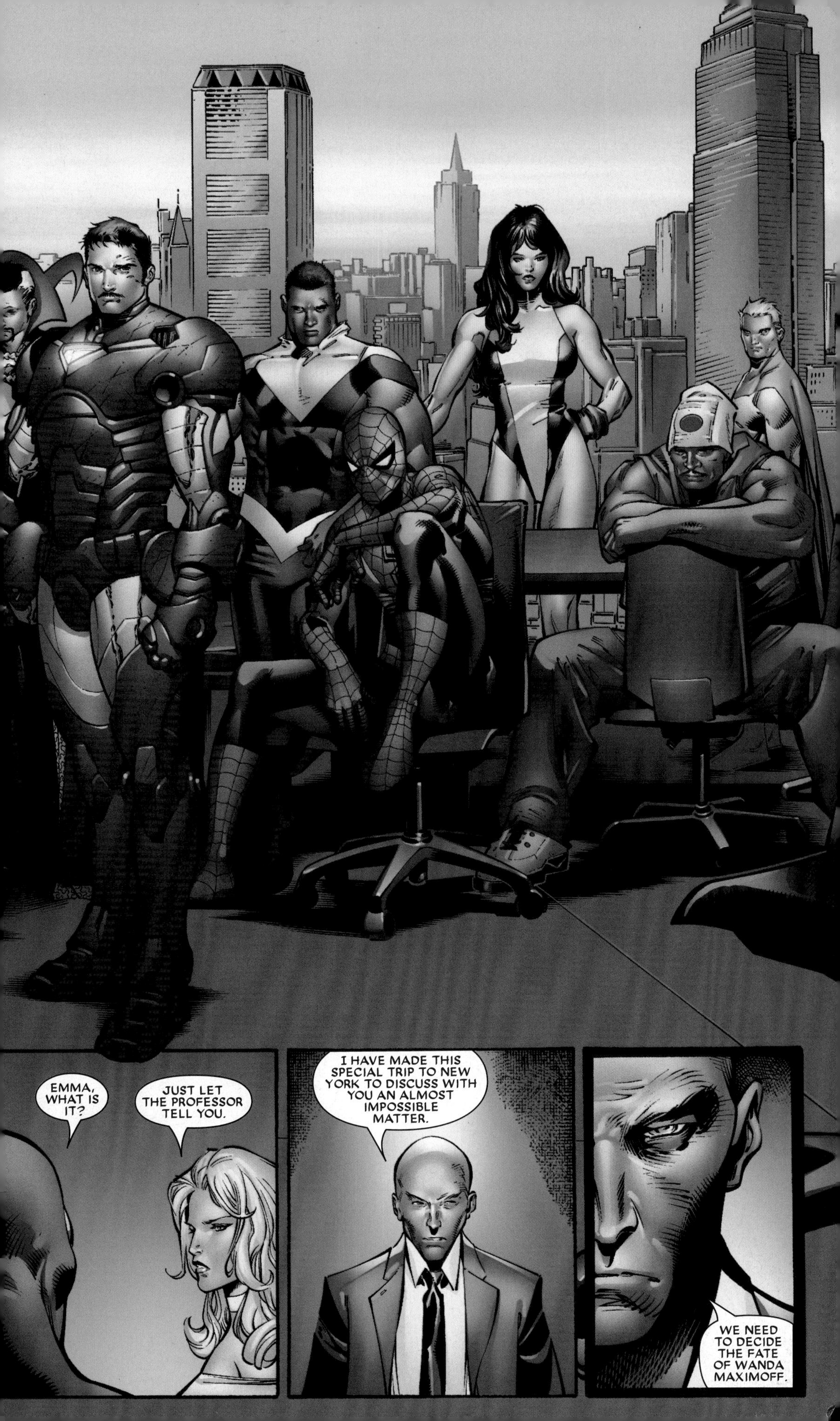
EMMA, WHAT IS IT?
JUST LET THE PROFESSOR TELL YOU.
I HAVE MADE THIS SPECIAL TRIP TO NEW YORK TO DISCUSS WITH YOU AN ALMOST IMPOSSIBLE MATTER.
WE NEED TO DECIDE THE FATE OF WANDA MAXIMOFF.

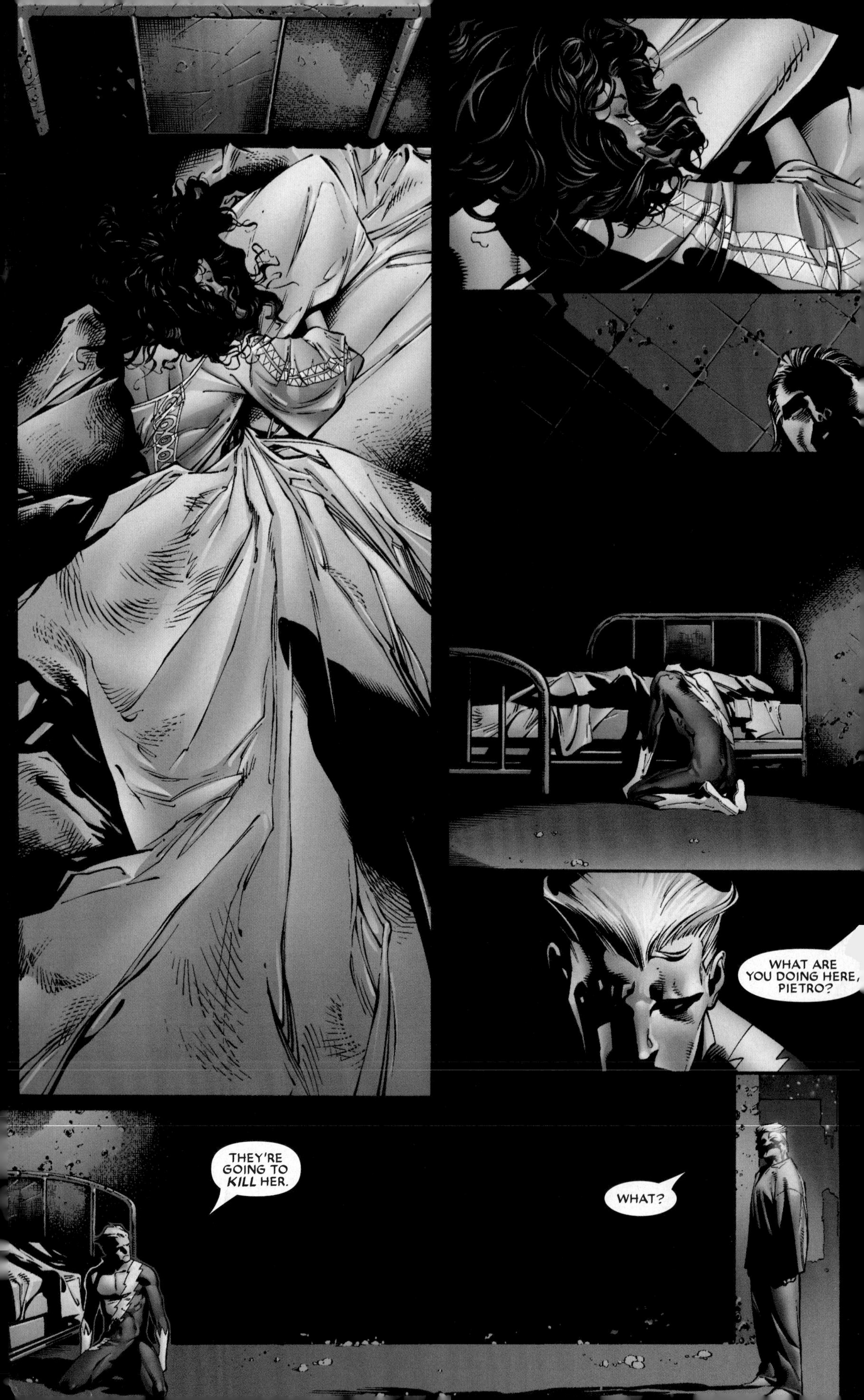
WHAT ARE YOU DOING HERE, PIETRO?
THEY'RE GOING TO KILL HER.
WHAT?

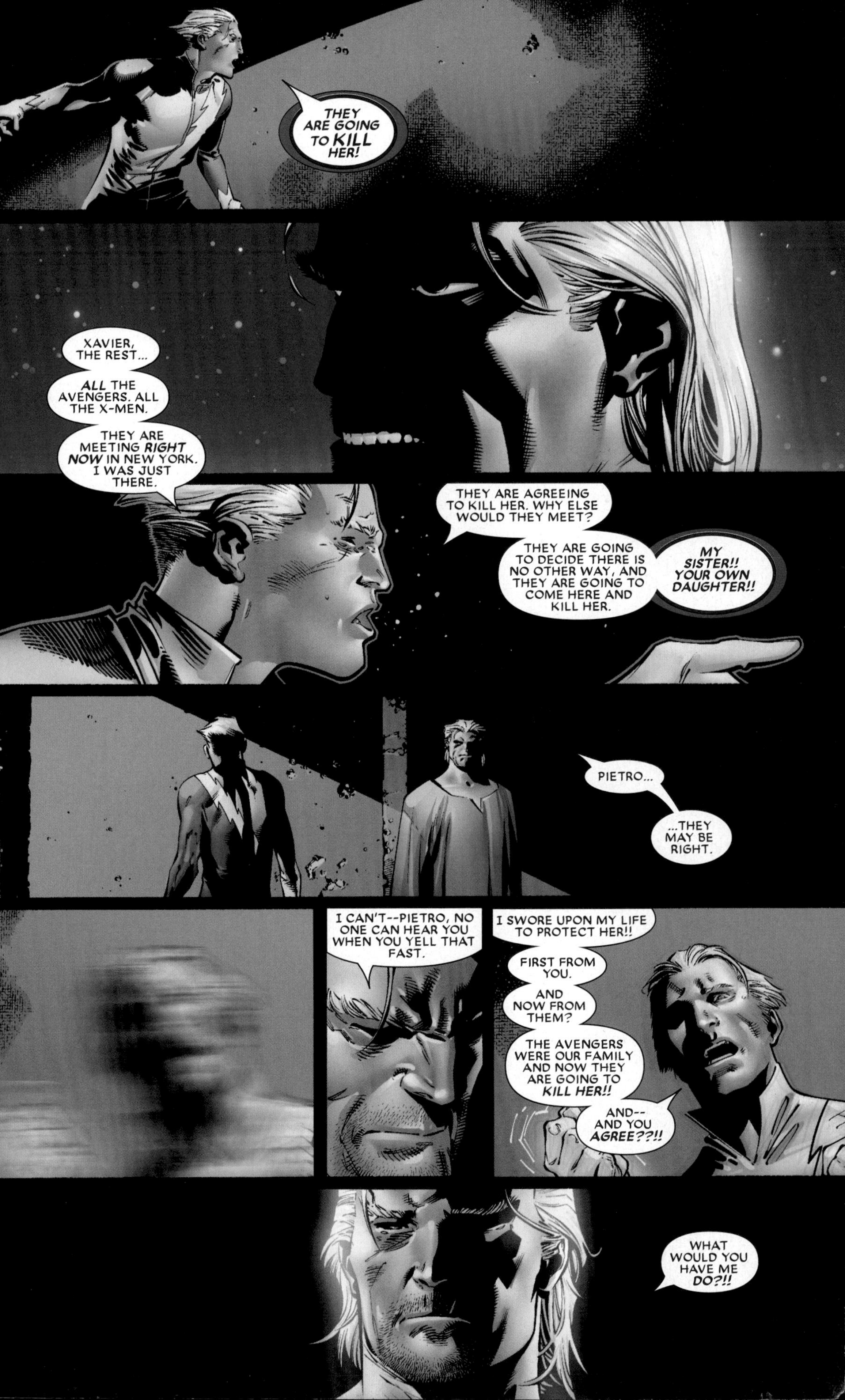
THEY ARE GOING TO KILL HER!
XAVIER, THE REST...
ALL THE AVENGERS. ALL THE X-MEN.
THEY ARE MEETING RIGHT NOW IN NEW YORK. I WAS JUST THERE.
THEY ARE AGREEING TO KILL HER. WHY ELSE WOULD THEY MEET?
THEY ARE GOING TO DECIDE THERE IS NO OTHER WAY, AND THEY ARE GOING TO COME HERE AND KILL HER.
MY SISTER!! YOUR OWN DAUGHTER!!
PIETRO...
...THEY MAY BE RIGHT.
I CAN'T--PIETRO, NO ONE CAN HEAR YOU WHEN YOU YELL THAT FAST.
I SWORE UPON MY LIFE TO PROTECT HER!!
FIRST FROM YOU.
AND NOW FROM THEM?
THE AVENGERS WERE OUR FAMILY AND NOW THEY ARE GOING TO KILL HER!!
AND-- AND YOU AGREE??!!
WHAT WOULD YOU HAVE ME DO?!!

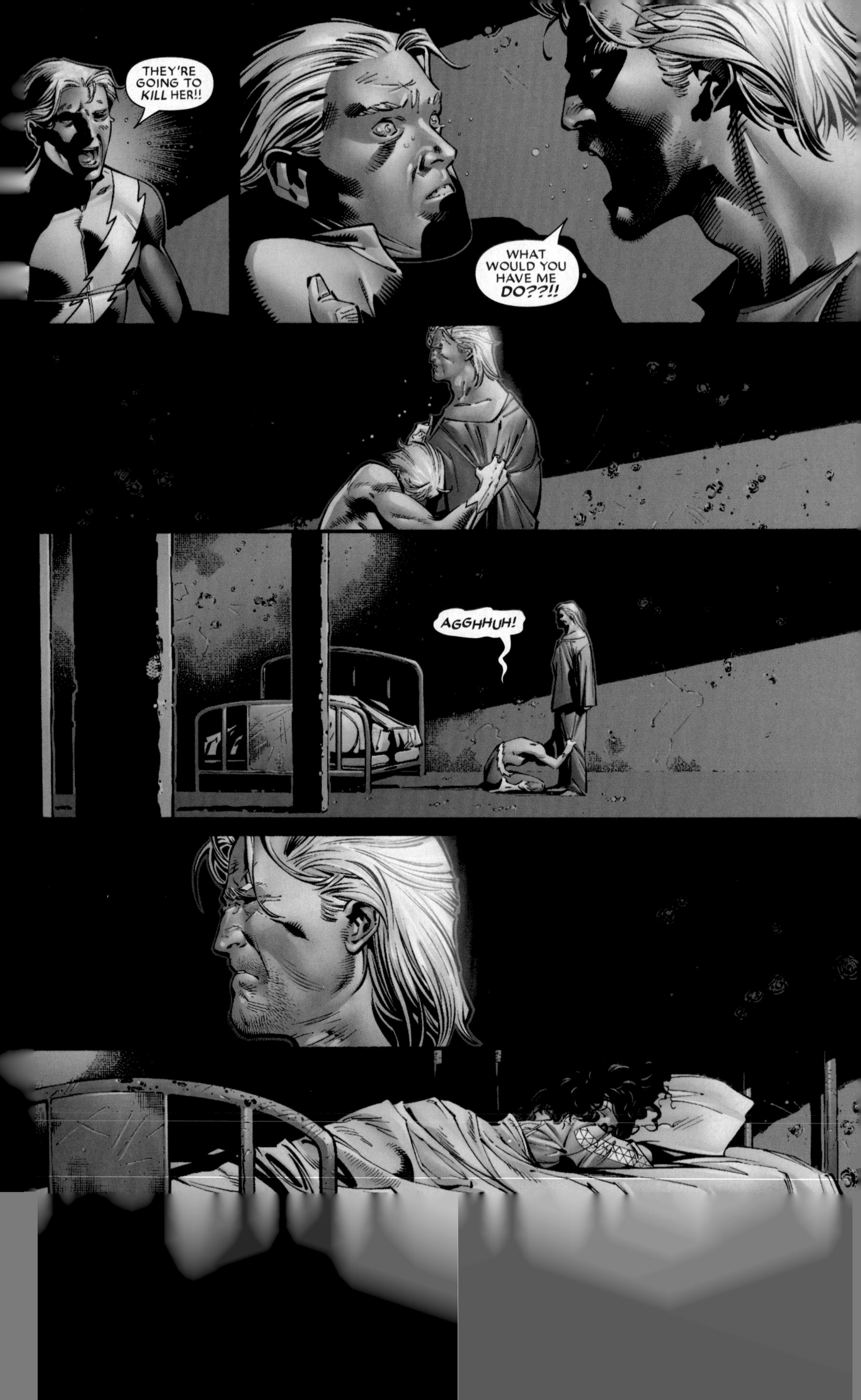
THEY'RE GOING TO KILL HER!!
WHAT WOULD YOU HAVE ME DO??!!
AGGHHUH!

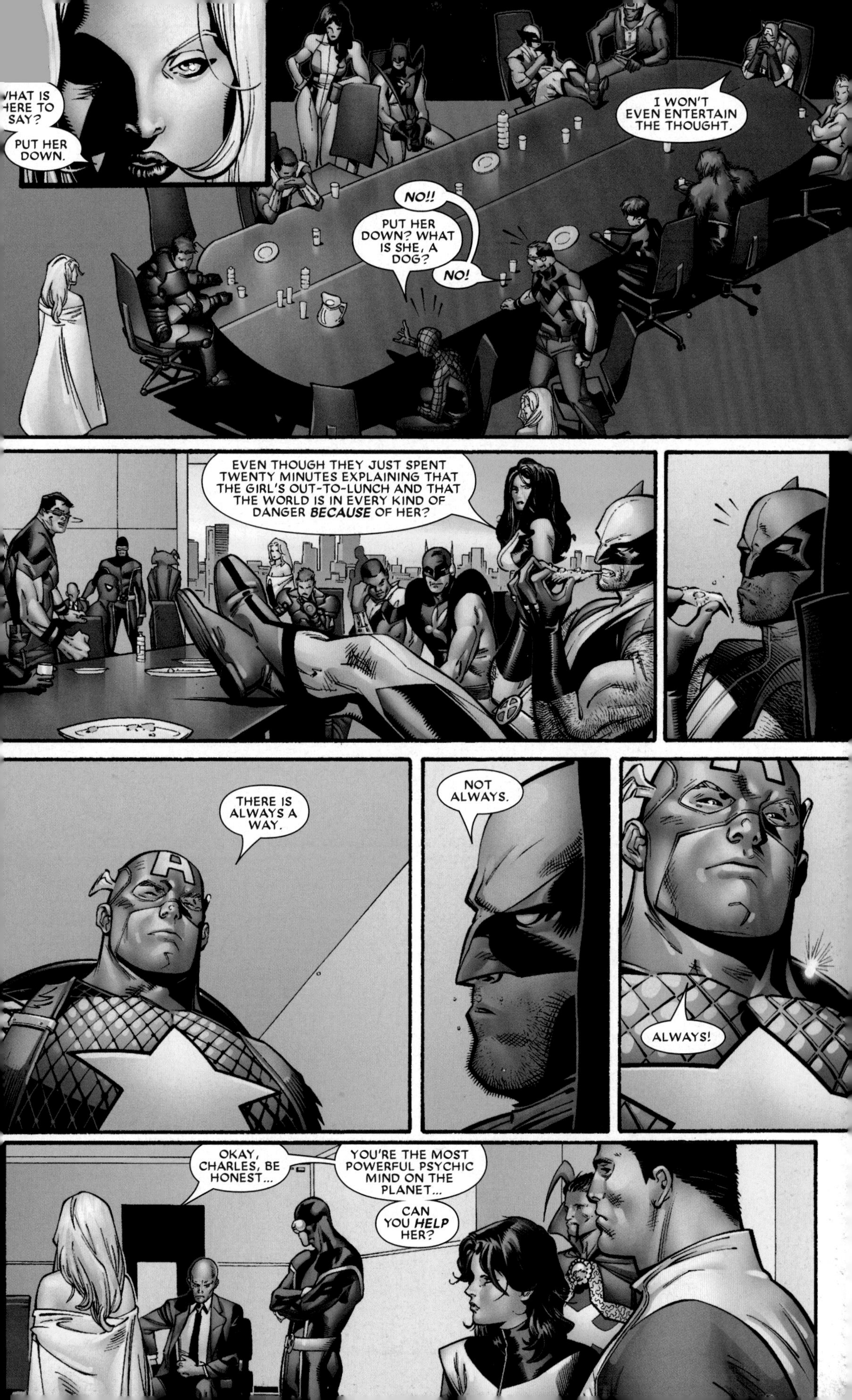
WHAT IS
HERE TO
SAY?
PUT HER
DOWN.
I WON'T
EVEN ENTERTAIN
THE THOUGHT.
NO!!
PUT HER
DOWN? WHAT
IS SHE, A
DOG?
NO!
EVEN THOUGH THEY JUST SPENT
TWENTY MINUTES EXPLAINING THAT
THE GIRL'S OUT-TO-LUNCH AND THAT
THE WORLD IS IN EVERY KIND OF
DANGER BECAUSE OF HER?
THERE IS
ALWAYS A
WAY.
NOT
ALWAYS.
ALWAYS!
OKAY,
CHARLES, BE
HONEST...
YOU'RE THE MOST
POWERFUL PSYCHIC
MIND ON THE
PLANET...
CAN
YOU HELP
HER?

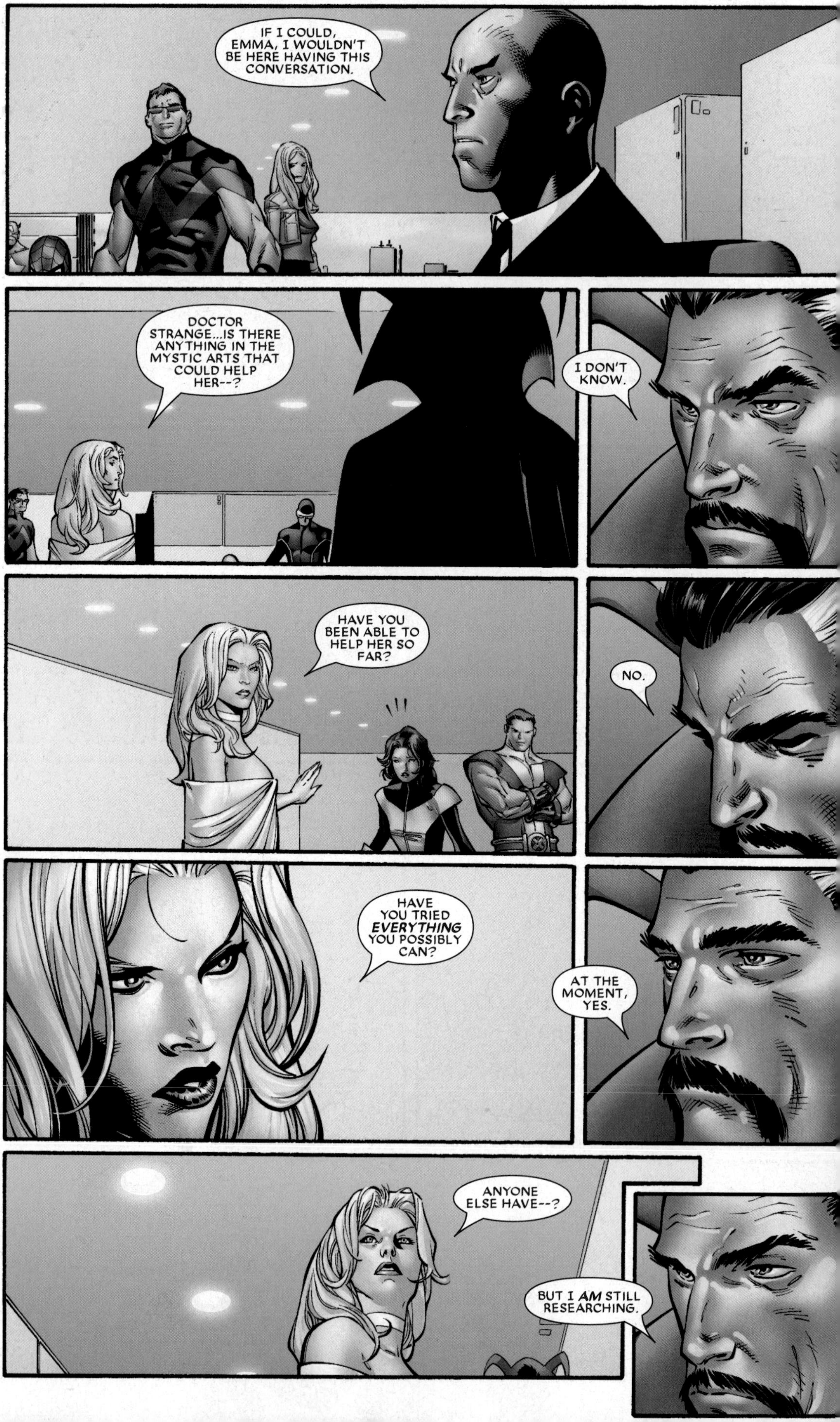
IF I COULD, EMMA, I WOULDN'T BE HERE HAVING THIS CONVERSATION.
DOCTOR STRANGE...IS THERE ANYTHING IN THE MYSTIC ARTS THAT COULD HELP HER--?
I DON'T KNOW.
HAVE YOU BEEN ABLE TO HELP HER SO FAR?
NO.
HAVE YOU TRIED *EVERYTHING* YOU POSSIBLY CAN?
AT THE MOMENT, YES.
ANYONE ELSE HAVE--?
BUT I *AM* STILL RESEARCHING.

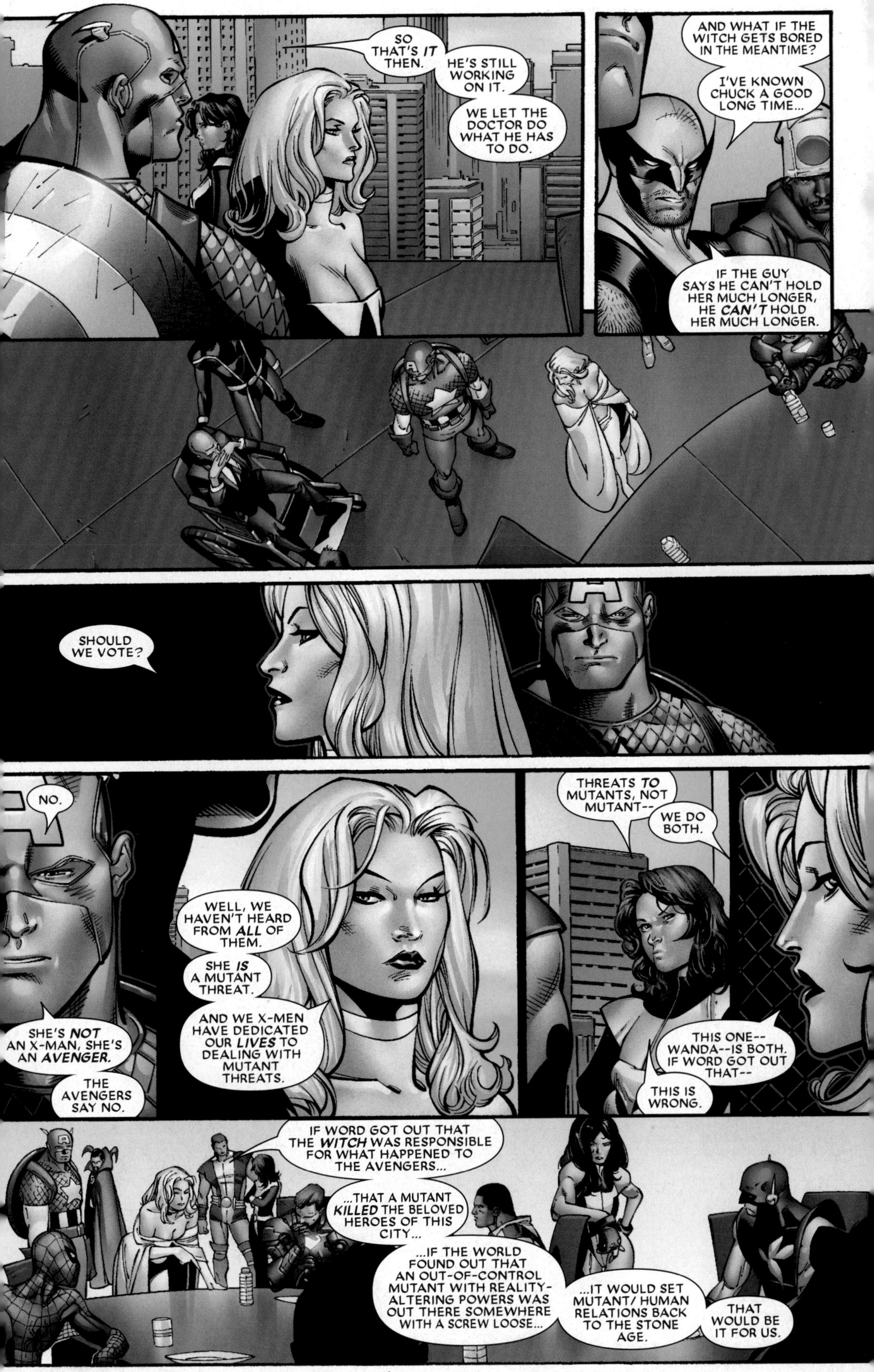

SO THAT'S IT THEN.
HE'S STILL WORKING ON IT.
WE LET THE DOCTOR DO WHAT HE HAS TO DO.
AND WHAT IF THE WITCH GETS BORED IN THE MEANTIME?
I'VE KNOWN CHUCK A GOOD LONG TIME...
IF THE GUY SAYS HE CAN'T HOLD HER MUCH LONGER, HE CAN'T HOLD HER MUCH LONGER.
SHOULD WE VOTE?
NO.
WELL, WE HAVEN'T HEARD FROM ALL OF THEM.
SHE IS A MUTANT THREAT.
AND WE X-MEN HAVE DEDICATED OUR LIVES TO DEALING WITH MUTANT THREATS.
SHE'S NOT AN X-MAN, SHE'S AN AVENGER.
THE AVENGERS SAY NO.
THREATS TO MUTANTS, NOT MUTANT--
WE DO BOTH.
THIS ONE-- WANDA--IS BOTH. IF WORD GOT OUT THAT--
THIS IS WRONG.
IF WORD GOT OUT THAT THE WITCH WAS RESPONSIBLE FOR WHAT HAPPENED TO THE AVENGERS...
...THAT A MUTANT KILLED THE BELOVED HEROES OF THIS CITY...
...IF THE WORLD FOUND OUT THAT AN OUT-OF-CONTROL MUTANT WITH REALITY-ALTERING POWERS WAS OUT THERE SOMEWHERE WITH A SCREW LOOSE...
...IT WOULD SET MUTANT/ HUMAN RELATIONS BACK TO THE STONE AGE.
THAT WOULD BE IT FOR US.

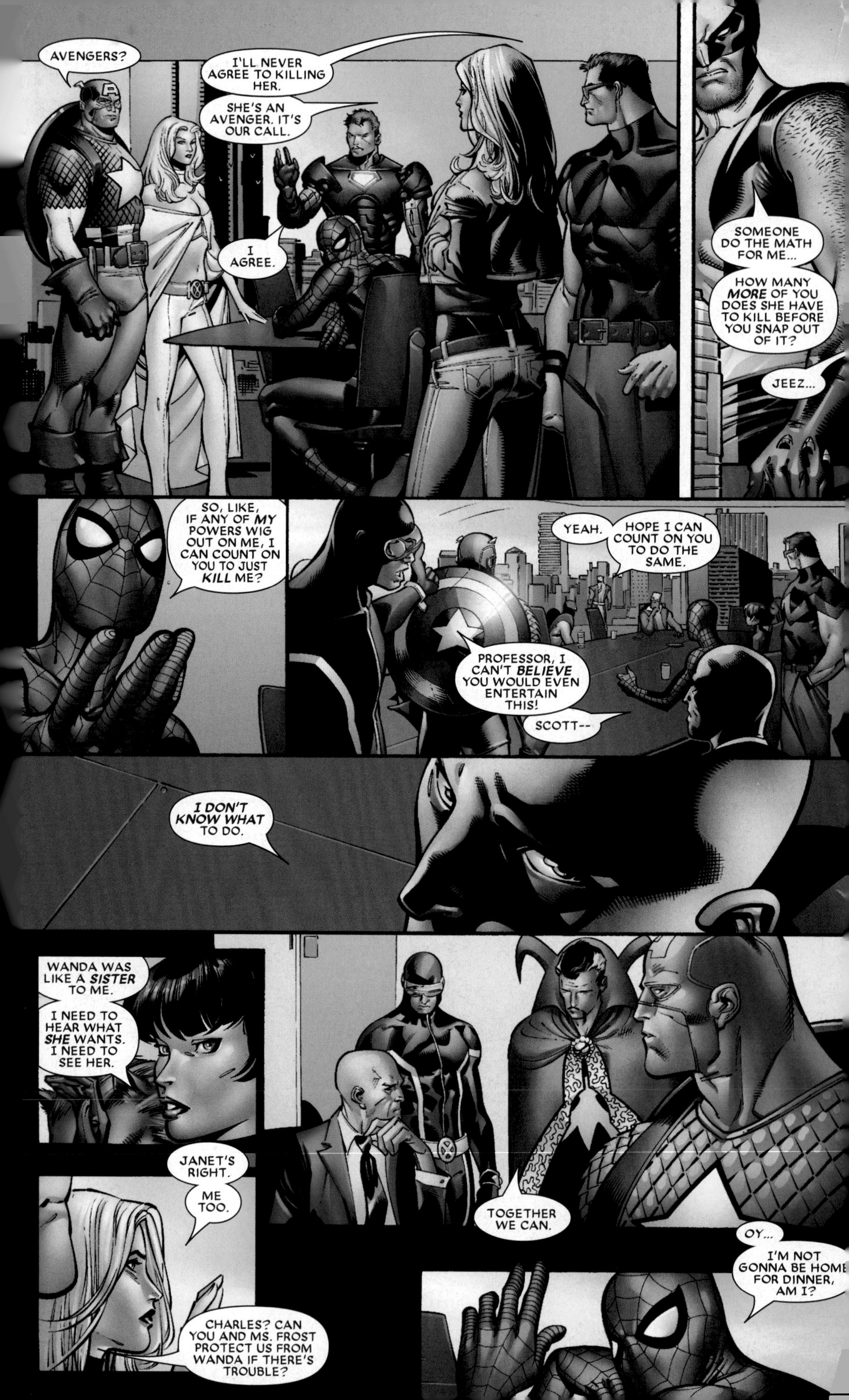
AVENGERS?
I'LL NEVER AGREE TO KILLING HER.
SHE'S AN AVENGER. IT'S OUR CALL.
I AGREE.
SOMEONE DO THE MATH FOR ME...
HOW MANY MORE OF YOU DOES SHE HAVE TO KILL BEFORE YOU SNAP OUT OF IT?
JEEZ...
SO, LIKE, IF ANY OF MY POWERS WIG OUT ON ME, I CAN COUNT ON YOU TO JUST KILL ME?
YEAH.
HOPE I CAN COUNT ON YOU TO DO THE SAME.
PROFESSOR, I CAN'T BELIEVE YOU WOULD EVEN ENTERTAIN THIS!
SCOTT--
I DON'T KNOW WHAT TO DO.
WANDA WAS LIKE A SISTER TO ME.
I NEED TO HEAR WHAT SHE WANTS. I NEED TO SEE HER.
JANET'S RIGHT.
ME TOO.
TOGETHER WE CAN.
CHARLES? CAN YOU AND MS. FROST PROTECT US FROM WANDA IF THERE'S TROUBLE?
OY...
I'M NOT GONNA BE HOME FOR DINNER, AM I?

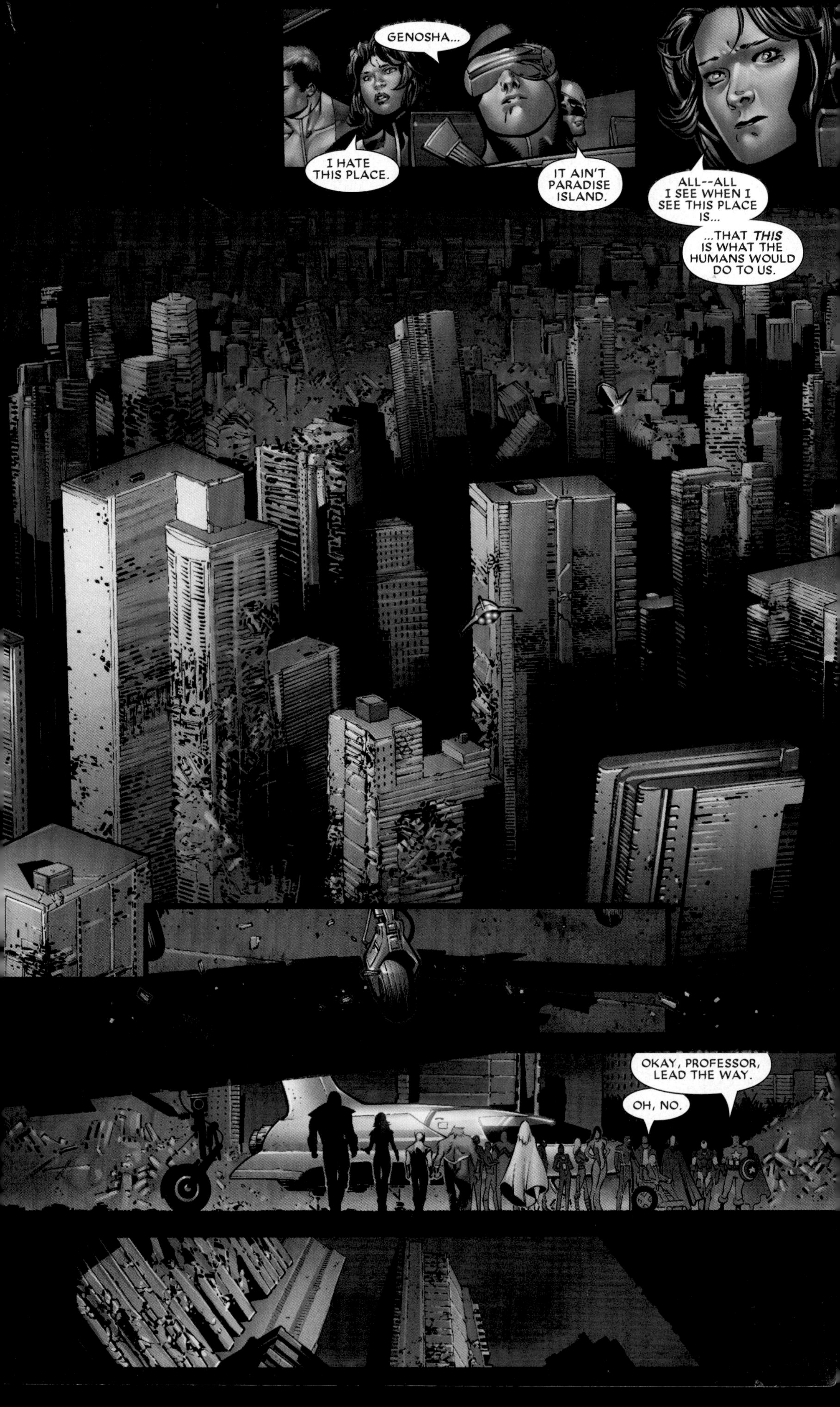

GENOSHA...
I HATE THIS PLACE.
IT AIN'T PARADISE ISLAND.
ALL--ALL I SEE WHEN I SEE THIS PLACE IS...
...THAT *THIS* IS WHAT THE HUMANS WOULD DO TO US.
OKAY, PROFESSOR, LEAD THE WAY.
OH, NO.

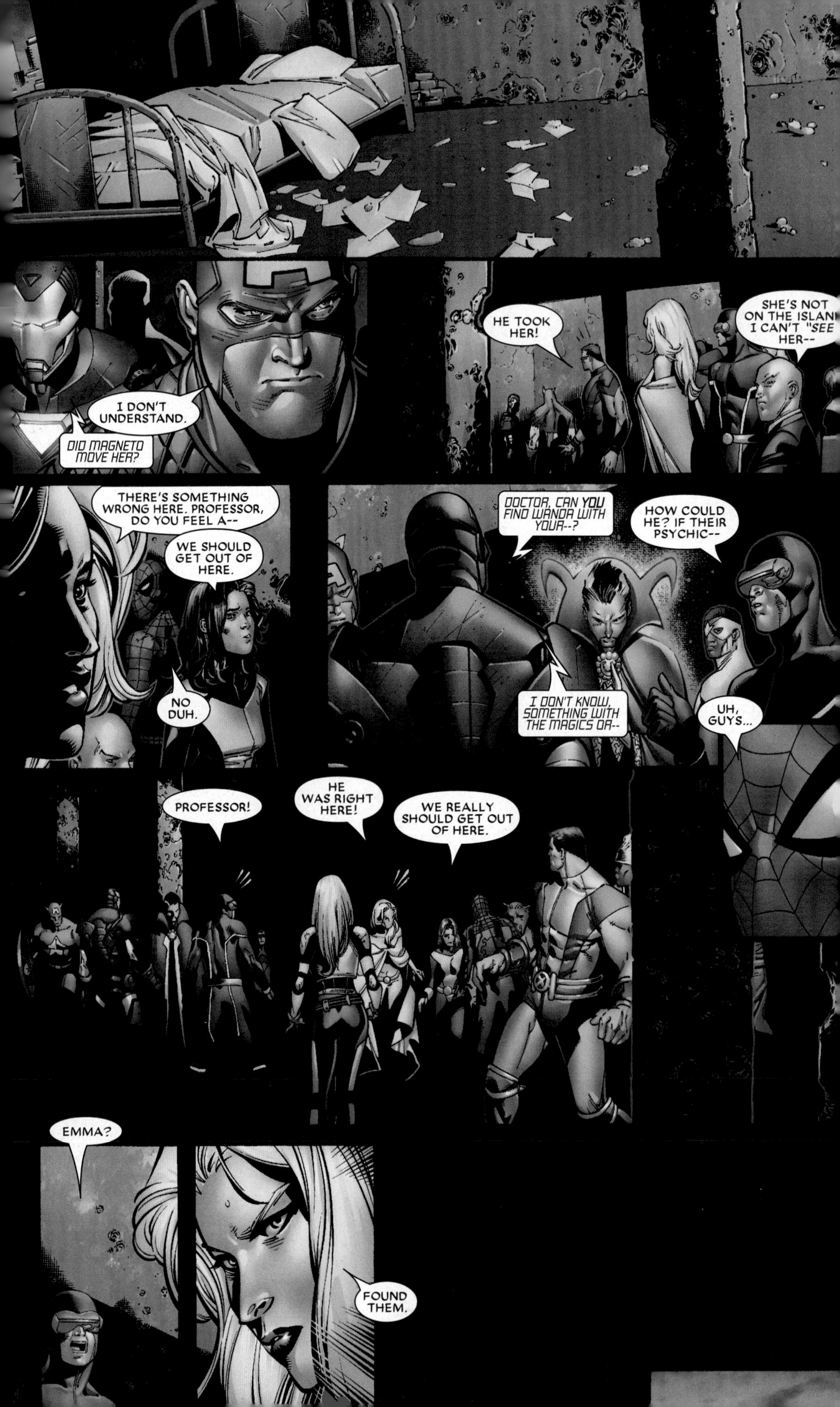

I DON'T UNDERSTAND.
DID MAGNETO MOVE HER?
HE TOOK HER!
SHE'S NOT ON THE ISLAN I CAN'T "SEE" HER--
THERE'S SOMETHING WRONG HERE. PROFESSOR, DO YOU FEEL A--
WE SHOULD GET OUT OF HERE.
NO DUH.
DOCTOR, CAN YOU FIND WANDA WITH YOUR--?
HOW COULD HE? IF THEIR PSYCHIC--
I DON'T KNOW. SOMETHING WITH THE MAGICS OR--
UH, GUYS...
PROFESSOR!
HE WAS RIGHT HERE!
WE REALLY SHOULD GET OUT OF HERE.
EMMA?
FOUND THEM.

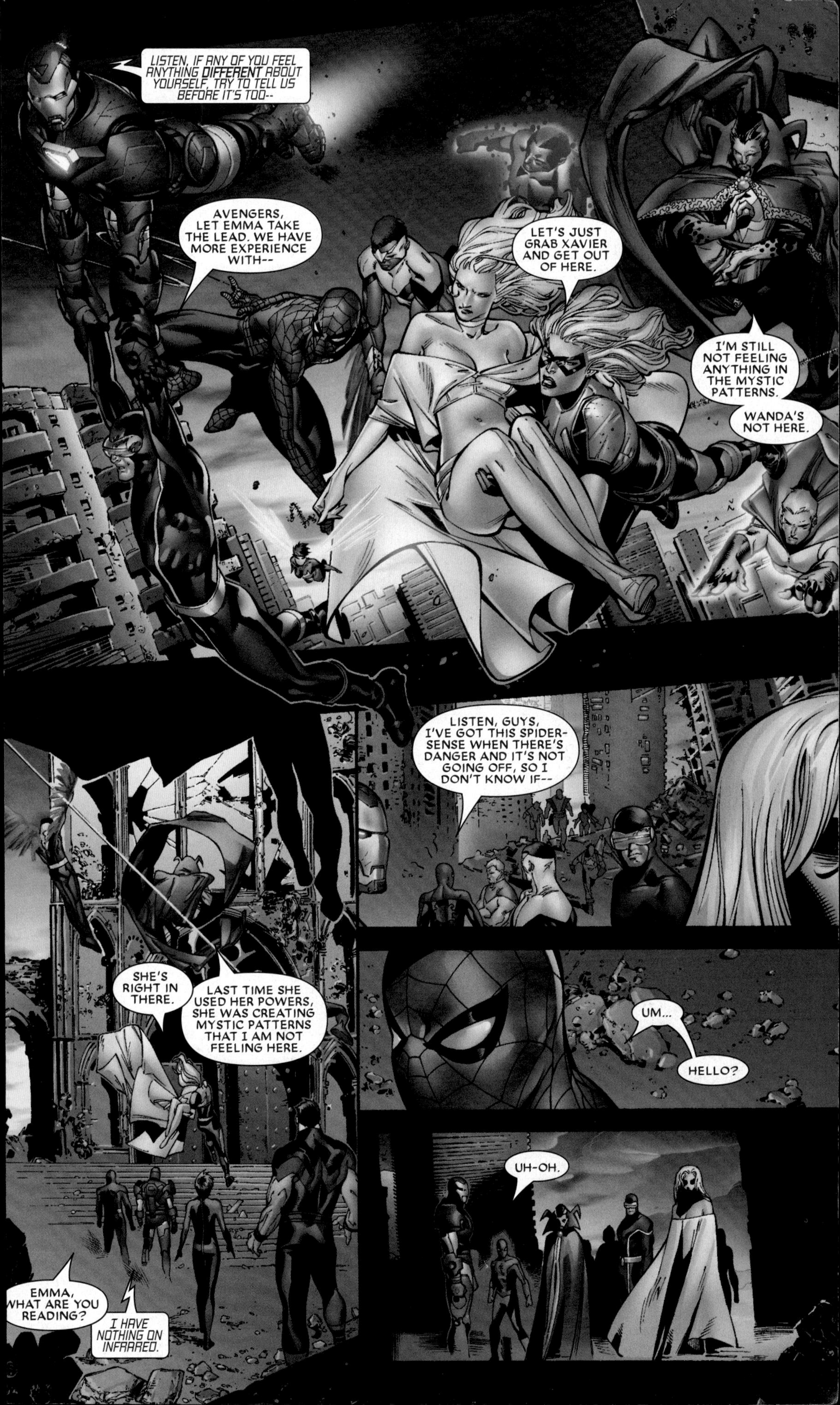

LISTEN, IF ANY OF YOU FEEL ANYTHING DIFFERENT ABOUT YOURSELF, TRY TO TELL US BEFORE IT'S TOO--
AVENGERS, LET EMMA TAKE THE LEAD. WE HAVE MORE EXPERIENCE WITH--
LET'S JUST GRAB XAVIER AND GET OUT OF HERE.
I'M STILL NOT FEELING ANYTHING IN THE MYSTIC PATTERNS.
WANDA'S NOT HERE.
SHE'S RIGHT IN THERE.
LAST TIME SHE USED HER POWERS, SHE WAS CREATING MYSTIC PATTERNS THAT I AM NOT FEELING HERE.
EMMA, WHAT ARE YOU READING?
I HAVE NOTHING ON INFRARED.
LISTEN, GUYS, I'VE GOT THIS SPIDER-SENSE WHEN THERE'S DANGER AND IT'S NOT GOING OFF, SO I DON'T KNOW IF--
UM...
HELLO?
UH-OH.

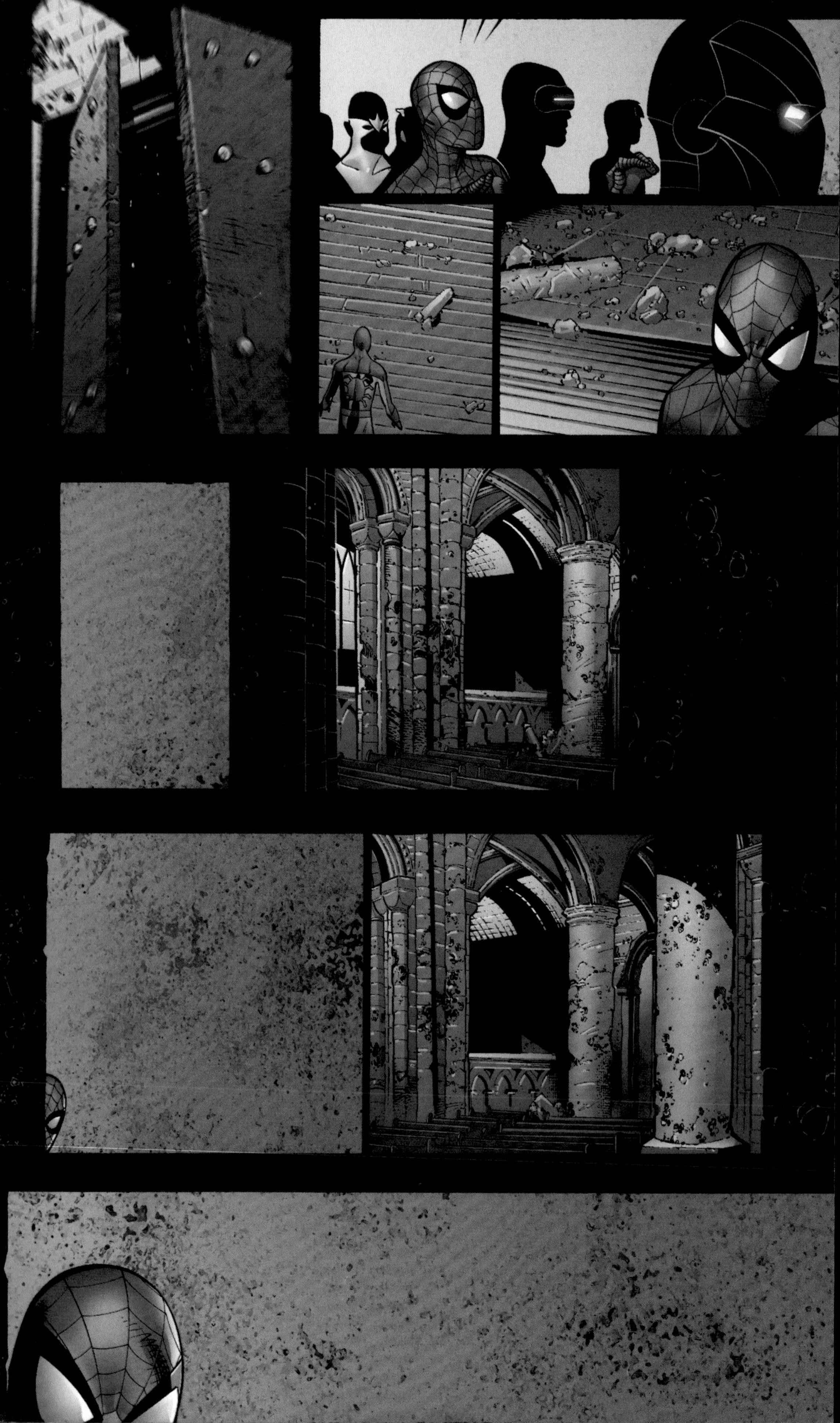

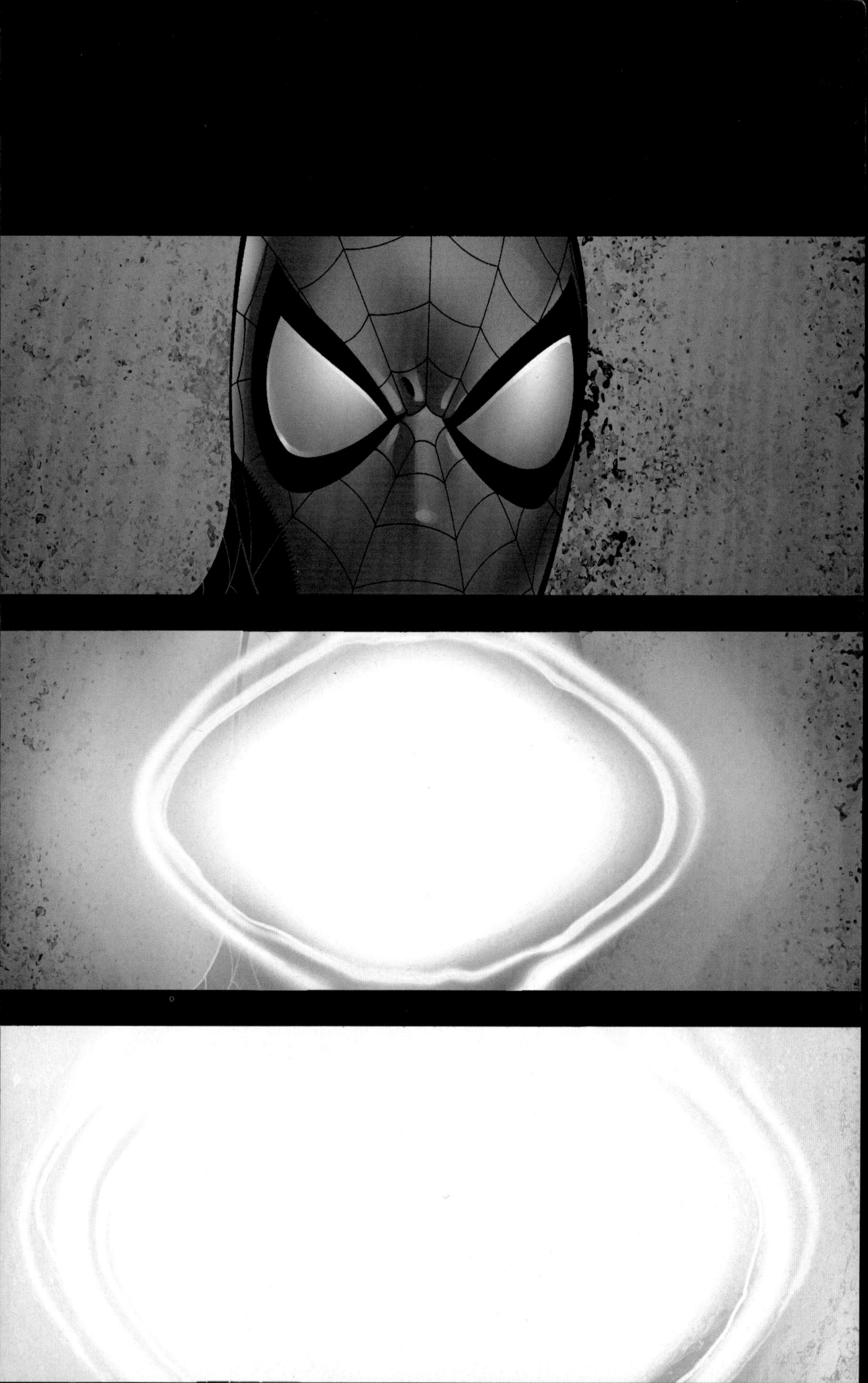

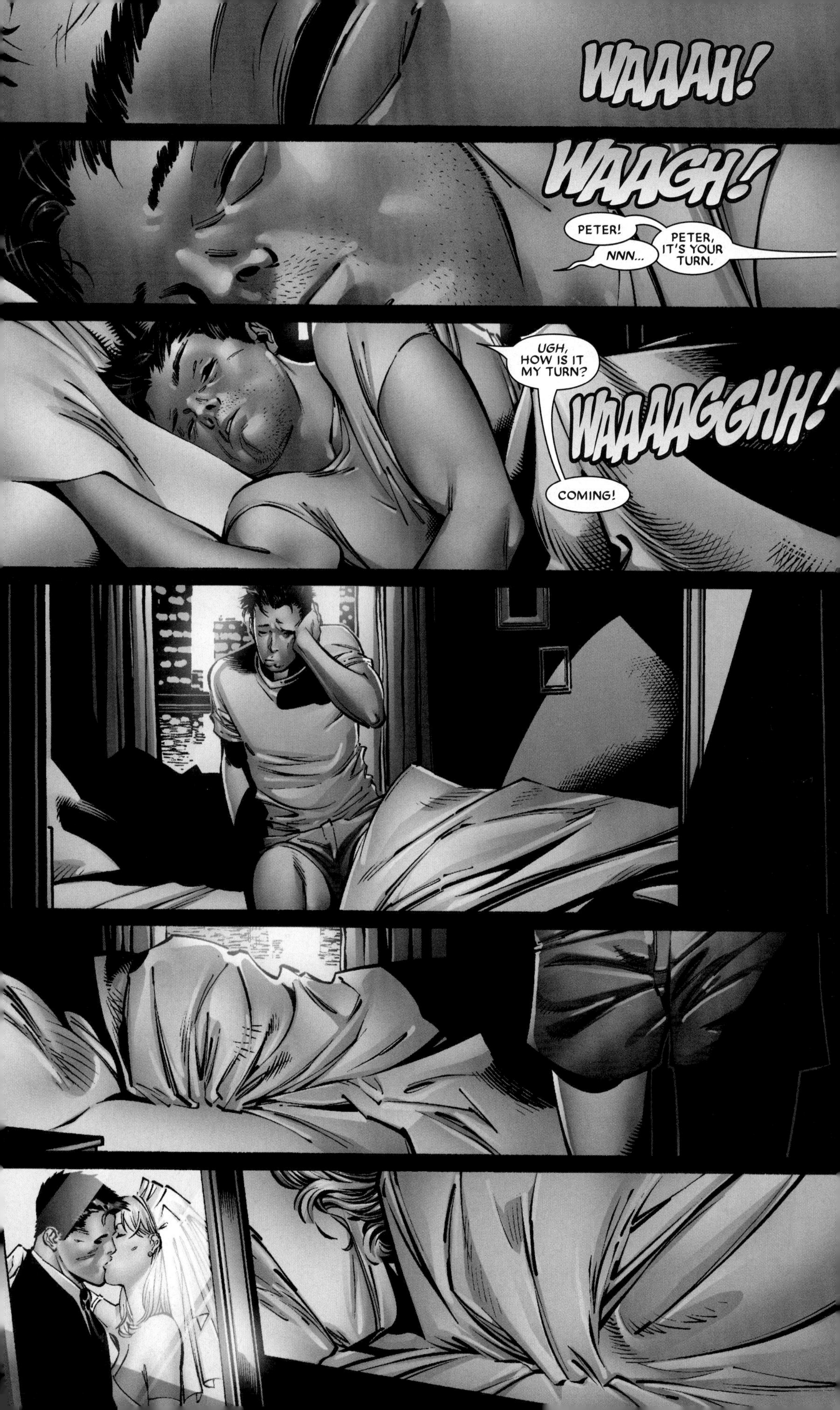
WAAAH!
WAAGH!
PETER!
NNN...
PETER, IT'S YOUR TURN.
UGH, HOW IS IT MY TURN?
WAAAAGGHH!
COMING!

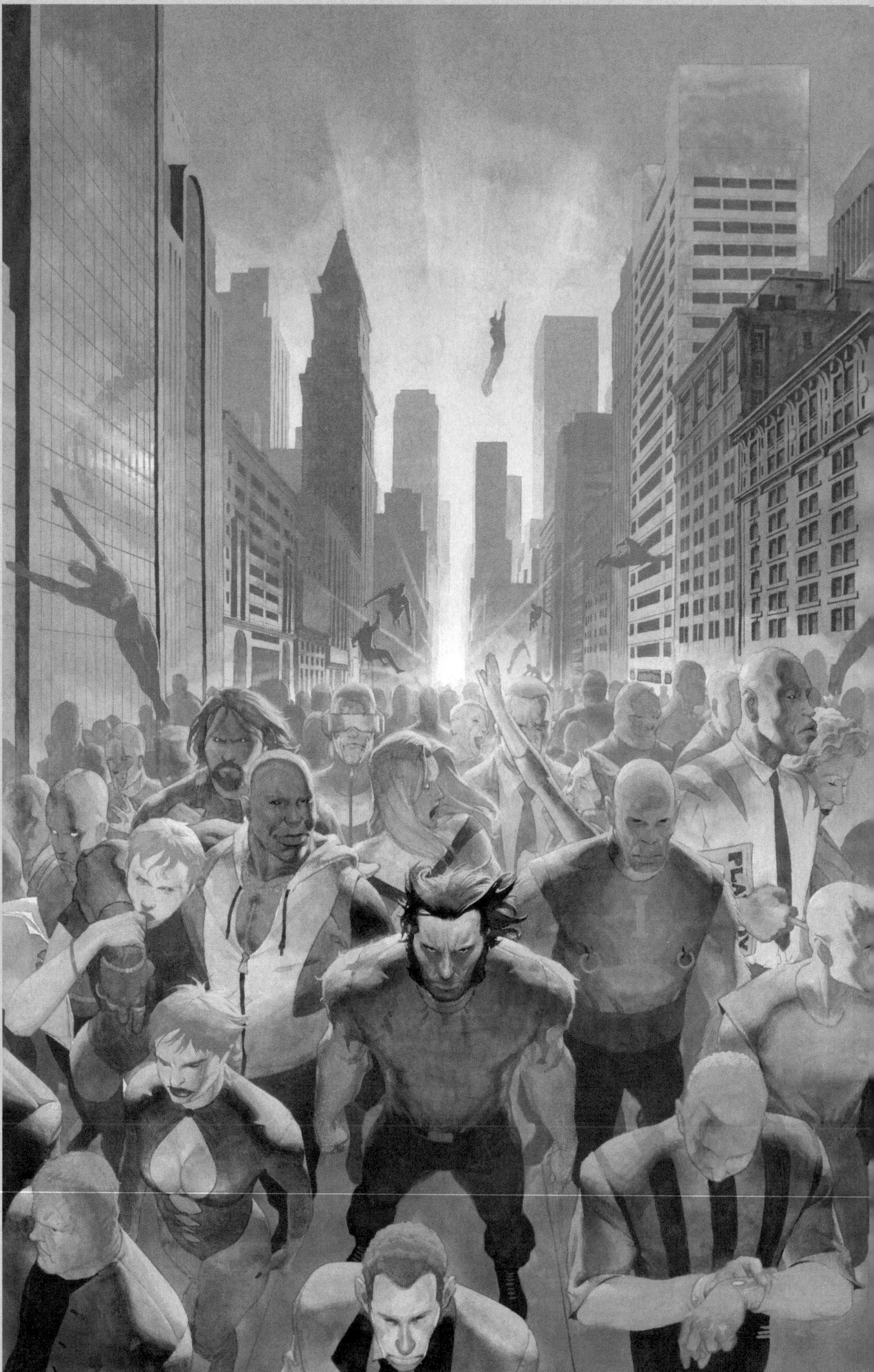

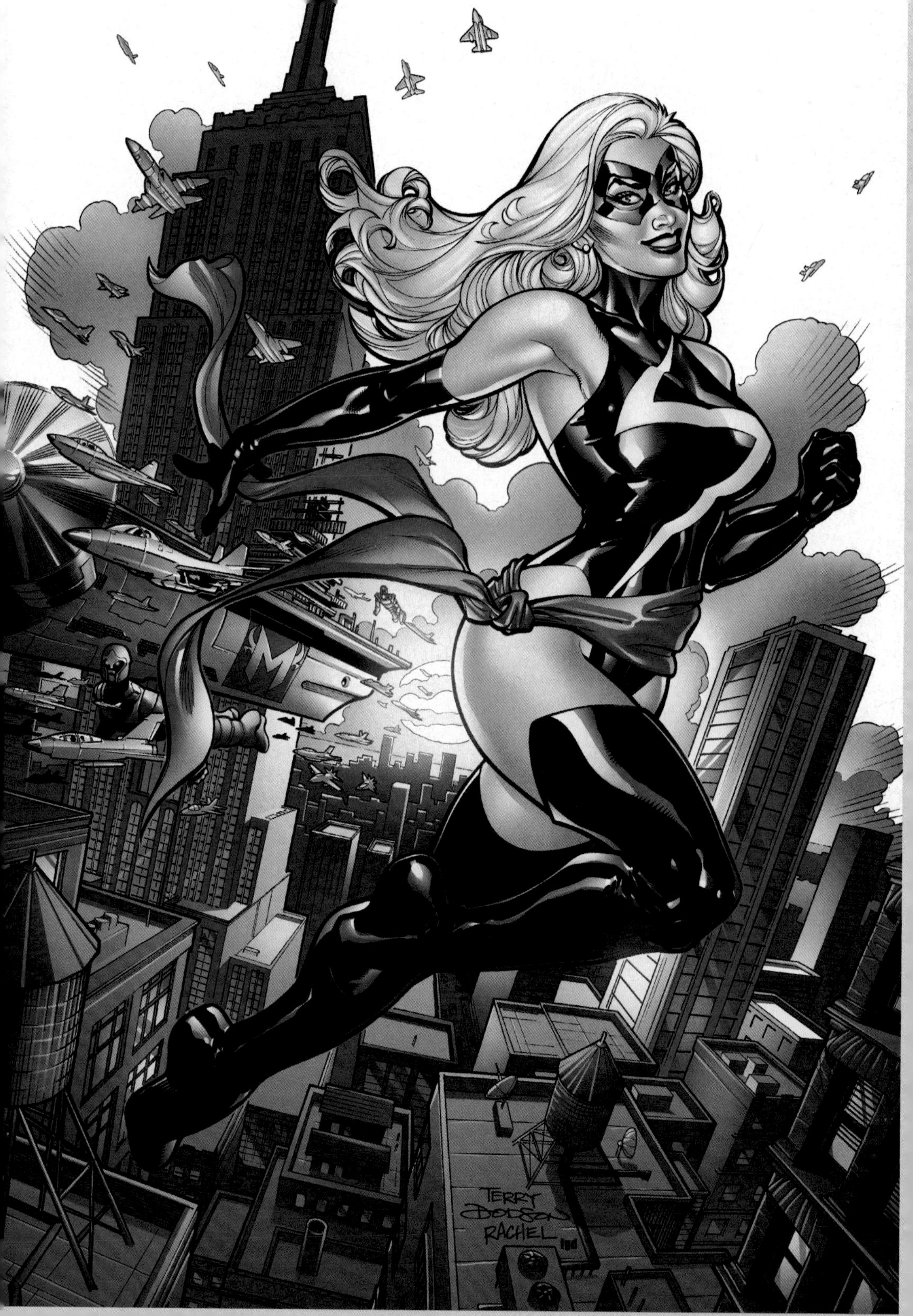
TERRY
DODSON
RACHEL

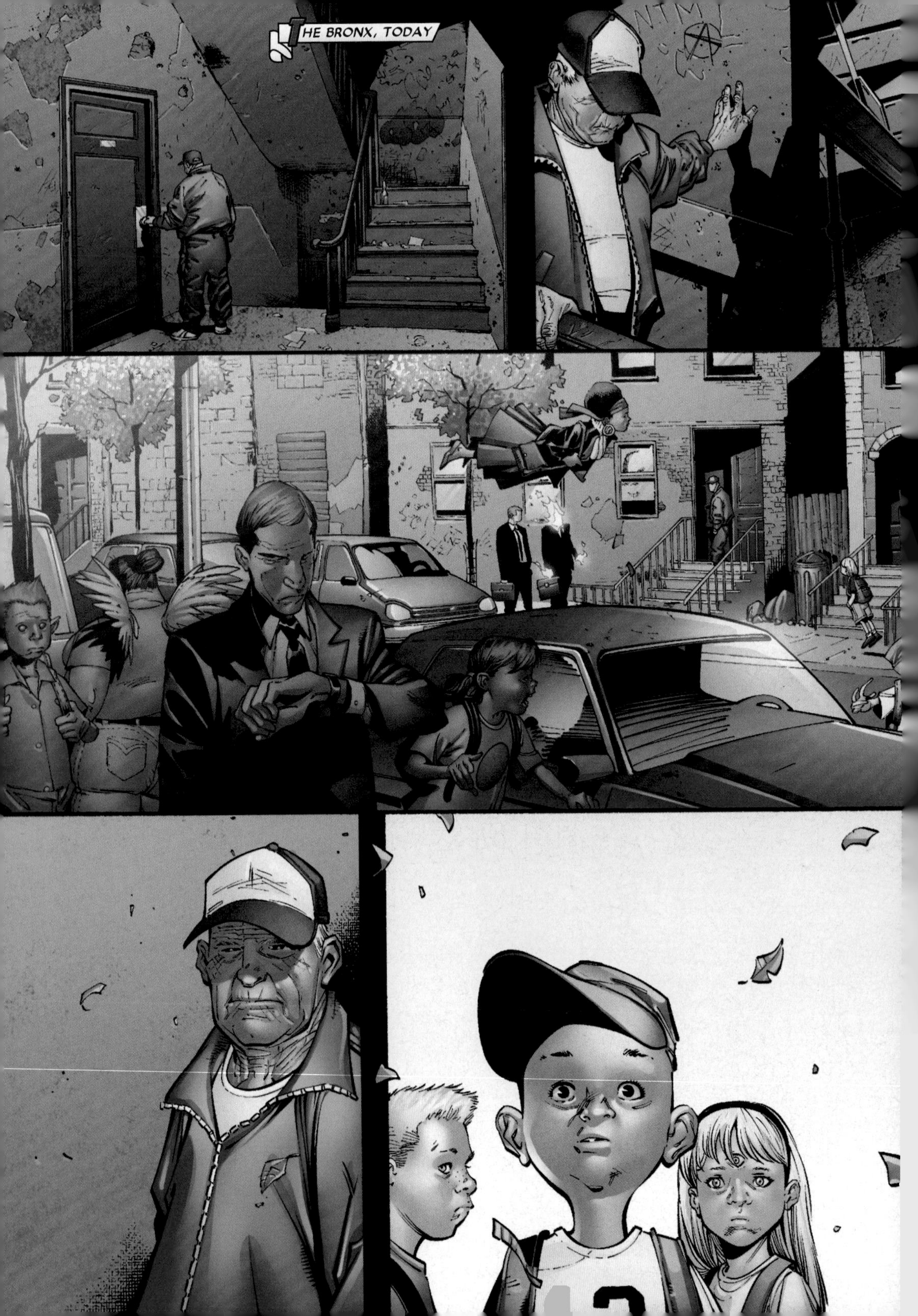
THE BRONX, TODAY

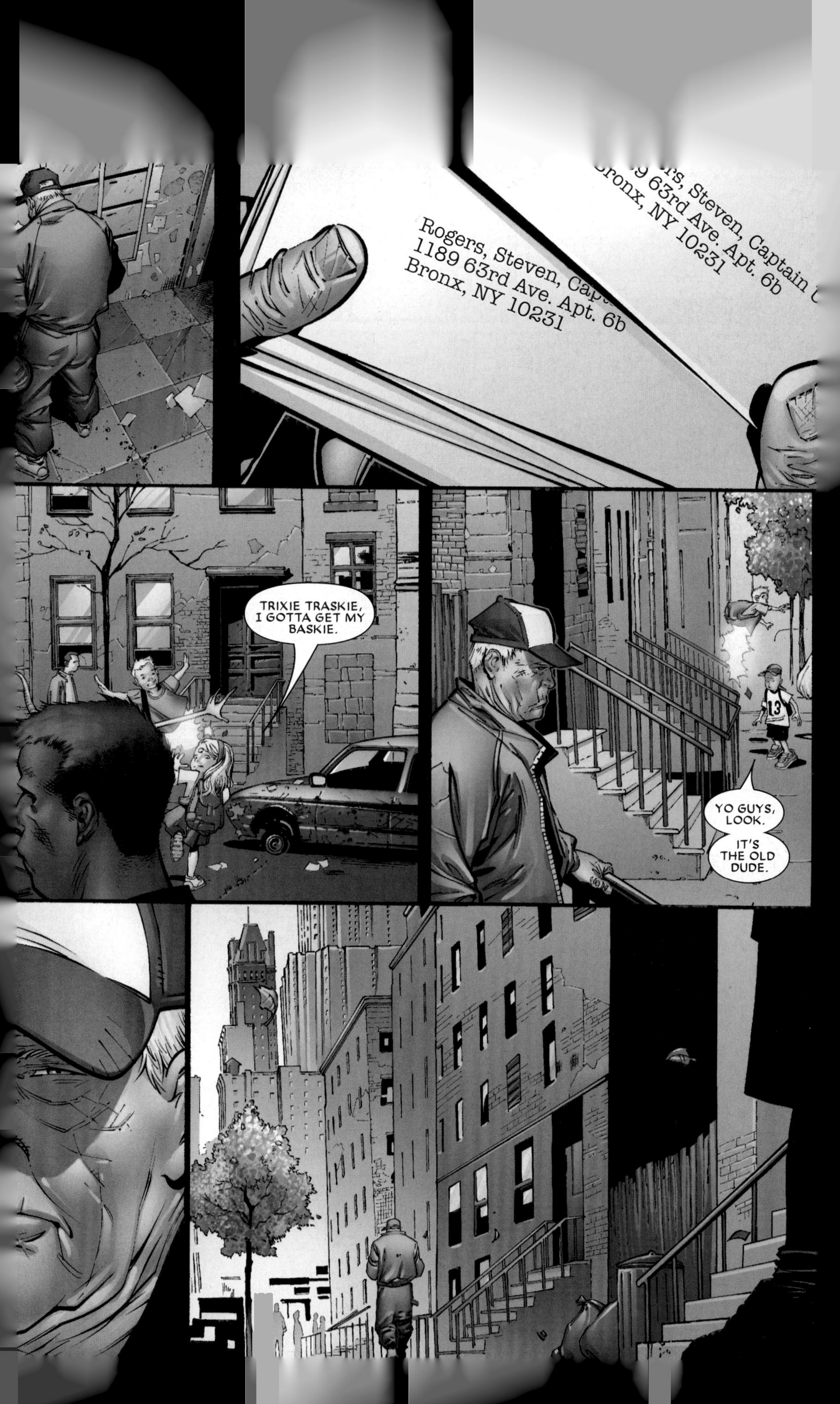
Rogers, Steven, Captain
1189 63rd Ave. Apt. 6b
Bronx, NY 10231
TRIXIE TRASKIE, I GOTTA GET MY BASKIE.
YO GUYS, LOOK.
IT'S THE OLD DUDE.

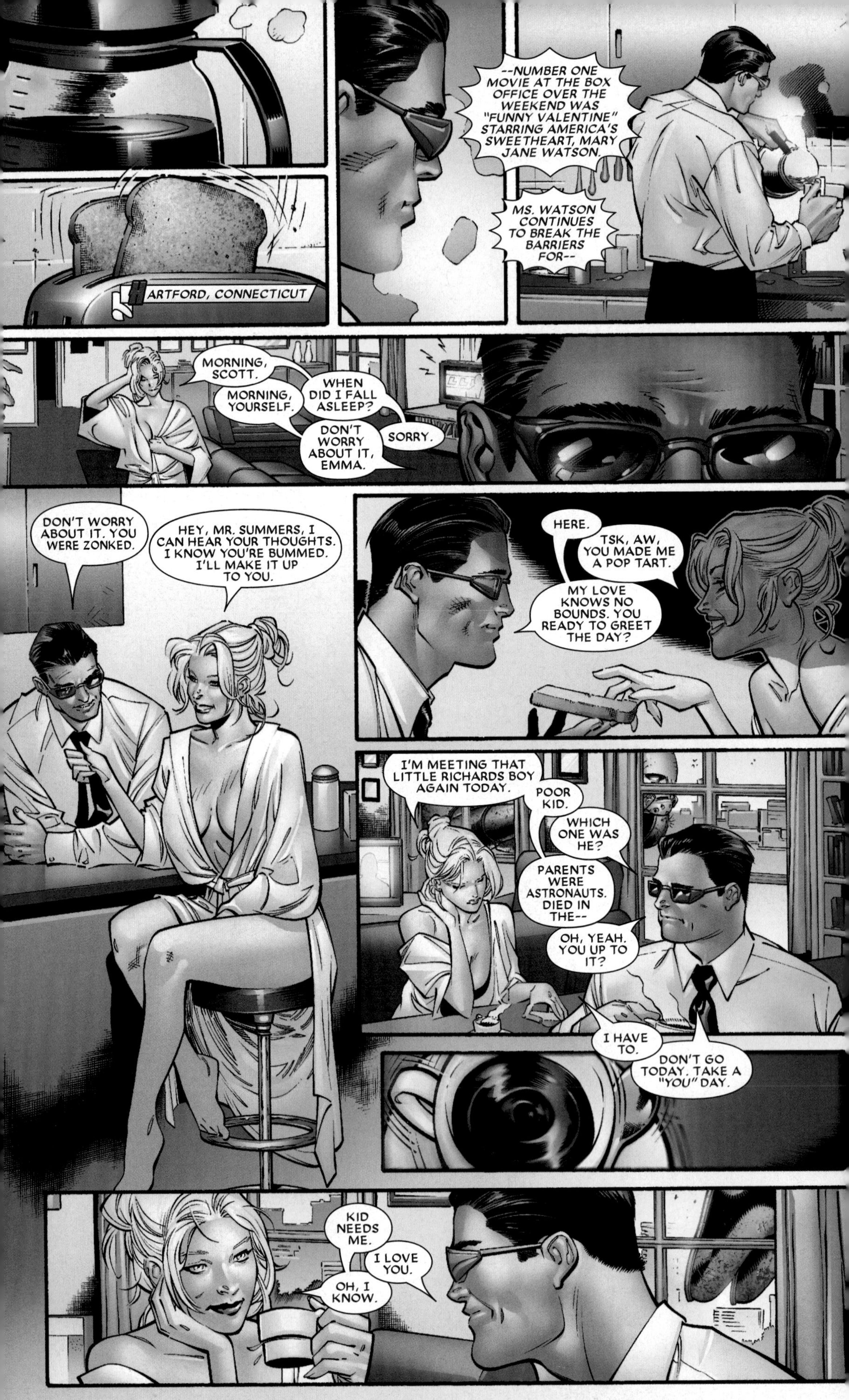

HARTFORD, CONNECTICUT
--NUMBER ONE MOVIE AT THE BOX OFFICE OVER THE WEEKEND WAS "FUNNY VALENTINE" STARRING AMERICA'S SWEETHEART, MARY JANE WATSON.
MS. WATSON CONTINUES TO BREAK THE BARRIERS FOR--
MORNING, SCOTT.
MORNING, YOURSELF.
WHEN DID I FALL ASLEEP?
DON'T WORRY ABOUT IT, EMMA.
SORRY.
DON'T WORRY ABOUT IT. YOU WERE ZONKED.
HEY, MR. SUMMERS, I CAN HEAR YOUR THOUGHTS. I KNOW YOU'RE BUMMED. I'LL MAKE IT UP TO YOU.
HERE.
TSK, AW, YOU MADE ME A POP TART.
MY LOVE KNOWS NO BOUNDS. YOU READY TO GREET THE DAY?
I'M MEETING THAT LITTLE RICHARDS BOY AGAIN TODAY.
POOR KID.
WHICH ONE WAS HE?
PARENTS WERE ASTRONAUTS. DIED IN THE--
OH, YEAH. YOU UP TO IT?
I HAVE TO.
DON'T GO TODAY. TAKE A "YOU" DAY.
KID NEEDS ME.
I LOVE YOU.
OH, I KNOW.

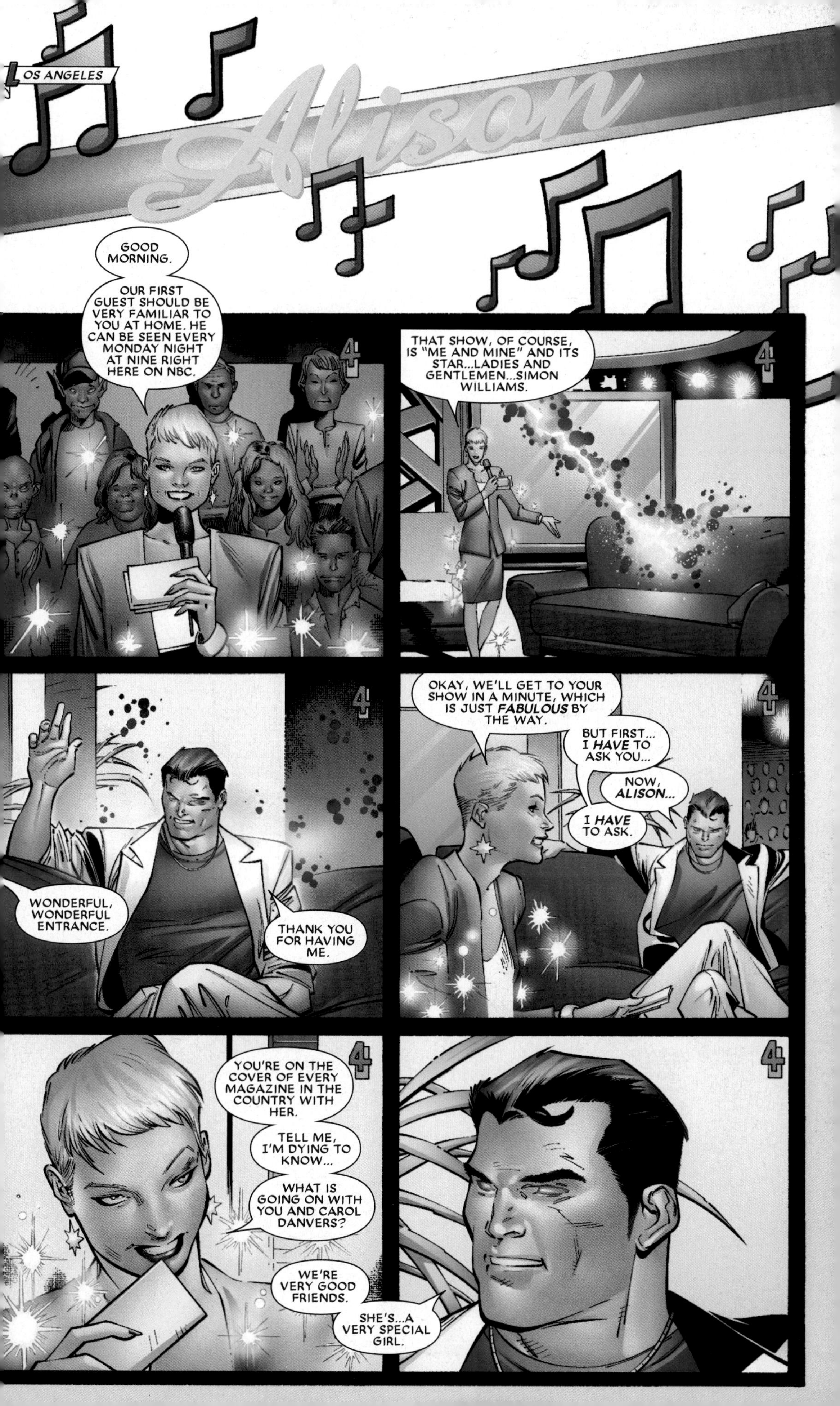

LOS ANGELES
Alison
GOOD MORNING.
OUR FIRST GUEST SHOULD BE VERY FAMILIAR TO YOU AT HOME. HE CAN BE SEEN EVERY MONDAY NIGHT AT NINE RIGHT HERE ON NBC.
THAT SHOW, OF COURSE, IS "ME AND MINE" AND ITS STAR...LADIES AND GENTLEMEN...SIMON WILLIAMS.
WONDERFUL, WONDERFUL ENTRANCE.
THANK YOU FOR HAVING ME.
OKAY, WE'LL GET TO YOUR SHOW IN A MINUTE, WHICH IS JUST FABULOUS BY THE WAY.
BUT FIRST... I HAVE TO ASK YOU...
NOW, ALISON...
I HAVE TO ASK.
YOU'RE ON THE COVER OF EVERY MAGAZINE IN THE COUNTRY WITH HER.
TELL ME, I'M DYING TO KNOW...
WHAT IS GOING ON WITH YOU AND CAROL DANVERS?
WE'RE VERY GOOD FRIENDS.
SHE'S...A VERY SPECIAL GIRL.

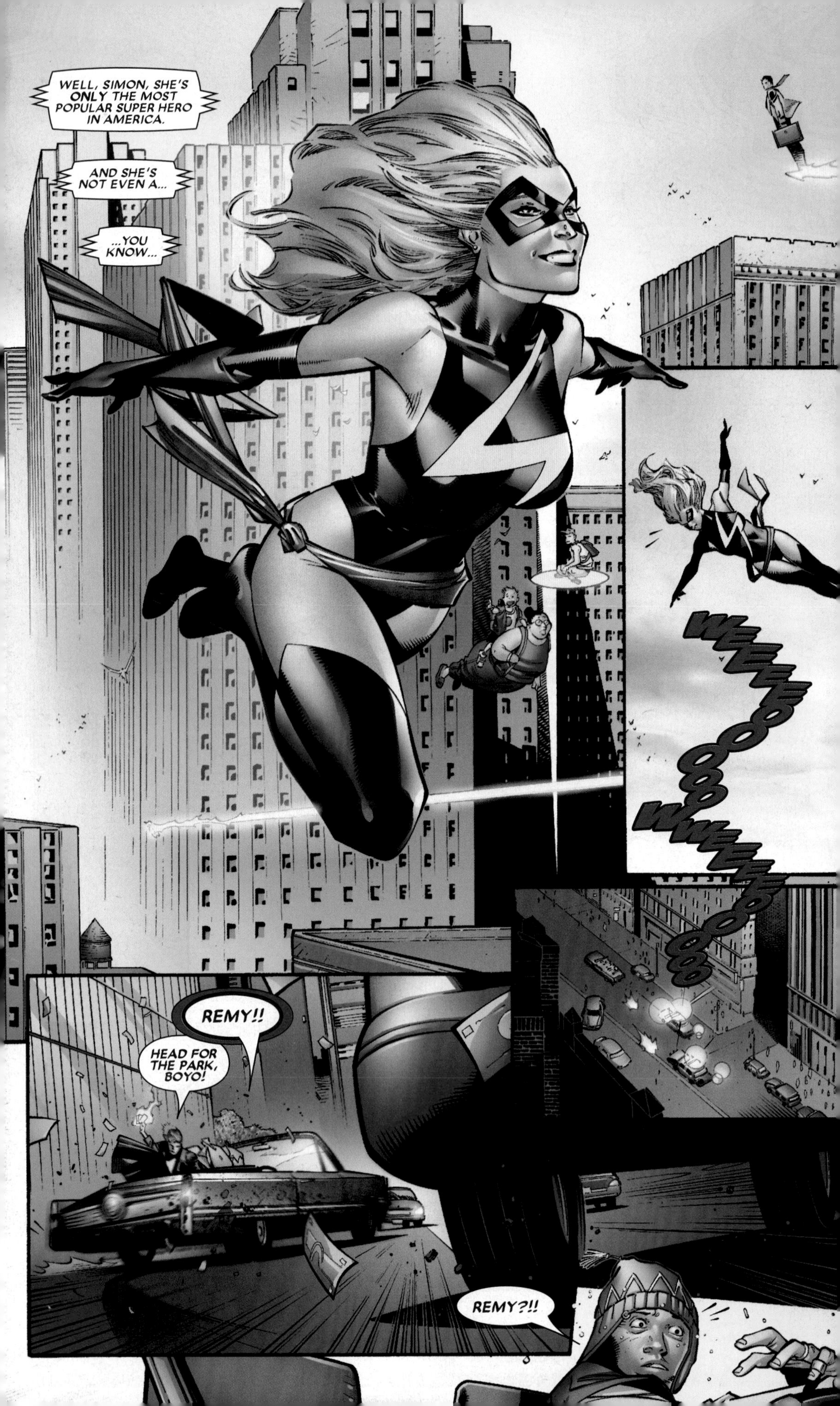
WELL, SIMON, SHE'S ONLY THE MOST POPULAR SUPER HERO IN AMERICA.
AND SHE'S NOT EVEN A...
...YOU KNOW...
WEEEEOOOOWWEEEEOOOO
REMY!!
HEAD FOR THE PARK, BOYO!
REMY?!!

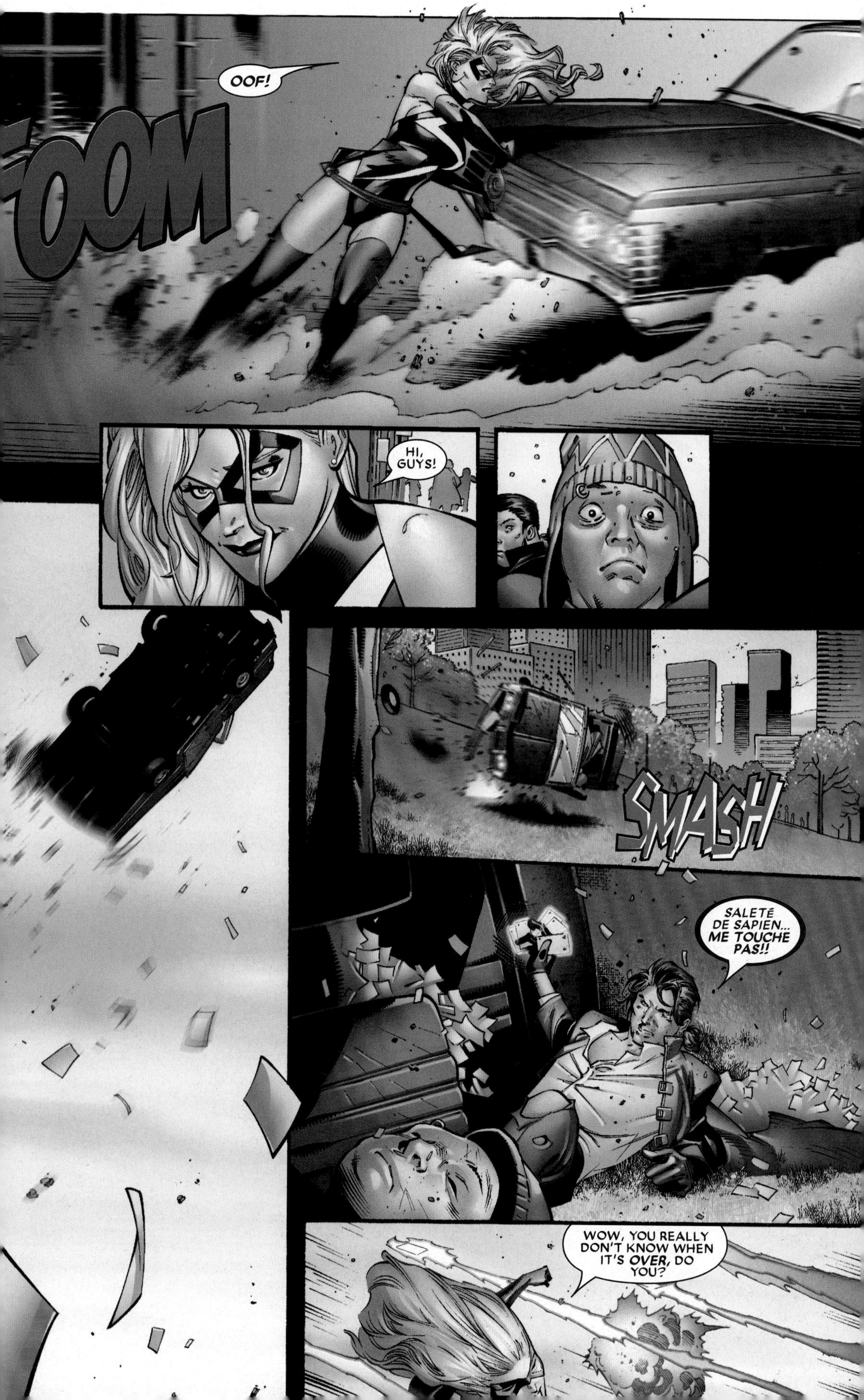
OOF!
FOOM
HI, GUYS!
SMASH
SALETÉ DE SAPIEN... ME TOUCHE PAS!!
WOW, YOU REALLY DON'T KNOW WHEN IT'S OVER, DO YOU?

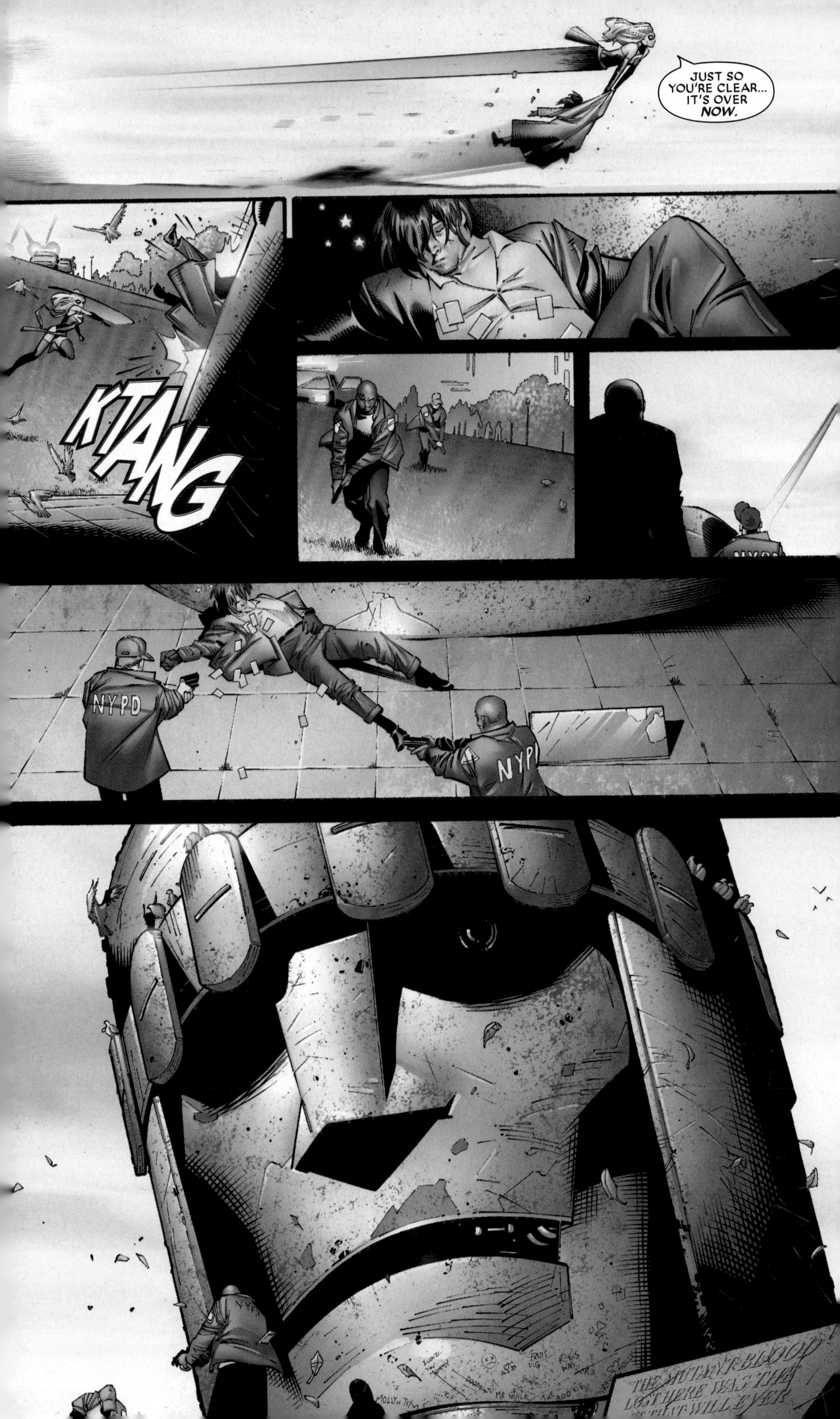
JUST SO YOU'RE CLEAR... IT'S OVER *NOW*.
KTANG
NYPD
NYPD
NYPD
I LOVE YOU TOMMY
MR GUILE
THE ROOKIE
MOLLY + TIM
THE MUTANT BLOOD
LOST HERE WAS THE

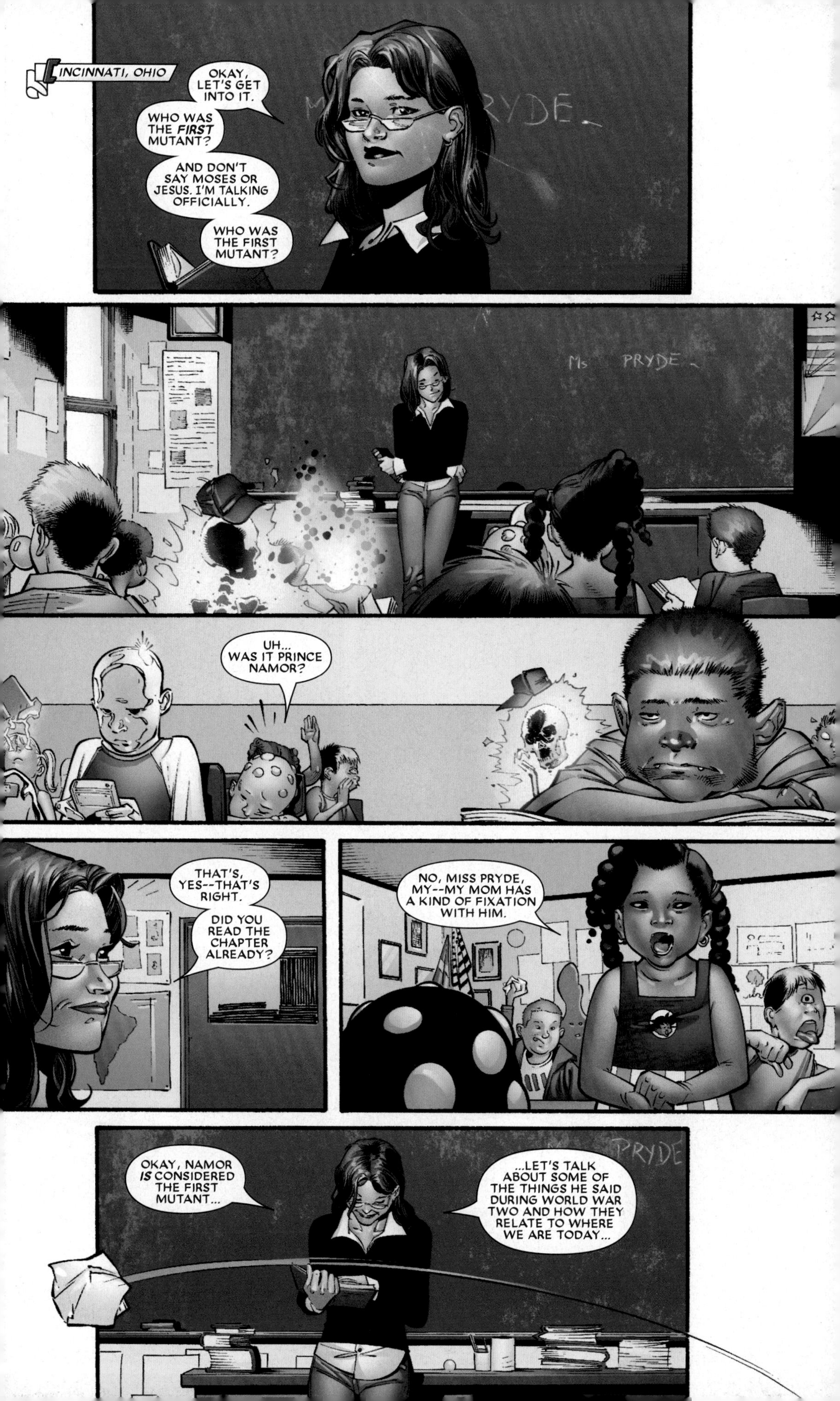
CINCINNATI, OHIO
OKAY, LET'S GET INTO IT.
WHO WAS THE *FIRST* MUTANT?
AND DON'T SAY MOSES OR JESUS. I'M TALKING OFFICIALLY.
WHO WAS THE FIRST MUTANT?
Ms PRYDE
UH... WAS IT PRINCE NAMOR?
THAT'S, YES--THAT'S RIGHT.
DID YOU READ THE CHAPTER ALREADY?
NO, MISS PRYDE, MY--MY MOM HAS A KIND OF FIXATION WITH HIM.
OKAY, NAMOR *IS* CONSIDERED THE FIRST MUTANT...
...LET'S TALK ABOUT SOME OF THE THINGS HE SAID DURING WORLD WAR TWO AND HOW THEY RELATE TO WHERE WE ARE TODAY...

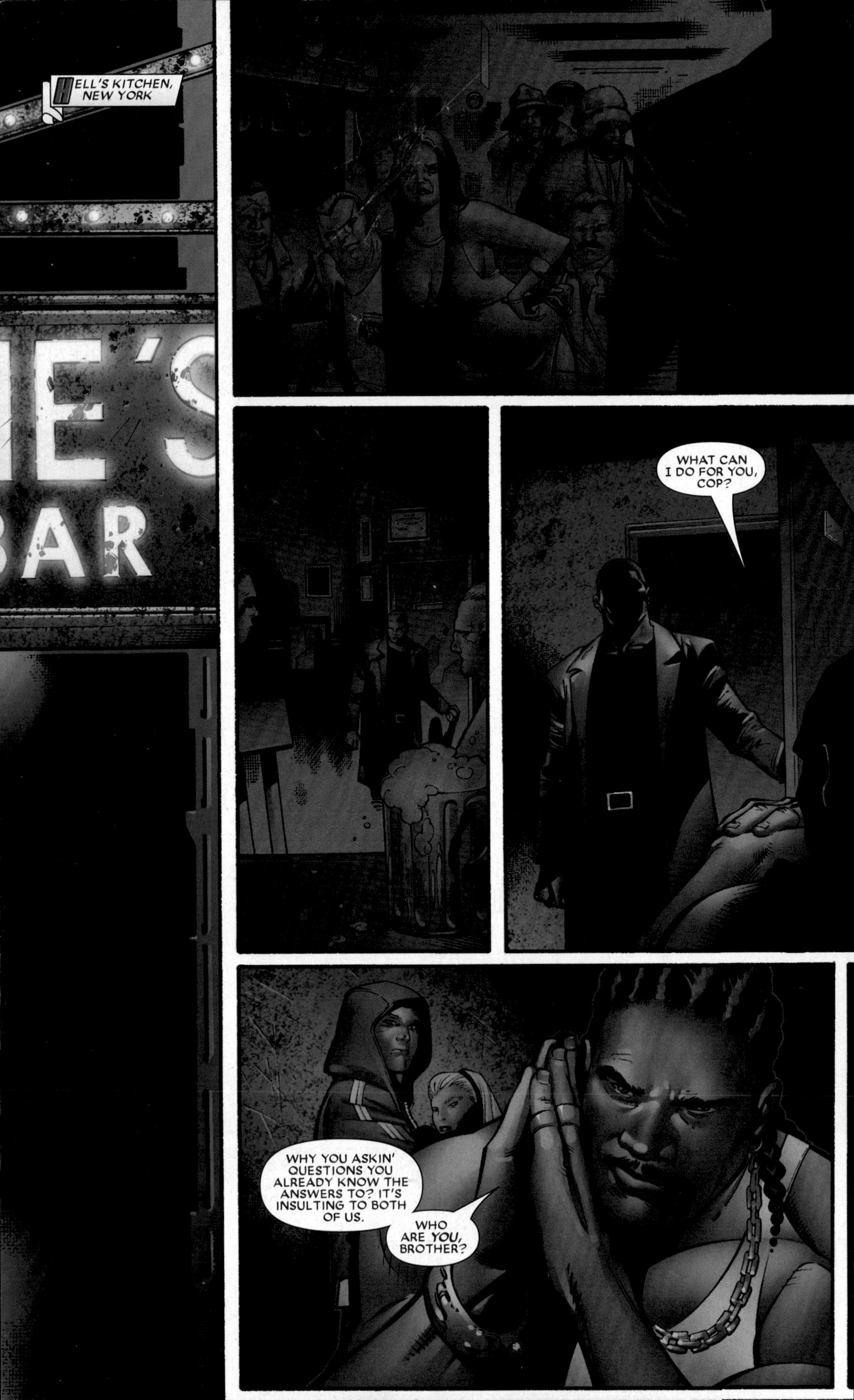
HELL'S KITCHEN, NEW YORK
E'S
BAR
WHAT CAN I DO FOR YOU, COP?
WHY YOU ASKIN' QUESTIONS YOU ALREADY KNOW THE ANSWERS TO? IT'S INSULTING TO BOTH OF US.
WHO ARE YOU, BROTHER?

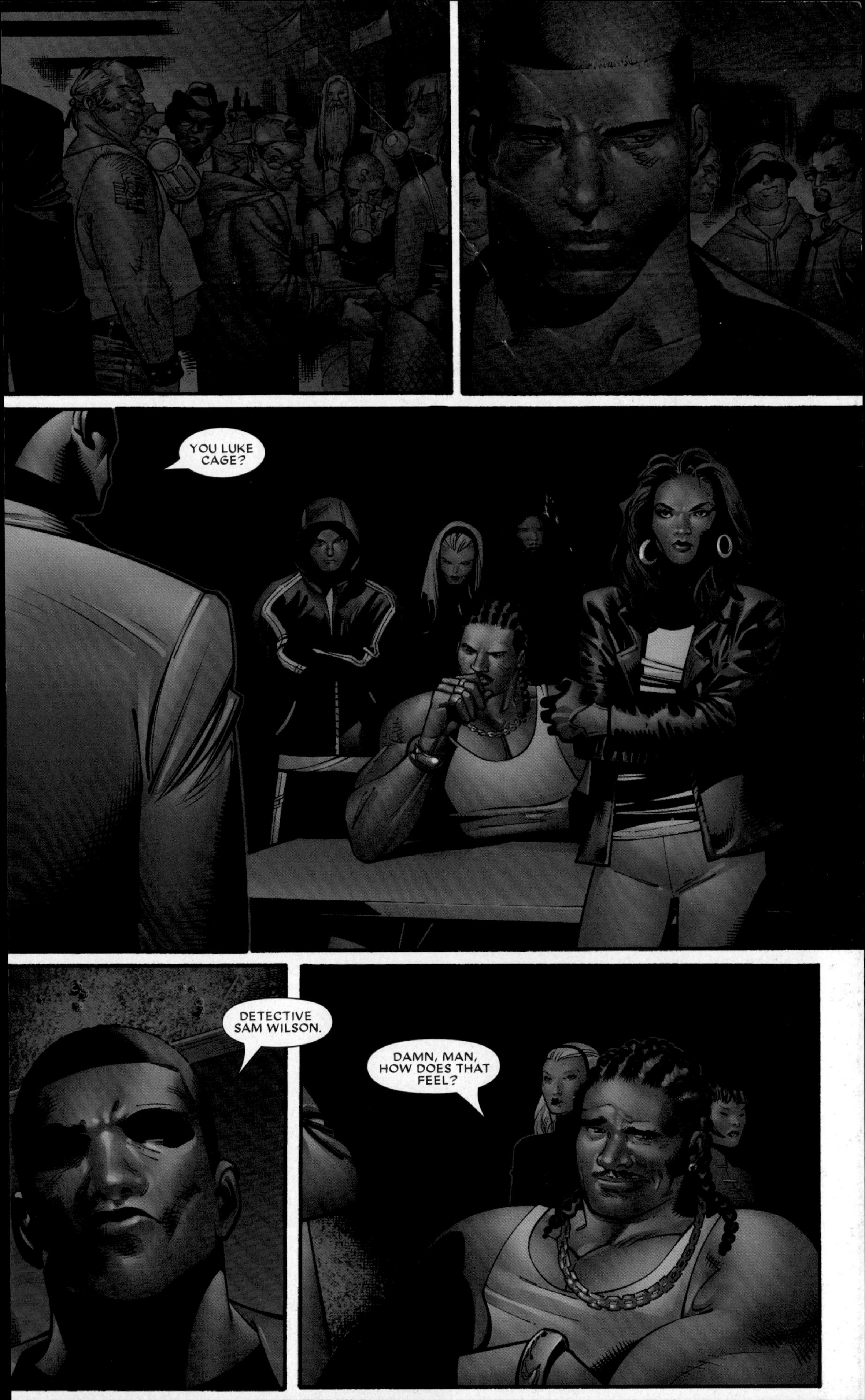
YOU LUKE CAGE?
DETECTIVE SAM WILSON.
DAMN, MAN, HOW DOES THAT FEEL?

HOW DOES *WHAT* FEEL?

COME ON... PUTTIN' A SAPIEN BROTHER IN HELL'S KITCHEN? YOU DON'T FEEL A BIT *USED* BY THE SYSTEM?

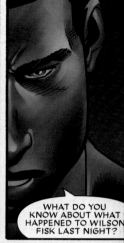

WHAT DO YOU KNOW ABOUT WHAT HAPPENED TO WILSON FISK LAST NIGHT?

HOW MANY PHOTO OPS THEY MAKE YOU DO A WEEK? BEING THE TOKEN SAPIEN.

YOU WANNA DO THIS AT THE STATION?

WHAT *HAPPENED* TO THE KINGPIN? I HAVEN'T TURNED ON A TV. SOMEONE *WHACK* HIM?

SOMEONE BEAT HIM INTO A COMA.

WHERE WERE YOU LAST NIGHT?

THIS IS FOR WHOEVER DID IT.

CLAP CLAP CLAP

SLEEPING. YOU SHOULD TRY IT...IF YOU CAN STILL DO IT.

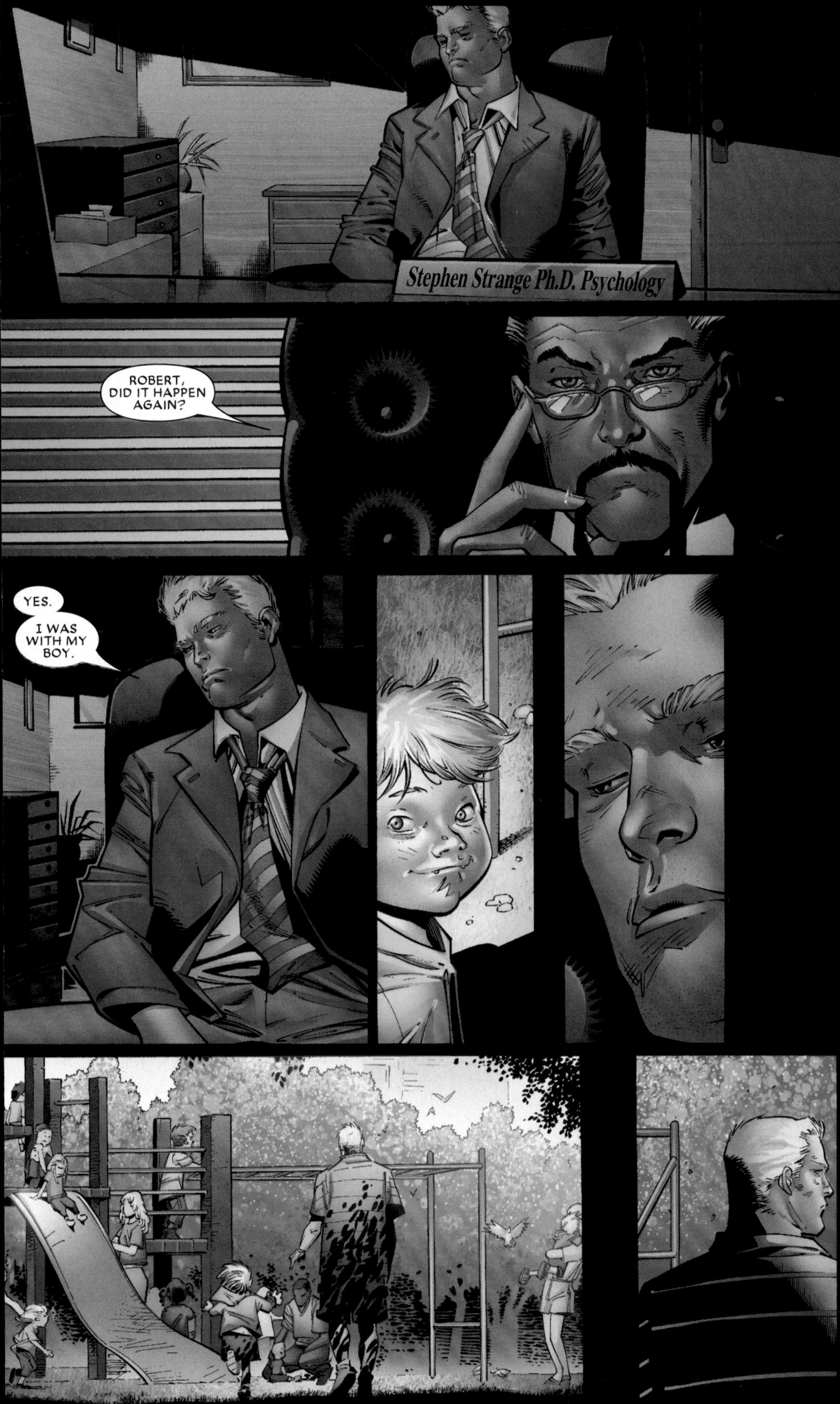
Stephen Strange Ph.D. Psychology
ROBERT, DID IT HAPPEN AGAIN?
YES.
I WAS WITH MY BOY.

AND THIS WALL OF BLACK...

...IT JUST DISAPPEARED?

BUT IT WAS THERE.

IT WASN'T-- I KNOW WHAT'S REAL. I'M NOT CRAZY. I KNOW WHAT'S REAL.

WHAT DO YOU THINK IT MEANT?

I. DON'T. KNOW.

AND HOW DOES THAT MAKE YOU FEEL?

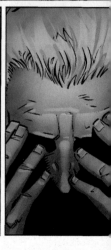

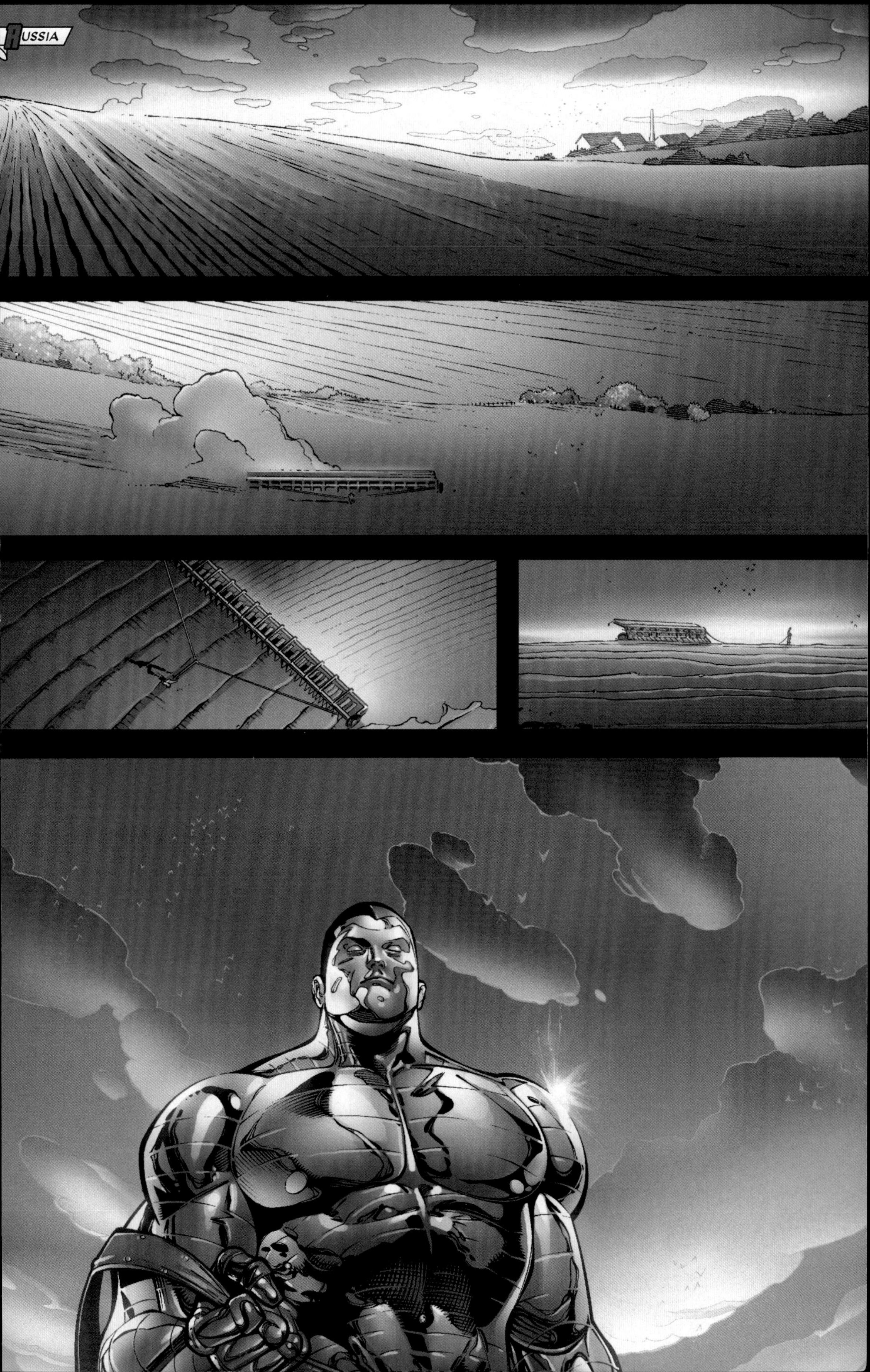
RUSSIA

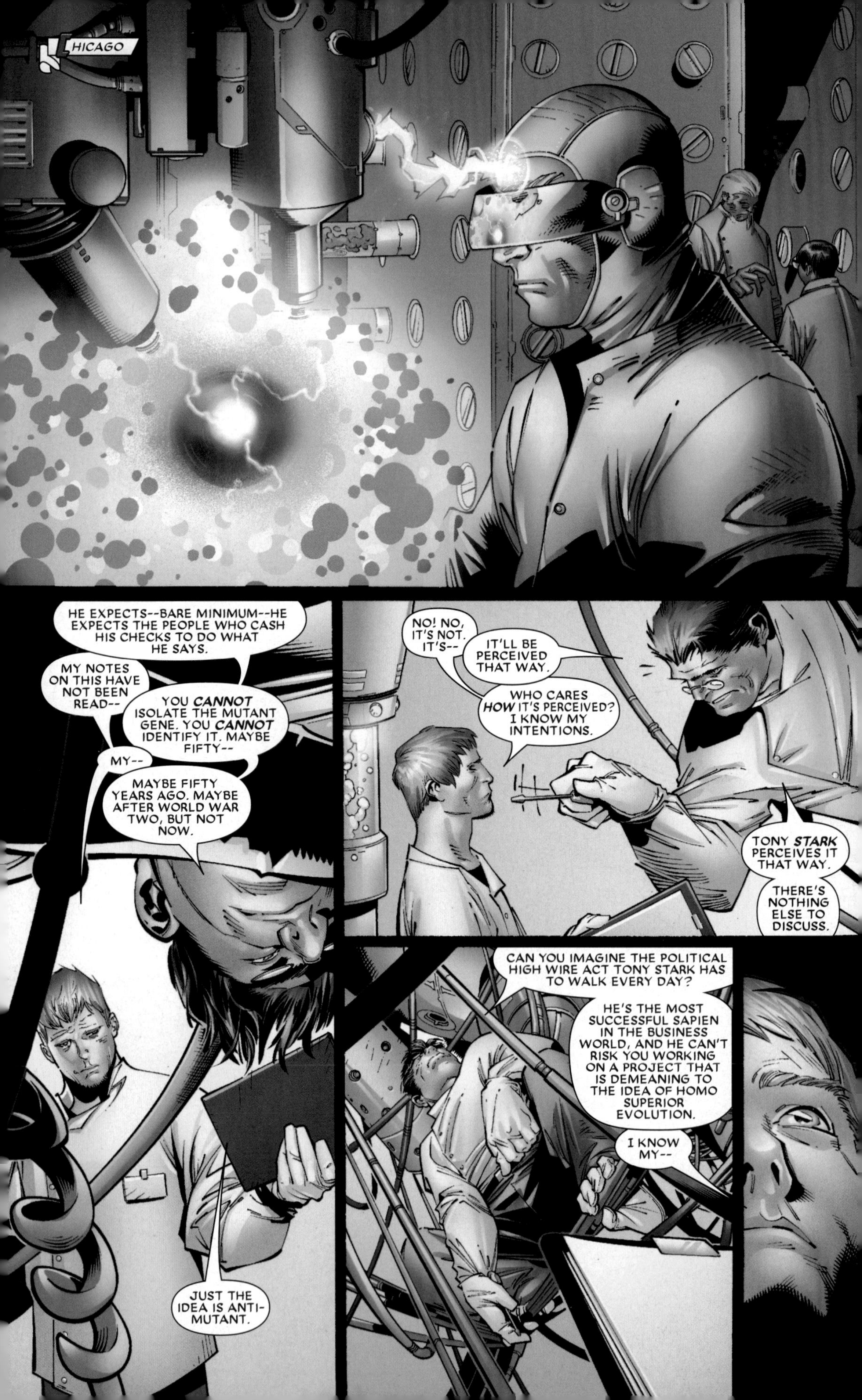
HICAGO
HE EXPECTS--BARE MINIMUM--HE EXPECTS THE PEOPLE WHO CASH HIS CHECKS TO DO WHAT HE SAYS.
MY NOTES ON THIS HAVE NOT BEEN READ--
YOU CANNOT ISOLATE THE MUTANT GENE. YOU CANNOT IDENTIFY IT. MAYBE FIFTY--
MY--
MAYBE FIFTY YEARS AGO. MAYBE AFTER WORLD WAR TWO, BUT NOT NOW.
JUST THE IDEA IS ANTI-MUTANT.
NO! NO, IT'S NOT. IT'S--
IT'LL BE PERCEIVED THAT WAY.
WHO CARES HOW IT'S PERCEIVED? I KNOW MY INTENTIONS.
TONY STARK PERCEIVES IT THAT WAY.
THERE'S NOTHING ELSE TO DISCUSS.
CAN YOU IMAGINE THE POLITICAL HIGH WIRE ACT TONY STARK HAS TO WALK EVERY DAY?
HE'S THE MOST SUCCESSFUL SAPIEN IN THE BUSINESS WORLD, AND HE CAN'T RISK YOU WORKING ON A PROJECT THAT IS DEMEANING TO THE IDEA OF HOMO SUPERIOR EVOLUTION.
I KNOW MY--

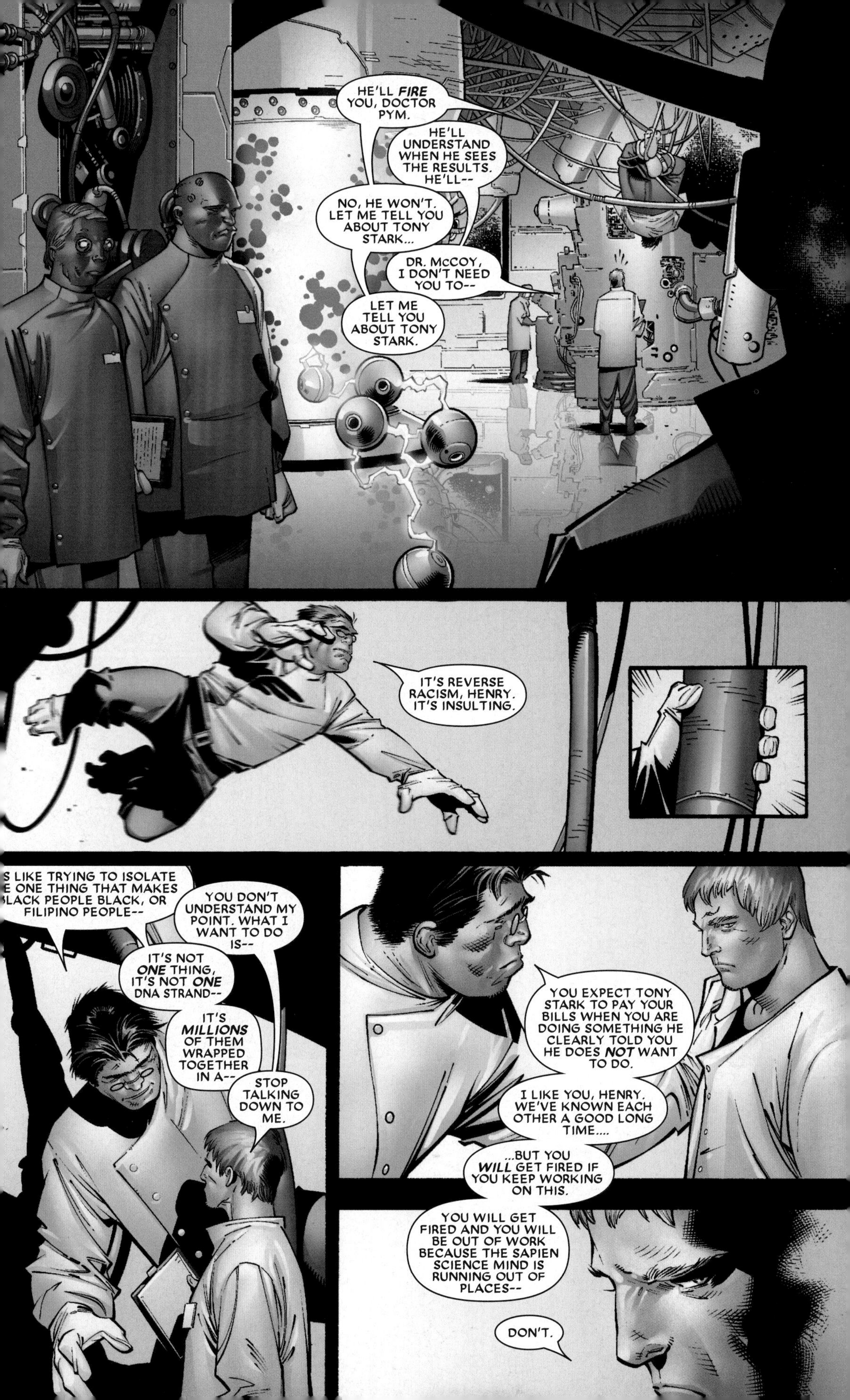
HE'LL FIRE YOU, DOCTOR PYM.
HE'LL UNDERSTAND WHEN HE SEES THE RESULTS. HE'LL--
NO, HE WON'T. LET ME TELL YOU ABOUT TONY STARK...
DR. McCOY, I DON'T NEED YOU TO--
LET ME TELL YOU ABOUT TONY STARK.
IT'S REVERSE RACISM, HENRY. IT'S INSULTING.
S LIKE TRYING TO ISOLATE E ONE THING THAT MAKES BLACK PEOPLE BLACK, OR FILIPINO PEOPLE--
YOU DON'T UNDERSTAND MY POINT. WHAT I WANT TO DO IS--
IT'S NOT ONE THING, IT'S NOT ONE DNA STRAND--
IT'S MILLIONS OF THEM WRAPPED TOGETHER IN A--
STOP TALKING DOWN TO ME.
YOU EXPECT TONY STARK TO PAY YOUR BILLS WHEN YOU ARE DOING SOMETHING HE CLEARLY TOLD YOU HE DOES NOT WANT TO DO.
I LIKE YOU, HENRY. WE'VE KNOWN EACH OTHER A GOOD LONG TIME....
...BUT YOU WILL GET FIRED IF YOU KEEP WORKING ON THIS.
YOU WILL GET FIRED AND YOU WILL BE OUT OF WORK BECAUSE THE SAPIEN SCIENCE MIND IS RUNNING OUT OF PLACES--
DON'T.

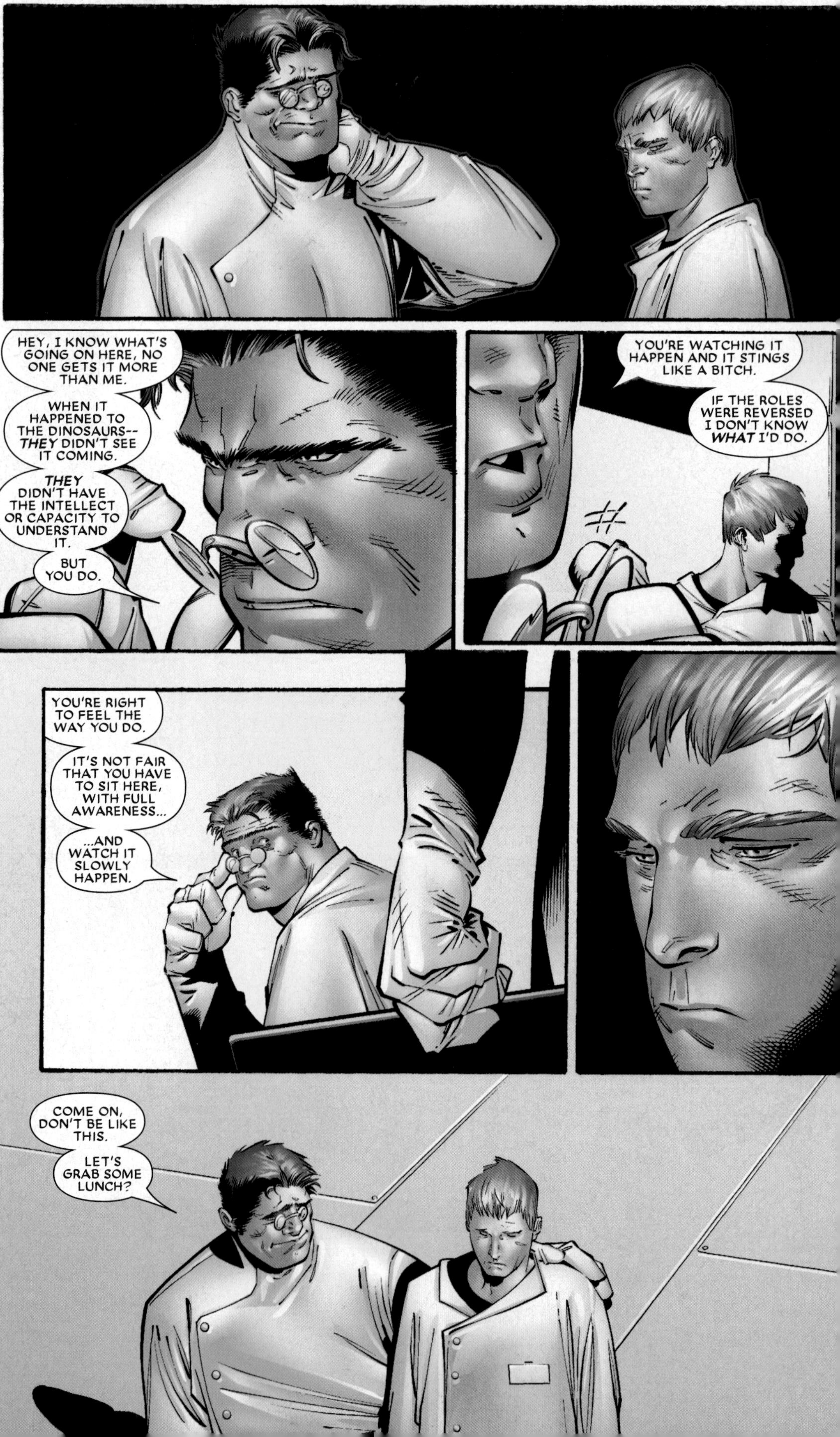
HEY, I KNOW WHAT'S GOING ON HERE, NO ONE GETS IT MORE THAN ME.
WHEN IT HAPPENED TO THE DINOSAURS-- *THEY* DIDN'T SEE IT COMING.
THEY DIDN'T HAVE THE INTELLECT OR CAPACITY TO UNDERSTAND IT.
BUT YOU DO.
YOU'RE WATCHING IT HAPPEN AND IT STINGS LIKE A BITCH.
IF THE ROLES WERE REVERSED I DON'T KNOW *WHAT* I'D DO.
YOU'RE RIGHT TO FEEL THE WAY YOU DO.
IT'S NOT FAIR THAT YOU HAVE TO SIT HERE, WITH FULL AWARENESS...
...AND WATCH IT SLOWLY HAPPEN.
COME ON, DON'T BE LIKE THIS.
LET'S GRAB SOME LUNCH?

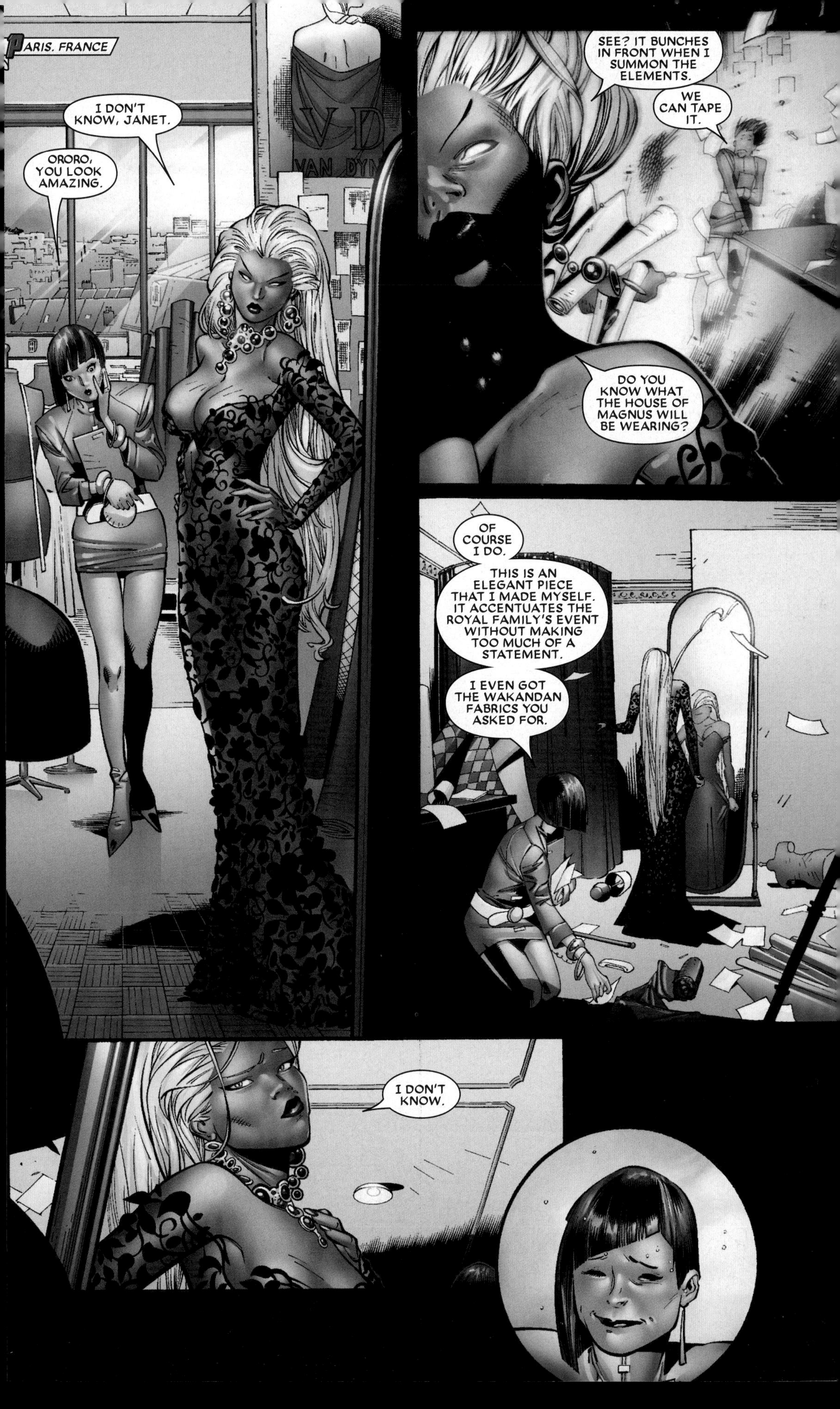
PARIS, FRANCE
ORORO, YOU LOOK AMAZING.
I DON'T KNOW, JANET.
SEE? IT BUNCHES IN FRONT WHEN I SUMMON THE ELEMENTS.
WE CAN TAPE IT.
DO YOU KNOW WHAT THE HOUSE OF MAGNUS WILL BE WEARING?
OF COURSE I DO.
THIS IS AN ELEGANT PIECE THAT I MADE MYSELF. IT ACCENTUATES THE ROYAL FAMILY'S EVENT WITHOUT MAKING TOO MUCH OF A STATEMENT.
I EVEN GOT THE WAKANDAN FABRICS YOU ASKED FOR.
I DON'T KNOW.

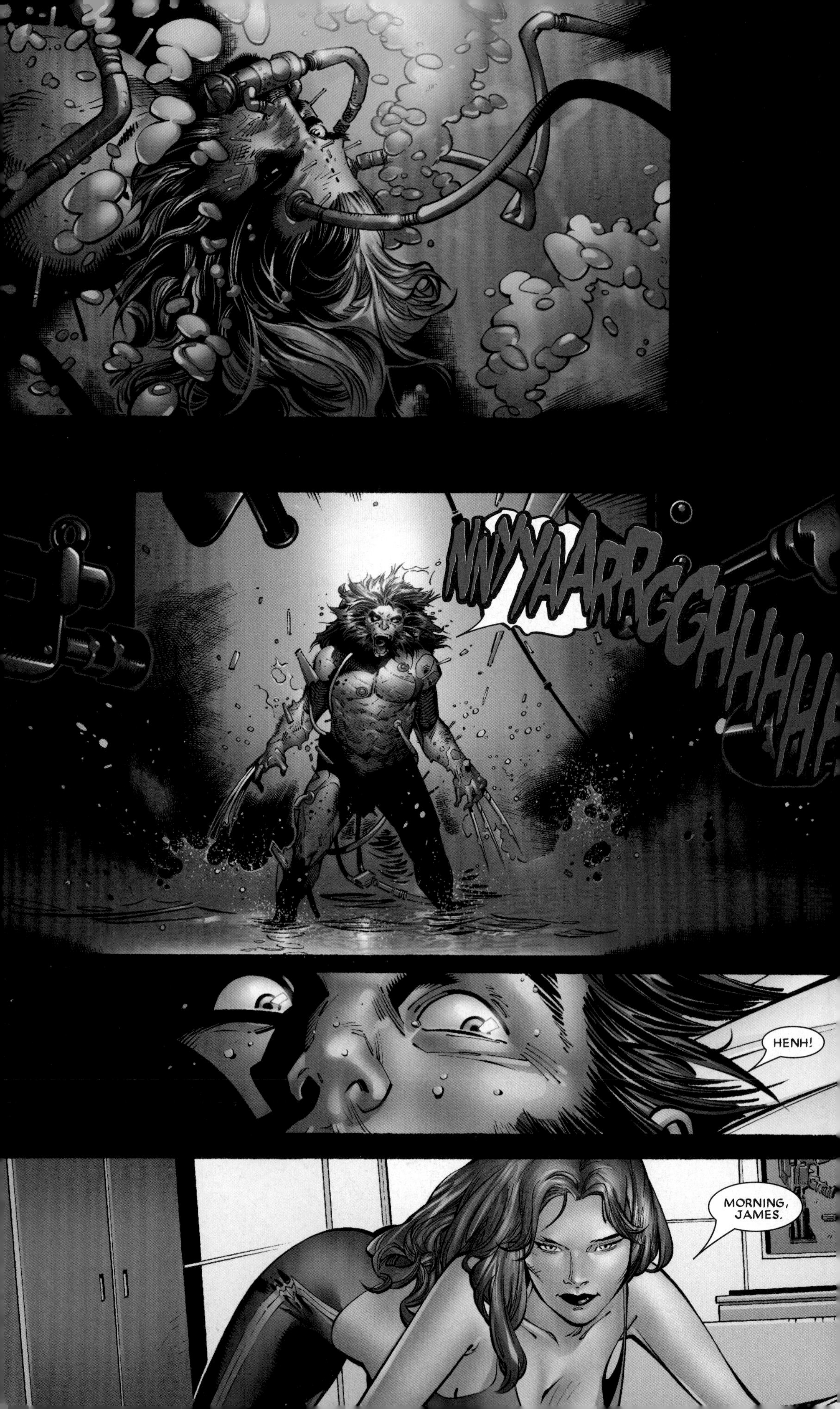

NNYYAARRGGHHHHH
HENH!
MORNING, JAMES.

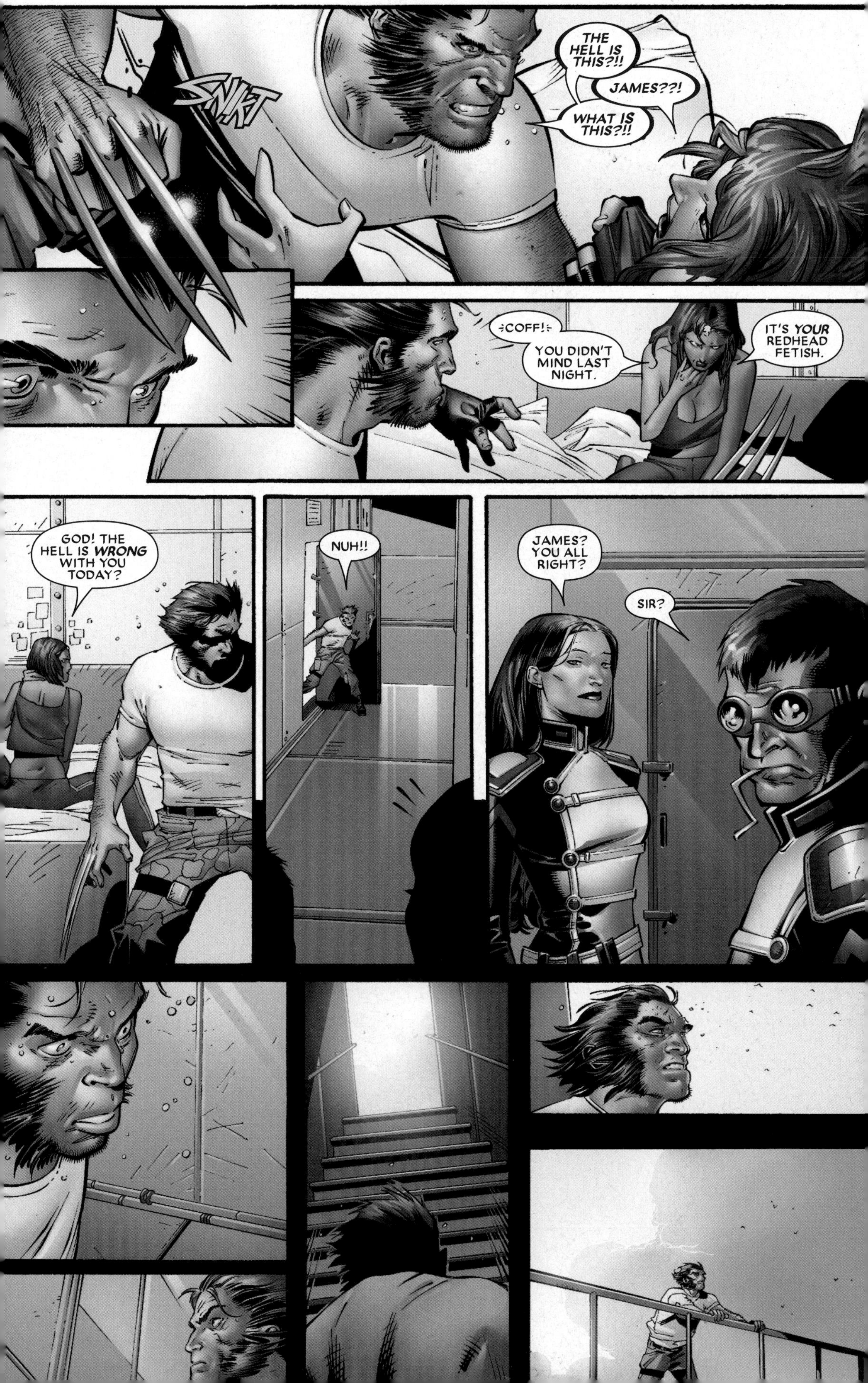
SNIKT
THE HELL IS THIS?!!
JAMES??!
WHAT IS THIS?!!
=COFF!=
YOU DIDN'T MIND LAST NIGHT.
IT'S YOUR REDHEAD FETISH.
GOD! THE HELL IS WRONG WITH YOU TODAY?
NUH!!
JAMES? YOU ALL RIGHT?
SIR?

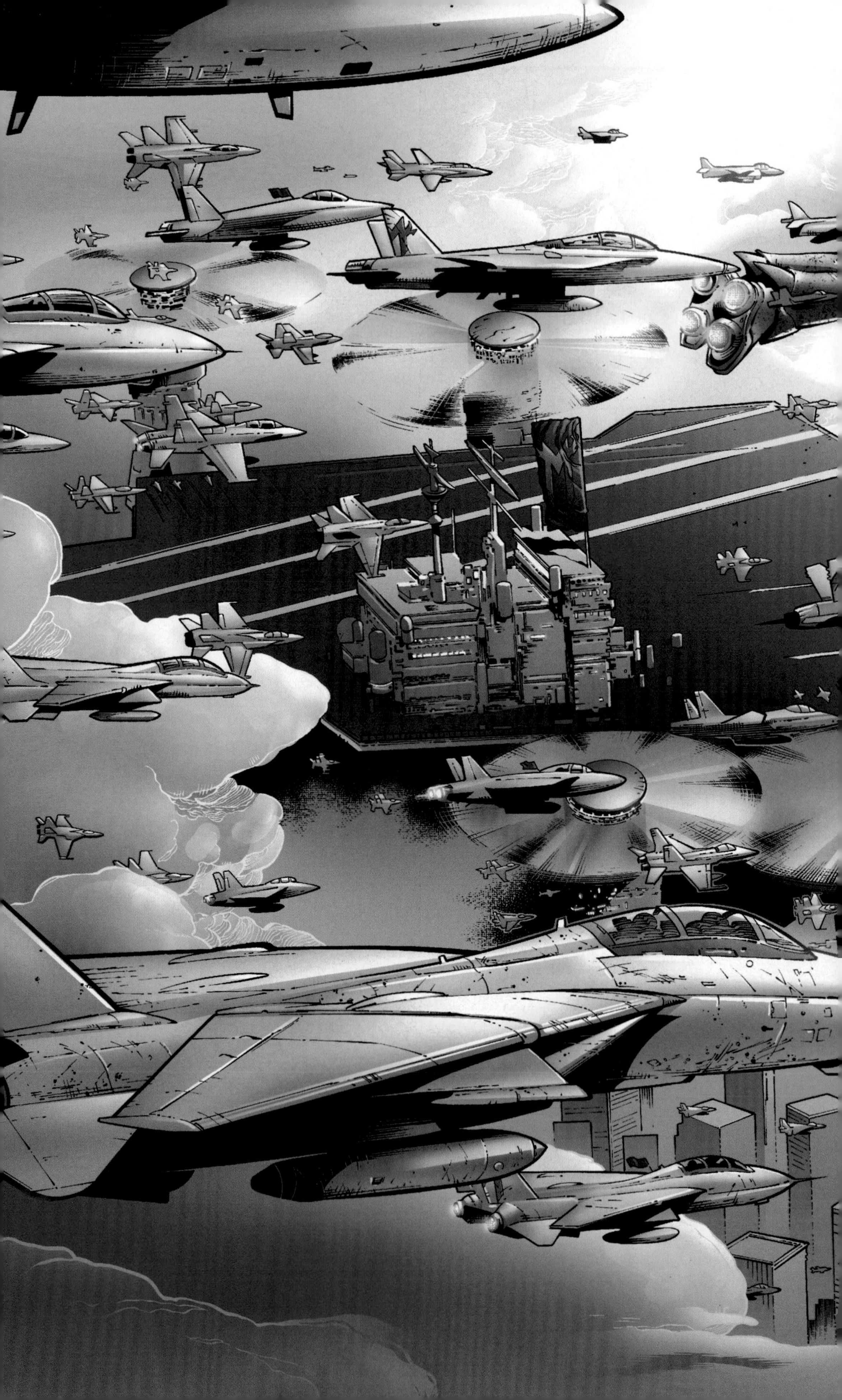

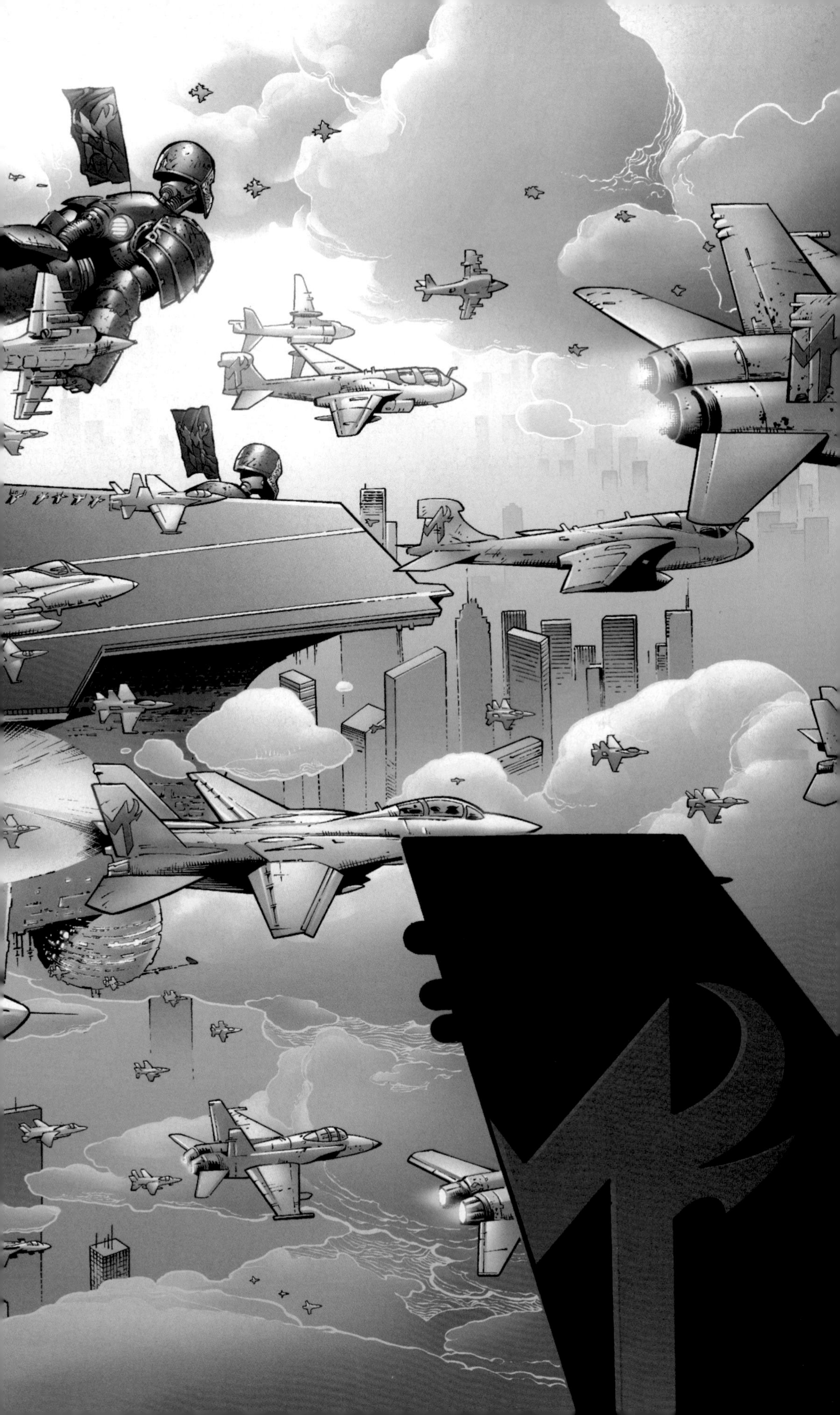

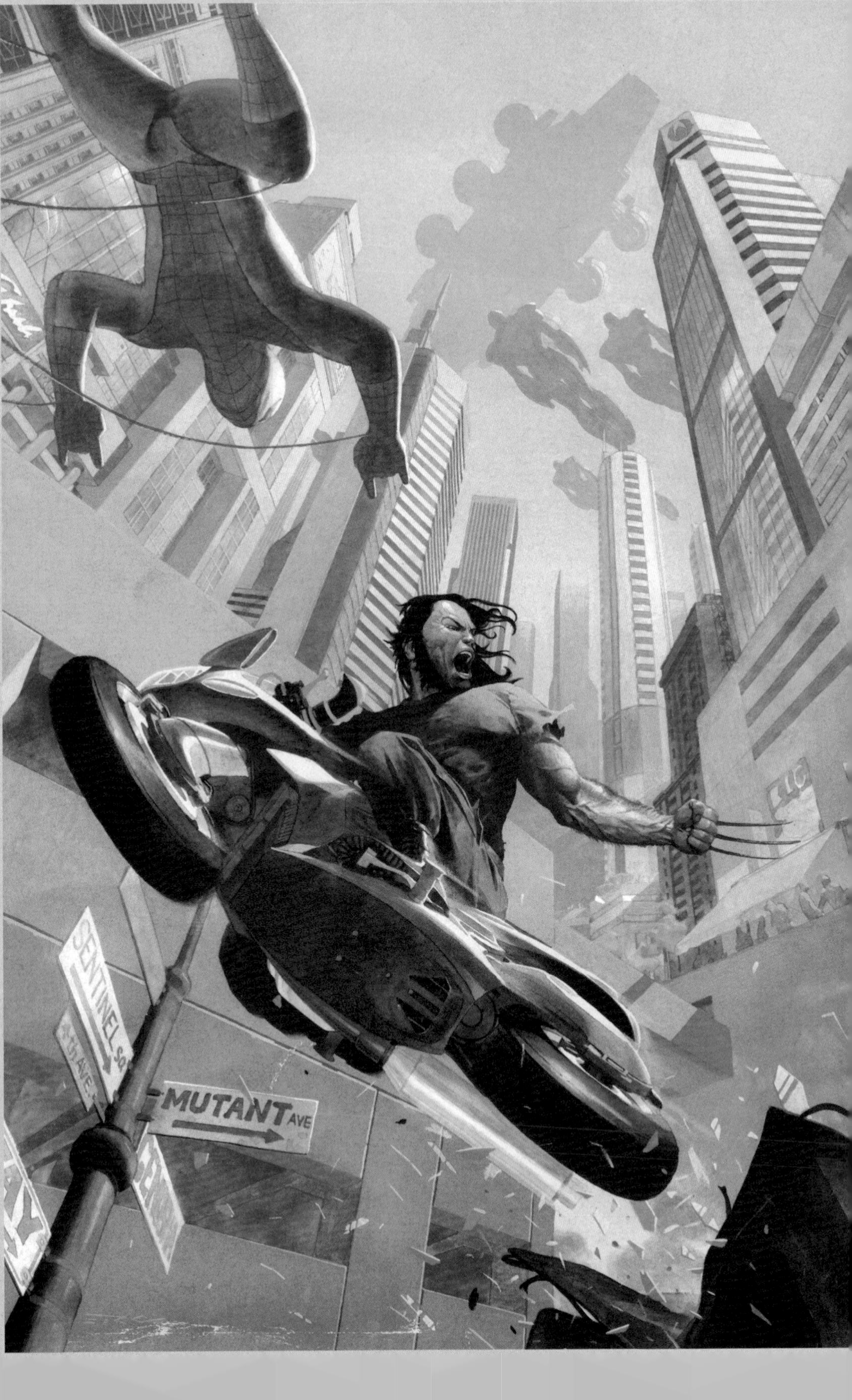
SENTINEL SQ
MUTANT AVE

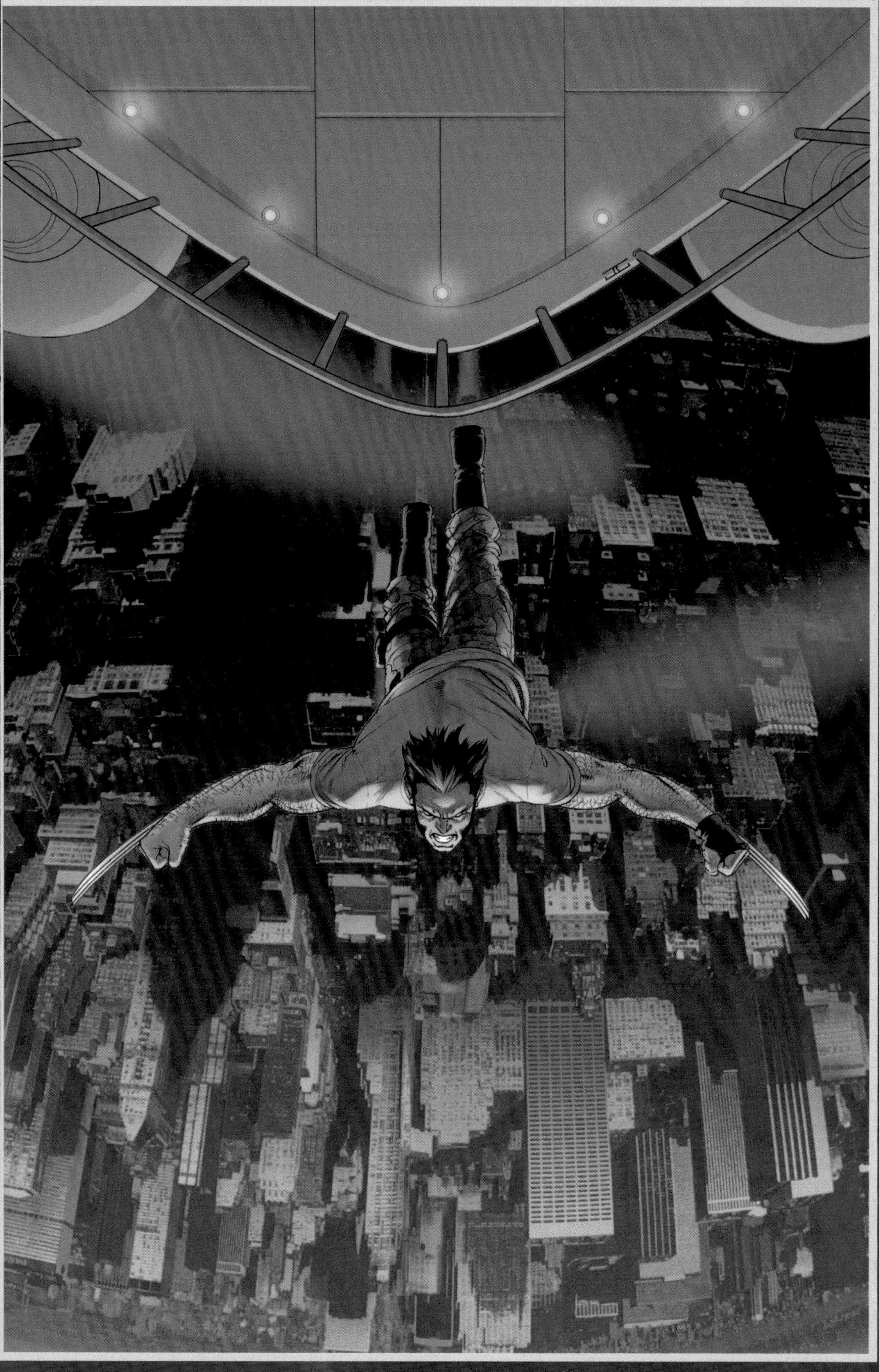

HOUSE OF M #3

Variant cover by John Cassaday & Laura Martin

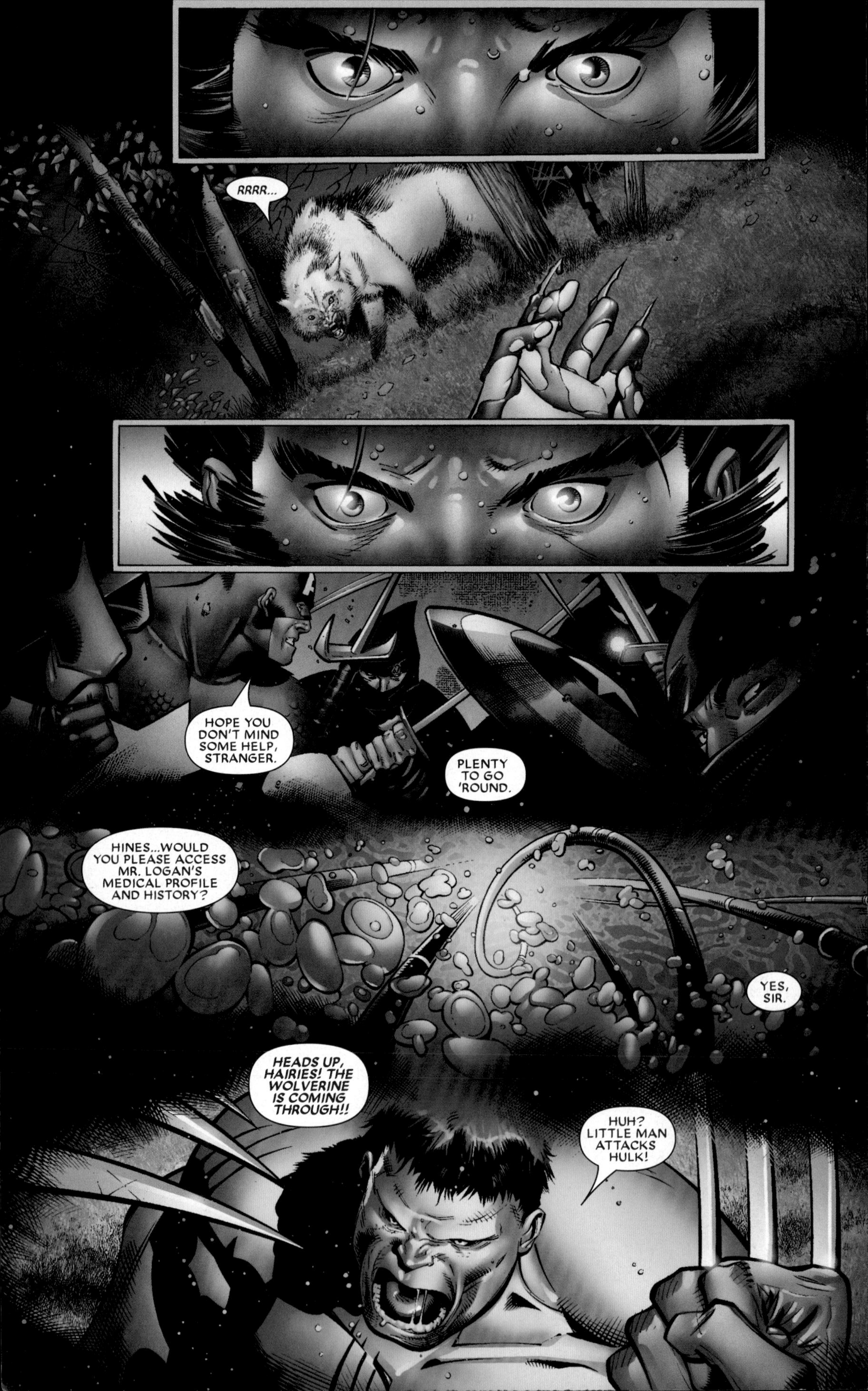
RRRR...
HOPE YOU DON'T MIND SOME HELP, STRANGER.
PLENTY TO GO 'ROUND.
HINES...WOULD YOU PLEASE ACCESS MR. LOGAN'S MEDICAL PROFILE AND HISTORY?
YES, SIR.
HEADS UP, HAIRIES! THE WOLVERINE IS COMING THROUGH!!
HUH? LITTLE MAN ATTACKS HULK!

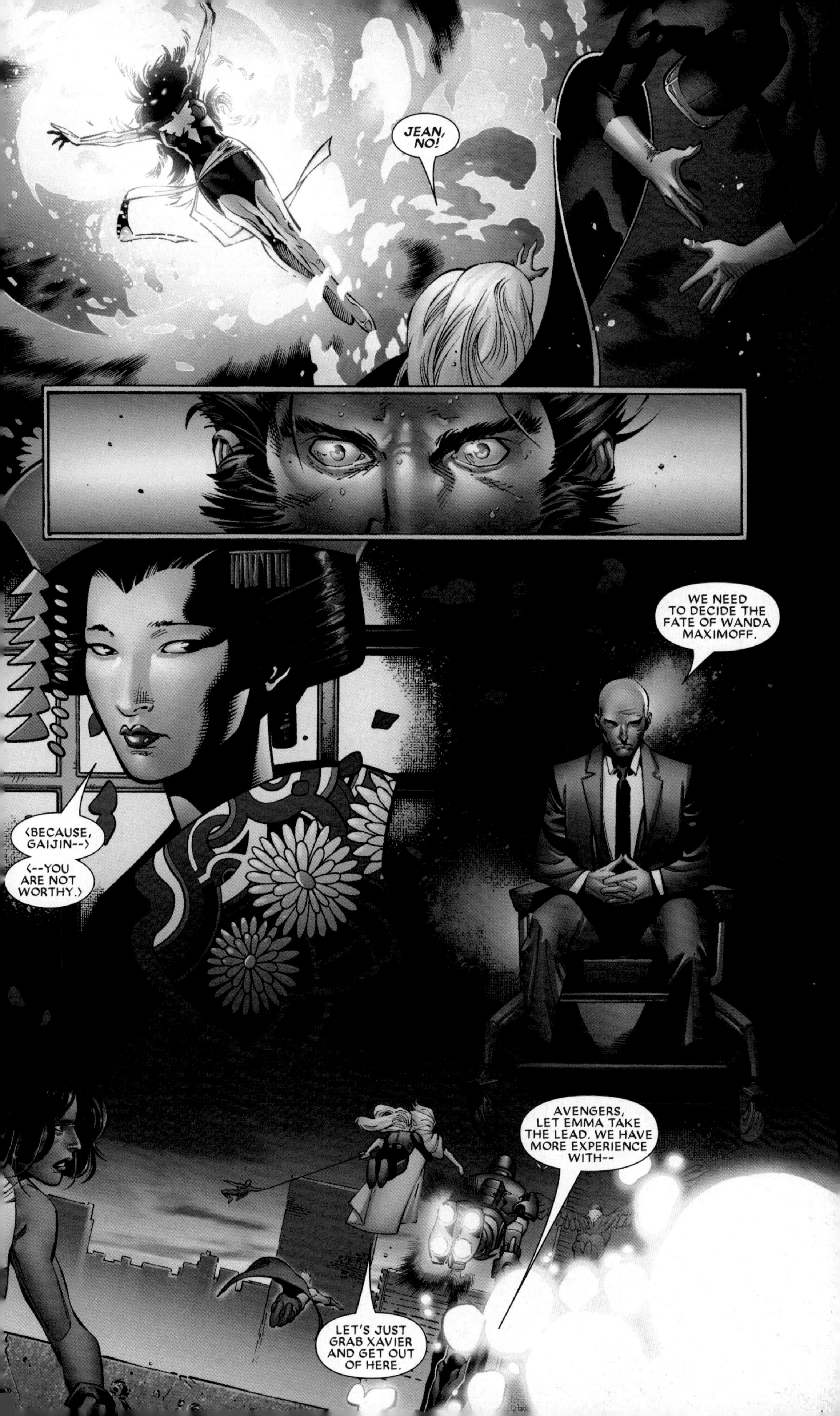
JEAN, NO!
WE NEED TO DECIDE THE FATE OF WANDA MAXIMOFF.
‹BECAUSE, GAIJIN--›
‹--YOU ARE NOT WORTHY.›
AVENGERS, LET EMMA TAKE THE LEAD. WE HAVE MORE EXPERIENCE WITH--
LET'S JUST GRAB XAVIER AND GET OUT OF HERE.

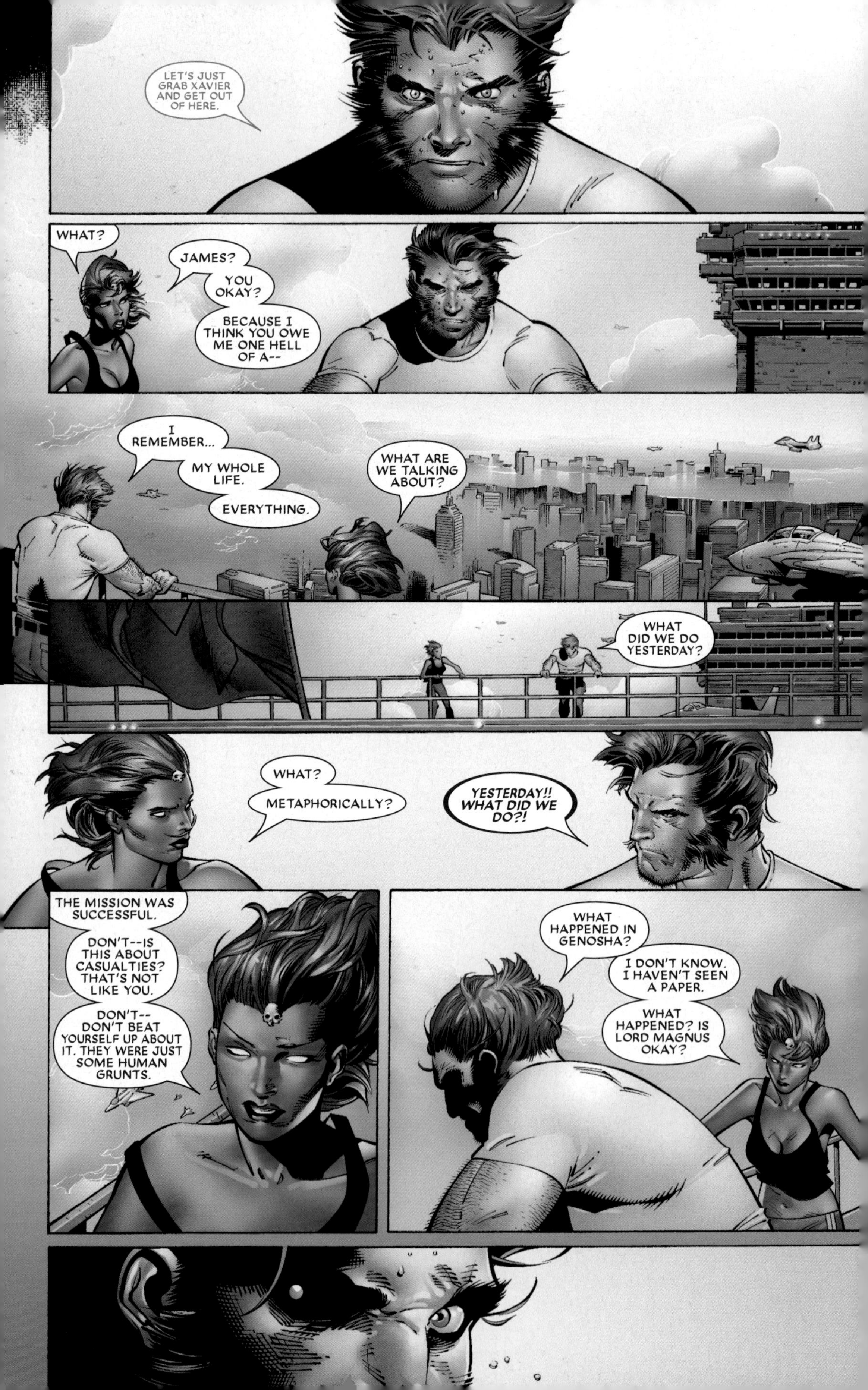
LET'S JUST GRAB XAVIER AND GET OUT OF HERE.
WHAT?
JAMES?
YOU OKAY?
BECAUSE I THINK YOU OWE ME ONE HELL OF A--
I REMEMBER...
MY WHOLE LIFE.
EVERYTHING.
WHAT ARE WE TALKING ABOUT?
WHAT DID WE DO YESTERDAY?
WHAT?
METAPHORICALLY?
YESTERDAY!! WHAT DID WE DO?!
THE MISSION WAS SUCCESSFUL.
DON'T--IS THIS ABOUT CASUALTIES? THAT'S NOT LIKE YOU.
DON'T-- DON'T BEAT YOURSELF UP ABOUT IT. THEY WERE JUST SOME HUMAN GRUNTS.
WHAT HAPPENED IN GENOSHA?
I DON'T KNOW. I HAVEN'T SEEN A PAPER.
WHAT HAPPENED? IS LORD MAGNUS OKAY?

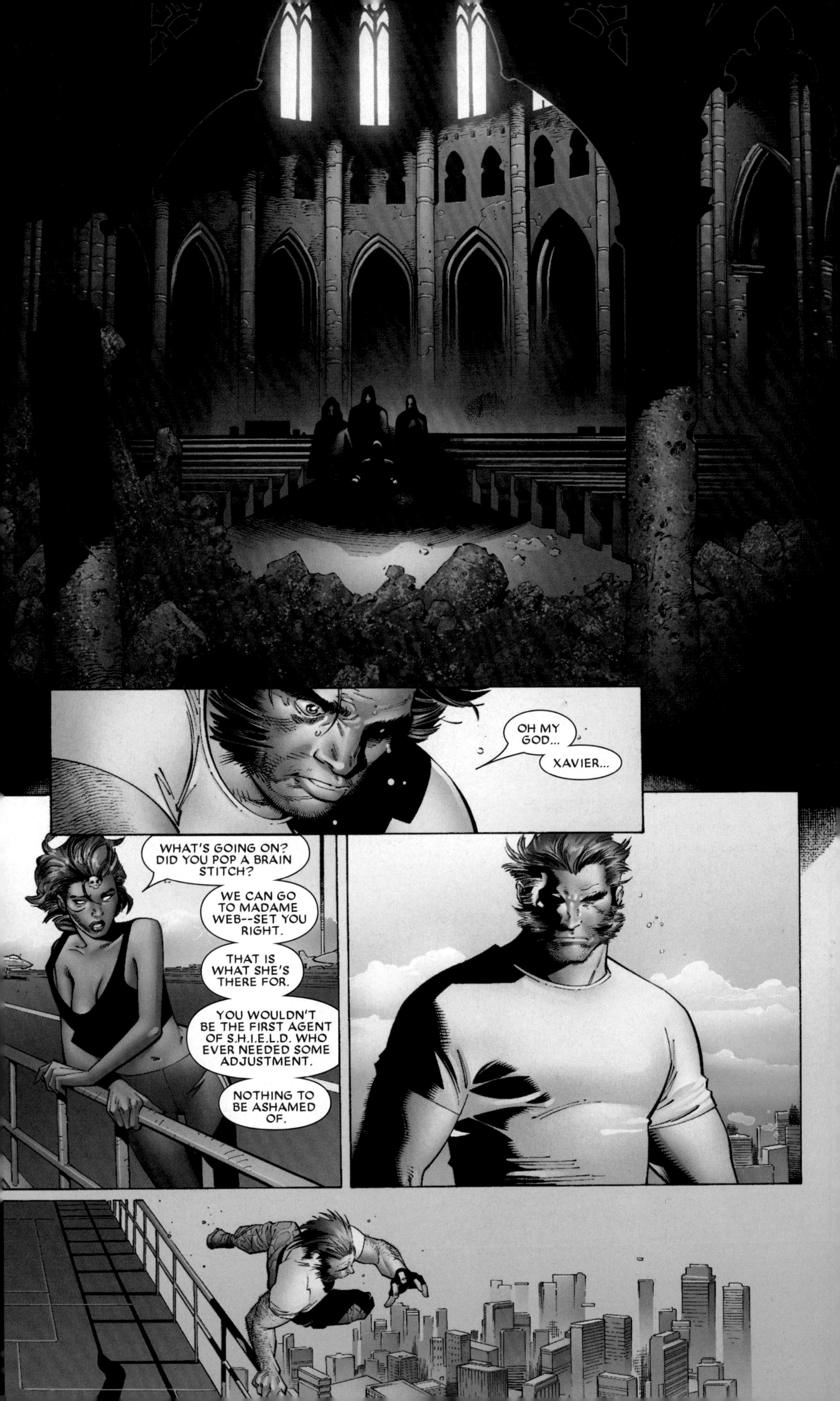
OH MY GOD...
XAVIER...
WHAT'S GOING ON? DID YOU POP A BRAIN STITCH?
WE CAN GO TO MADAME WEB--SET YOU RIGHT.
THAT IS WHAT SHE'S THERE FOR.
YOU WOULDN'T BE THE FIRST AGENT OF S.H.I.E.L.D. WHO EVER NEEDED SOME ADJUSTMENT.
NOTHING TO BE ASHAMED OF.

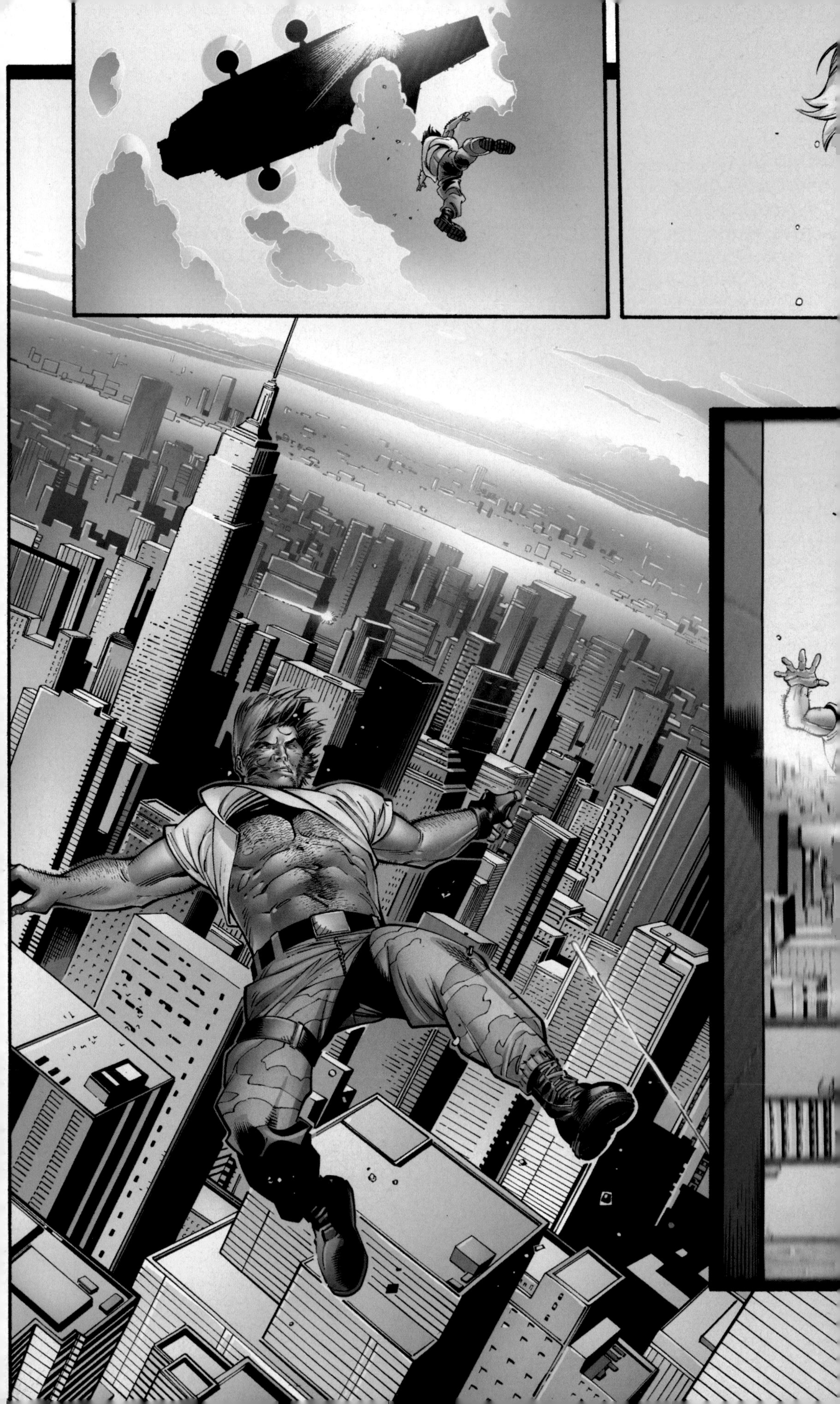

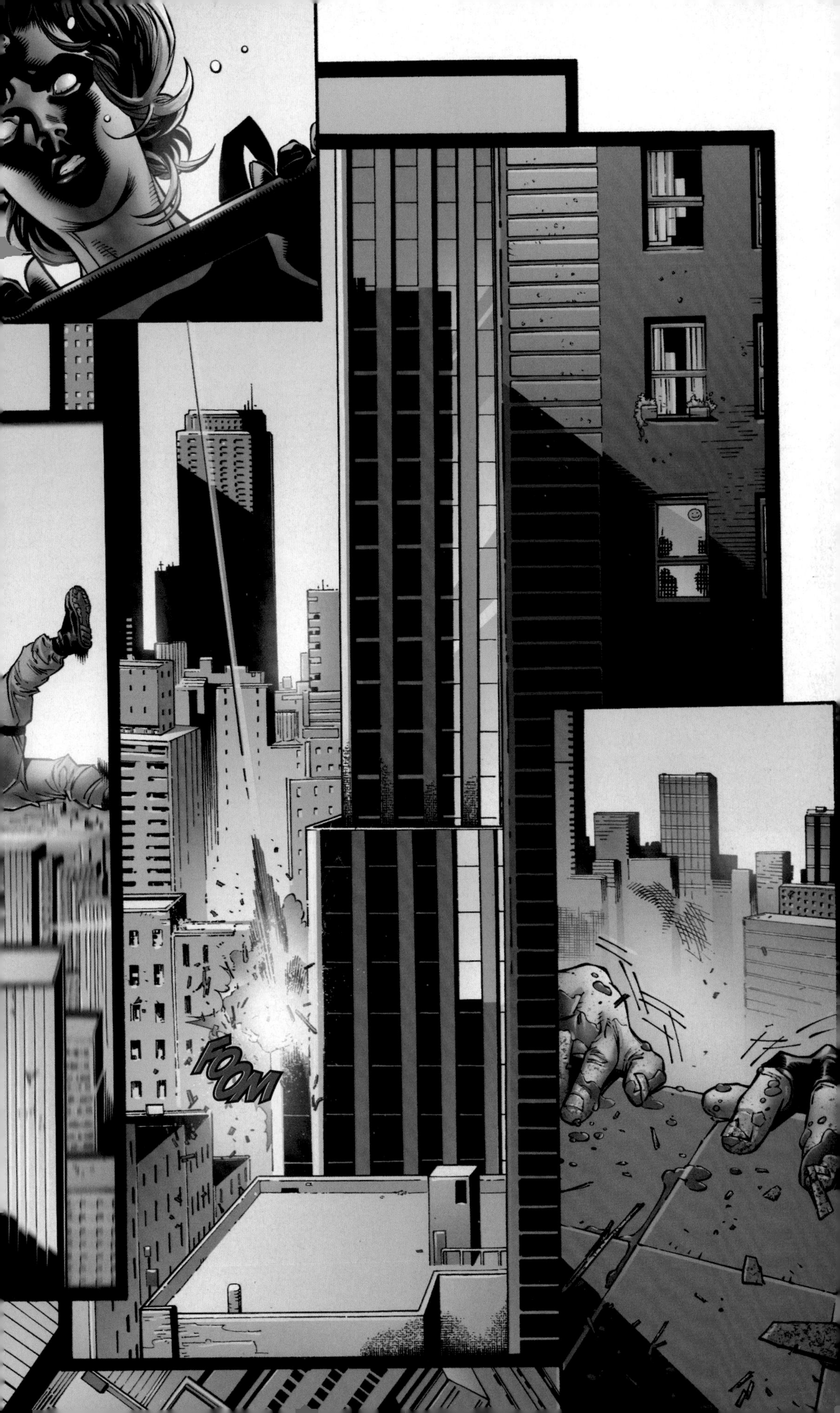
FOOM

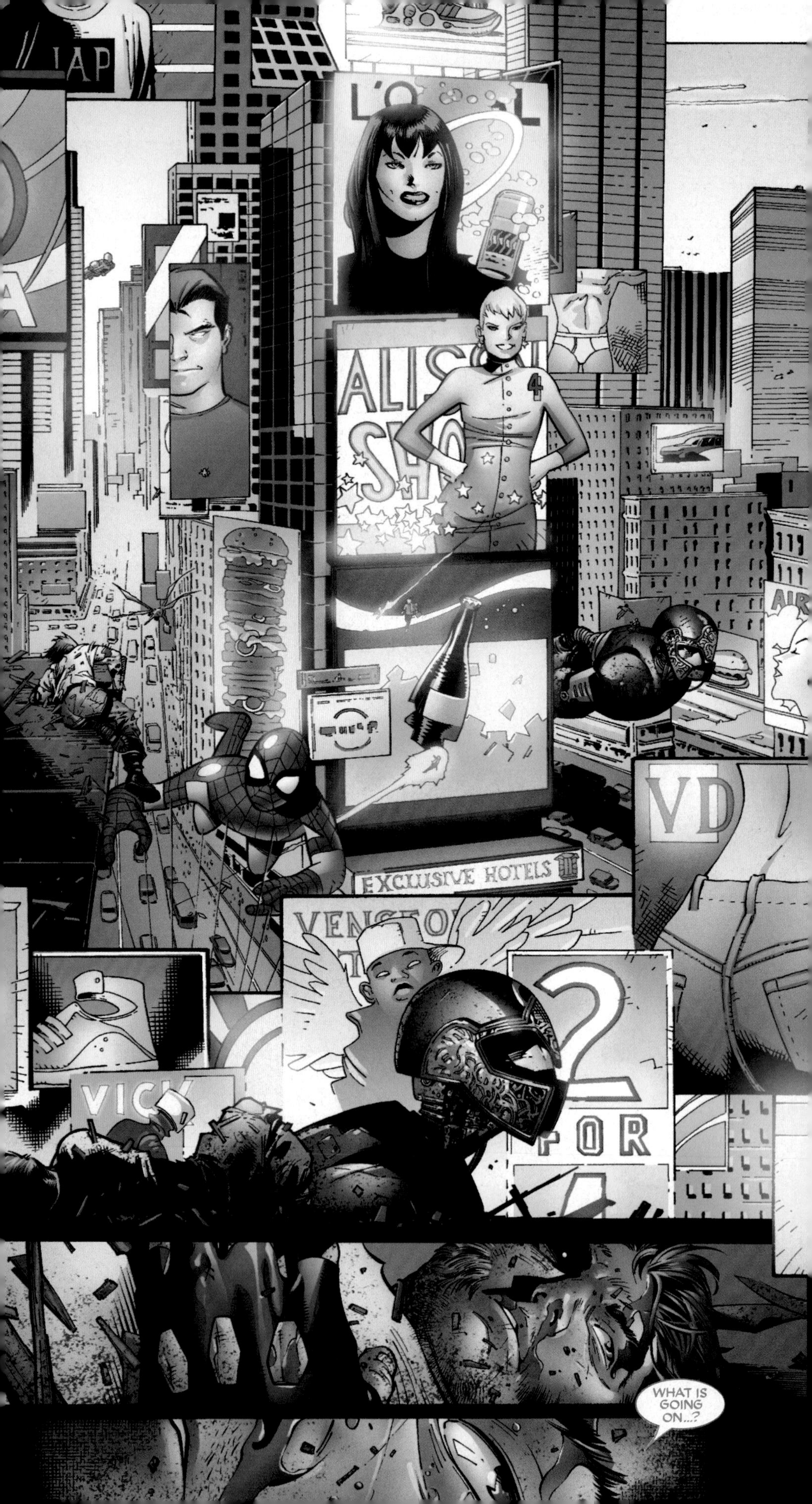

EXCLUSIVE HOTELS
VD
VICK
FOR
WHAT IS GOING ON...?

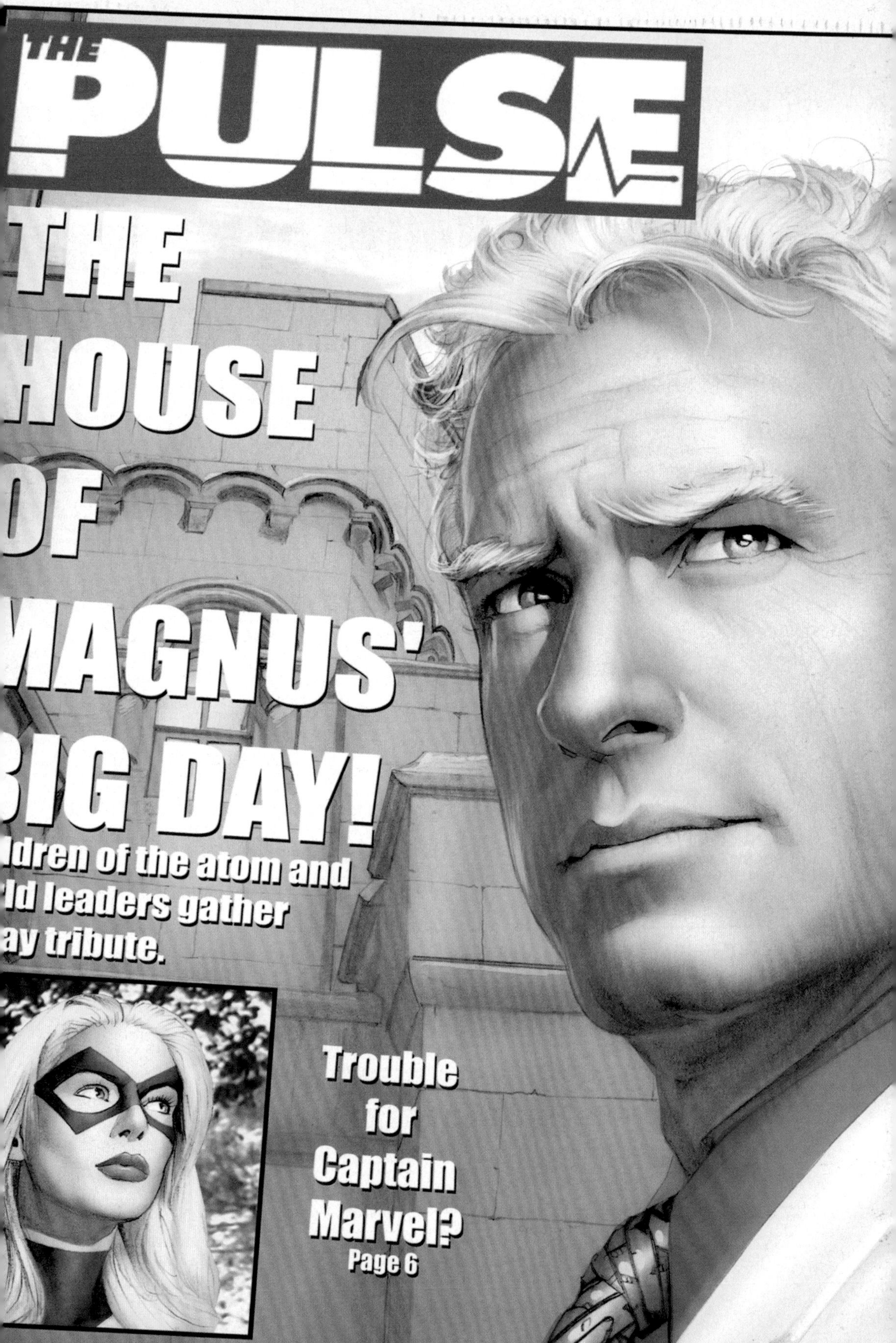
THE PULSE
THE HOUSE OF MAGNUS' BIG DAY!
ldren of the atom and
rld leaders gather
ay tribute.
Trouble for Captain Marvel?
Page 6

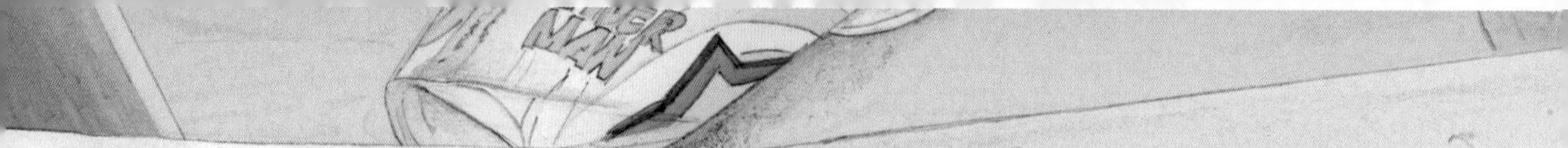

Pulse Weekend Extra

Don't start your day without it!

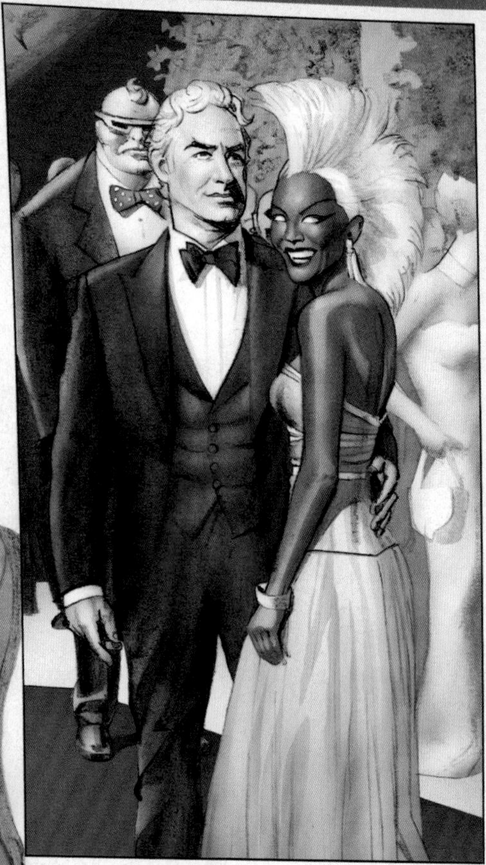

House of M's **Eric Magnus** and **Princess Ororo** of Kenya will be among the dignitaries celebrating thirty years of freedom from oppression by Sapiens.

House of Magnus gala this weekend

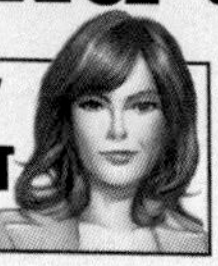

BETTY BRANT

Eric Magnus will be the center of attention, once again! This time at a charity gala in his honor hosted by the British Royal family.

Prince Namor, King T'Challa, Lord Victor Von Doom, Kree Private Genis-Vell, Princess Ororo of Kenya and a smorgasbord of international glitterati are expected to pay tribute to the man in a once-in-a-lifetime event commemorating the anniversary of the rebellion against homo sapien oppressors that held the world captive for decades.

The event has been put together by Magnus's children, all of whom will be in attendance. Security will be tight as a highly publicized event like this makes a prime target for sapien relation sympathizers. Rumors of several underground movements using this event to make a statement of violence against the house of Magnus have been circulating for weeks, but sources close to the event say that no such threats have surfaced and that "we do not live in fear."

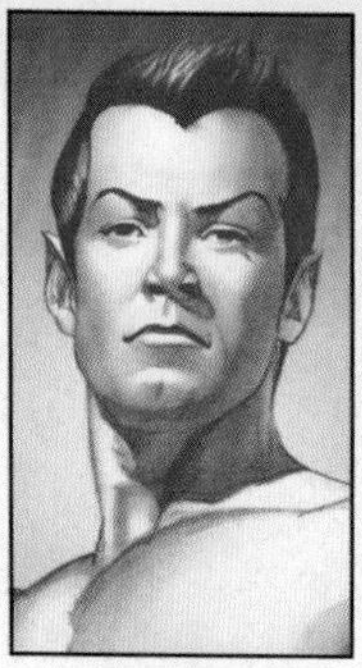

Prince Namor, ruler of Atlantis will be attending.

Born in the Nazi death camp in Auschwitz, Poland and the only member of his family to survive the camp, Magnus discovered himself to be one of the earliest reported mutants. Because of his all-encompassing powers over Earth's magnetic fields, Magnus became an early target in anti-mutant propaganda where he was given the mocking name Magneto.

Magnus struggled through a number of sapien attacks over the years with various world governments and the media branding him a mutant terrorist New Yorkers know, on August 1979, Eric Magnus came under attack by the original and highl controversial mutant-hunting Sentinels. This spectacular figh over the skies of New York Cit ended with Magnus unveiling proof of a worldwide multi-governmental anti-mutan conspiracy that funneled all the way up to our elected world leaders of the time, including American President Richard Nixon.

It was soon after the famed Sentinel takedown that the U.N granted Magneto sovereignty c the newly established island of Genosha as the world capital o mutant population.

Since then, with the homo supe population growing so quickly believed it will overtake the sa population by the year 2013, Magneto's power base has restructured the world governments to include the pro-mutant life agenda into any and all law making.

Look for full coverage of the e in the weekend edition of The Pulse along with an exclusive color photo essay of the red ca arrivals.

lew technique eyed in mutant stem-cell deba

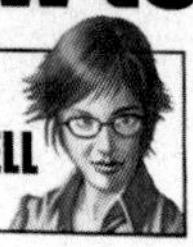

KAT FARRELL

With the nation deadlocked over the questionable morality of using mutated homo superior embryos for research for human medical treatments, a high ranking member of the President's Council on Nu-Bioethics is developing a proposal that might allow scientists to create the equivalent of homo superior embryonic stem cells without destroying mutant embryos, offering a potential path out of the controversy.

Dr. Otto Octavius, a bioethicist and staunch opponent of research on mutant embryos, has developed a procedure called altered (Continued 15-B)

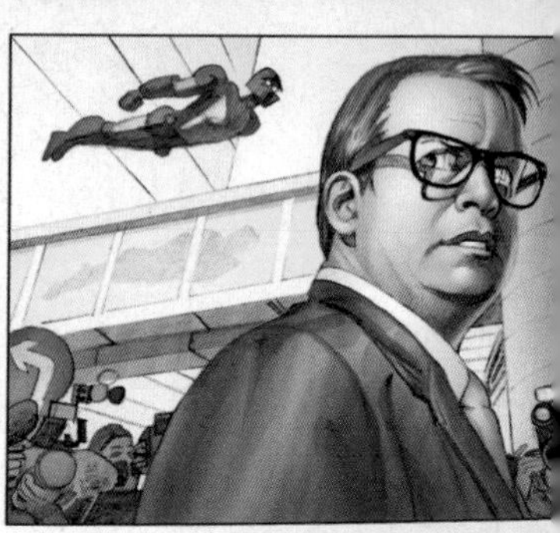

Doctor Otto Octavius revealed his new procedure known as "altered".

Hydra splinter group claims responsibility for kidnapping

By Ben Urich

A woman who goes by the name Madame Hydra released a statement to the press via a web site claiming responsibility for the abduction of Mariko Harada, daughter of Japanese businessman Keniuchio Harada. The statement claims that Harada is actually the leader of the Japanese crime cartel Clan Yashida. Harada has denied these claims on numerous occasion and points to his legitimate business ventures both here in America and abroad.

Mariko Harada, 11, was last seen being dragged into a red van containing at least five masked males right outside the Baxter Building, NYPD Sgt. Jasper Sitwell said:

The girl is believed to be in imminent danger. Madame Hydra's statement included the words: "this girl's mutant blood will spill in the streets if the Harada family does not forfeit their profits in the Indonesian MGH drug trade."

The Harada family, through a statement, said: "this devastating turn of events is nothing short of blackmail. The Harada family does not profit from the international drug trade. This is the work of psychotics. Please, we beg you, give us our innocent daughter back. If she is not returned unharmed, there will be no end to the retaliation."

Mariko is described as 4 feet tall, weighing 65 pounds, with black hair and black eyes, and wearing a white sweater and black jeans.

Anyone with information is asked to contact the nearest law-enforcement agency.

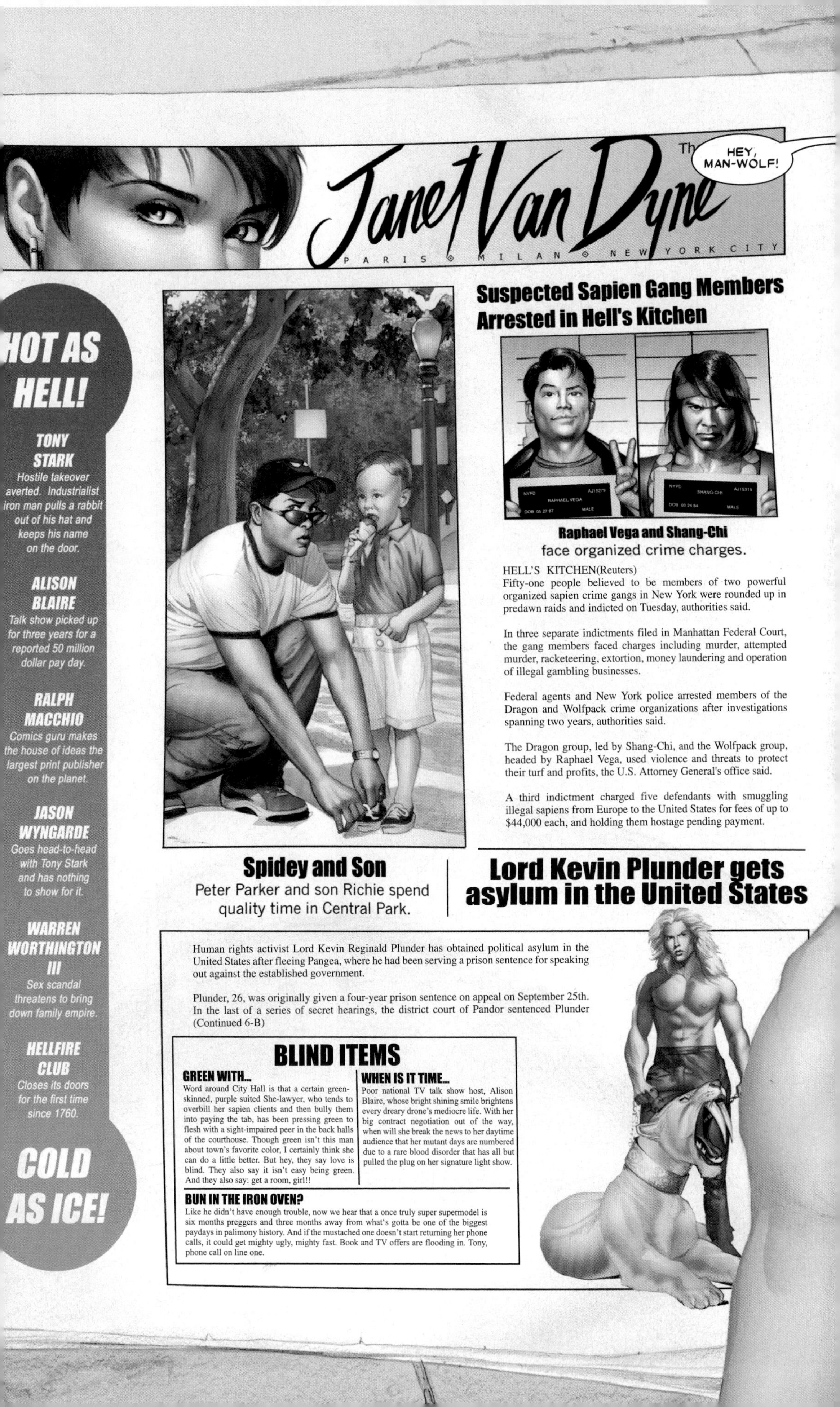
HEY, MAN-WOLF!

Janet Van Dyne

P A R I S ◇ M I L A N ◇ N E W Y O R K C I T Y

HOT AS HELL!

TONY STARK
Hostile takeover averted. Industrialist iron man pulls a rabbit out of his hat and keeps his name on the door.

ALISON BLAIRE
Talk show picked up for three years for a reported 50 million dollar pay day.

RALPH MACCHIO
Comics guru makes the house of ideas the largest print publisher on the planet.

COLD AS ICE!

JASON WYNGARDE
Goes head-to-head with Tony Stark and has nothing to show for it.

WARREN WORTHINGTON III
Sex scandal threatens to bring down family empire.

HELLFIRE CLUB
Closes its doors for the first time since 1760.

Suspected Sapien Gang Members Arrested in Hell's Kitchen

Raphael Vega and Shang-Chi
face organized crime charges.

HELL'S KITCHEN(Reuters)
Fifty-one people believed to be members of two powerful organized sapien crime gangs in New York were rounded up in predawn raids and indicted on Tuesday, authorities said.

In three separate indictments filed in Manhattan Federal Court, the gang members faced charges including murder, attempted murder, racketeering, extortion, money laundering and operation of illegal gambling businesses.

Federal agents and New York police arrested members of the Dragon and Wolfpack crime organizations after investigations spanning two years, authorities said.

The Dragon group, led by Shang-Chi, and the Wolfpack group, headed by Raphael Vega, used violence and threats to protect their turf and profits, the U.S. Attorney General's office said.

A third indictment charged five defendants with smuggling illegal sapiens from Europe to the United States for fees of up to $44,000 each, and holding them hostage pending payment.

Spidey and Son

Peter Parker and son Richie spend quality time in Central Park.

Lord Kevin Plunder gets asylum in the United States

Human rights activist Lord Kevin Reginald Plunder has obtained political asylum in the United States after fleeing Pangea, where he had been serving a prison sentence for speaking out against the established government.

Plunder, 26, was originally given a four-year prison sentence on appeal on September 25th. In the last of a series of secret hearings, the district court of Pandor sentenced Plunder (Continued 6-B)

BLIND ITEMS

GREEN WITH...
Word around City Hall is that a certain green-skinned, purple suited She-lawyer, who tends to overbill her sapien clients and then bully them into paying the tab, has been pressing green to flesh with a sight-impaired peer in the back halls of the courthouse. Though green isn't this man about town's favorite color, I certainly think she can do a little better. But hey, they say love is blind. They also say it isn't easy being green. And they also say: get a room, girl!!

WHEN IS IT TIME...
Poor national TV talk show host, Alison Blaire, whose bright shining smile brightens every dreary drone's mediocre life. With her big contract negotiation out of the way, when will she break the news to her daytime audience that her mutant days are numbered due to a rare blood disorder that has all but pulled the plug on her signature light show.

BUN IN THE IRON OVEN?
Like he didn't have enough trouble, now we hear that a once truly super supermodel is six months preggers and three months away from what's gotta be one of the biggest paydays in palimony history. And if the mustached one doesn't start returning her phone calls, it could get mighty ugly, mighty fast. Book and TV offers are flooding in. Tony, phone call on line one.

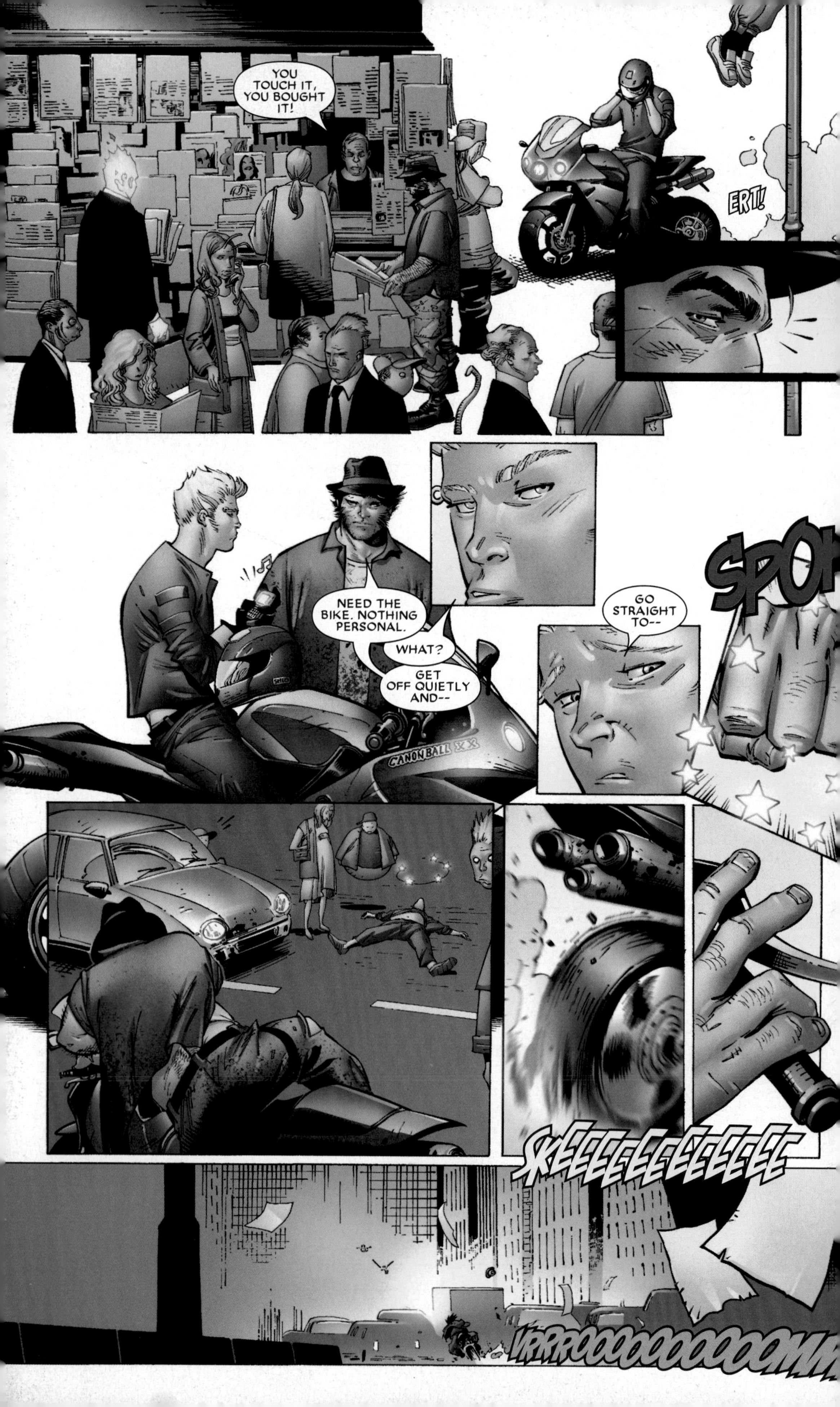
YOU TOUCH IT, YOU BOUGHT IT!
ERT!
NEED THE BIKE. NOTHING PERSONAL.
WHAT?
GET OFF QUIETLY AND--
GO STRAIGHT TO--
SPO
CANONBALL XX
SKEEEEEEEEEEEEE
VRRRROOOOOOOOOOOM

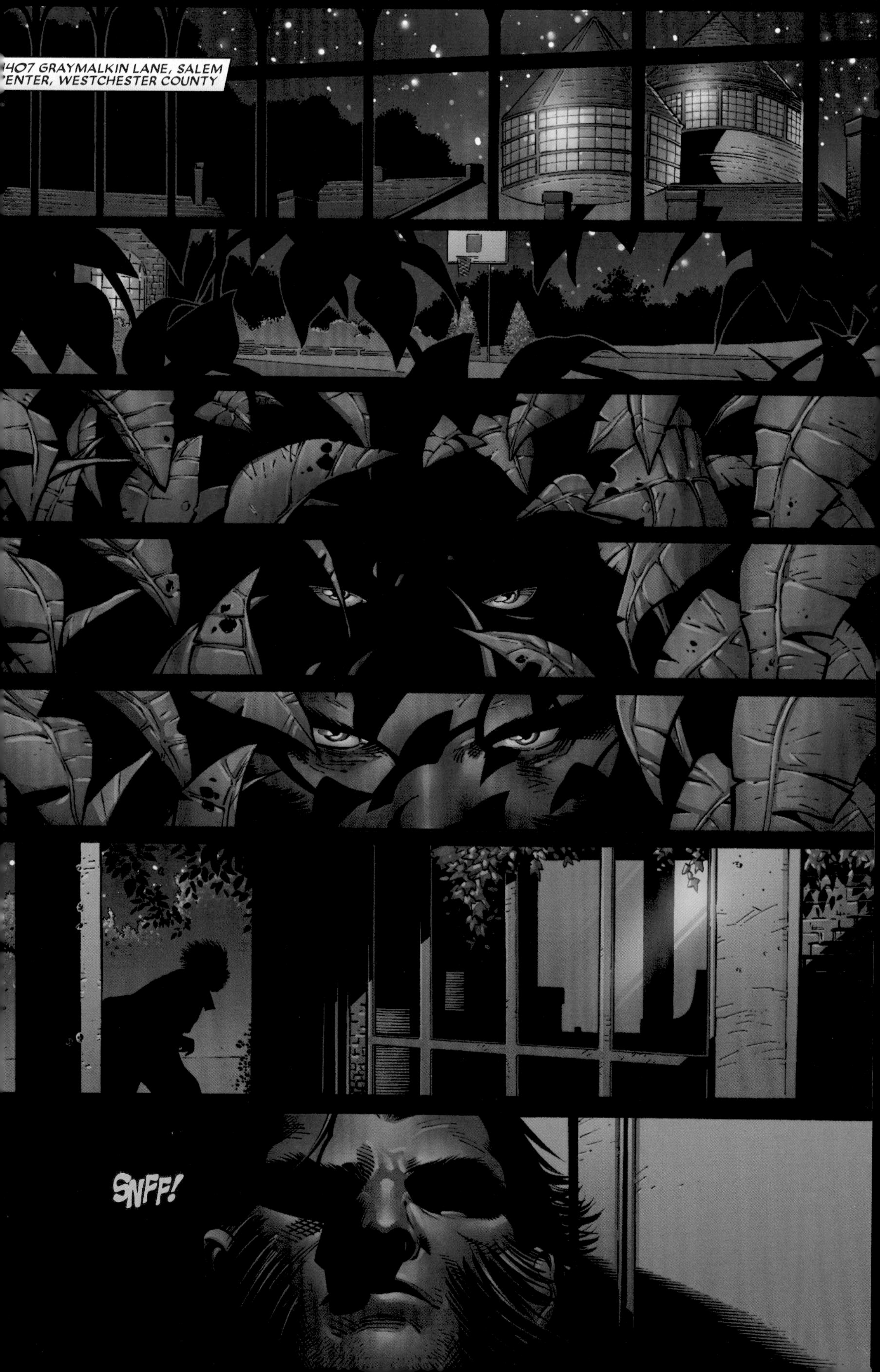
1407 GRAYMALKIN LANE, SALEM CENTER, WESTCHESTER COUNTY
SNFF!

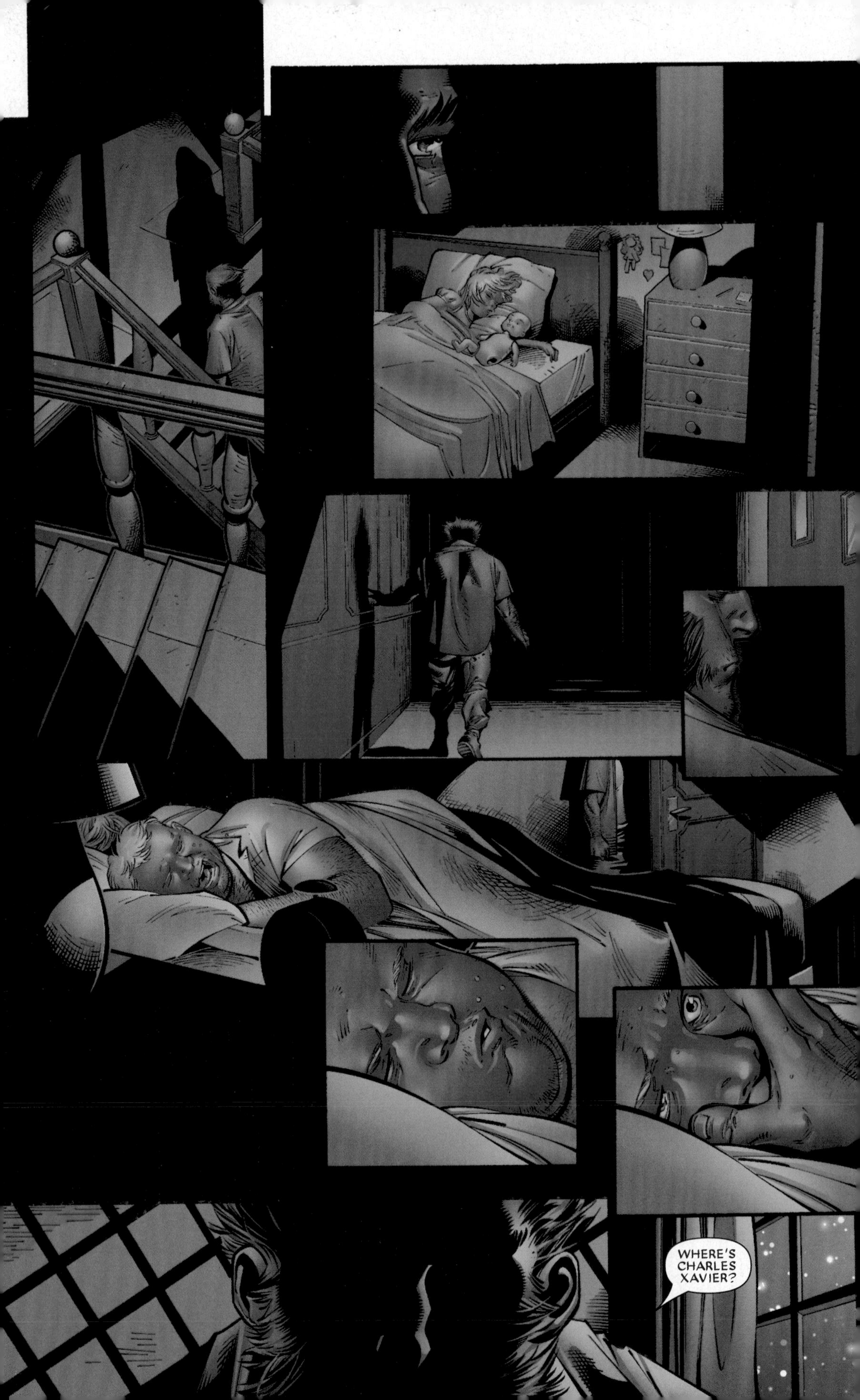
WHERE'S CHARLES XAVIER?

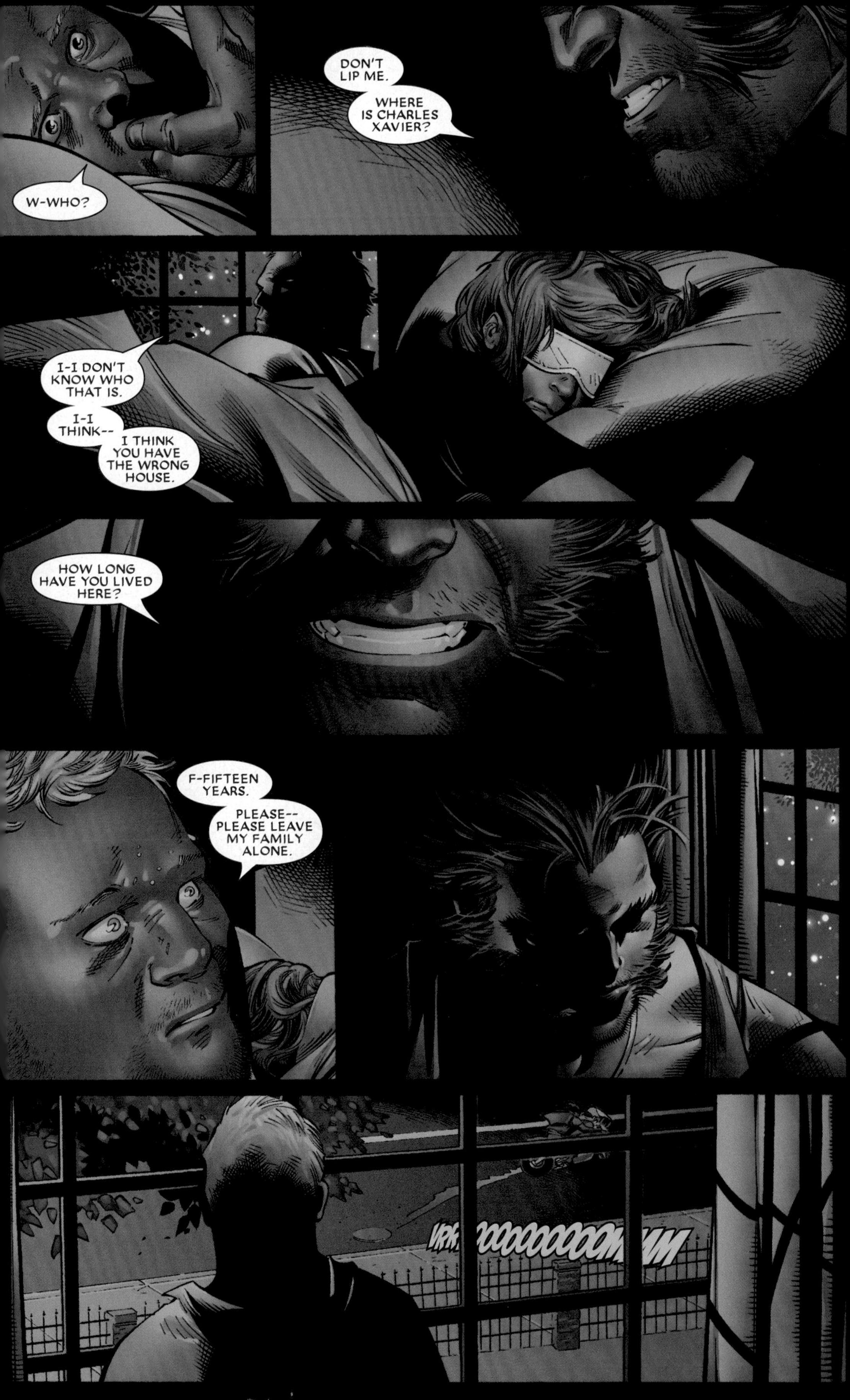

W-WHO?
DON'T LIP ME.
WHERE IS CHARLES XAVIER?
I-I DON'T KNOW WHO THAT IS.
I-I THINK--
I THINK YOU HAVE THE WRONG HOUSE.
HOW LONG HAVE YOU LIVED HERE?
F-FIFTEEN YEARS.
PLEASE-- PLEASE LEAVE MY FAMILY ALONE.
VRRROOOOOOOOOOMMMM

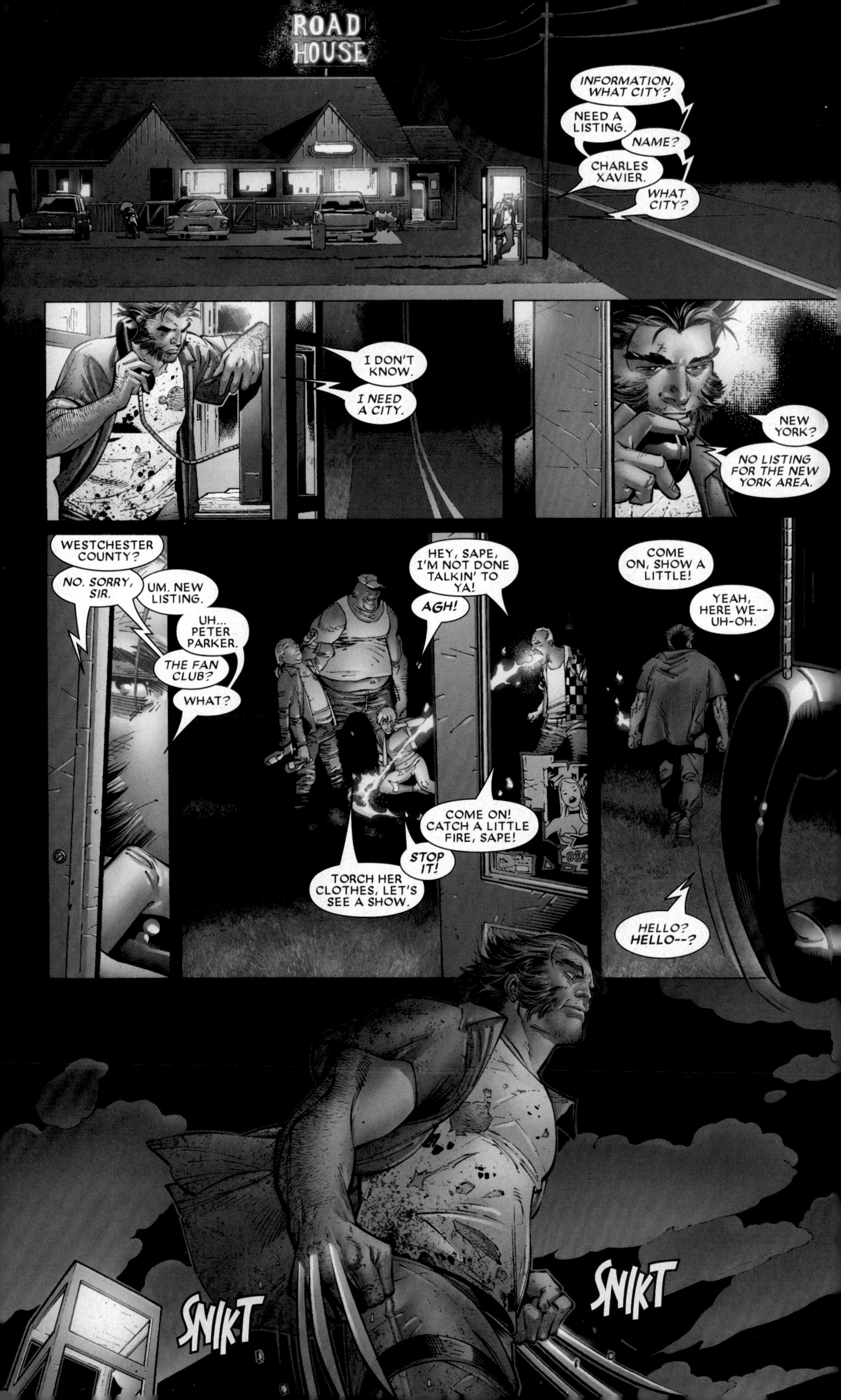

ROAD HOUSE
INFORMATION, WHAT CITY?
NEED A LISTING.
NAME?
CHARLES XAVIER.
WHAT CITY?
I DON'T KNOW.
I NEED A CITY.
NEW YORK?
NO LISTING FOR THE NEW YORK AREA.
WESTCHESTER COUNTY?
NO. SORRY, SIR.
UM. NEW LISTING.
UH... PETER PARKER.
THE FAN CLUB?
WHAT?
HEY, SAPE, I'M NOT DONE TALKIN' TO YA!
AGH!
COME ON! CATCH A LITTLE FIRE, SAPE!
STOP IT!
TORCH HER CLOTHES, LET'S SEE A SHOW.
COME ON, SHOW A LITTLE!
YEAH, HERE WE-- UH-OH.
HELLO? HELLO--?
SNIKT
SNIKT

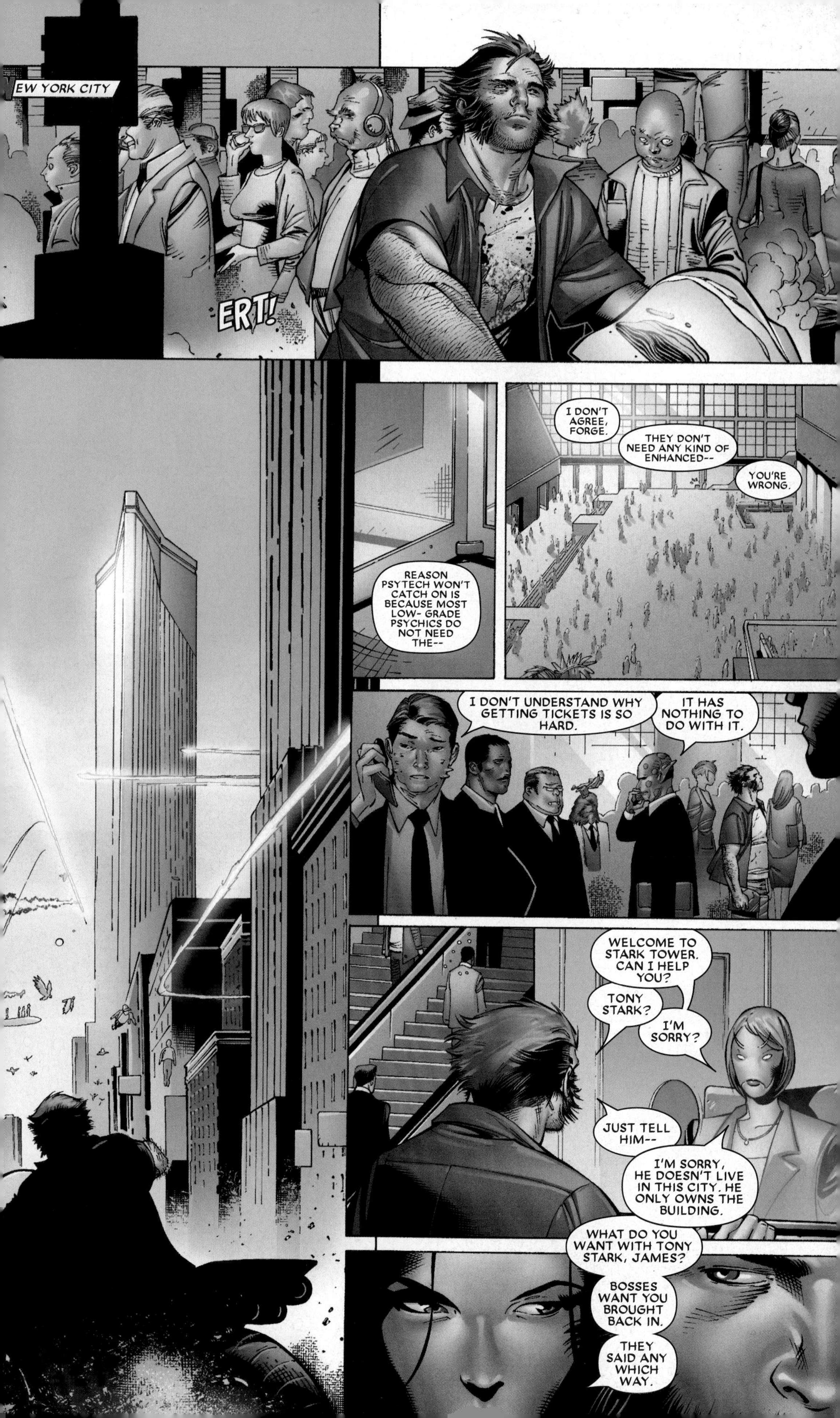
NEW YORK CITY
ERT!
REASON PSYTECH WON'T CATCH ON IS BECAUSE MOST LOW- GRADE PSYCHICS DO NOT NEED THE--
I DON'T AGREE, FORGE.
THEY DON'T NEED ANY KIND OF ENHANCED--
YOU'RE WRONG.
I DON'T UNDERSTAND WHY GETTING TICKETS IS SO HARD.
IT HAS NOTHING TO DO WITH IT.
WELCOME TO STARK TOWER. CAN I HELP YOU?
TONY STARK?
I'M SORRY?
JUST TELL HIM--
I'M SORRY, HE DOESN'T LIVE IN THIS CITY. HE ONLY OWNS THE BUILDING.
WHAT DO YOU WANT WITH TONY STARK, JAMES?
BOSSES WANT YOU BROUGHT BACK IN.
THEY SAID ANY WHICH WAY.

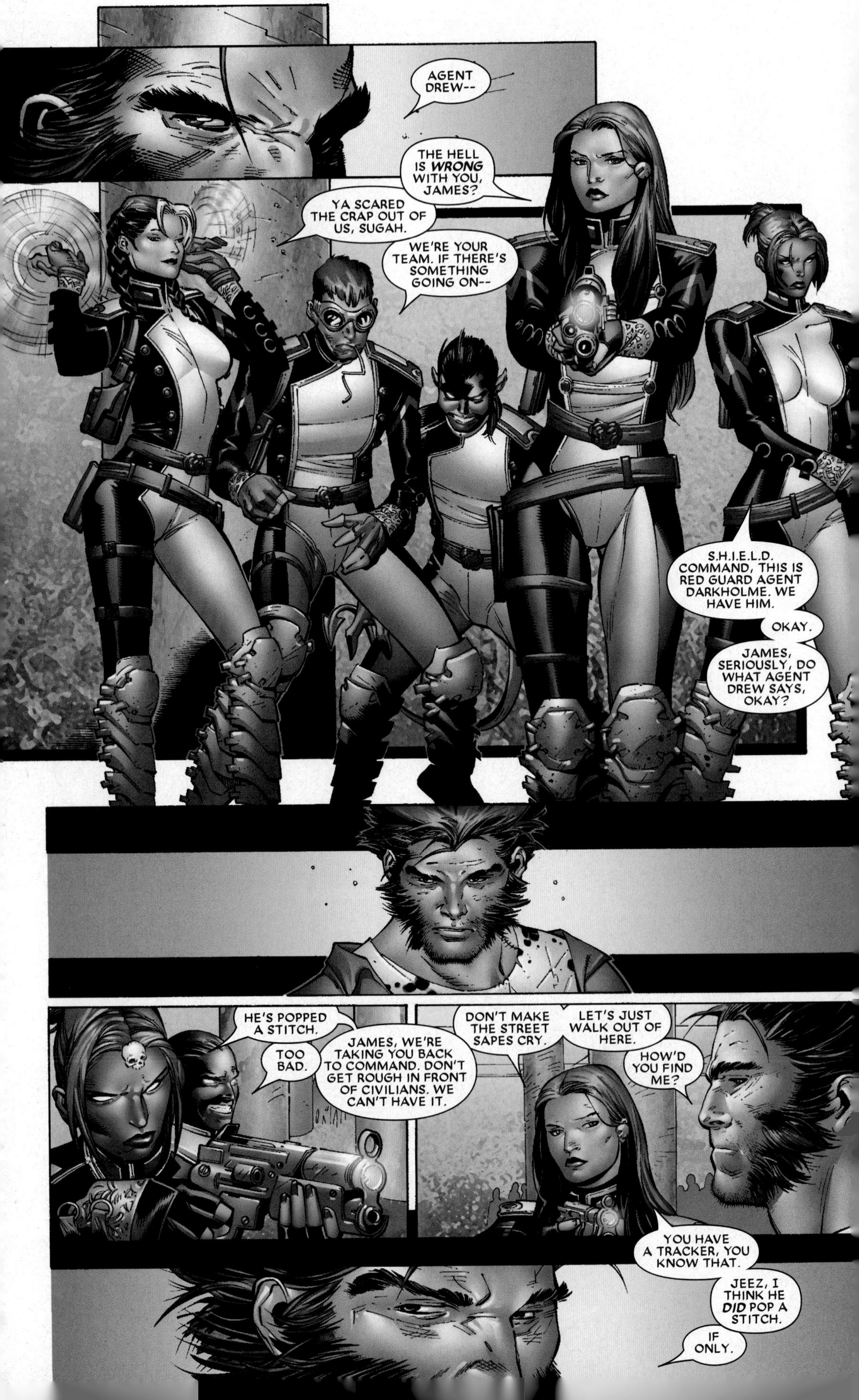
AGENT DREW--
THE HELL IS *WRONG* WITH YOU, JAMES?
YA SCARED THE CRAP OUT OF US, SUGAH.
WE'RE YOUR TEAM. IF THERE'S SOMETHING GOING ON--
S.H.I.E.L.D. COMMAND, THIS IS RED GUARD AGENT DARKHOLME. WE HAVE HIM.
OKAY.
JAMES, SERIOUSLY, DO WHAT AGENT DREW SAYS, OKAY?
HE'S POPPED A STITCH.
TOO BAD.
JAMES, WE'RE TAKING YOU BACK TO COMMAND. DON'T GET ROUGH IN FRONT OF CIVILIANS. WE CAN'T HAVE IT.
DON'T MAKE THE STREET SAPES CRY.
LET'S JUST WALK OUT OF HERE.
HOW'D YOU FIND ME?
YOU HAVE A TRACKER, YOU KNOW THAT.
JEEZ, I THINK HE *DID* POP A STITCH.
IF ONLY.

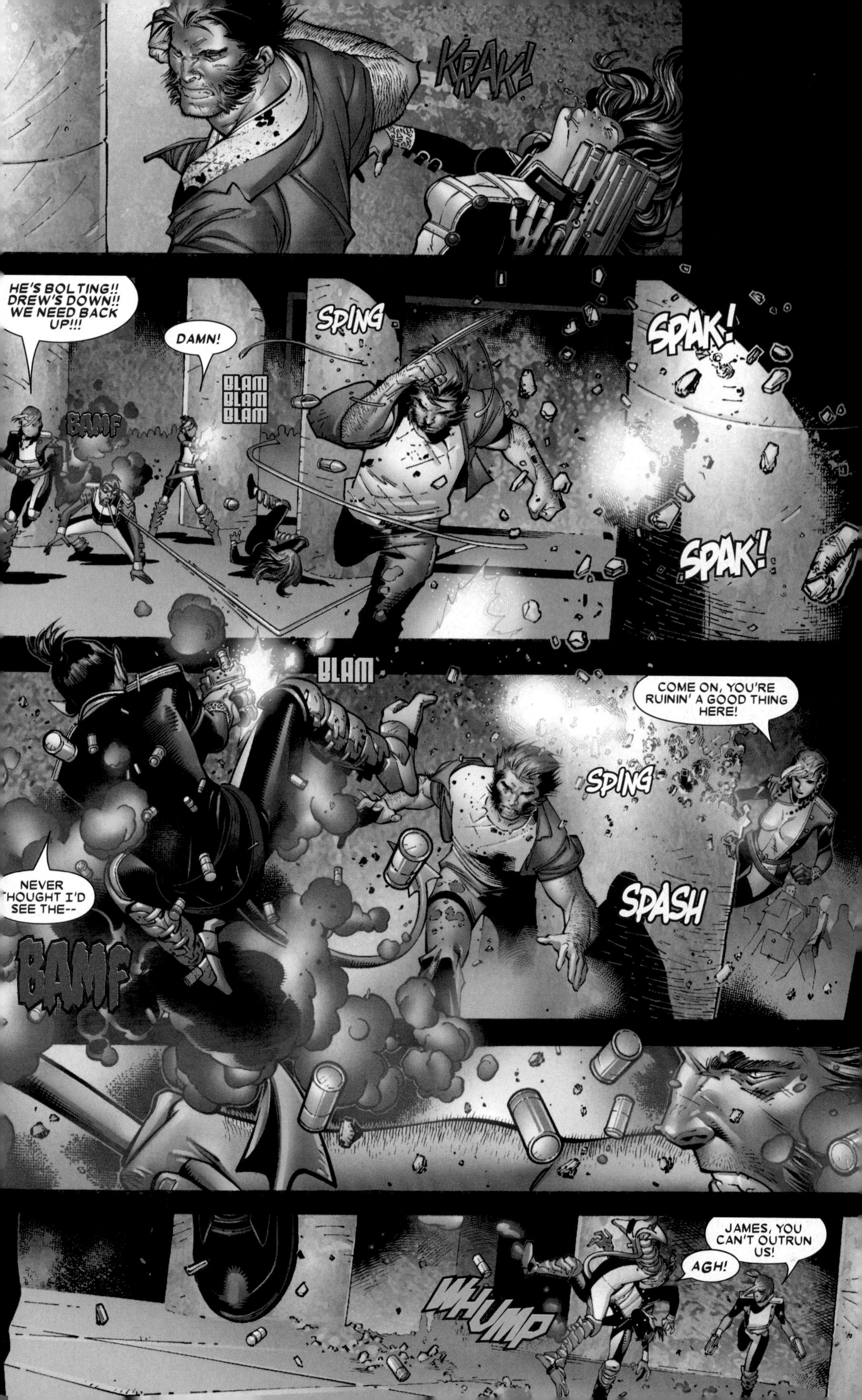
KRAK!
HE'S BOLTING!! DREW'S DOWN!! WE NEED BACK UP!!!
DAMN!
BAMF
BLAM BLAM BLAM
SPING
SPAK!
SPAK!
BLAM
COME ON, YOU'RE RUININ' A GOOD THING HERE!
SPING
NEVER THOUGHT I'D SEE THE--
SPASH
BAMF
WHUMP
JAMES, YOU CAN'T OUTRUN US!
AGH!

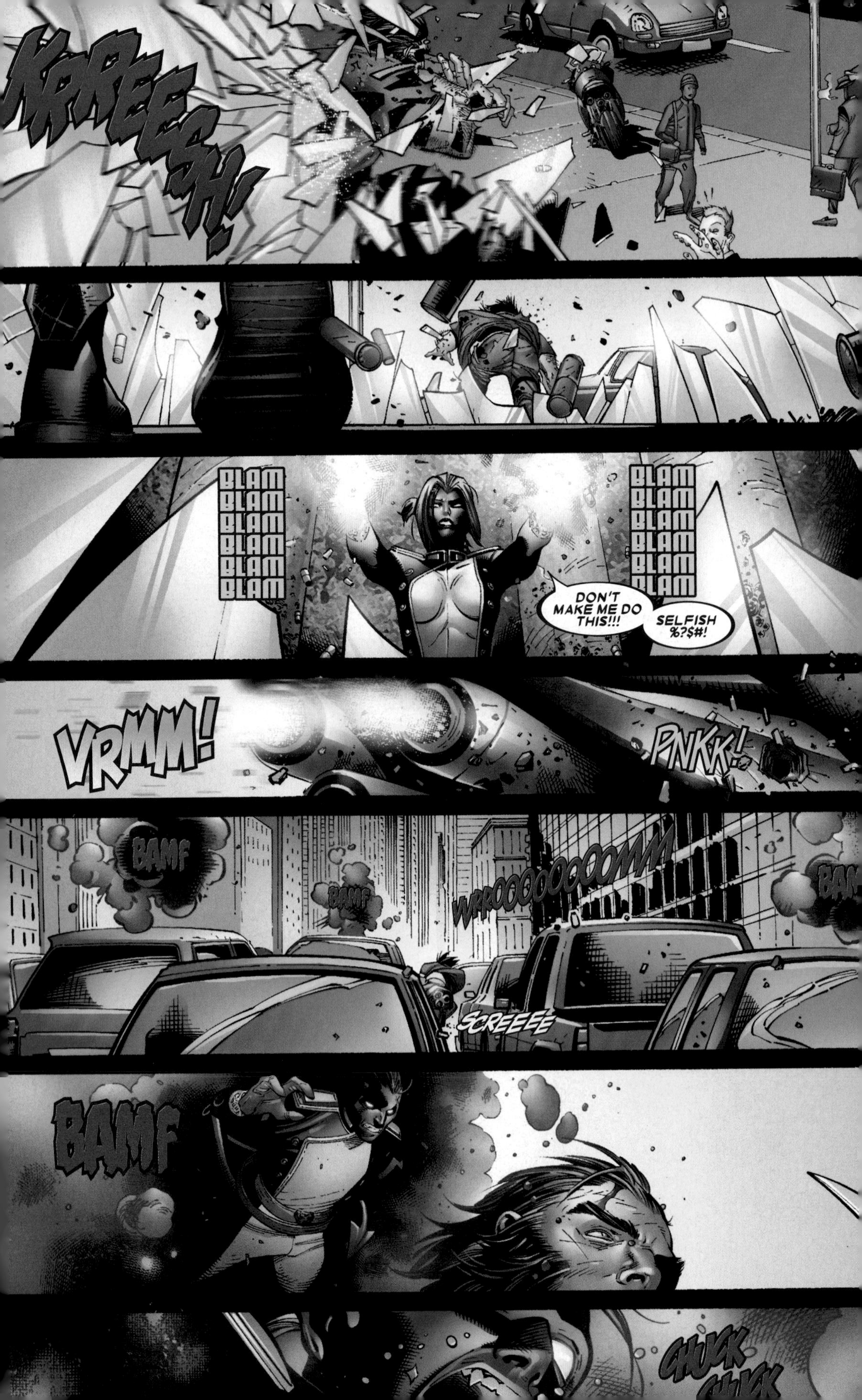
KRREESH!
BLAM
BLAM
BLAM
BLAM
BLAM
BLAM
BLAM
BLAM
BLAM
BLAM
BLAM
BLAM
DON'T MAKE ME DO THIS!!!
SELFISH %?$#!
VRMM!
PNKK!
BAMF
BAMF
VRROOOOOOOOOMM
SCREEEE
BAMF
CHUCK

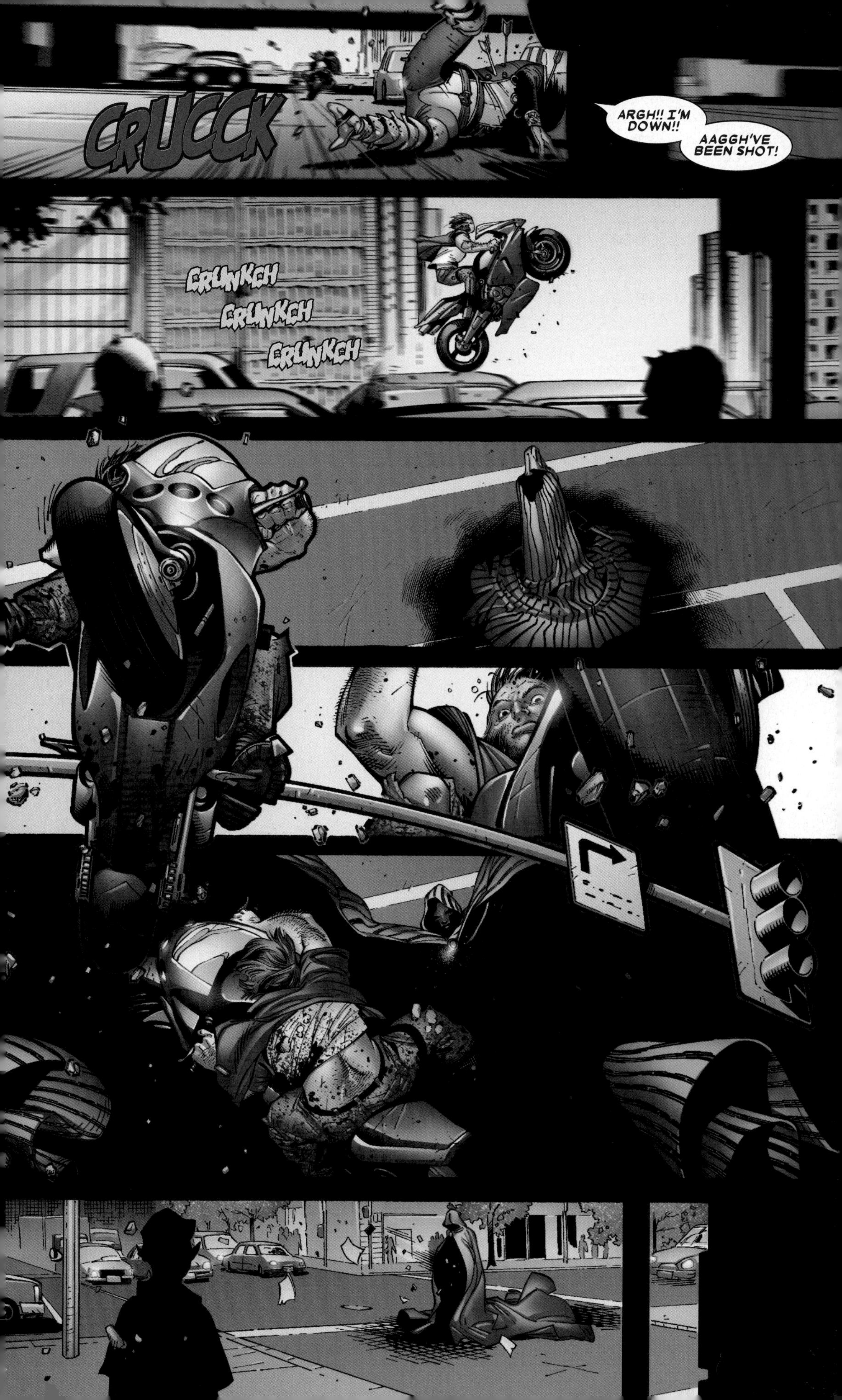
CRUCCK
ARGH!! I'M DOWN!!
AAGGH'VE BEEN SHOT!
CRUNKCH
CRUNKCH
CRUNKCH

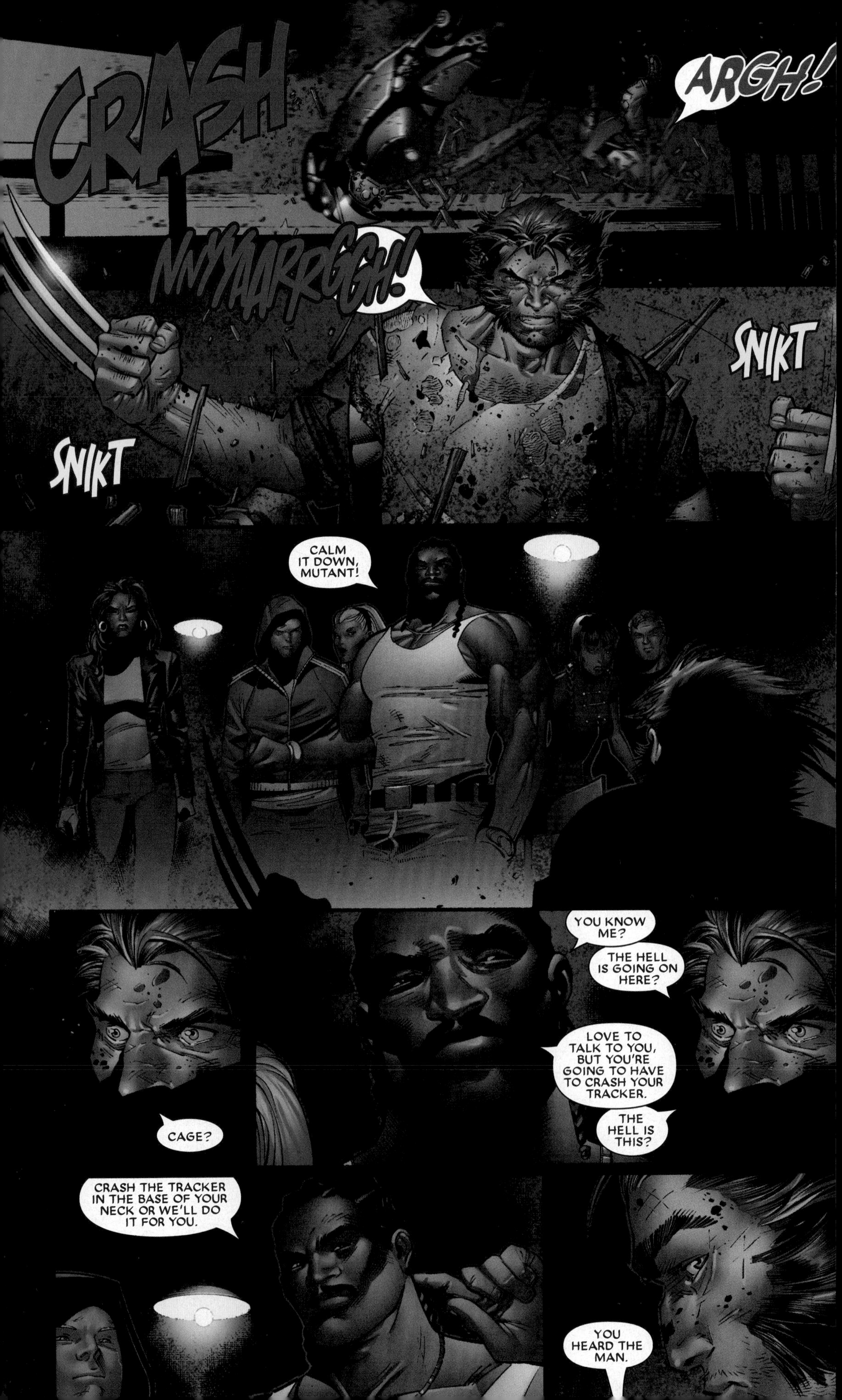

CRASH
ARGH!
NNYYAARRGGH!
SNIKT
SNIKT
CALM IT DOWN, MUTANT!
CAGE?
YOU KNOW ME?
THE HELL IS GOING ON HERE?
LOVE TO TALK TO YOU, BUT YOU'RE GOING TO HAVE TO CRASH YOUR TRACKER.
THE HELL IS THIS?
CRASH THE TRACKER IN THE BASE OF YOUR NECK OR WE'LL DO IT FOR YOU.
YOU HEARD THE MAN.

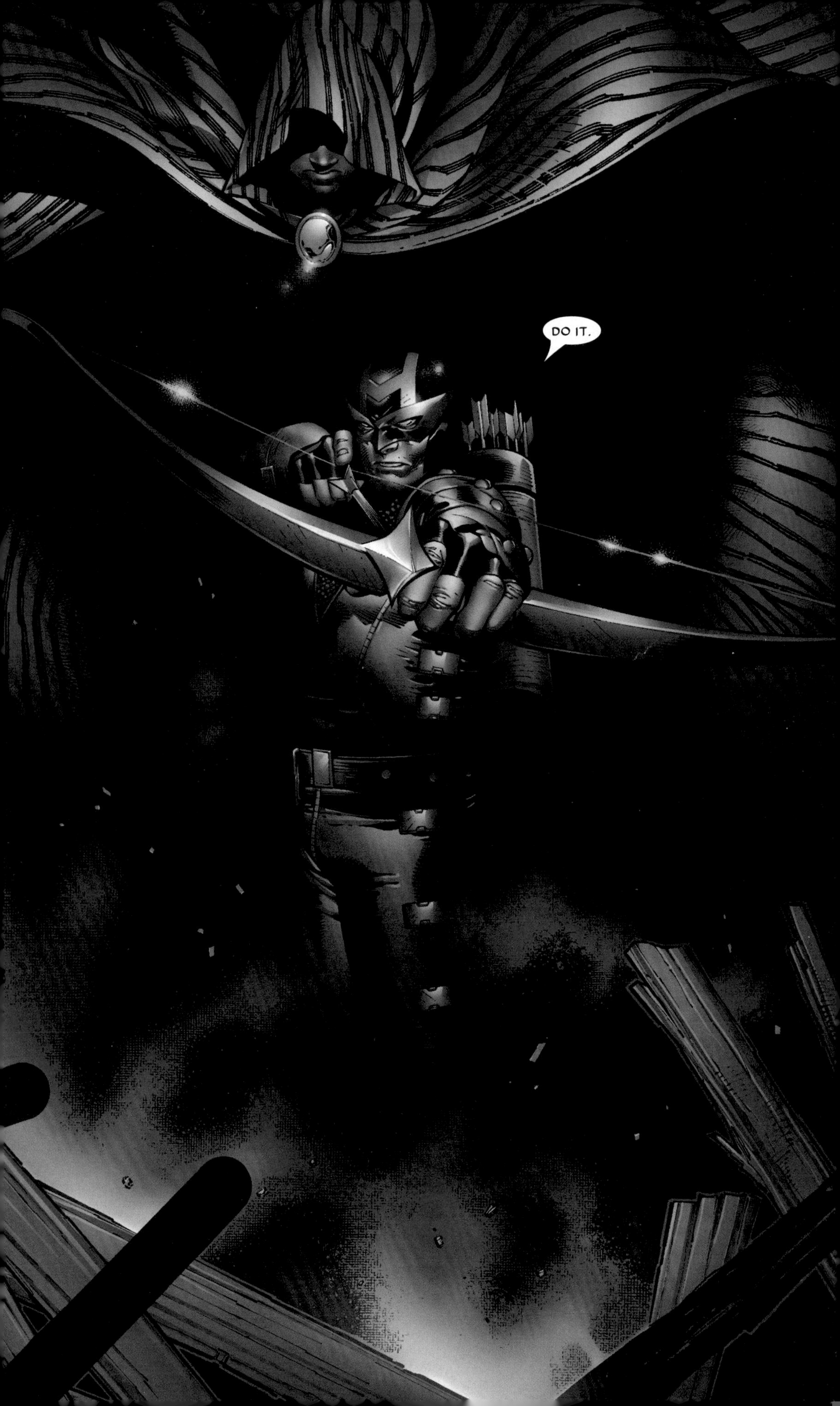
DO IT.

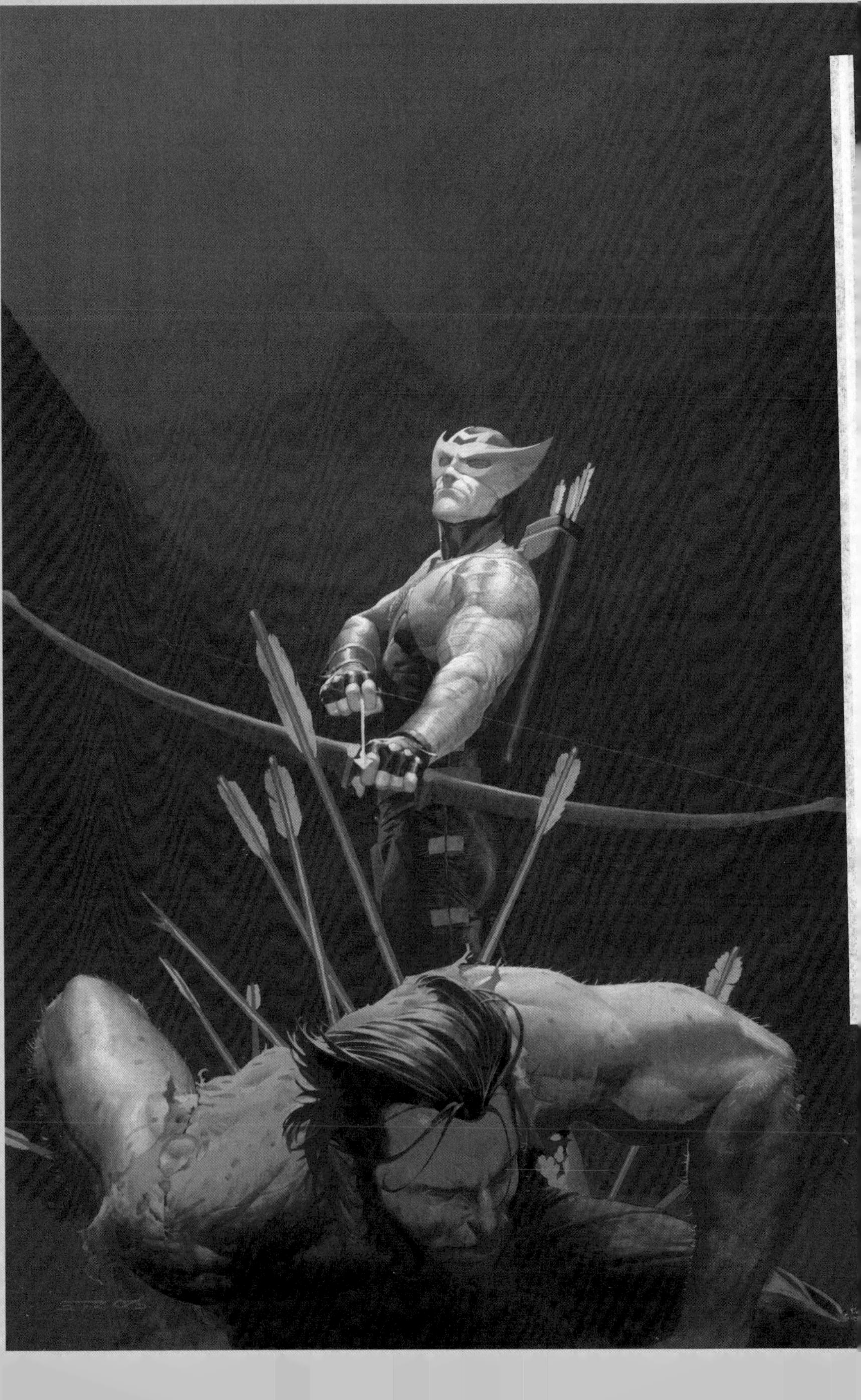

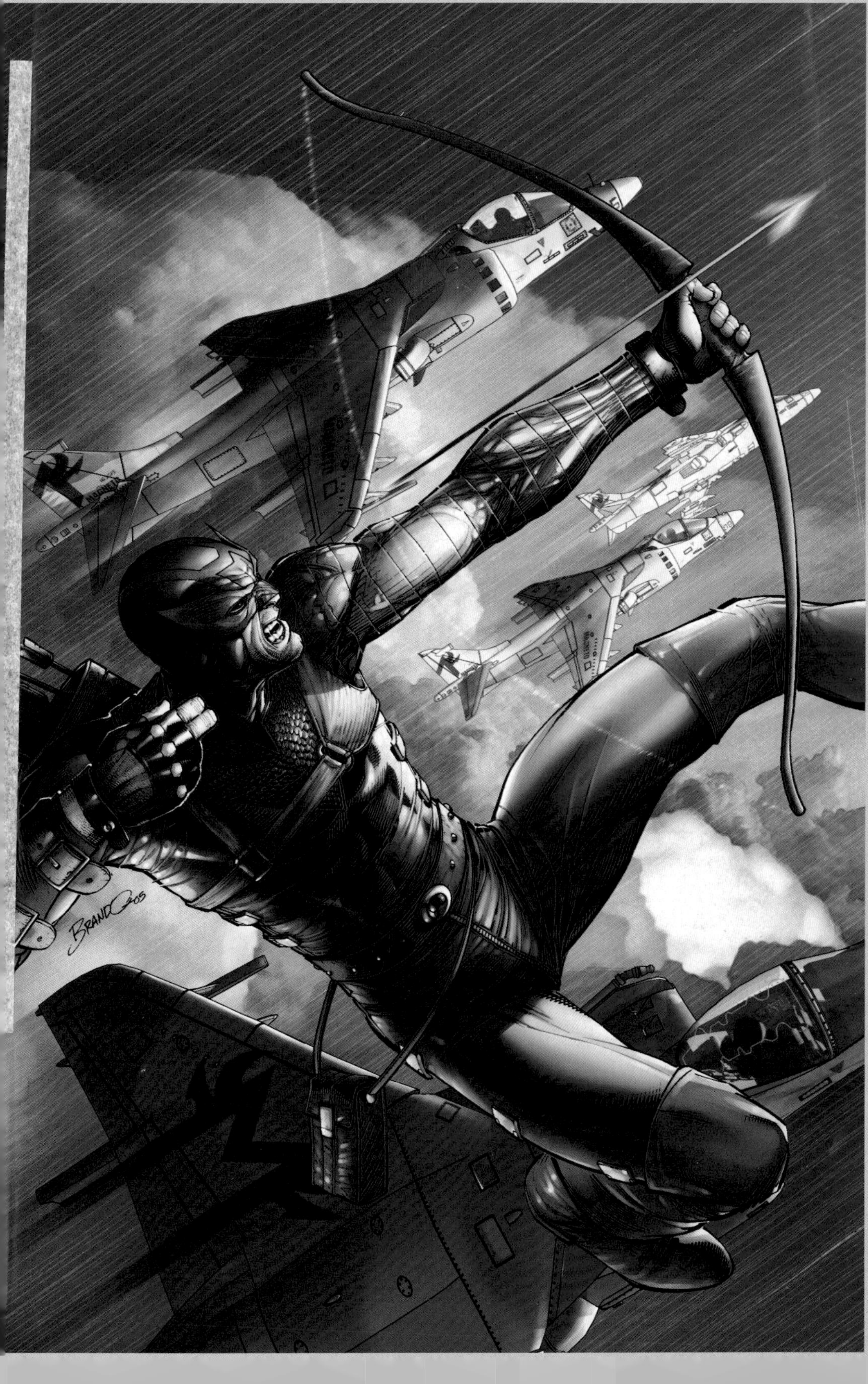

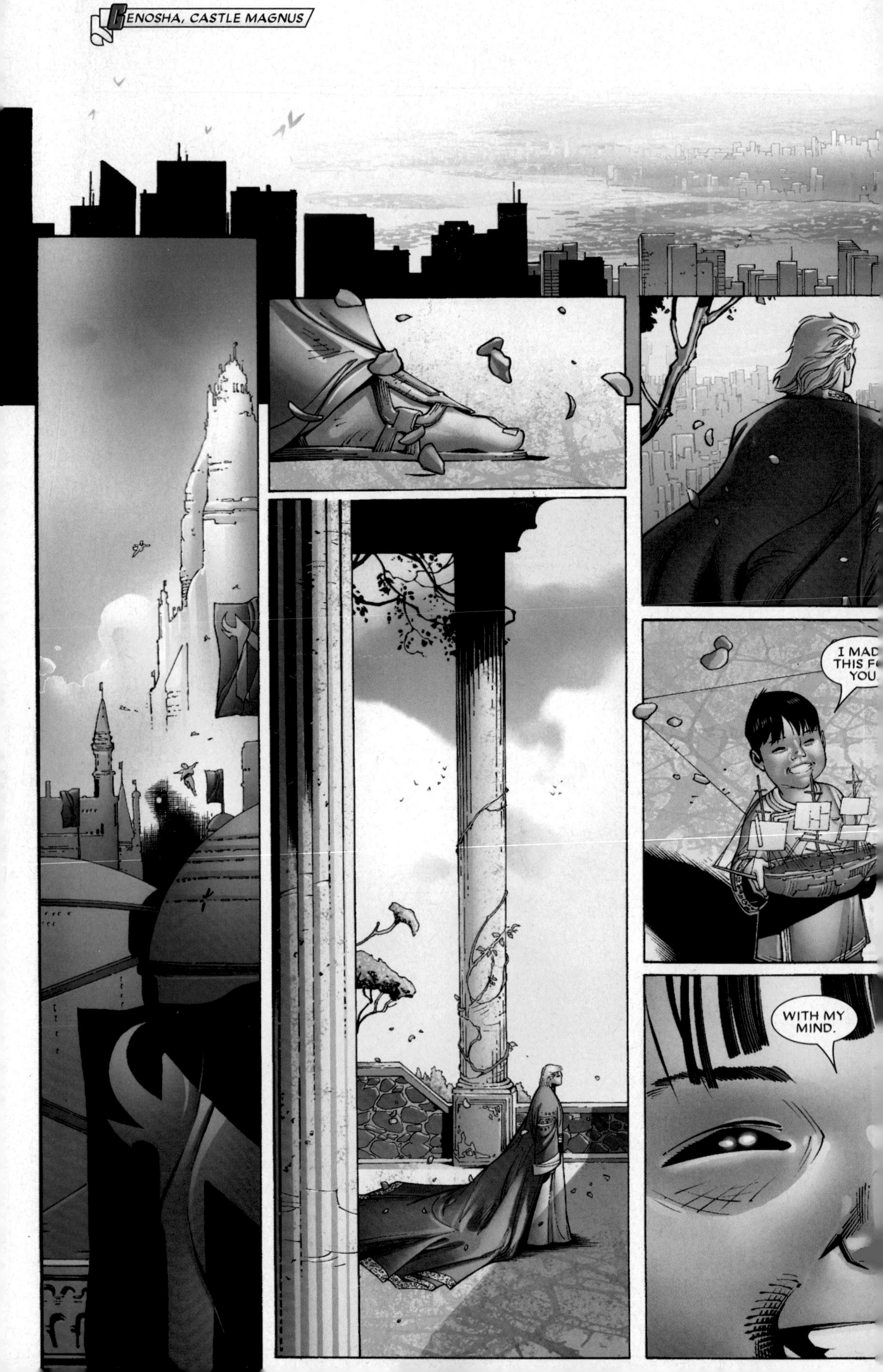
GENOSHA, CASTLE MAGNUS
I MAD
THIS F
YOU.
WITH MY
MIND.

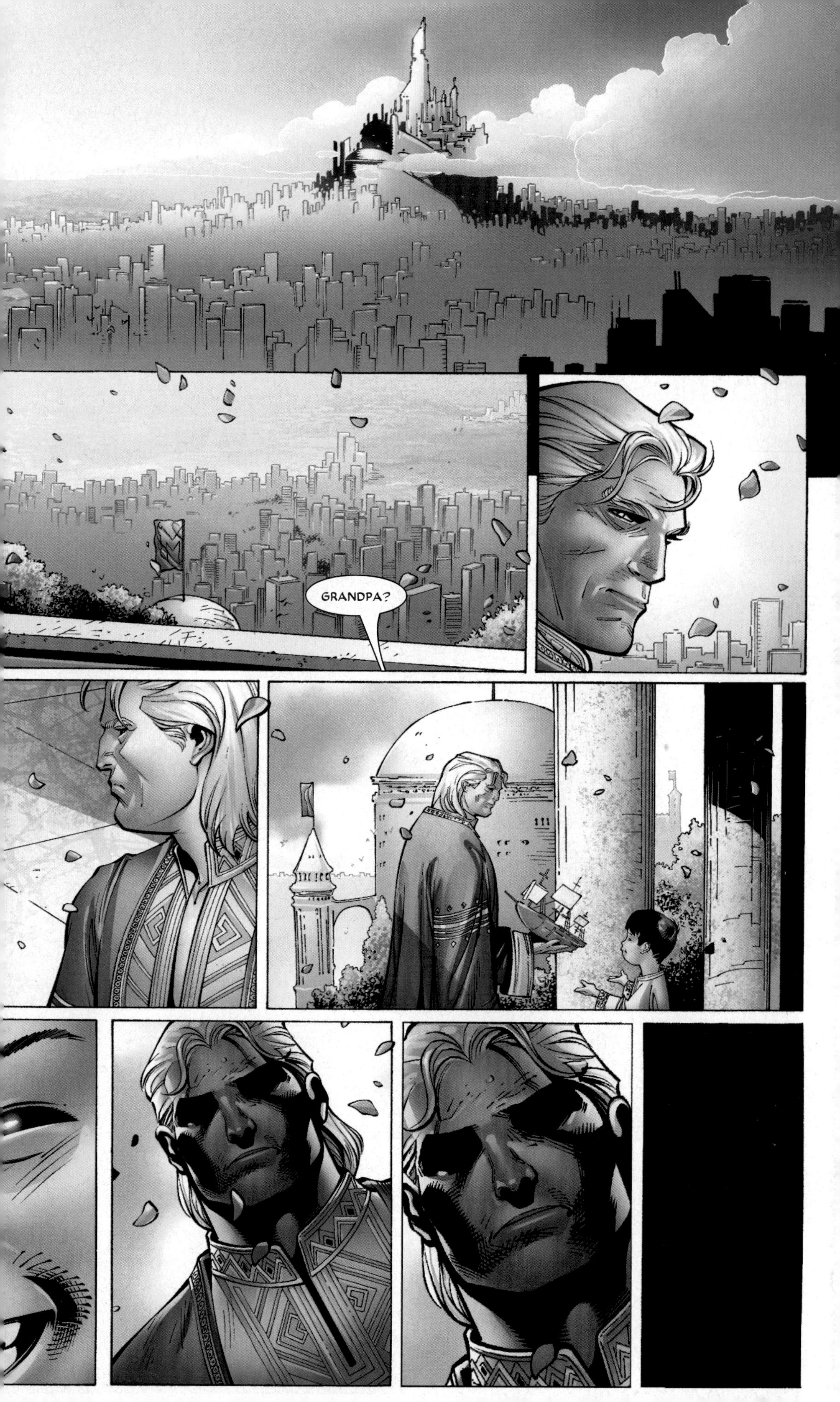
GRANDPA?

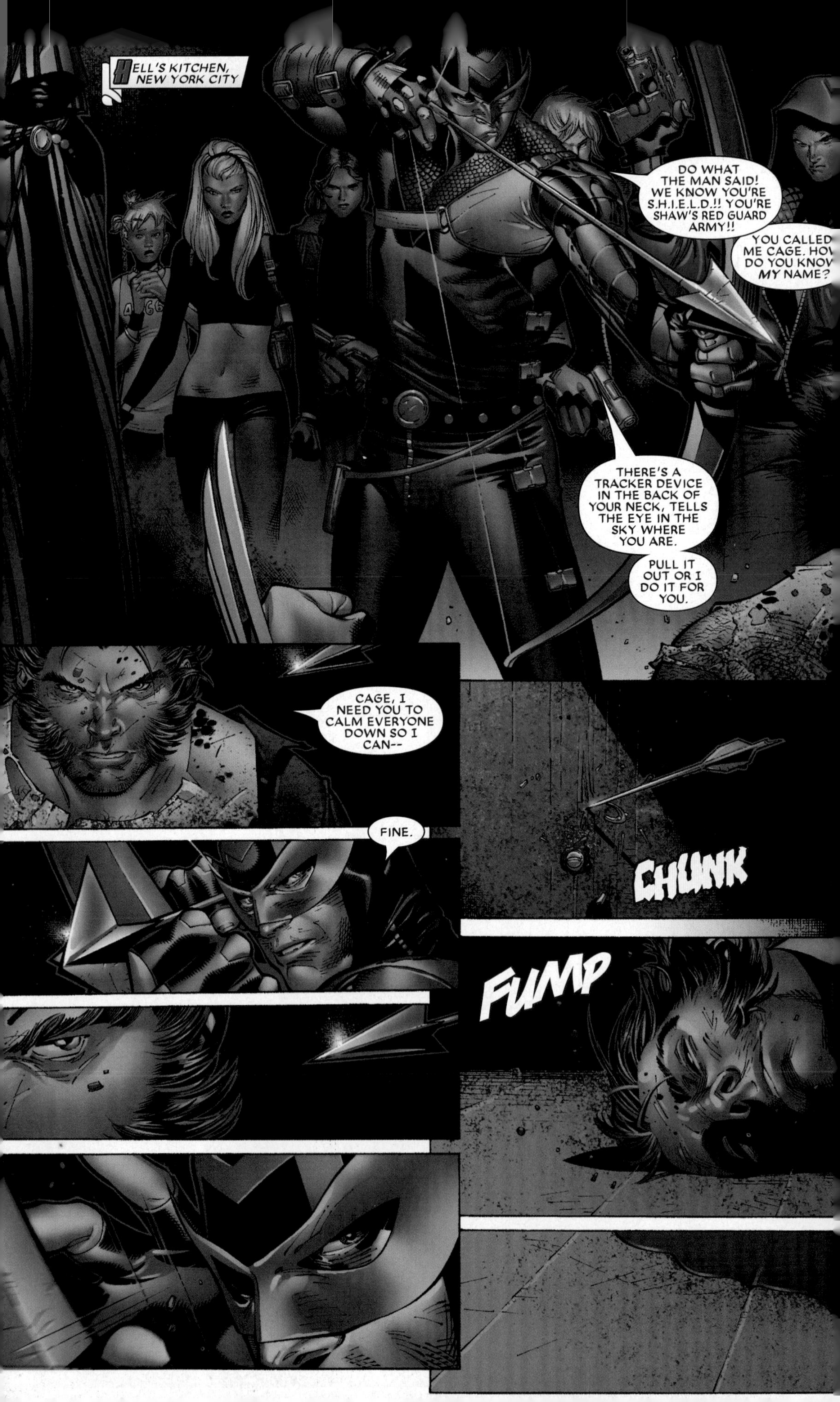
HELL'S KITCHEN, NEW YORK CITY
DO WHAT THE MAN SAID! WE KNOW YOU'RE S.H.I.E.L.D.!! YOU'RE SHAW'S RED GUARD ARMY!!
YOU CALLED ME CAGE. HOW DO YOU KNOW MY NAME?
THERE'S A TRACKER DEVICE IN THE BACK OF YOUR NECK, TELLS THE EYE IN THE SKY WHERE YOU ARE.
PULL IT OUT OR I DO IT FOR YOU.
CAGE, I NEED YOU TO CALM EVERYONE DOWN SO I CAN--
FINE.
CHUNK
FUMP

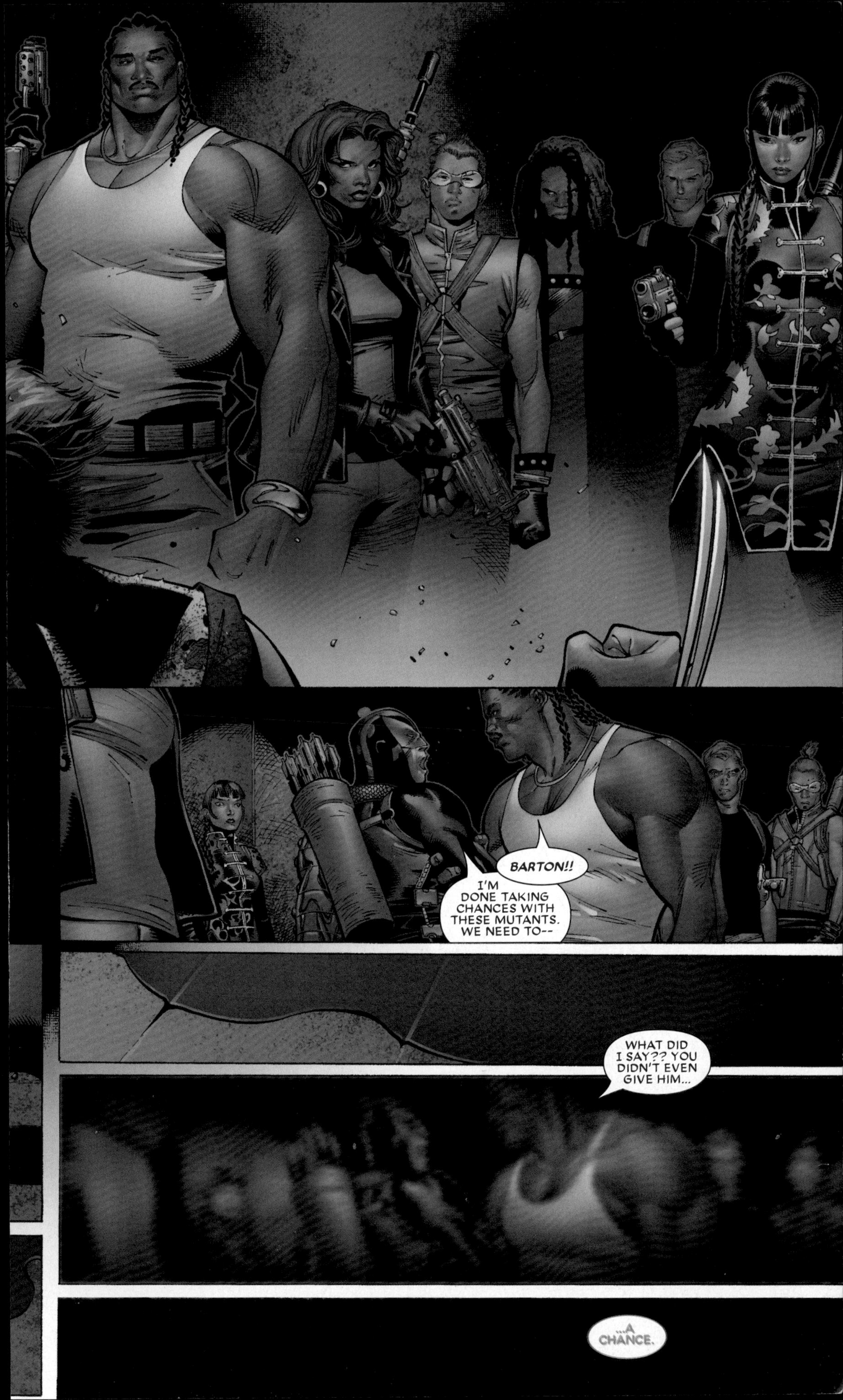
BARTON!!
I'M DONE TAKING CHANCES WITH THESE MUTANTS. WE NEED TO--
WHAT DID I SAY?? YOU DIDN'T EVEN GIVE HIM...
...A CHANCE.

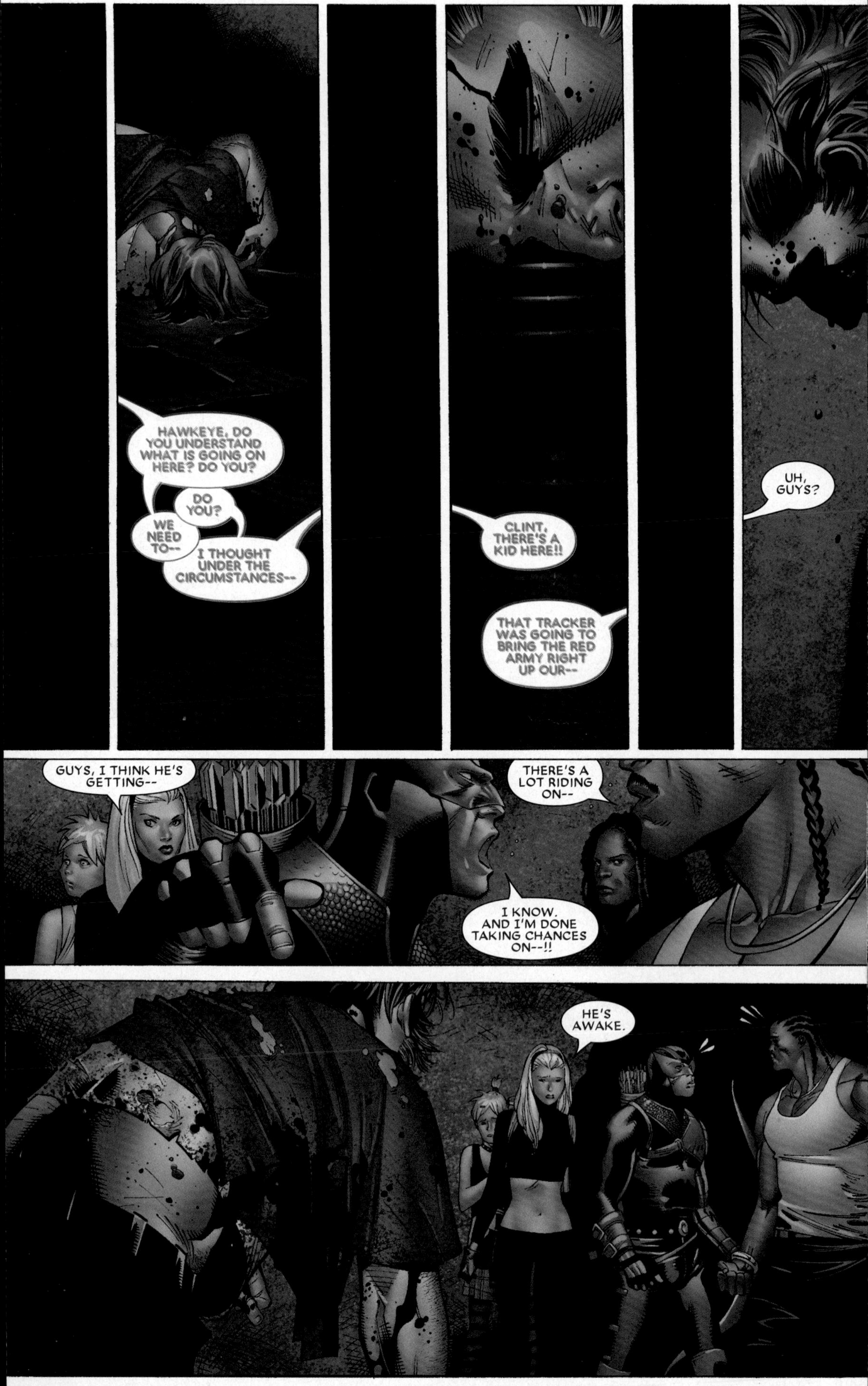
HAWKEYE, DO YOU UNDERSTAND WHAT IS GOING ON HERE? DO YOU?
DO YOU?
WE NEED TO--
I THOUGHT UNDER THE CIRCUMSTANCES--
CLINT, THERE'S A KID HERE!!
THAT TRACKER WAS GOING TO BRING THE RED ARMY RIGHT UP OUR--
UH, GUYS?
GUYS, I THINK HE'S GETTING--
THERE'S A LOT RIDING ON--
I KNOW. AND I'M DONE TAKING CHANCES ON--!!
HE'S AWAKE.

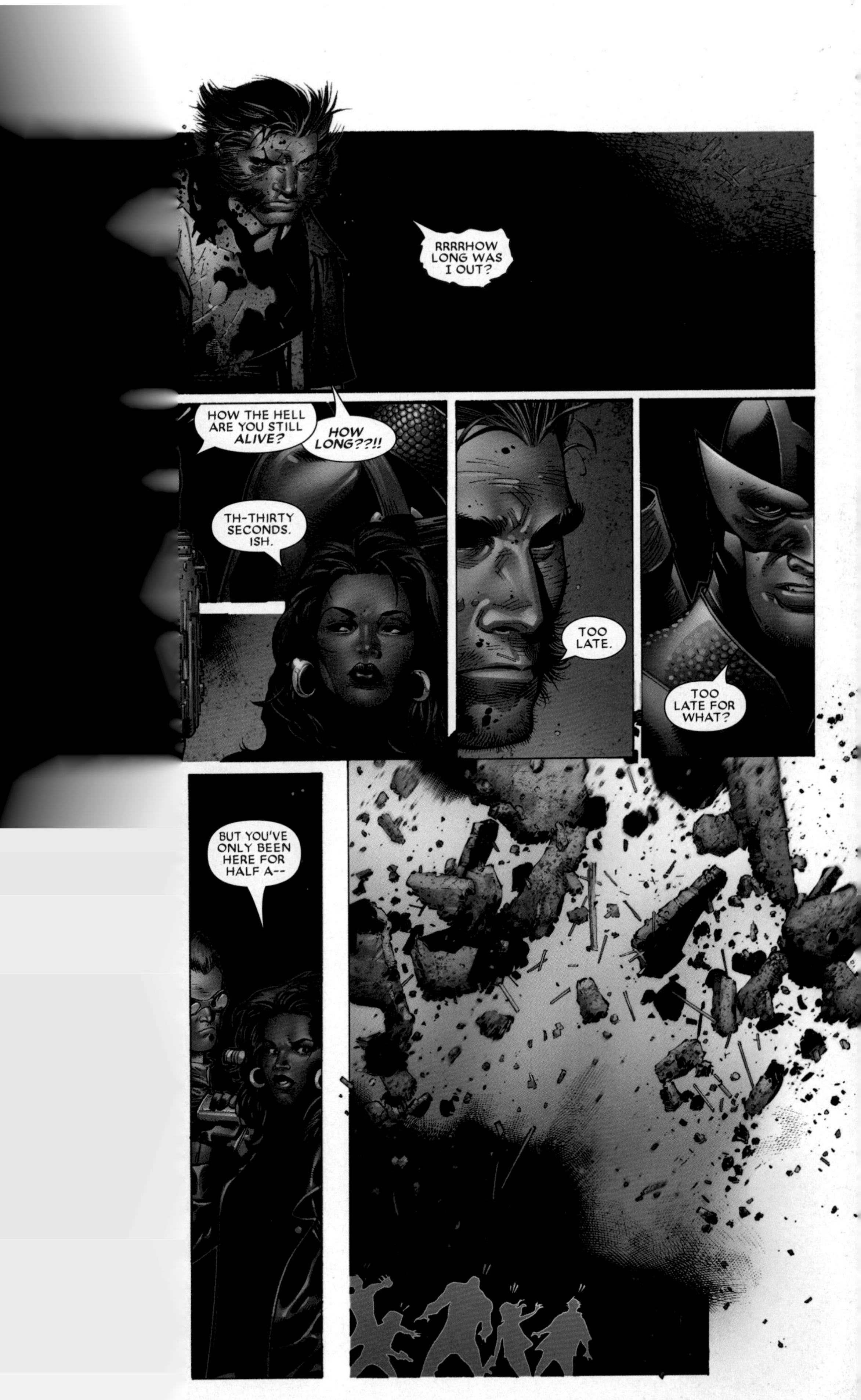
RRRRHOW LONG WAS I OUT?
HOW THE HELL ARE YOU STILL ALIVE?
HOW LONG??!!
TH-THIRTY SECONDS. ISH.
TOO LATE.
TOO LATE FOR WHAT?
BUT YOU'VE ONLY BEEN HERE FOR HALF A--

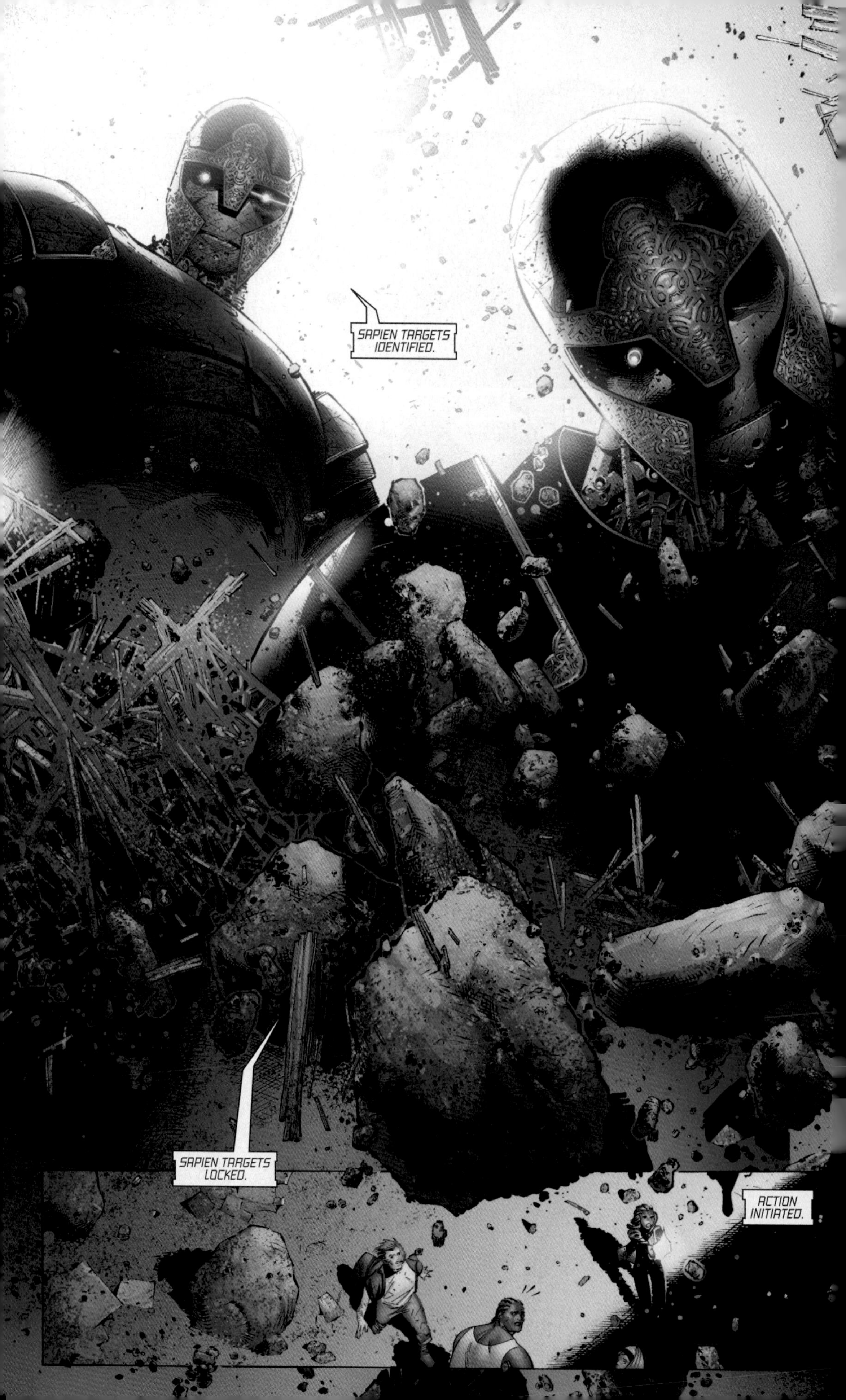
SAPIEN TARGETS IDENTIFIED.
SAPIEN TARGETS LOCKED.
ACTION INITIATED.

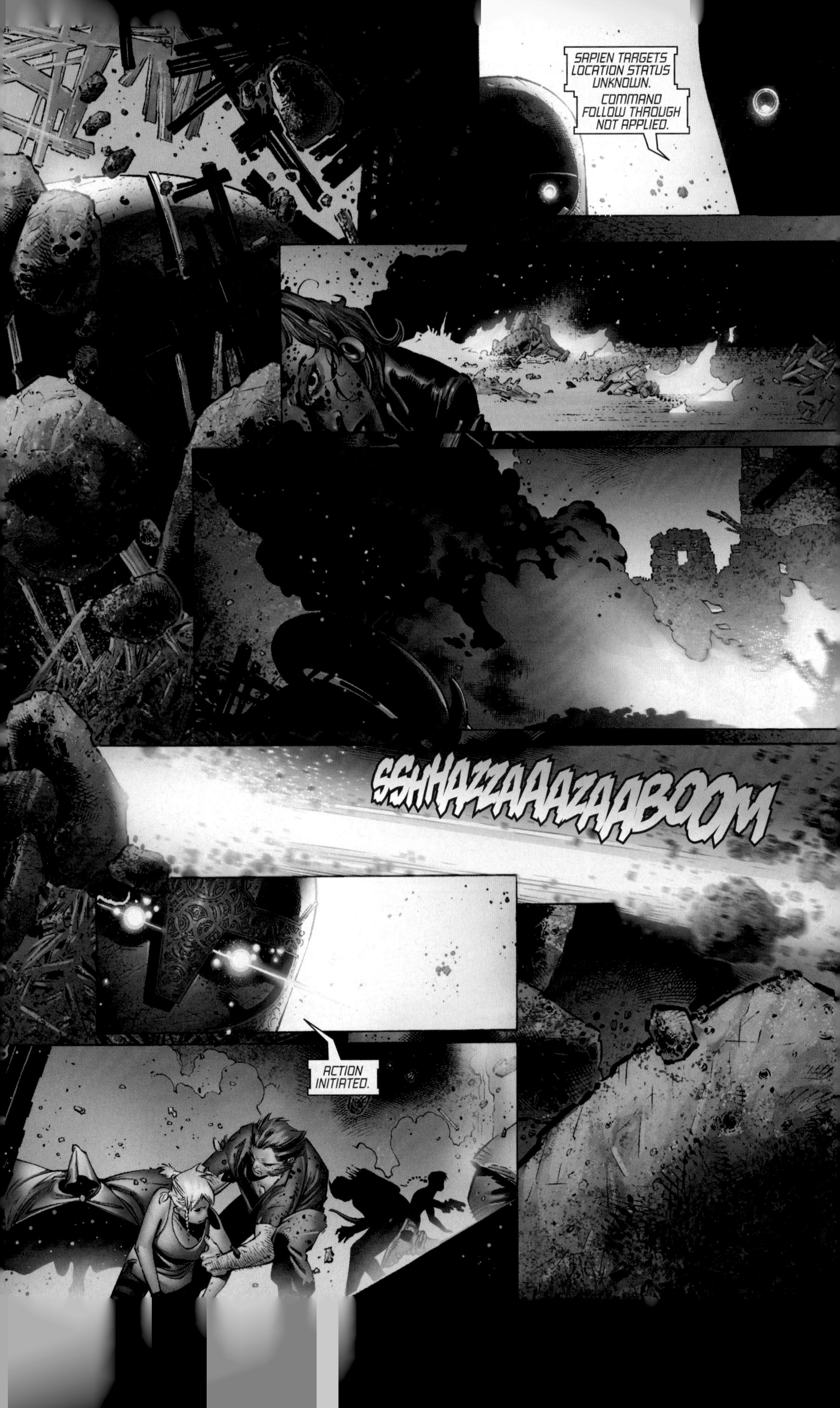
SAPIEN TARGETS LOCATION STATUS UNKNOWN.
COMMAND FOLLOW THROUGH NOT APPLIED.
SSHHAZZAAAAZAABOOM
ACTION INITIATED.

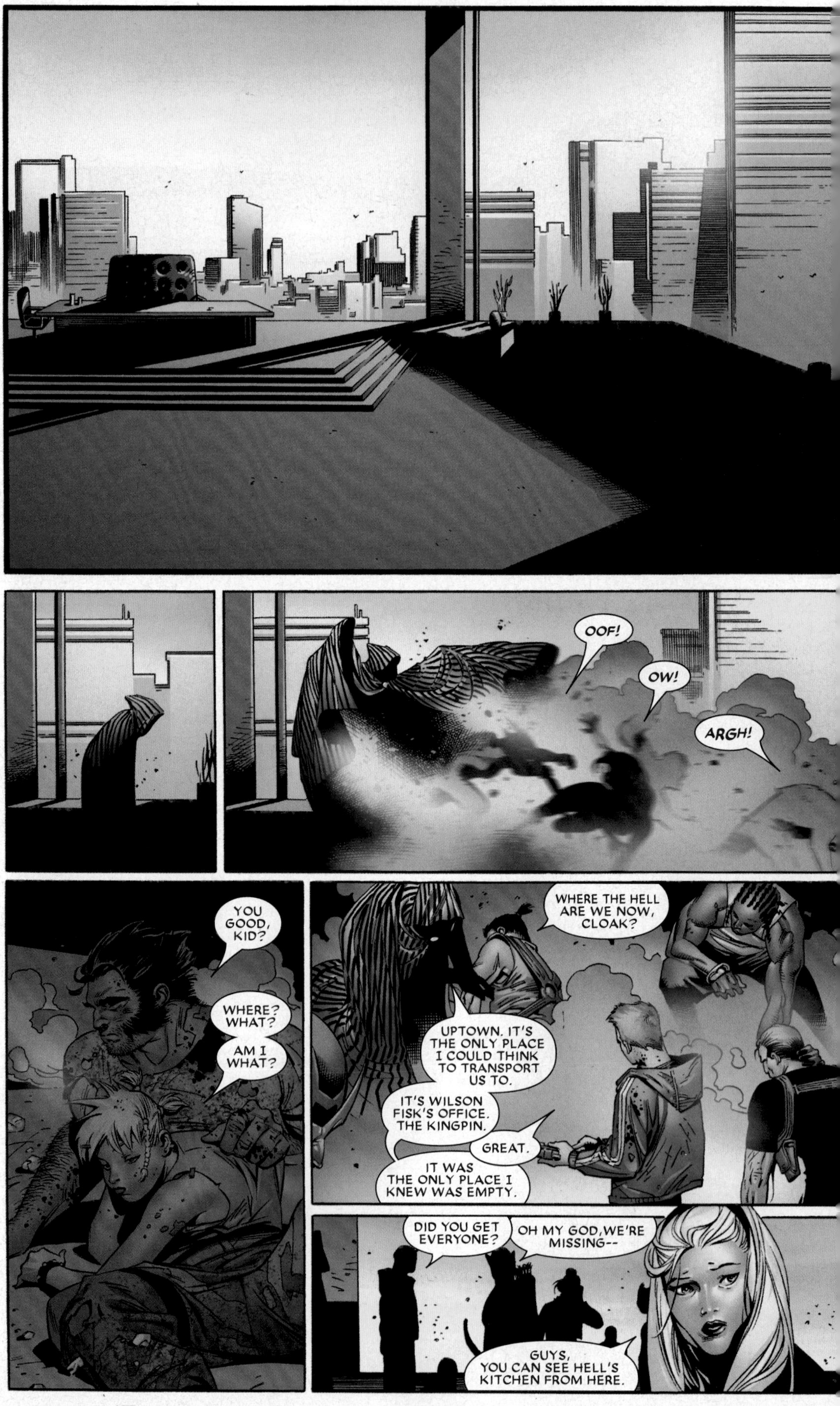
OOF!
OW!
ARGH!
YOU GOOD, KID?
WHERE? WHAT?
AM I WHAT?
WHERE THE HELL ARE WE NOW, CLOAK?
UPTOWN. IT'S THE ONLY PLACE I COULD THINK TO TRANSPORT US TO.
IT'S WILSON FISK'S OFFICE. THE KINGPIN.
GREAT.
IT WAS THE ONLY PLACE I KNEW WAS EMPTY.
DID YOU GET EVERYONE?
OH MY GOD, WE'RE MISSING--
GUYS, YOU CAN SEE HELL'S KITCHEN FROM HERE.

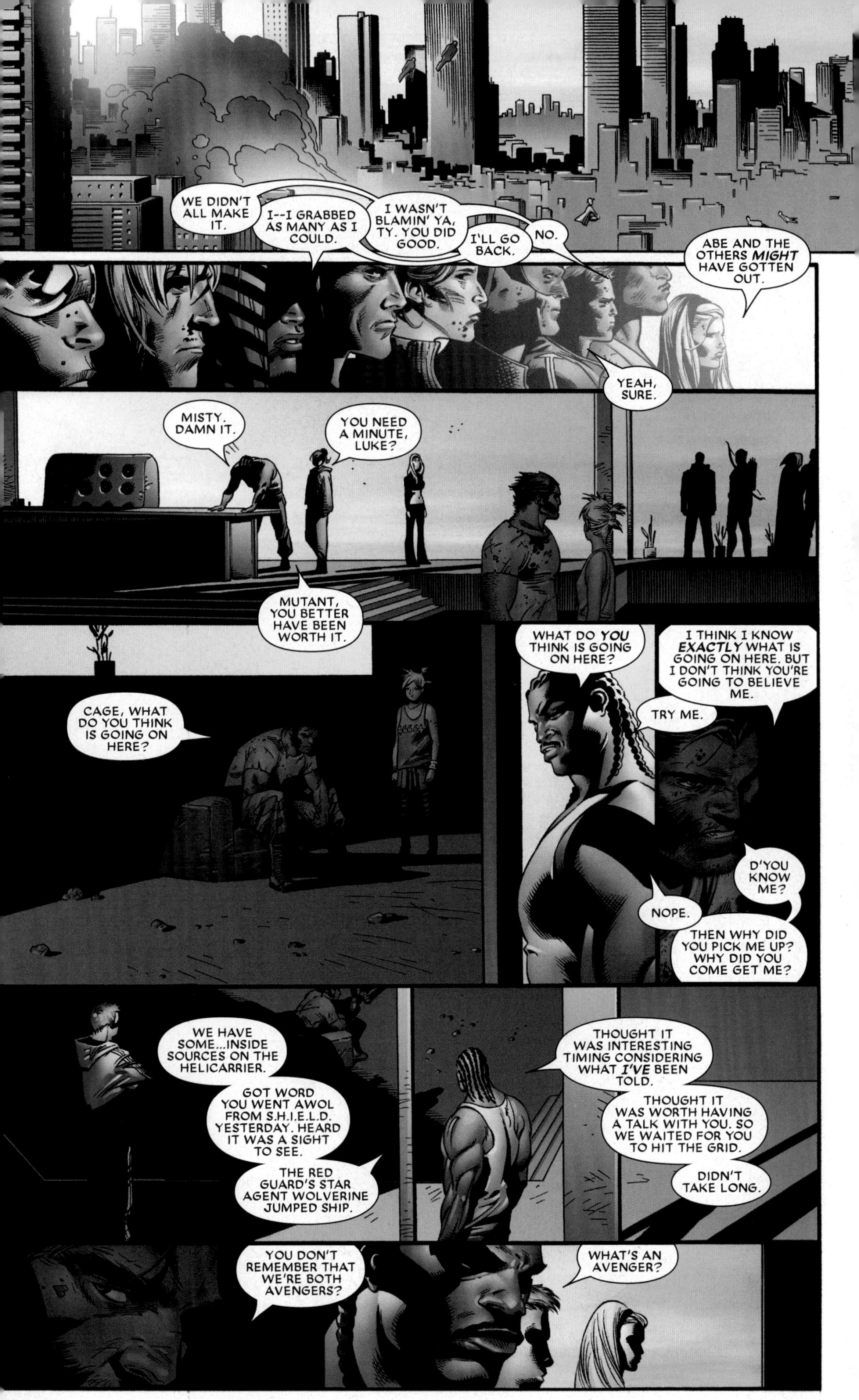
WE DIDN'T ALL MAKE IT.
I--I GRABBED AS MANY AS I COULD.
I WASN'T BLAMIN' YA, TY. YOU DID GOOD.
I'LL GO BACK.
NO.
ABE AND THE OTHERS *MIGHT* HAVE GOTTEN OUT.
YEAH, SURE.
MISTY. DAMN IT.
YOU NEED A MINUTE, LUKE?
MUTANT, YOU BETTER HAVE BEEN WORTH IT.
CAGE, WHAT DO YOU THINK IS GOING ON HERE?
WHAT DO *YOU* THINK IS GOING ON HERE?
I THINK I KNOW *EXACTLY* WHAT IS GOING ON HERE. BUT I DON'T THINK YOU'RE GOING TO BELIEVE ME.
TRY ME.
D'YOU KNOW ME?
NOPE.
THEN WHY DID YOU PICK ME UP? WHY DID YOU COME GET ME?
WE HAVE SOME...INSIDE SOURCES ON THE HELICARRIER.
GOT WORD YOU WENT AWOL FROM S.H.I.E.L.D. YESTERDAY. HEARD IT WAS A SIGHT TO SEE.
THE RED GUARD'S STAR AGENT WOLVERINE JUMPED SHIP.
THOUGHT IT WAS INTERESTING TIMING CONSIDERING WHAT *I'VE* BEEN TOLD.
THOUGHT IT WAS WORTH HAVING A TALK WITH YOU. SO WE WAITED FOR YOU TO HIT THE GRID.
DIDN'T TAKE LONG.
YOU DON'T REMEMBER THAT WE'RE BOTH AVENGERS?
WHAT'S AN AVENGER?

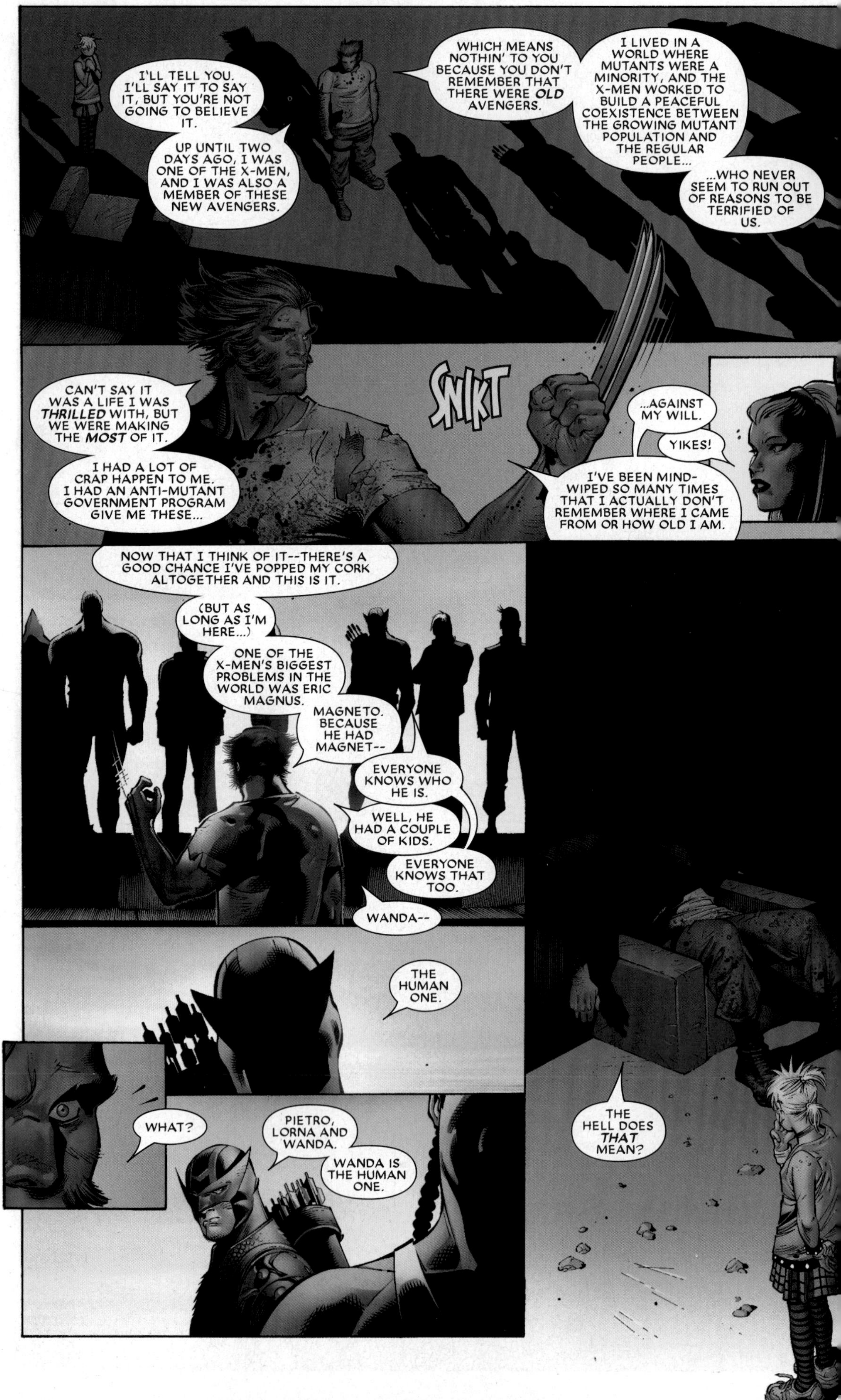
I'LL TELL YOU. I'LL SAY IT TO SAY IT, BUT YOU'RE NOT GOING TO BELIEVE IT.
UP UNTIL TWO DAYS AGO, I WAS ONE OF THE X-MEN, AND I WAS ALSO A MEMBER OF THESE NEW AVENGERS.
WHICH MEANS NOTHIN' TO YOU BECAUSE YOU DON'T REMEMBER THAT THERE WERE OLD AVENGERS.
I LIVED IN A WORLD WHERE MUTANTS WERE A MINORITY, AND THE X-MEN WORKED TO BUILD A PEACEFUL COEXISTENCE BETWEEN THE GROWING MUTANT POPULATION AND THE REGULAR PEOPLE...
...WHO NEVER SEEM TO RUN OUT OF REASONS TO BE TERRIFIED OF US.
CAN'T SAY IT WAS A LIFE I WAS THRILLED WITH, BUT WE WERE MAKING THE MOST OF IT.
I HAD A LOT OF CRAP HAPPEN TO ME. I HAD AN ANTI-MUTANT GOVERNMENT PROGRAM GIVE ME THESE...
SNIKT
...AGAINST MY WILL.
YIKES!
I'VE BEEN MIND-WIPED SO MANY TIMES THAT I ACTUALLY DON'T REMEMBER WHERE I CAME FROM OR HOW OLD I AM.
NOW THAT I THINK OF IT--THERE'S A GOOD CHANCE I'VE POPPED MY CORK ALTOGETHER AND THIS IS IT.
(BUT AS LONG AS I'M HERE...)
ONE OF THE X-MEN'S BIGGEST PROBLEMS IN THE WORLD WAS ERIC MAGNUS.
MAGNETO. BECAUSE HE HAD MAGNET--
EVERYONE KNOWS WHO HE IS.
WELL, HE HAD A COUPLE OF KIDS.
EVERYONE KNOWS THAT TOO.
WANDA--
THE HUMAN ONE.
WHAT?
PIETRO, LORNA AND WANDA.
WANDA IS THE HUMAN ONE.
THE HELL DOES THAT MEAN?

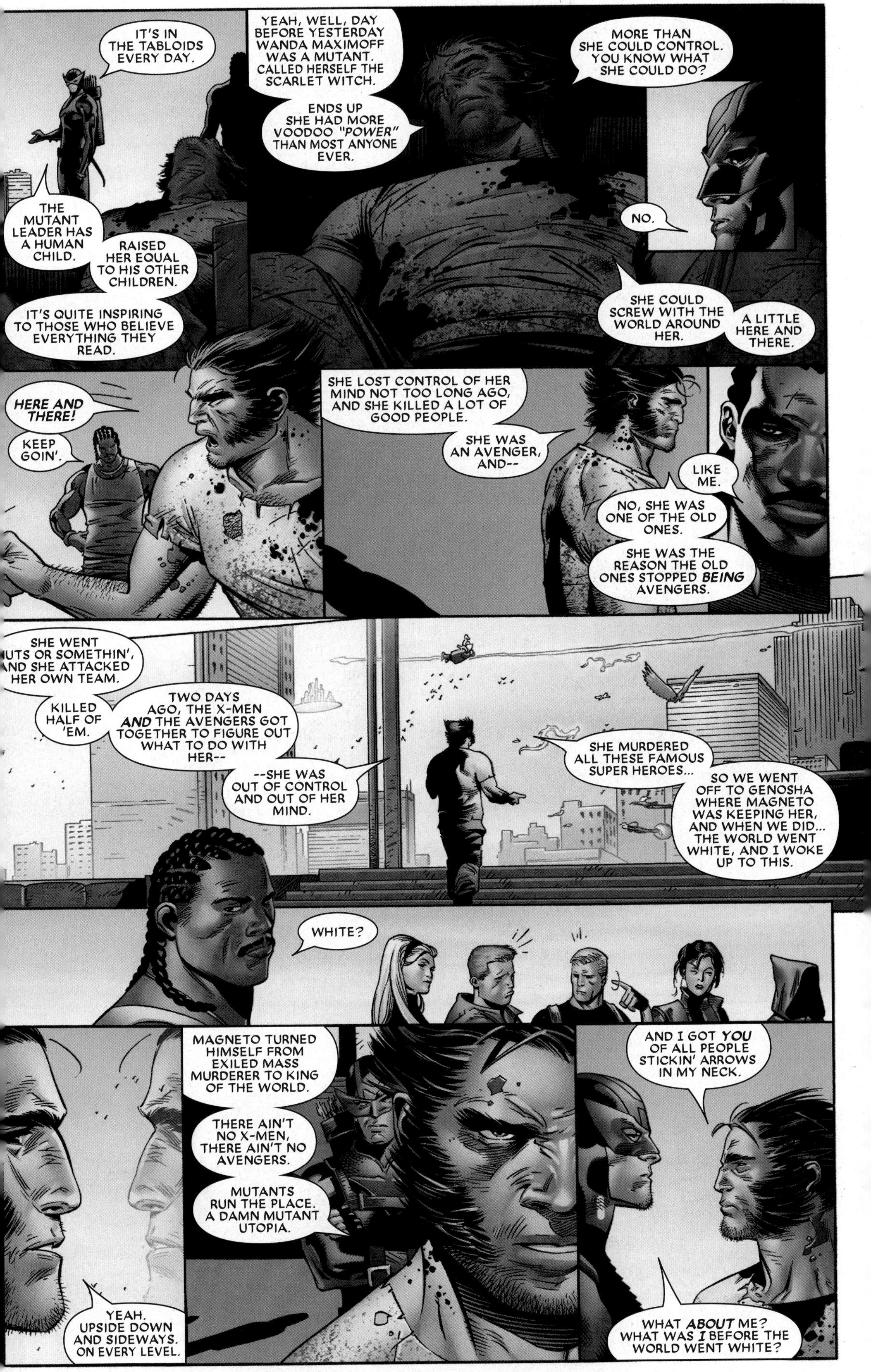

IT'S IN THE TABLOIDS EVERY DAY.
THE MUTANT LEADER HAS A HUMAN CHILD.
RAISED HER EQUAL TO HIS OTHER CHILDREN.
IT'S QUITE INSPIRING TO THOSE WHO BELIEVE EVERYTHING THEY READ.
YEAH, WELL, DAY BEFORE YESTERDAY WANDA MAXIMOFF WAS A MUTANT. CALLED HERSELF THE SCARLET WITCH.
ENDS UP SHE HAD MORE VOODOO "POWER" THAN MOST ANYONE EVER.
MORE THAN SHE COULD CONTROL. YOU KNOW WHAT SHE COULD DO?
NO.
SHE COULD SCREW WITH THE WORLD AROUND HER.
A LITTLE HERE AND THERE.
HERE AND THERE!
KEEP GOIN'.
SHE LOST CONTROL OF HER MIND NOT TOO LONG AGO, AND SHE KILLED A LOT OF GOOD PEOPLE.
SHE WAS AN AVENGER, AND--
LIKE ME.
NO, SHE WAS ONE OF THE OLD ONES.
SHE WAS THE REASON THE OLD ONES STOPPED BEING AVENGERS.
SHE WENT UTS OR SOMETHIN', ND SHE ATTACKED HER OWN TEAM.
KILLED HALF OF 'EM.
TWO DAYS AGO, THE X-MEN AND THE AVENGERS GOT TOGETHER TO FIGURE OUT WHAT TO DO WITH HER--
--SHE WAS OUT OF CONTROL AND OUT OF HER MIND.
SHE MURDERED ALL THESE FAMOUS SUPER HEROES...
SO WE WENT OFF TO GENOSHA WHERE MAGNETO WAS KEEPING HER, AND WHEN WE DID... THE WORLD WENT WHITE, AND I WOKE UP TO THIS.
WHITE?
YEAH. UPSIDE DOWN AND SIDEWAYS. ON EVERY LEVEL.
MAGNETO TURNED HIMSELF FROM EXILED MASS MURDERER TO KING OF THE WORLD.
THERE AIN'T NO X-MEN, THERE AIN'T NO AVENGERS.
MUTANTS RUN THE PLACE. A DAMN MUTANT UTOPIA.
AND I GOT YOU OF ALL PEOPLE STICKIN' ARROWS IN MY NECK.
WHAT ABOUT ME? WHAT WAS I BEFORE THE WORLD WENT WHITE?

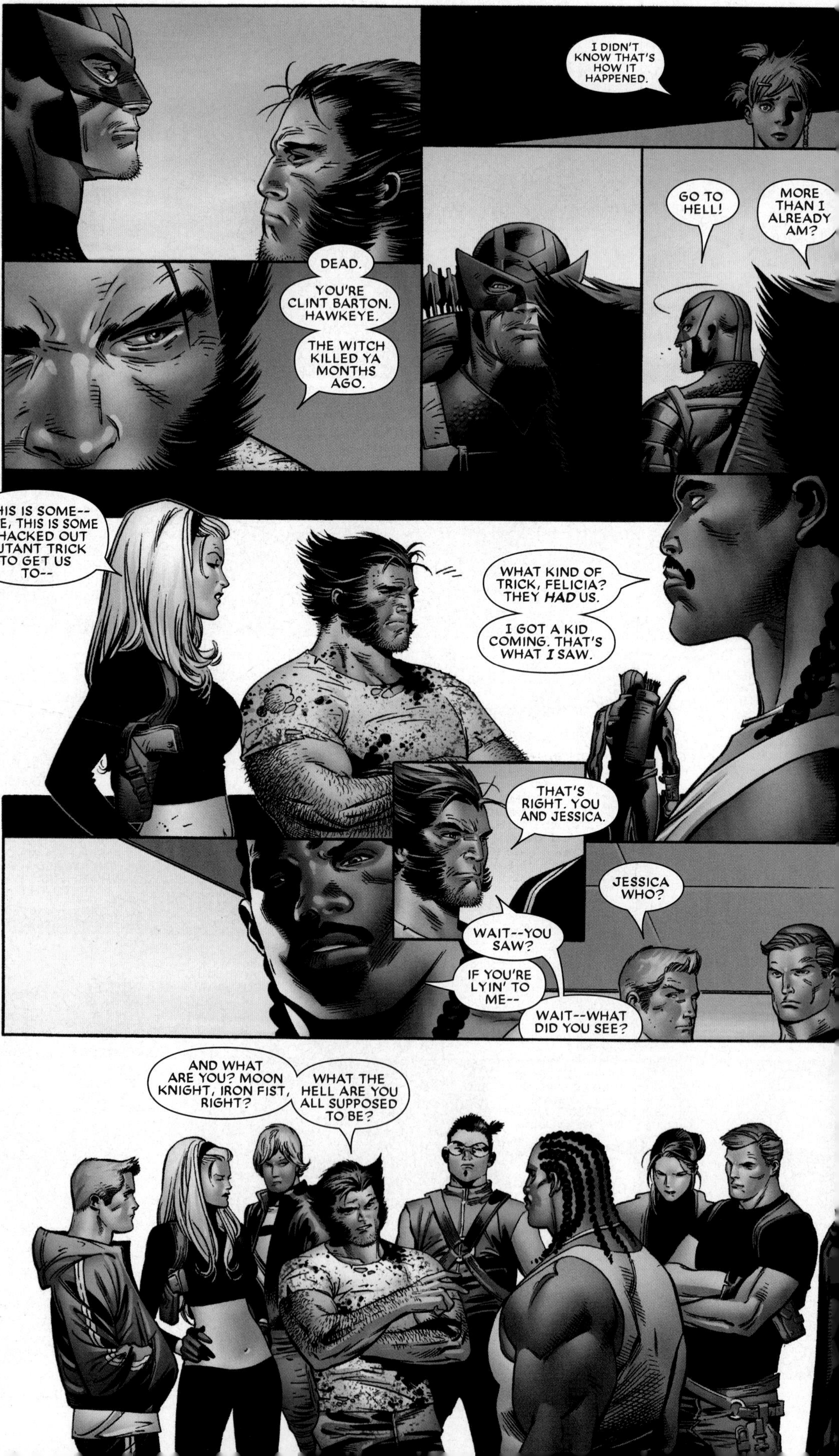
I DIDN'T KNOW THAT'S HOW IT HAPPENED.
DEAD.
YOU'RE CLINT BARTON. HAWKEYE.
THE WITCH KILLED YA MONTHS AGO.
GO TO HELL!
MORE THAN I ALREADY AM?
THIS IS SOME-- CAGE, THIS IS SOME WHACKED OUT MUTANT TRICK TO GET US TO--
WHAT KIND OF TRICK, FELICIA? THEY HAD US.
I GOT A KID COMING. THAT'S WHAT I SAW.
THAT'S RIGHT. YOU AND JESSICA.
JESSICA WHO?
WAIT--YOU SAW?
IF YOU'RE LYIN' TO ME--
WAIT--WHAT DID YOU SEE?
AND WHAT ARE YOU? MOON KNIGHT, IRON FIST, RIGHT?
WHAT THE HELL ARE YOU ALL SUPPOSED TO BE?

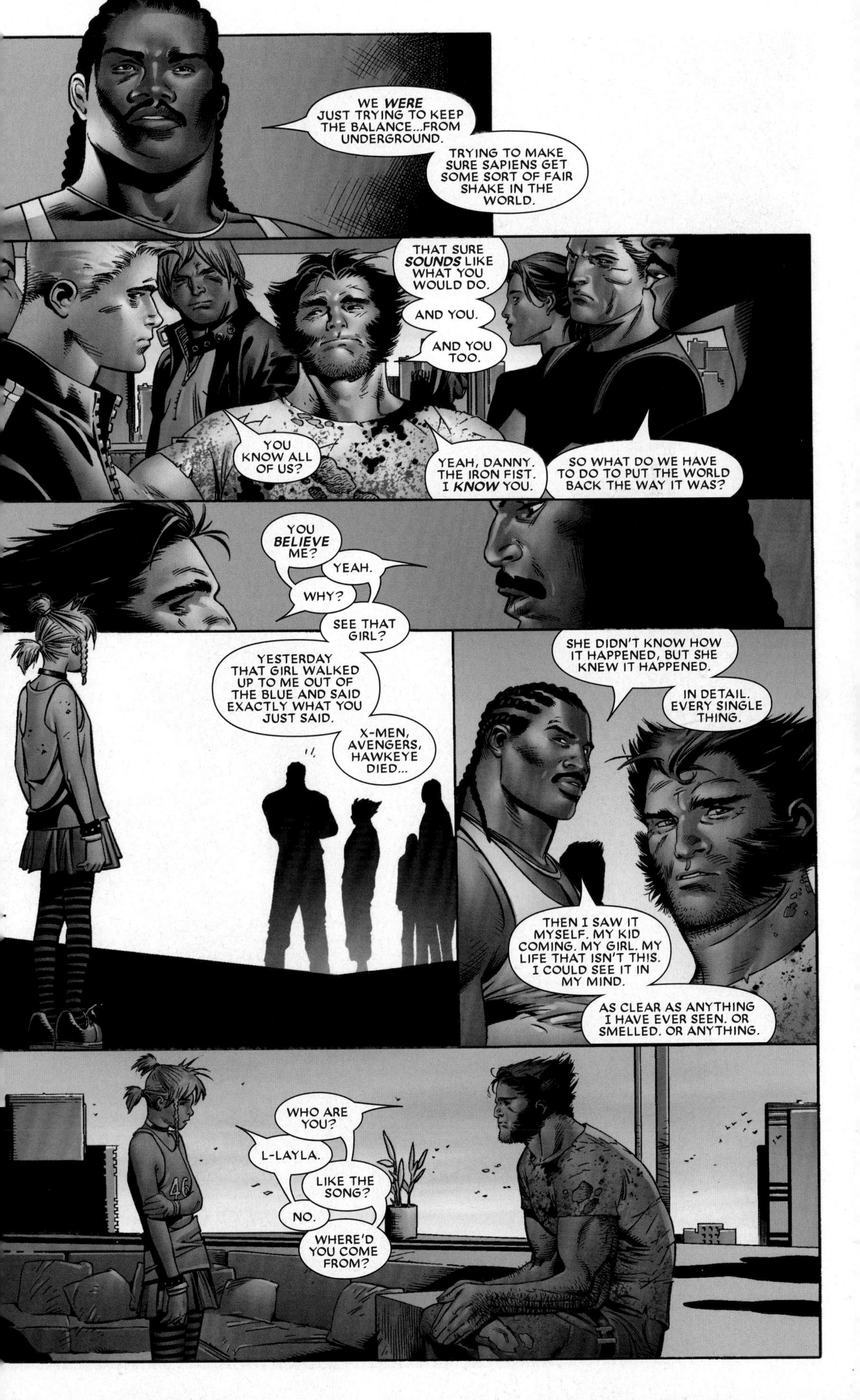
WE *WERE* JUST TRYING TO KEEP THE BALANCE...FROM UNDERGROUND.
TRYING TO MAKE SURE SAPIENS GET SOME SORT OF FAIR SHAKE IN THE WORLD.
THAT SURE *SOUNDS* LIKE WHAT YOU WOULD DO.
AND YOU.
AND YOU TOO.
YOU KNOW ALL OF US?
YEAH, DANNY. THE IRON FIST. I *KNOW* YOU.
SO WHAT DO WE HAVE TO DO TO PUT THE WORLD BACK THE WAY IT WAS?
YOU *BELIEVE* ME?
YEAH.
WHY?
SEE THAT GIRL?
YESTERDAY THAT GIRL WALKED UP TO ME OUT OF THE BLUE AND SAID EXACTLY WHAT YOU JUST SAID.
X-MEN, AVENGERS, HAWKEYE DIED...
SHE DIDN'T KNOW HOW IT HAPPENED, BUT SHE KNEW IT HAPPENED.
IN DETAIL. EVERY SINGLE THING.
THEN I SAW IT MYSELF. MY KID COMING. MY GIRL. MY LIFE THAT ISN'T THIS. I COULD SEE IT IN MY MIND.
AS CLEAR AS ANYTHING I HAVE EVER SEEN. OR SMELLED. OR ANYTHING.
WHO ARE YOU?
L-LAYLA.
LIKE THE SONG?
NO.
WHERE'D YOU COME FROM?

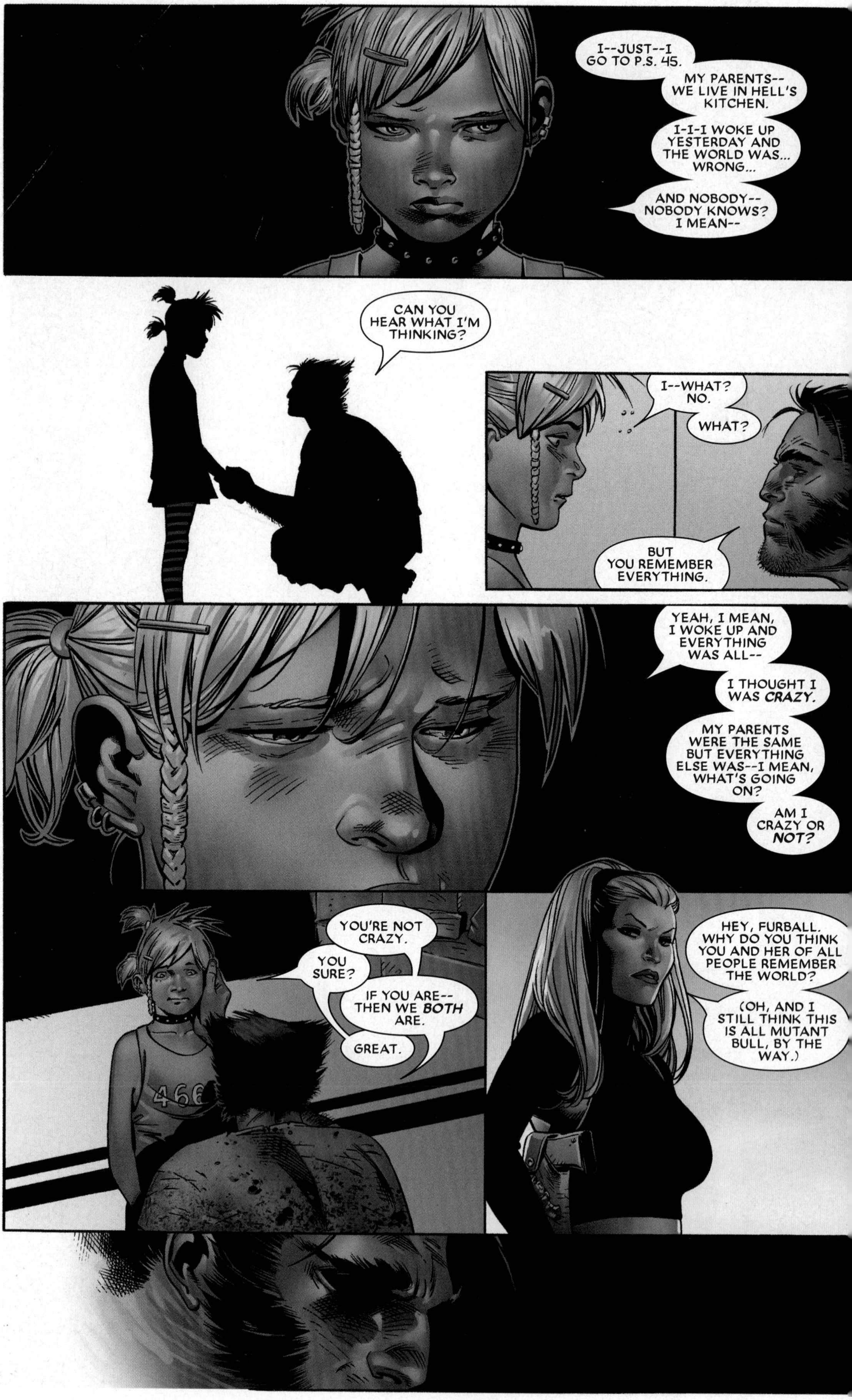
I--JUST--I GO TO P.S. 45.
MY PARENTS-- WE LIVE IN HELL'S KITCHEN.
I-I-I WOKE UP YESTERDAY AND THE WORLD WAS... WRONG...
AND NOBODY-- NOBODY KNOWS? I MEAN--
CAN YOU HEAR WHAT I'M THINKING?
I--WHAT? NO.
WHAT?
BUT YOU REMEMBER EVERYTHING.
YEAH, I MEAN, I WOKE UP AND EVERYTHING WAS ALL--
I THOUGHT I WAS *CRAZY.*
MY PARENTS WERE THE SAME BUT EVERYTHING ELSE WAS--I MEAN, WHAT'S GOING ON?
AM I CRAZY OR *NOT?*
YOU'RE NOT CRAZY.
YOU SURE?
IF YOU ARE-- THEN WE *BOTH* ARE.
GREAT.
HEY, FURBALL. WHY DO YOU THINK YOU AND HER OF ALL PEOPLE REMEMBER THE WORLD?
(OH, AND I STILL THINK THIS IS ALL MUTANT BULL, BY THE WAY.)

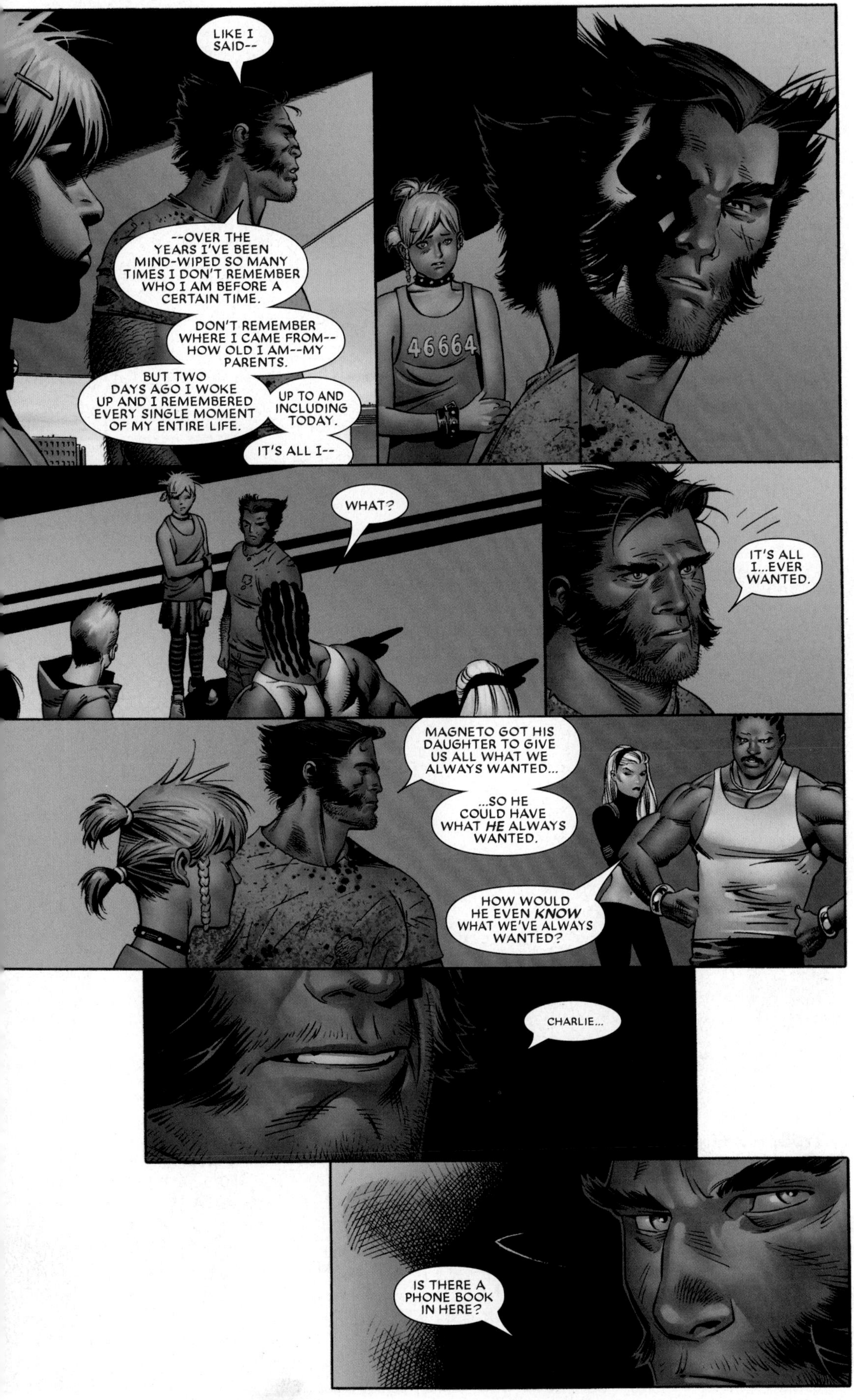
LIKE I SAID--
--OVER THE YEARS I'VE BEEN MIND-WIPED SO MANY TIMES I DON'T REMEMBER WHO I AM BEFORE A CERTAIN TIME.
DON'T REMEMBER WHERE I CAME FROM--HOW OLD I AM--MY PARENTS.
BUT TWO DAYS AGO I WOKE UP AND I REMEMBERED EVERY SINGLE MOMENT OF MY ENTIRE LIFE.
UP TO AND INCLUDING TODAY.
IT'S ALL I--
46664
WHAT?
IT'S ALL I...EVER WANTED.
MAGNETO GOT HIS DAUGHTER TO GIVE US ALL WHAT WE ALWAYS WANTED...
...SO HE COULD HAVE WHAT *HE* ALWAYS WANTED.
HOW WOULD HE EVEN *KNOW* WHAT WE'VE ALWAYS WANTED?
CHARLIE...
IS THERE A PHONE BOOK IN HERE?

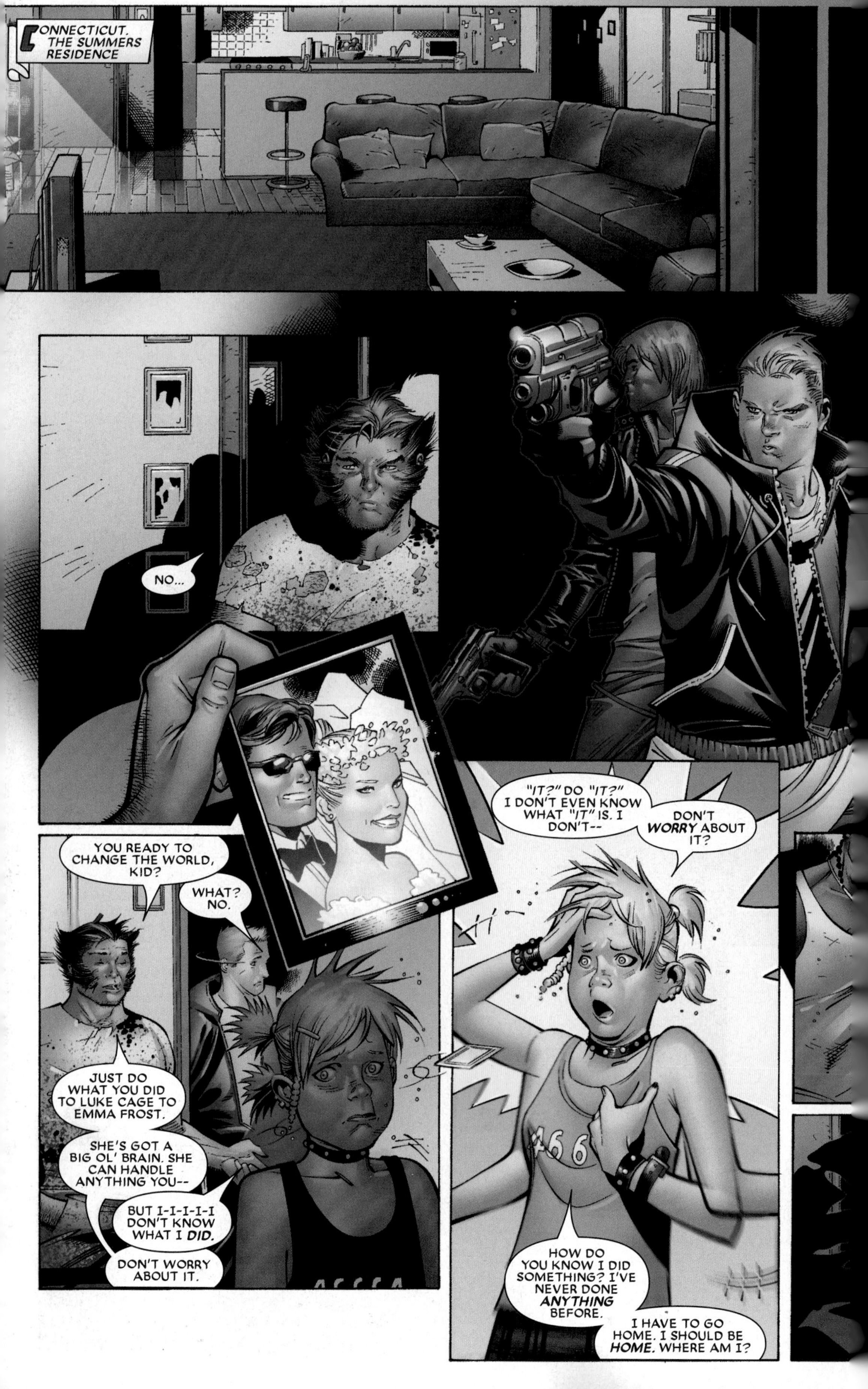
CONNECTICUT. THE SUMMERS RESIDENCE
NO...
YOU READY TO CHANGE THE WORLD, KID?
WHAT? NO.
JUST DO WHAT YOU DID TO LUKE CAGE TO EMMA FROST.
SHE'S GOT A BIG OL' BRAIN. SHE CAN HANDLE ANYTHING YOU--
BUT I-I-I-I-I DON'T KNOW WHAT I DID.
DON'T WORRY ABOUT IT.
"IT?" DO "IT?" I DON'T EVEN KNOW WHAT "IT"--IS. I DON'T--
DON'T WORRY ABOUT IT?
HOW DO YOU KNOW I DID SOMETHING? I'VE NEVER DONE ANYTHING BEFORE.
I HAVE TO GO HOME. I SHOULD BE HOME. WHERE AM I?

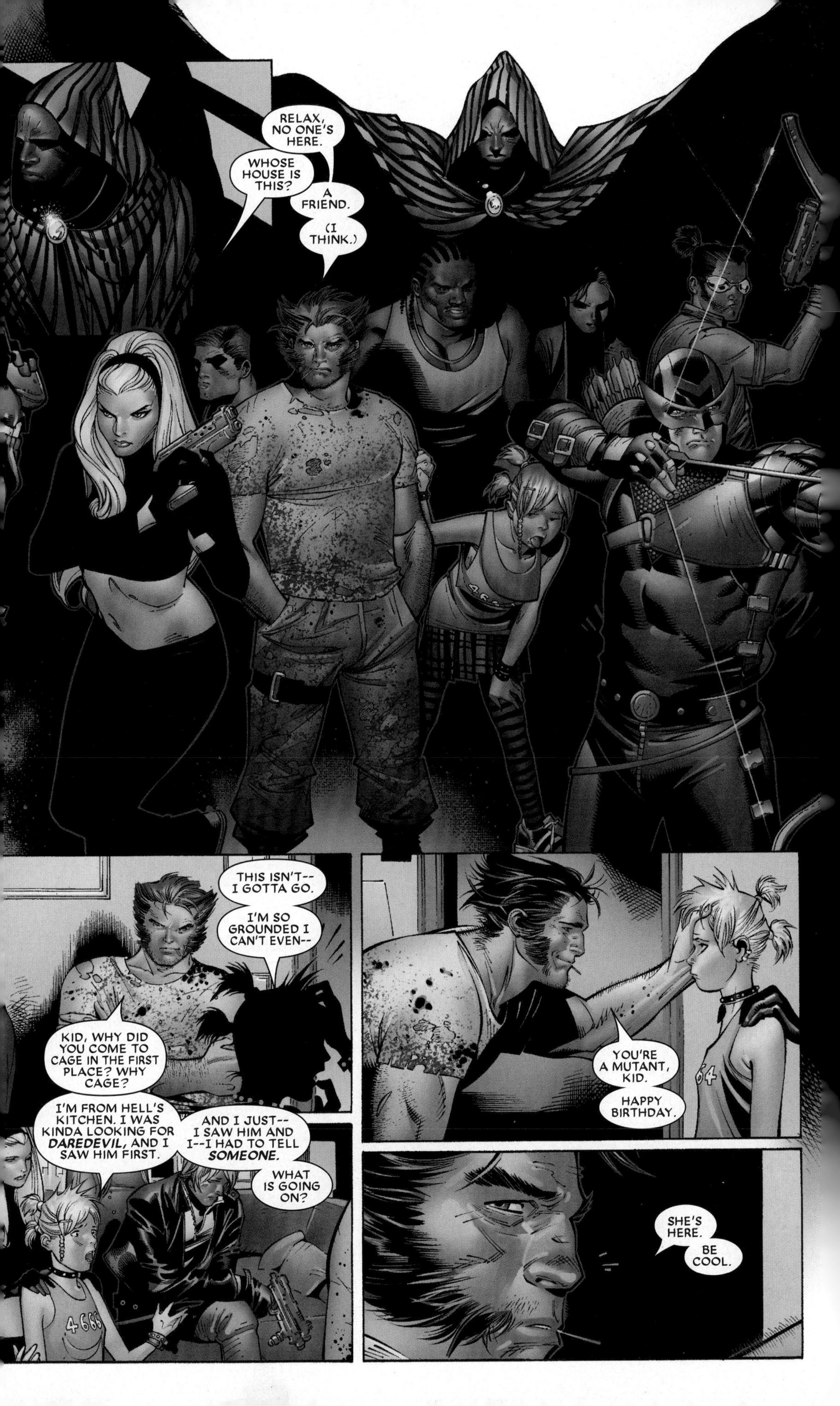

RELAX, NO ONE'S HERE.
WHOSE HOUSE IS THIS?
A FRIEND.
(I THINK.)
THIS ISN'T-- I GOTTA GO.
I'M SO GROUNDED I CAN'T EVEN--
KID, WHY DID YOU COME TO CAGE IN THE FIRST PLACE? WHY CAGE?
I'M FROM HELL'S KITCHEN. I WAS KINDA LOOKING FOR DAREDEVIL, AND I SAW HIM FIRST.
AND I JUST-- I SAW HIM AND I--I HAD TO TELL SOMEONE.
WHAT IS GOING ON?
YOU'RE A MUTANT, KID.
HAPPY BIRTHDAY.
SHE'S HERE.
BE COOL.

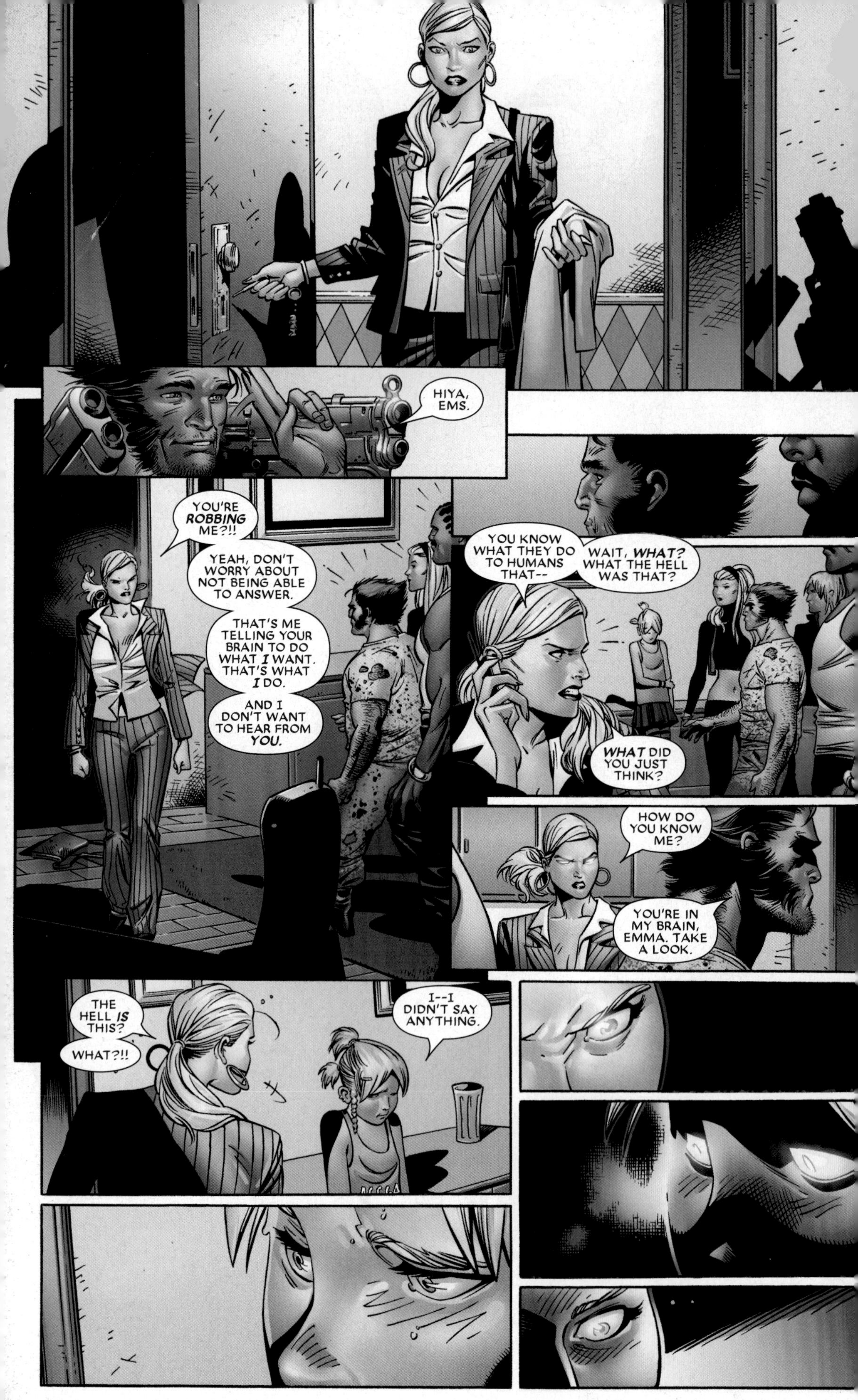
HIYA, EMS.
YOU'RE ROBBING ME?!!
YEAH, DON'T WORRY ABOUT NOT BEING ABLE TO ANSWER.
THAT'S ME TELLING YOUR BRAIN TO DO WHAT I WANT. THAT'S WHAT I DO.
AND I DON'T WANT TO HEAR FROM YOU.
YOU KNOW WHAT THEY DO TO HUMANS THAT--
WAIT, WHAT? WHAT THE HELL WAS THAT?
WHAT DID YOU JUST THINK?
HOW DO YOU KNOW ME?
YOU'RE IN MY BRAIN, EMMA. TAKE A LOOK.
THE HELL IS THIS?
WHAT?!!
I--I DIDN'T SAY ANYTHING.

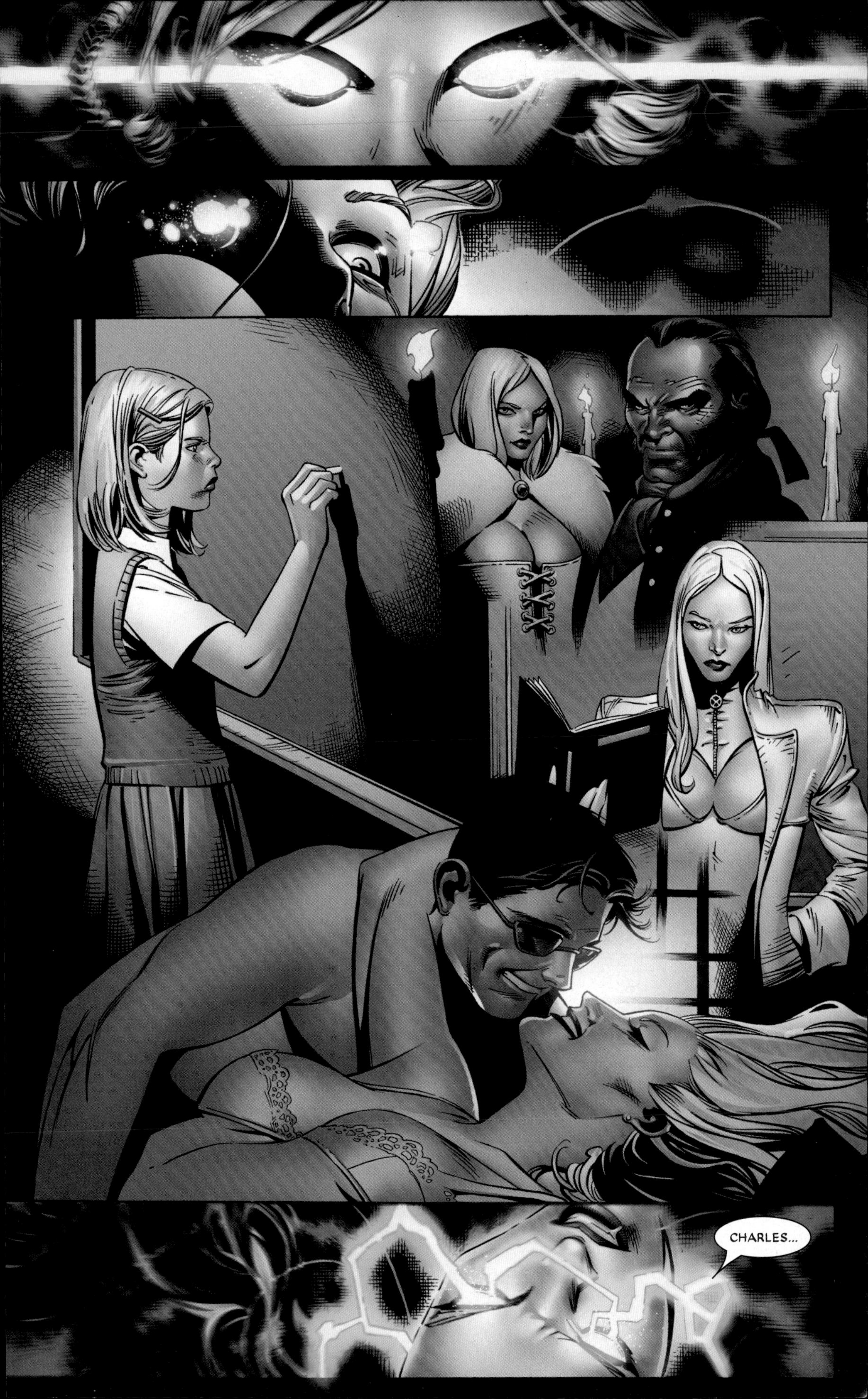
CHARLES...

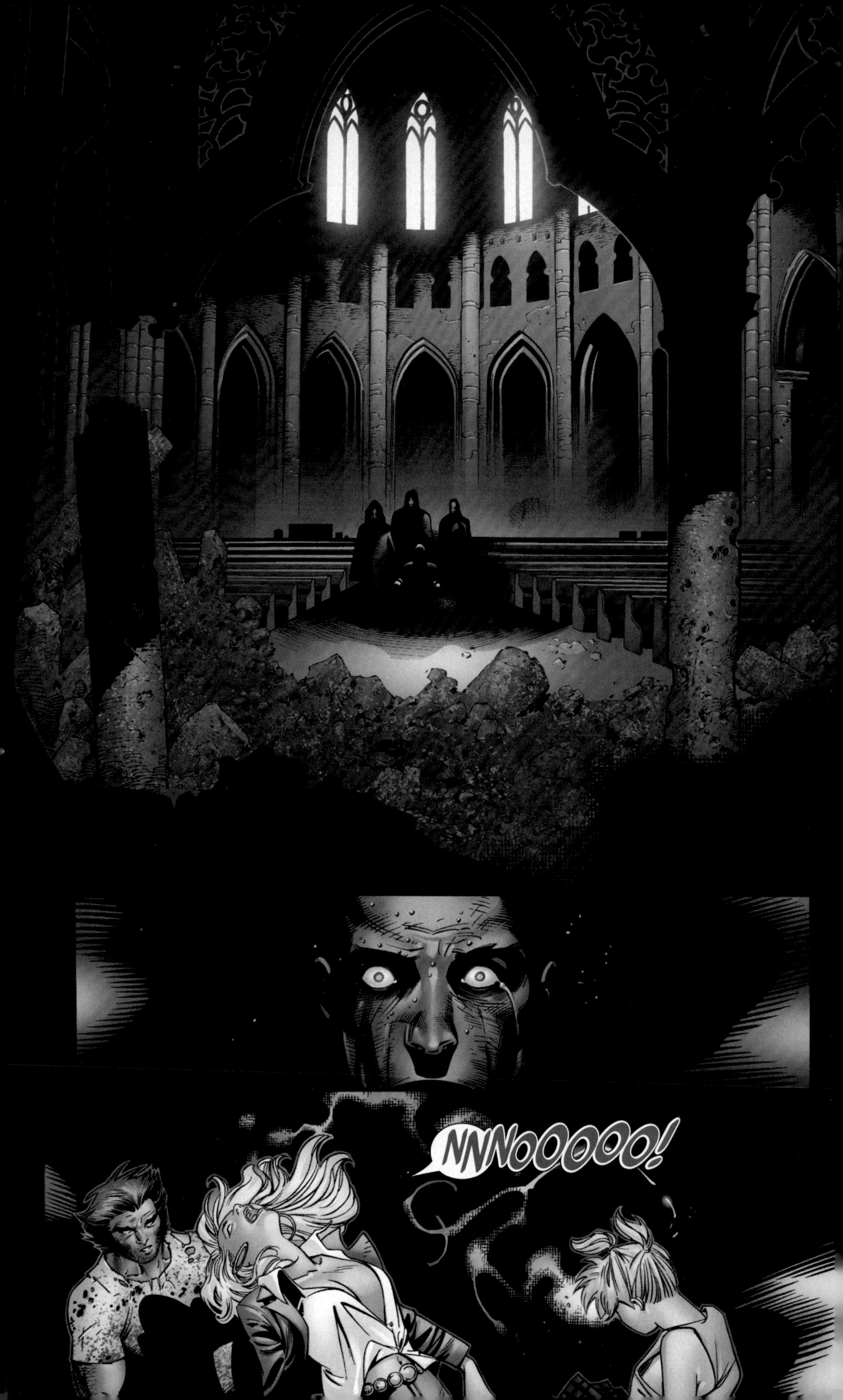
NNNOOOOO!

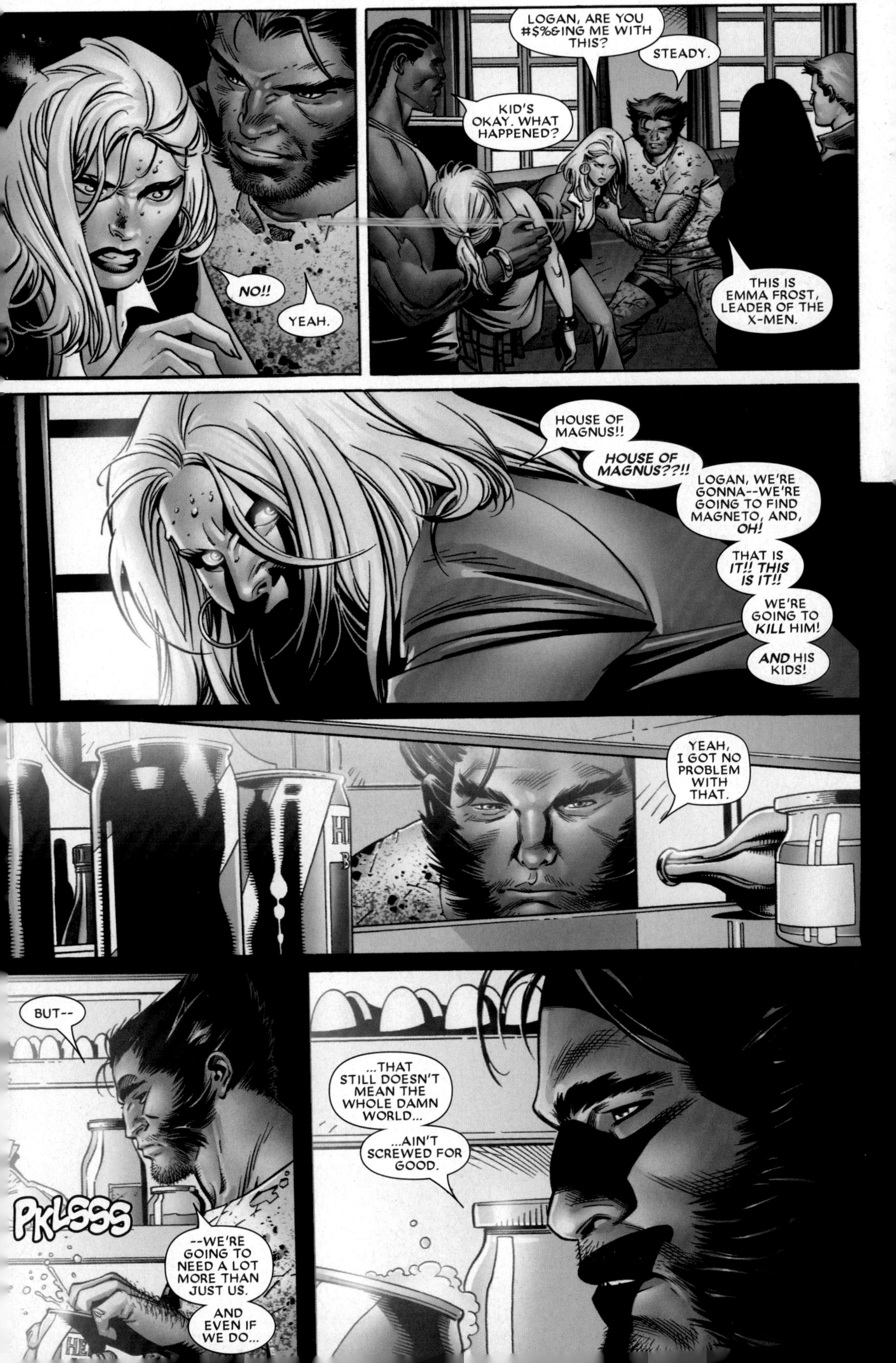
NO!!
YEAH.
LOGAN, ARE YOU #$%&ING ME WITH THIS?
STEADY.
KID'S OKAY. WHAT HAPPENED?
THIS IS EMMA FROST, LEADER OF THE X-MEN.
HOUSE OF MAGNUS!!
HOUSE OF MAGNUS??!!
LOGAN, WE'RE GONNA--WE'RE GOING TO FIND MAGNETO, AND, OH!
THAT IS IT!! THIS IS IT!!
WE'RE GOING TO KILL HIM!
AND HIS KIDS!
YEAH, I GOT NO PROBLEM WITH THAT.
BUT--
PKLSSS
--WE'RE GOING TO NEED A LOT MORE THAN JUST US.
AND EVEN IF WE DO...
...THAT STILL DOESN'T MEAN THE WHOLE DAMN WORLD...
...AIN'T SCREWED FOR GOOD.

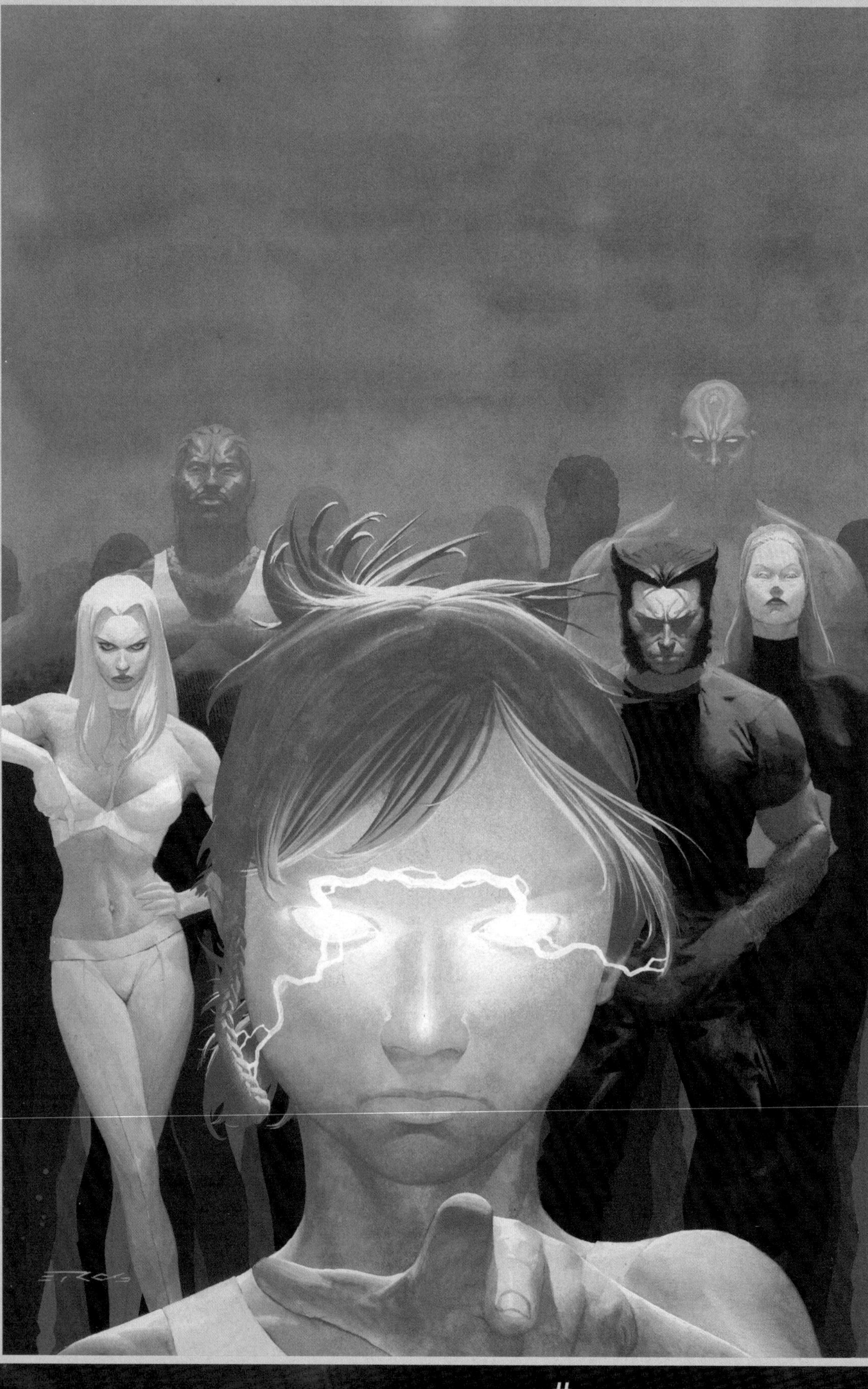

HOUSE OF M #5

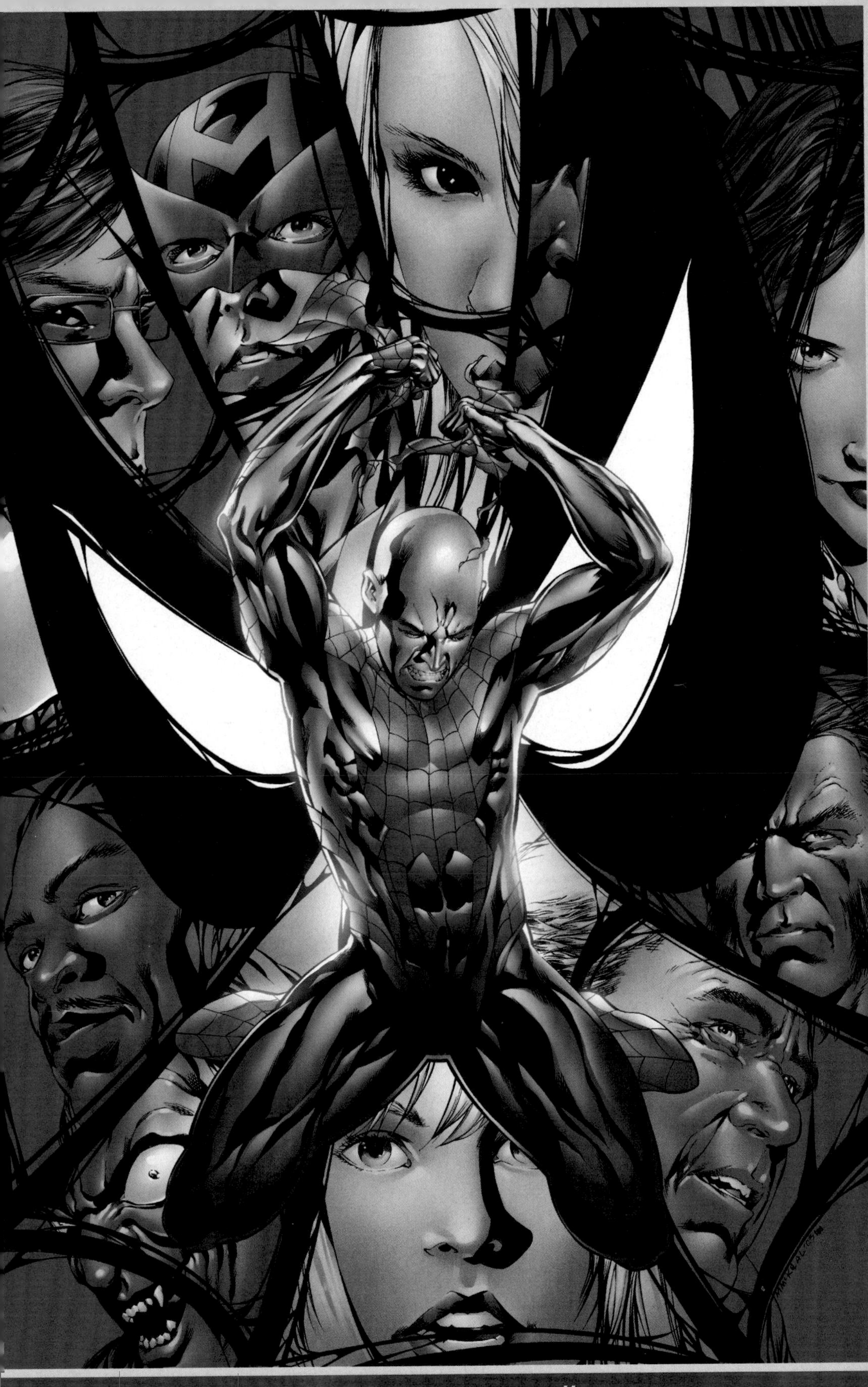

Variant cover [redacted]

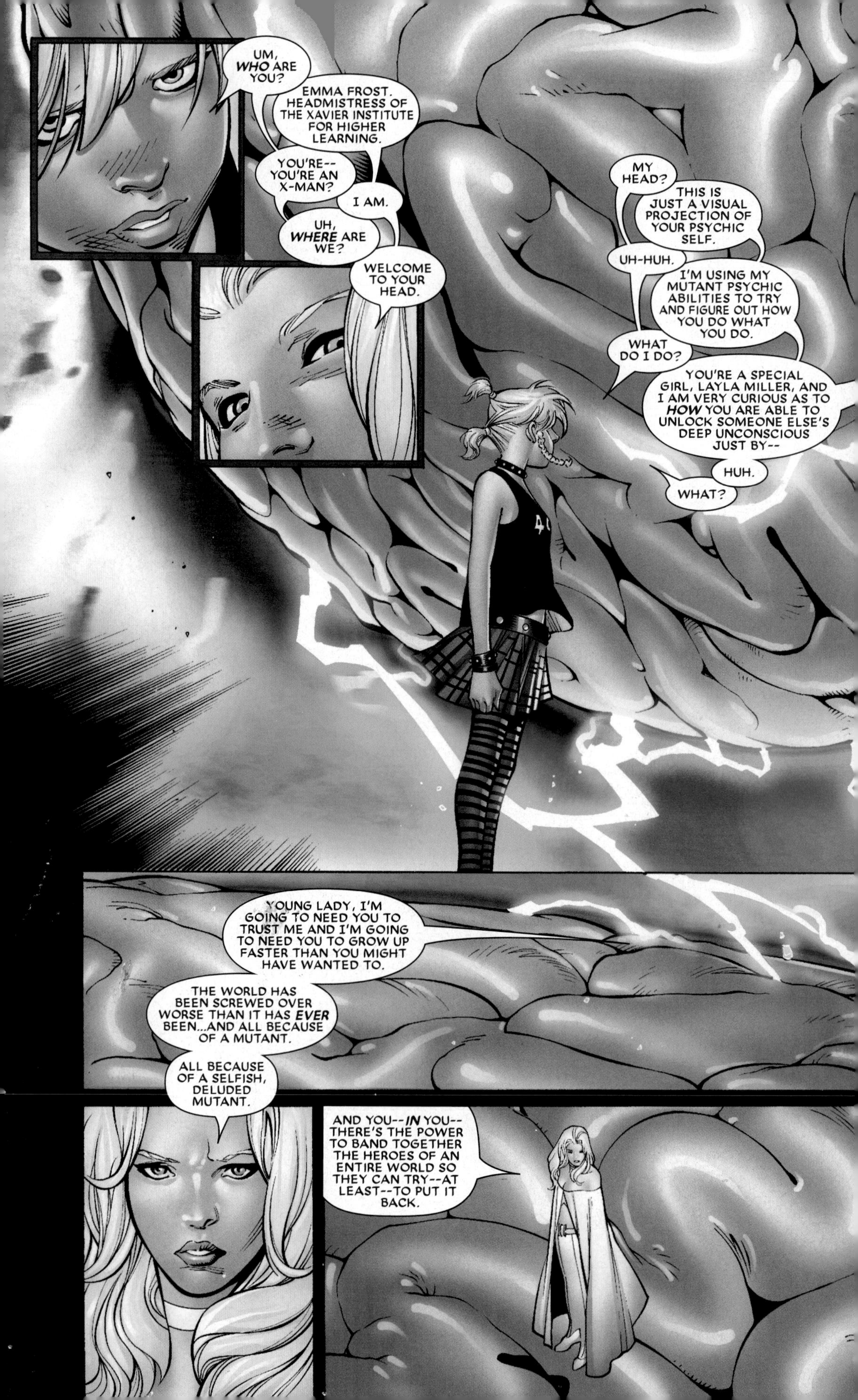
UM, WHO ARE YOU?
EMMA FROST. HEADMISTRESS OF THE XAVIER INSTITUTE FOR HIGHER LEARNING.
YOU'RE-- YOU'RE AN X-MAN?
I AM.
UH, WHERE ARE WE?
WELCOME TO YOUR HEAD.
MY HEAD?
THIS IS JUST A VISUAL PROJECTION OF YOUR PSYCHIC SELF.
UH-HUH.
I'M USING MY MUTANT PSYCHIC ABILITIES TO TRY AND FIGURE OUT HOW YOU DO WHAT YOU DO.
WHAT DO I DO?
YOU'RE A SPECIAL GIRL, LAYLA MILLER, AND I AM VERY CURIOUS AS TO HOW YOU ARE ABLE TO UNLOCK SOMEONE ELSE'S DEEP UNCONSCIOUS JUST BY--
HUH.
WHAT?
YOUNG LADY, I'M GOING TO NEED YOU TO TRUST ME AND I'M GOING TO NEED YOU TO GROW UP FASTER THAN YOU MIGHT HAVE WANTED TO.
THE WORLD HAS BEEN SCREWED OVER WORSE THAN IT HAS EVER BEEN...AND ALL BECAUSE OF A MUTANT.
ALL BECAUSE OF A SELFISH, DELUDED MUTANT.
AND YOU--IN YOU--THERE'S THE POWER TO BAND TOGETHER THE HEROES OF AN ENTIRE WORLD SO THEY CAN TRY--AT LEAST--TO PUT IT BACK.

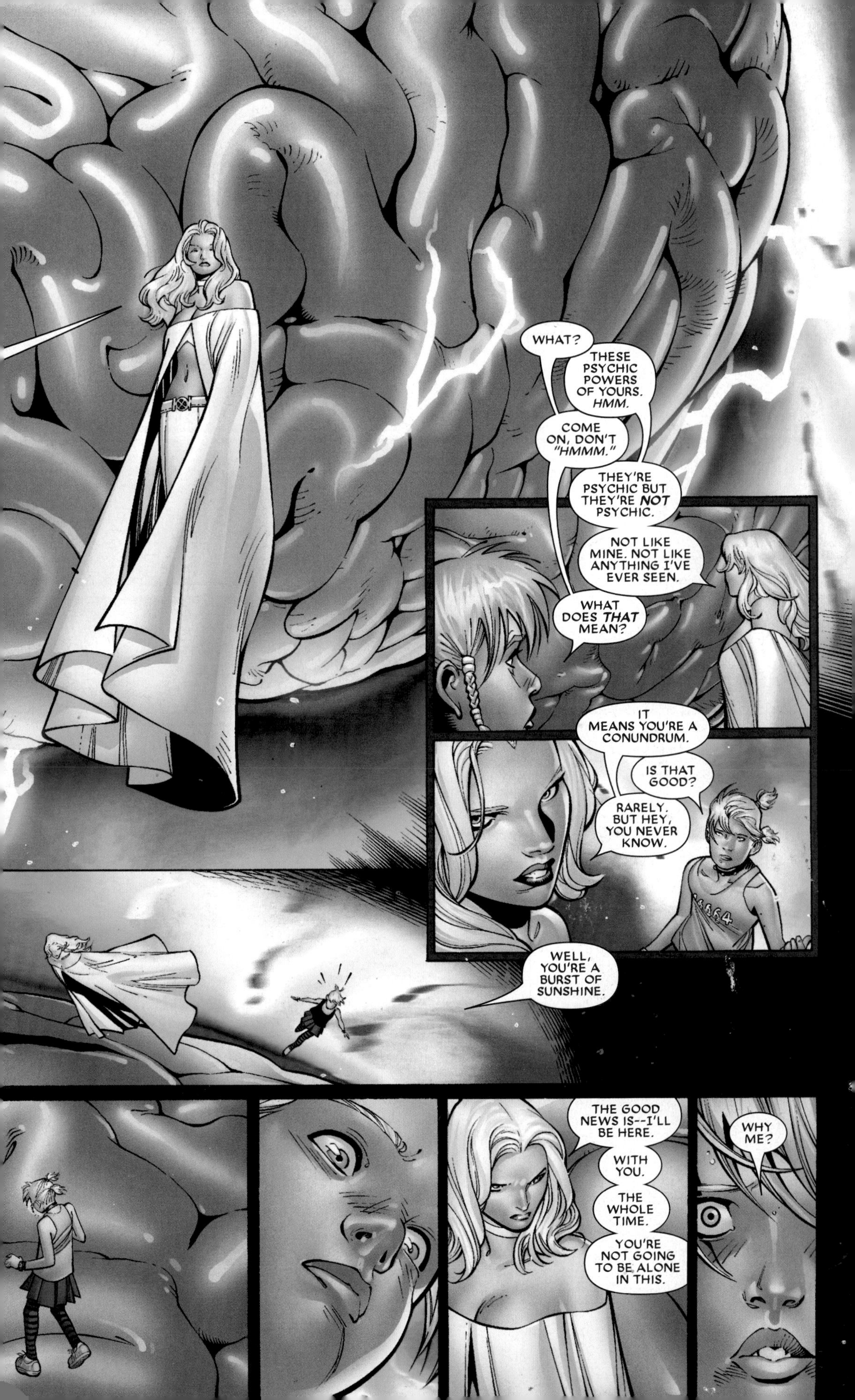
WHAT?
THESE PSYCHIC POWERS OF YOURS. *HMM.*
COME ON, DON'T *"HMMM."*
THEY'RE PSYCHIC BUT THEY'RE ***NOT*** PSYCHIC.
NOT LIKE MINE. NOT LIKE ANYTHING I'VE EVER SEEN.
WHAT DOES ***THAT*** MEAN?
IT MEANS YOU'RE A CONUNDRUM.
IS THAT GOOD?
RARELY. BUT HEY, YOU NEVER KNOW.
WELL, YOU'RE A BURST OF SUNSHINE.
THE GOOD NEWS IS--I'LL BE HERE.
WITH YOU.
THE WHOLE TIME.
YOU'RE NOT GOING TO BE ALONE IN THIS.
WHY ME?

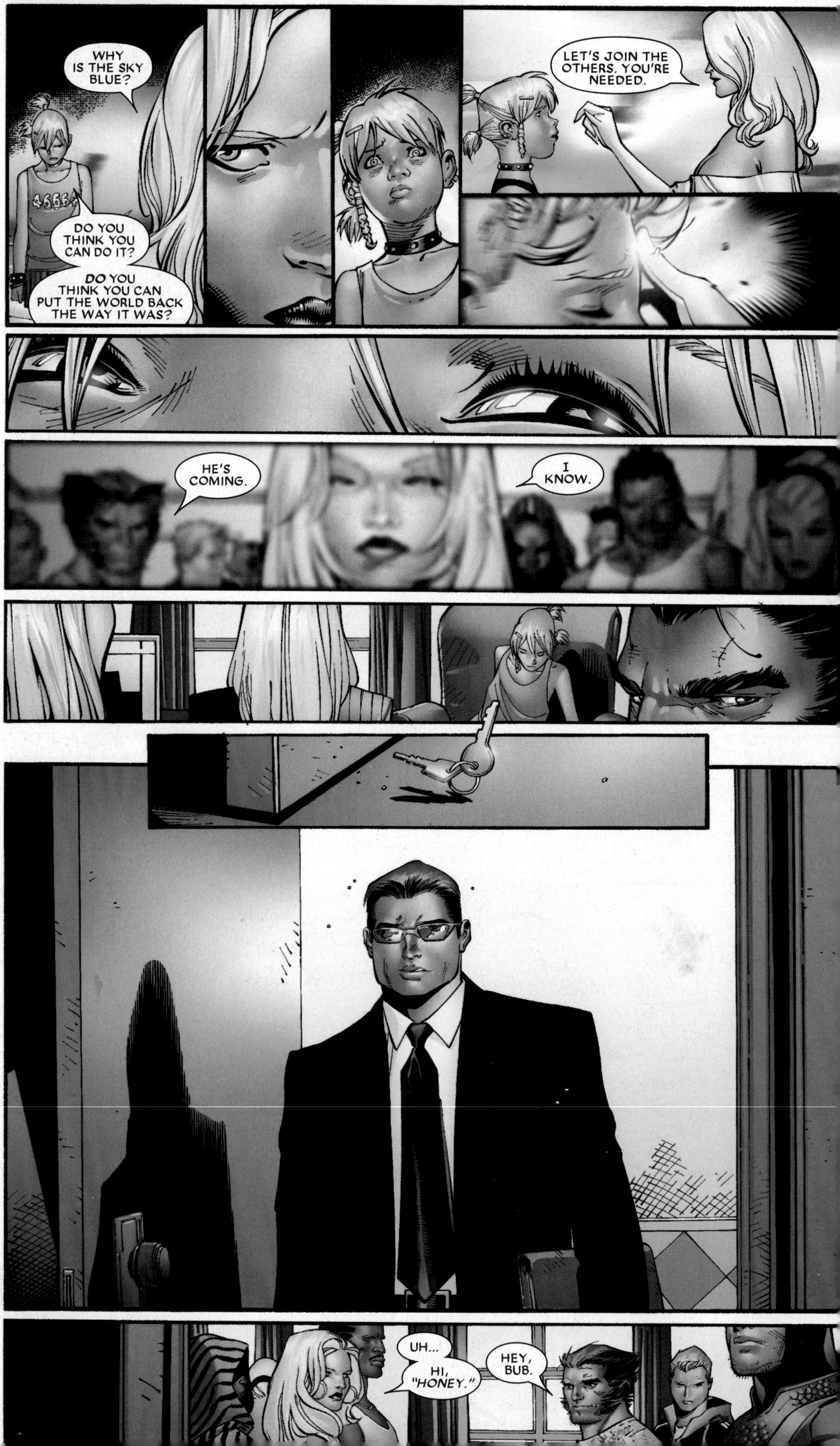
WHY IS THE SKY BLUE?
DO YOU THINK YOU CAN DO IT?
DO YOU THINK YOU CAN PUT THE WORLD BACK THE WAY IT WAS?
LET'S JOIN THE OTHERS. YOU'RE NEEDED.
HE'S COMING.
I KNOW.
UH...
HI, "HONEY."
HEY, BUB.

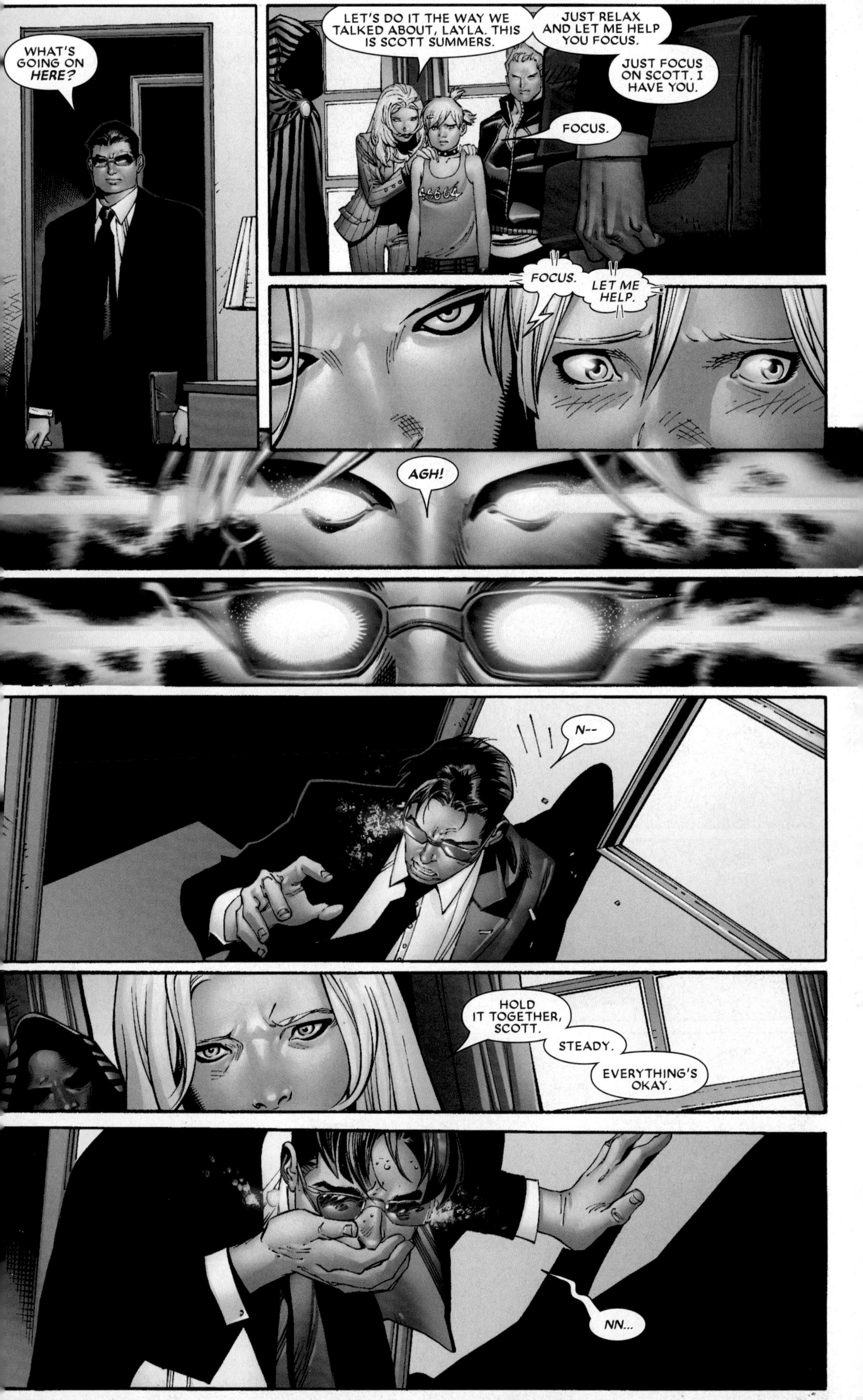
WHAT'S GOING ON *HERE?*
LET'S DO IT THE WAY WE TALKED ABOUT, LAYLA. THIS IS SCOTT SUMMERS.
JUST RELAX AND LET ME HELP YOU FOCUS.
JUST FOCUS ON SCOTT. I HAVE YOU.
FOCUS.
FOCUS.
LET ME HELP.
AGH!
N--
HOLD IT TOGETHER, SCOTT.
STEADY.
EVERYTHING'S OKAY.
NN...

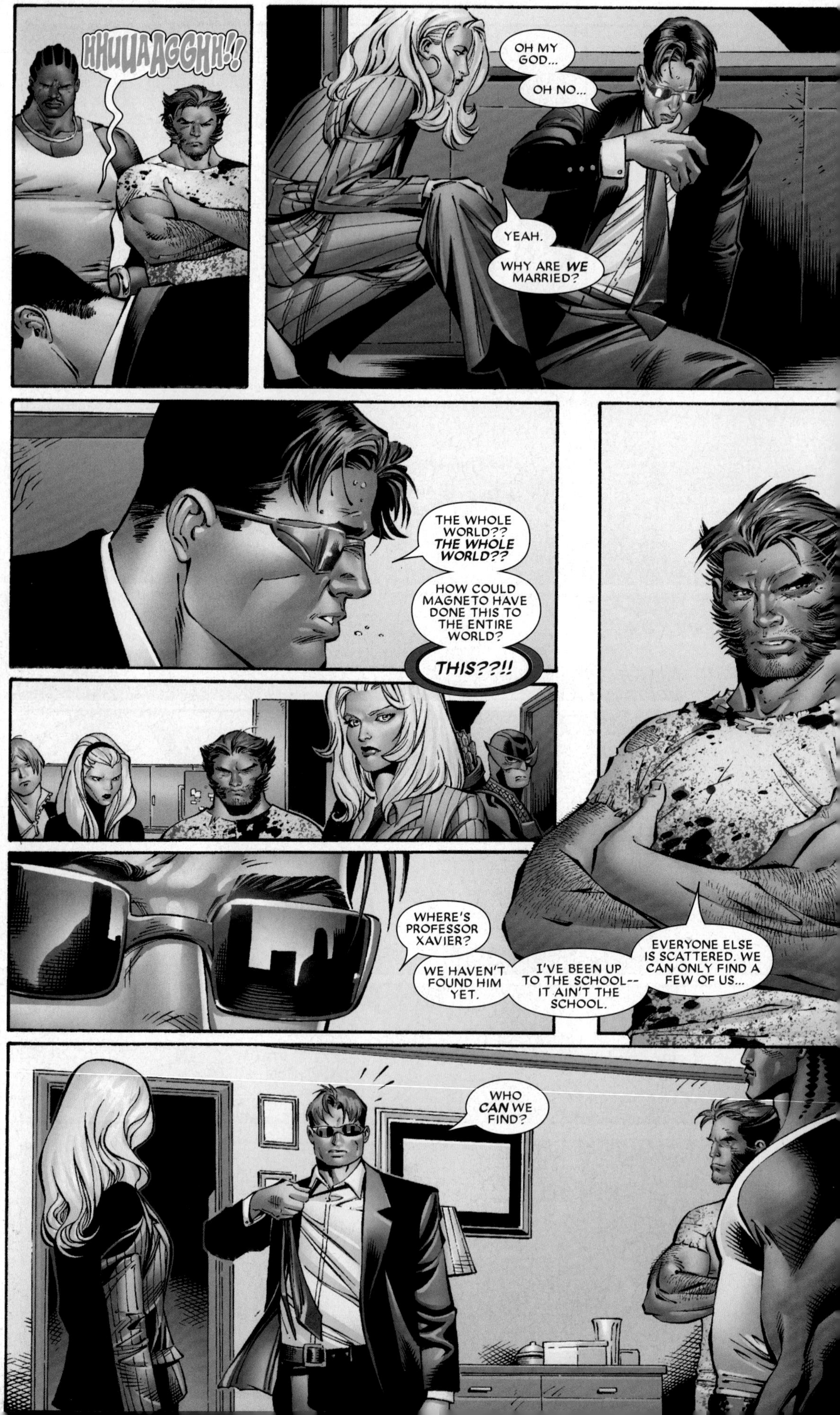
HHUUAAGGHH!!
OH MY GOD...
OH NO...
YEAH.
WHY ARE *WE* MARRIED?
THE WHOLE WORLD?? *THE WHOLE WORLD??*
HOW COULD MAGNETO HAVE DONE THIS TO THE ENTIRE WORLD?
THIS??!!
WHERE'S PROFESSOR XAVIER?
WE HAVEN'T FOUND HIM YET.
I'VE BEEN UP TO THE SCHOOL-- IT AIN'T THE SCHOOL.
EVERYONE ELSE IS SCATTERED. WE CAN ONLY FIND A FEW OF US...
WHO *CAN* WE FIND?

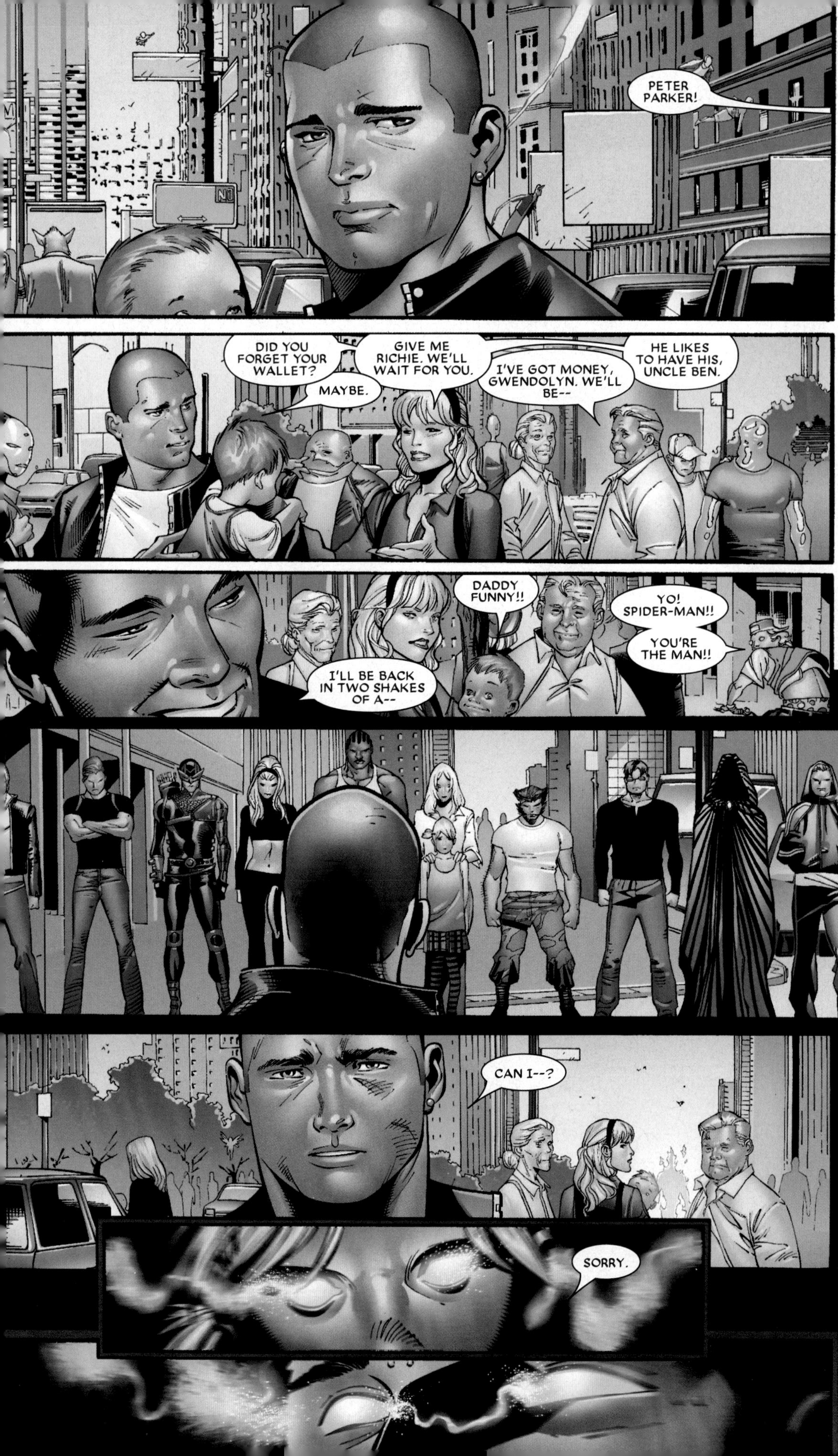
PETER PARKER!
DID YOU FORGET YOUR WALLET?
MAYBE.
GIVE ME RICHIE. WE'LL WAIT FOR YOU.
I'VE GOT MONEY, GWENDOLYN. WE'LL BE--
HE LIKES TO HAVE HIS, UNCLE BEN.
DADDY FUNNY!!
I'LL BE BACK IN TWO SHAKES OF A--
YO! SPIDER-MAN!!
YOU'RE THE MAN!!
CAN I--?
SORRY.

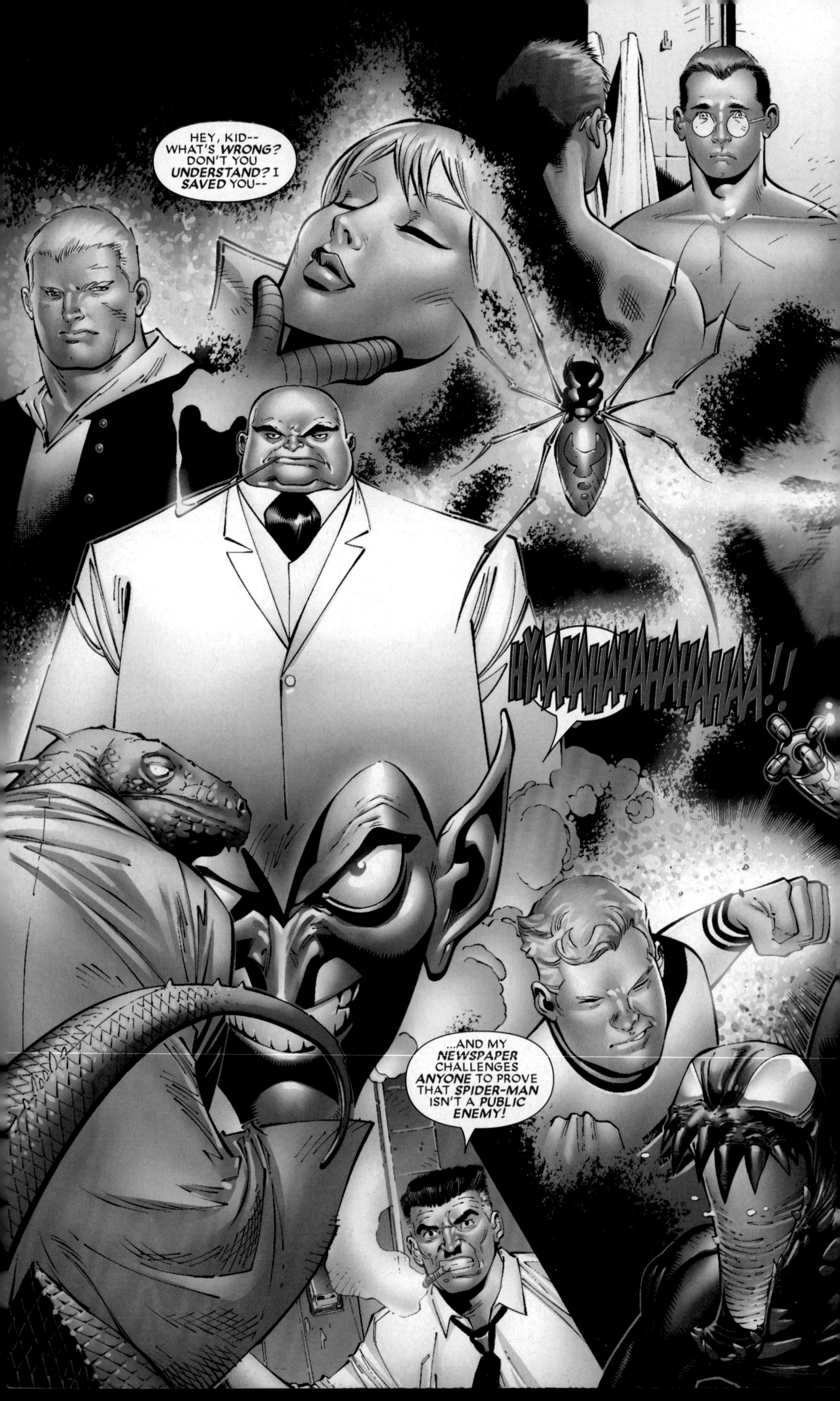
HEY, KID-- WHAT'S WRONG? DON'T YOU UNDERSTAND? I SAVED YOU--
HYAAHAHAHAHAHAHAA!!
...AND MY NEWSPAPER CHALLENGES ANYONE TO PROVE THAT SPIDER-MAN ISN'T A PUBLIC ENEMY!

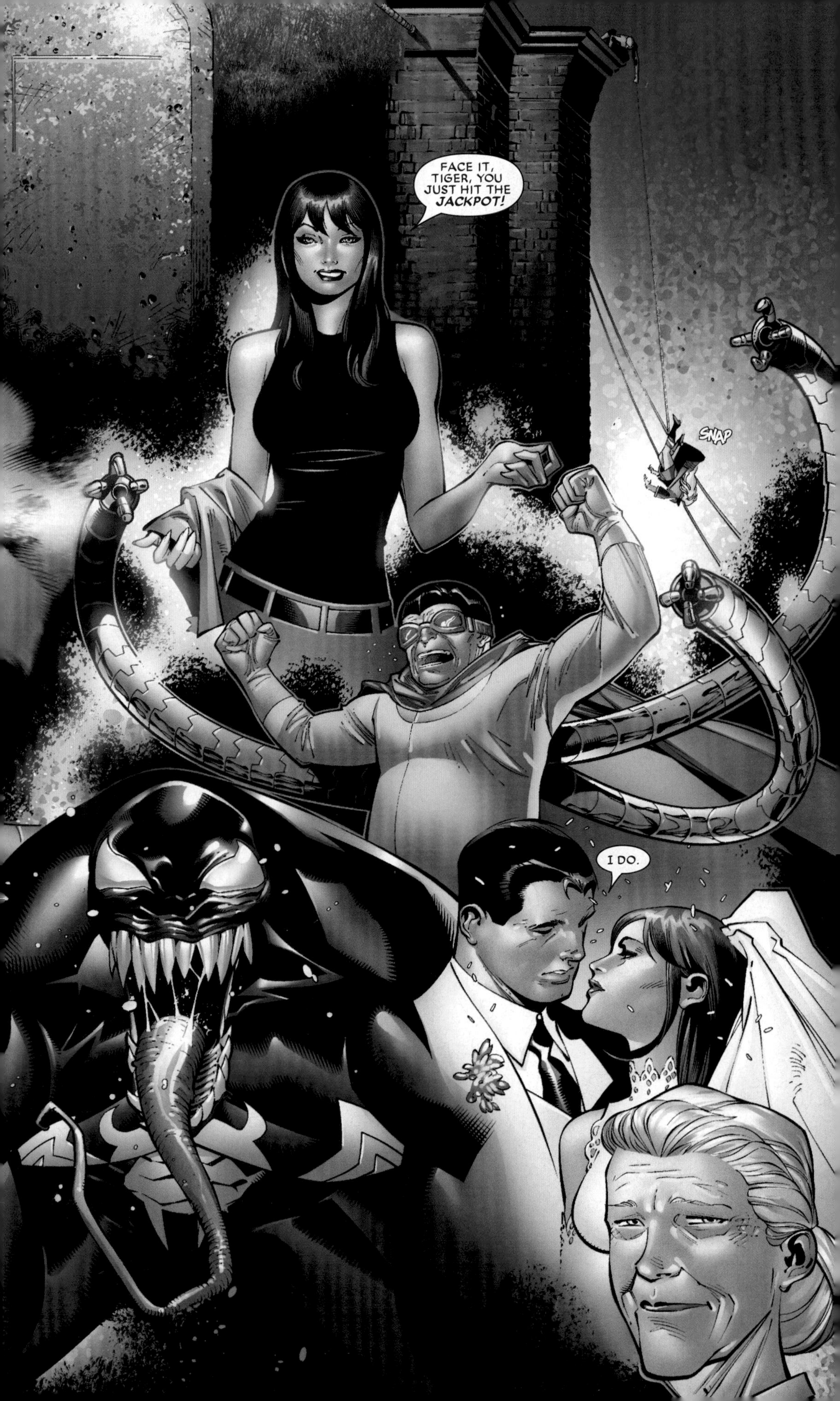

FACE IT, TIGER, YOU JUST HIT THE JACKPOT!
SNAP
I DO.

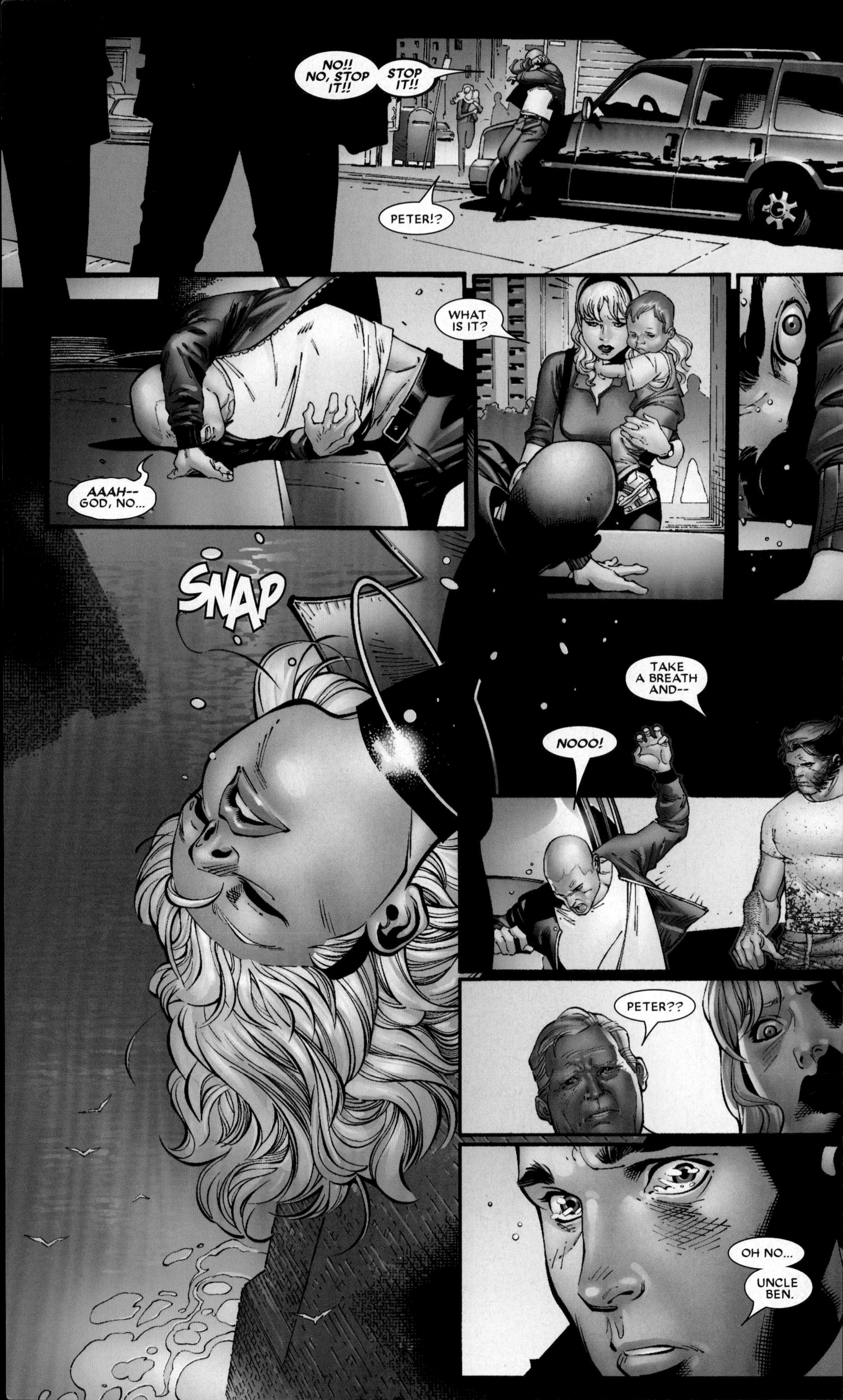
NO!! NO, STOP IT!!
STOP IT!!
PETER!?
AAAH-- GOD, NO...
WHAT IS IT?
SNAP
TAKE A BREATH AND--
NOOO!
PETER??
OH NO...
UNCLE BEN.

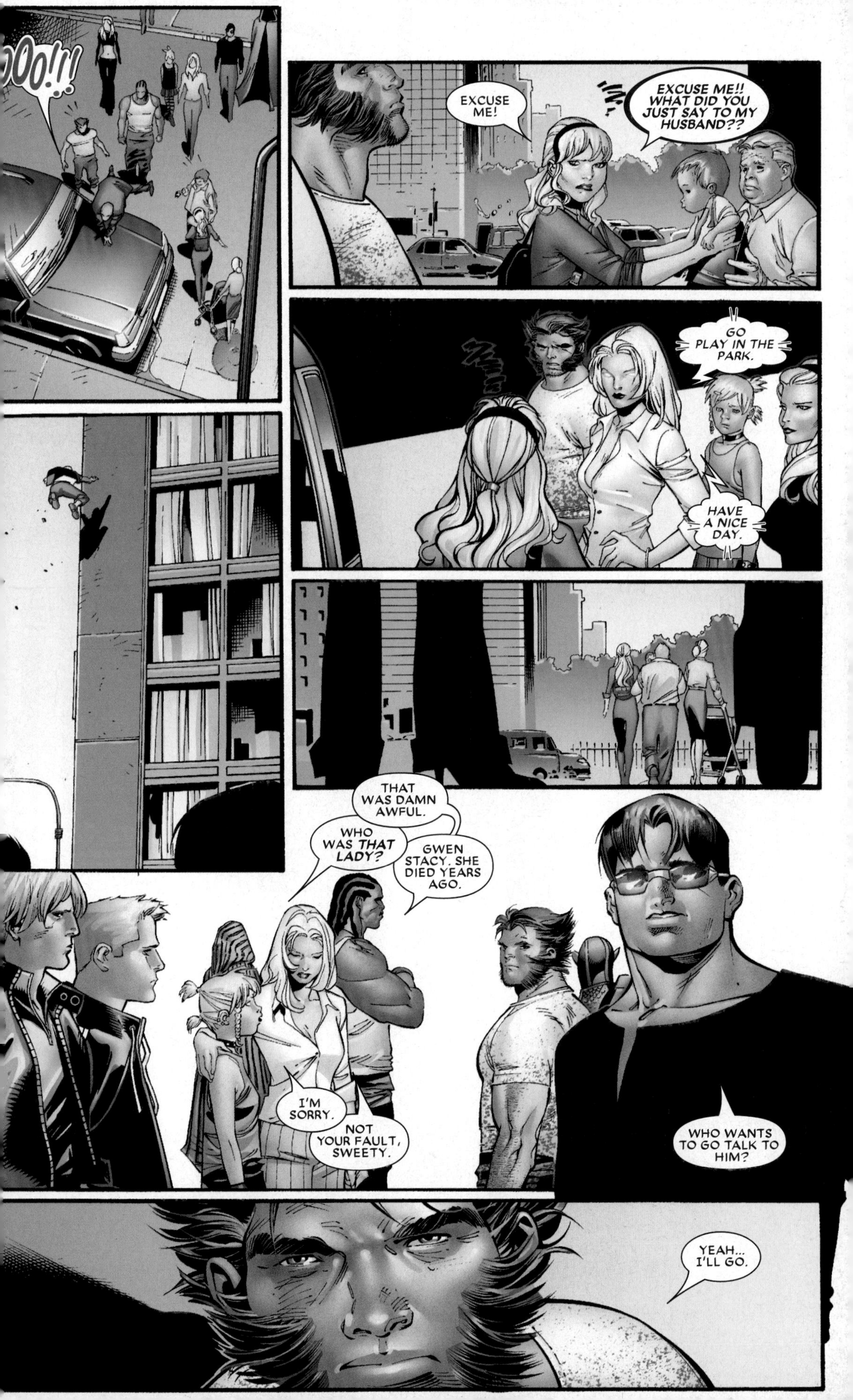
OOO!!!
EXCUSE ME!
EXCUSE ME!! WHAT DID YOU JUST SAY TO MY HUSBAND??
GO PLAY IN THE PARK.
HAVE A NICE DAY.
THAT WAS DAMN AWFUL.
WHO WAS THAT LADY?
GWEN STACY. SHE DIED YEARS AGO.
I'M SORRY.
NOT YOUR FAULT, SWEETY.
WHO WANTS TO GO TALK TO HIM?
YEAH... I'LL GO.

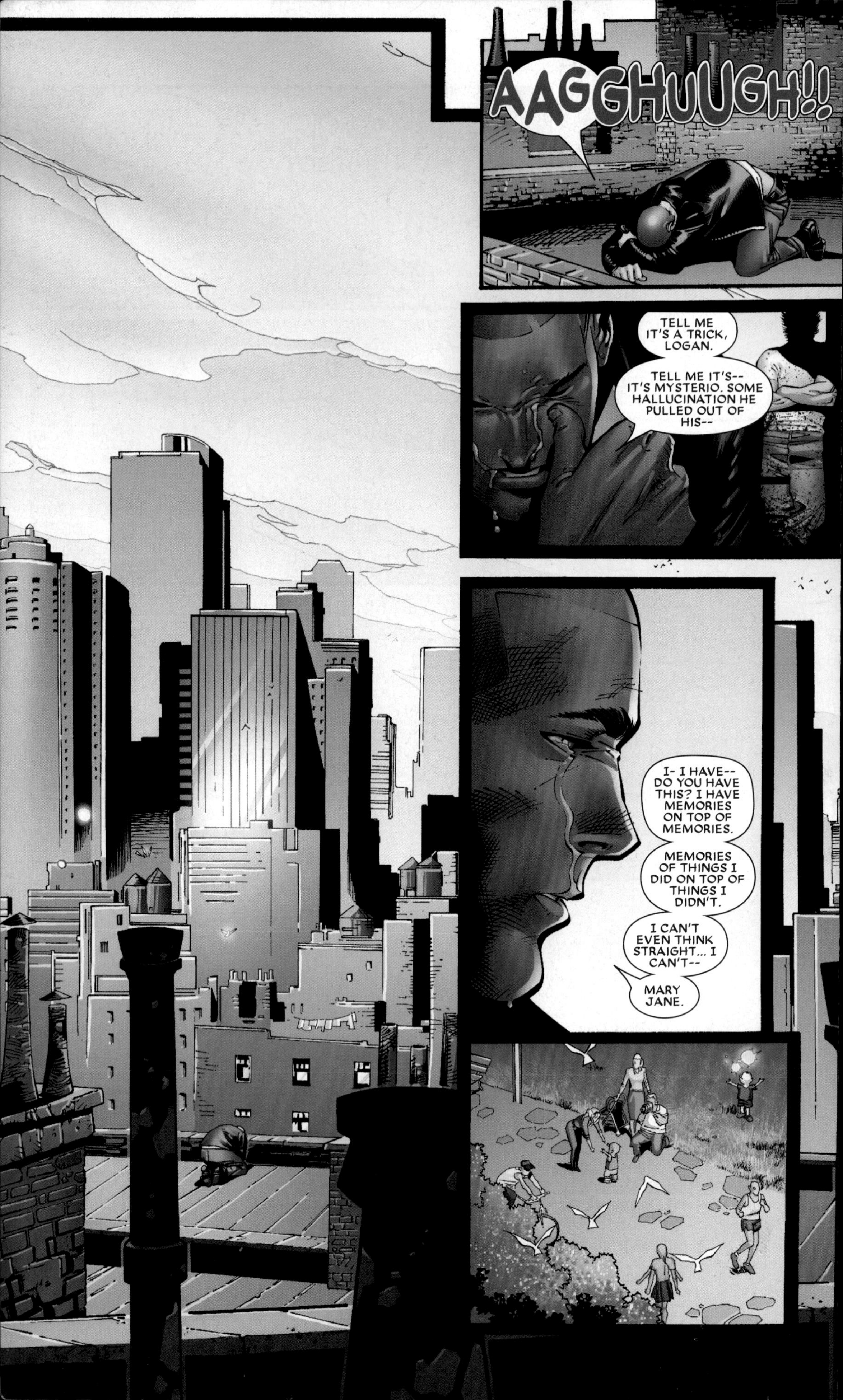
AAGGHUUGH!!
TELL ME IT'S A TRICK, LOGAN.
TELL ME IT'S-- IT'S MYSTERIO. SOME HALLUCINATION HE PULLED OUT OF HIS--
I- I HAVE-- DO YOU HAVE THIS? I HAVE MEMORIES ON TOP OF MEMORIES.
MEMORIES OF THINGS I DID ON TOP OF THINGS I DIDN'T.
I CAN'T EVEN THINK STRAIGHT... I CAN'T--
MARY JANE.

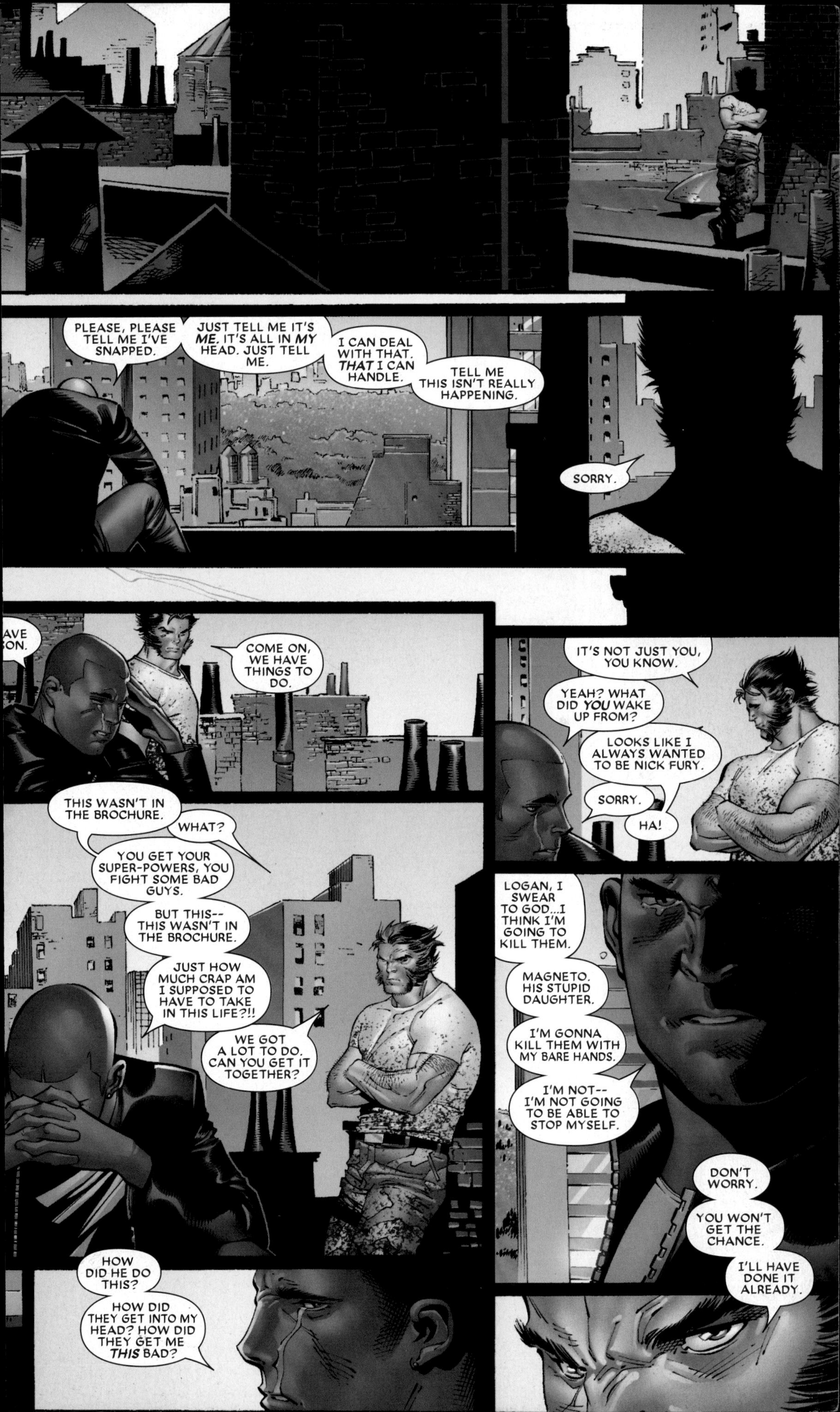

PLEASE, PLEASE TELL ME I'VE SNAPPED.
JUST TELL ME IT'S *ME.* IT'S ALL IN *MY* HEAD. JUST TELL ME.
I CAN DEAL WITH THAT. *THAT* I CAN HANDLE.
TELL ME THIS ISN'T REALLY HAPPENING.
SORRY.
COME ON, WE HAVE THINGS TO DO.
IT'S NOT JUST YOU, YOU KNOW.
YEAH? WHAT DID *YOU* WAKE UP FROM?
LOOKS LIKE I ALWAYS WANTED TO BE NICK FURY.
SORRY.
HA!
THIS WASN'T IN THE BROCHURE.
WHAT?
YOU GET YOUR SUPER-POWERS, YOU FIGHT SOME BAD GUYS.
BUT THIS-- THIS WASN'T IN THE BROCHURE.
JUST HOW MUCH CRAP AM I SUPPOSED TO HAVE TO TAKE IN THIS LIFE?!!
WE GOT A LOT TO DO. CAN YOU GET IT TOGETHER?
LOGAN, I SWEAR TO GOD...I THINK I'M GOING TO KILL THEM.
MAGNETO. HIS STUPID DAUGHTER.
I'M GONNA KILL THEM WITH MY BARE HANDS.
I'M NOT-- I'M NOT GOING TO BE ABLE TO STOP MYSELF.
DON'T WORRY.
YOU WON'T GET THE CHANCE.
I'LL HAVE DONE IT ALREADY.
HOW DID HE DO THIS?
HOW DID THEY GET INTO MY HEAD? HOW DID THEY GET ME *THIS* BAD?

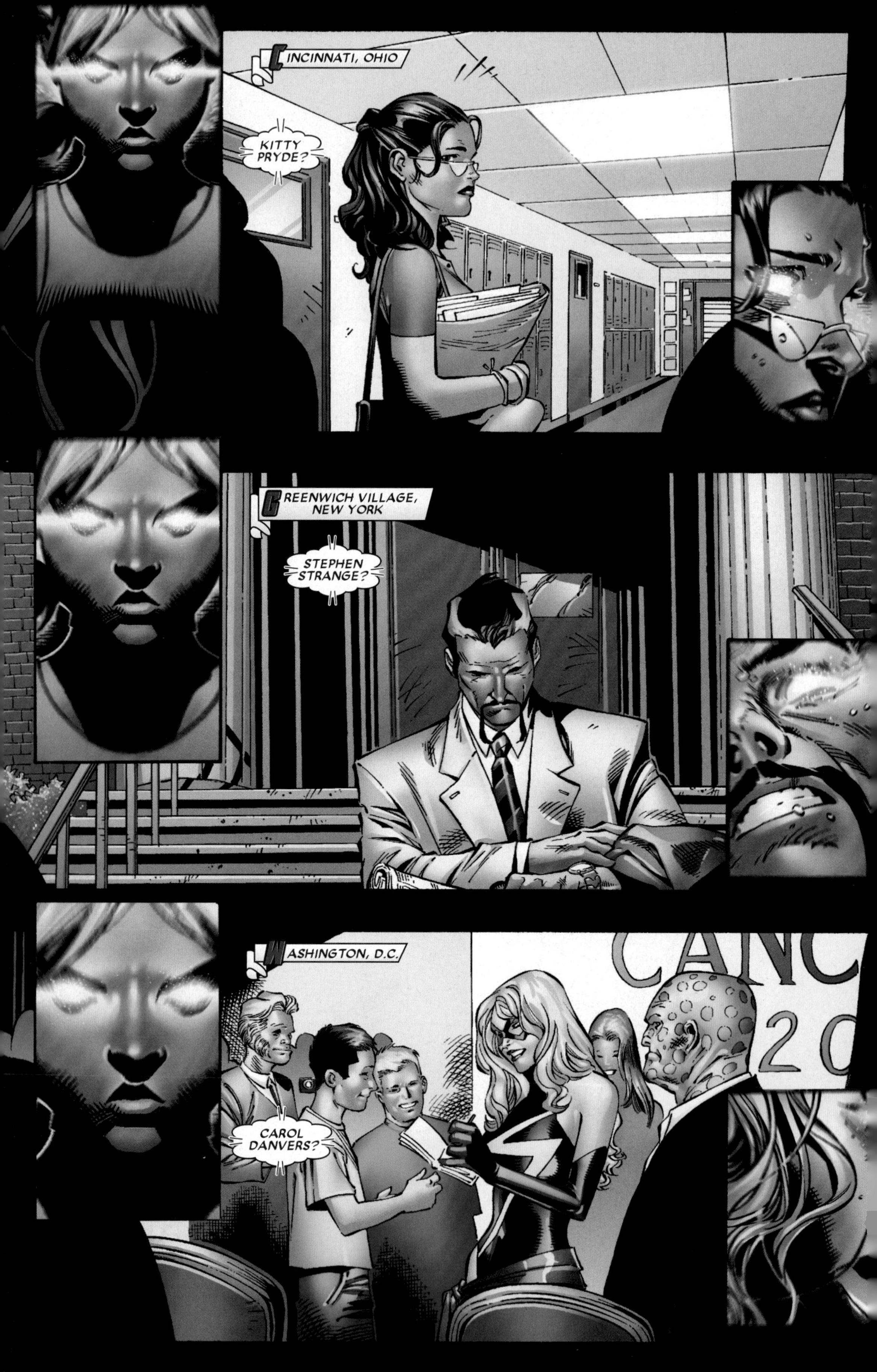
CINCINNATI, OHIO
KITTY PRYDE?
GREENWICH VILLAGE, NEW YORK
STEPHEN STRANGE?
WASHINGTON, D.C.
CAROL DANVERS?

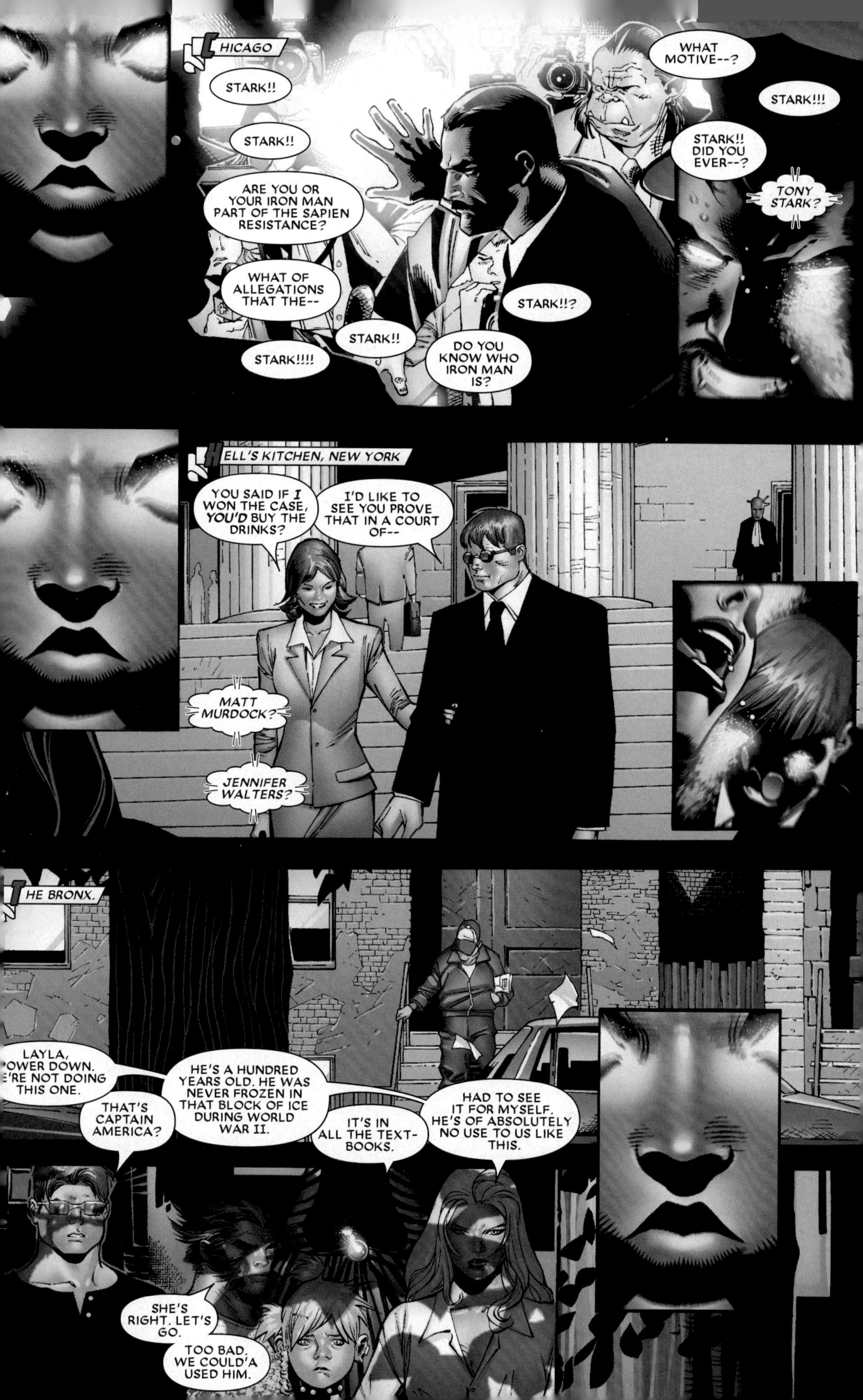
CHICAGO
STARK!!
STARK!!
ARE YOU OR YOUR IRON MAN PART OF THE SAPIEN RESISTANCE?
WHAT OF ALLEGATIONS THAT THE--
STARK!!!!
STARK!!
DO YOU KNOW WHO IRON MAN IS?
STARK!!?
WHAT MOTIVE--?
STARK!!!
STARK!! DID YOU EVER--?
TONY STARK?
HELL'S KITCHEN, NEW YORK
YOU SAID IF I WON THE CASE, YOU'D BUY THE DRINKS?
I'D LIKE TO SEE YOU PROVE THAT IN A COURT OF--
MATT MURDOCK?
JENNIFER WALTERS?
THE BRONX.
LAYLA, POWER DOWN. WE'RE NOT DOING THIS ONE.
THAT'S CAPTAIN AMERICA?
HE'S A HUNDRED YEARS OLD. HE WAS NEVER FROZEN IN THAT BLOCK OF ICE DURING WORLD WAR II.
IT'S IN ALL THE TEXT-BOOKS.
HAD TO SEE IT FOR MYSELF. HE'S OF ABSOLUTELY NO USE TO US LIKE THIS.
SHE'S RIGHT. LET'S GO.
TOO BAD. WE COULD'A USED HIM.

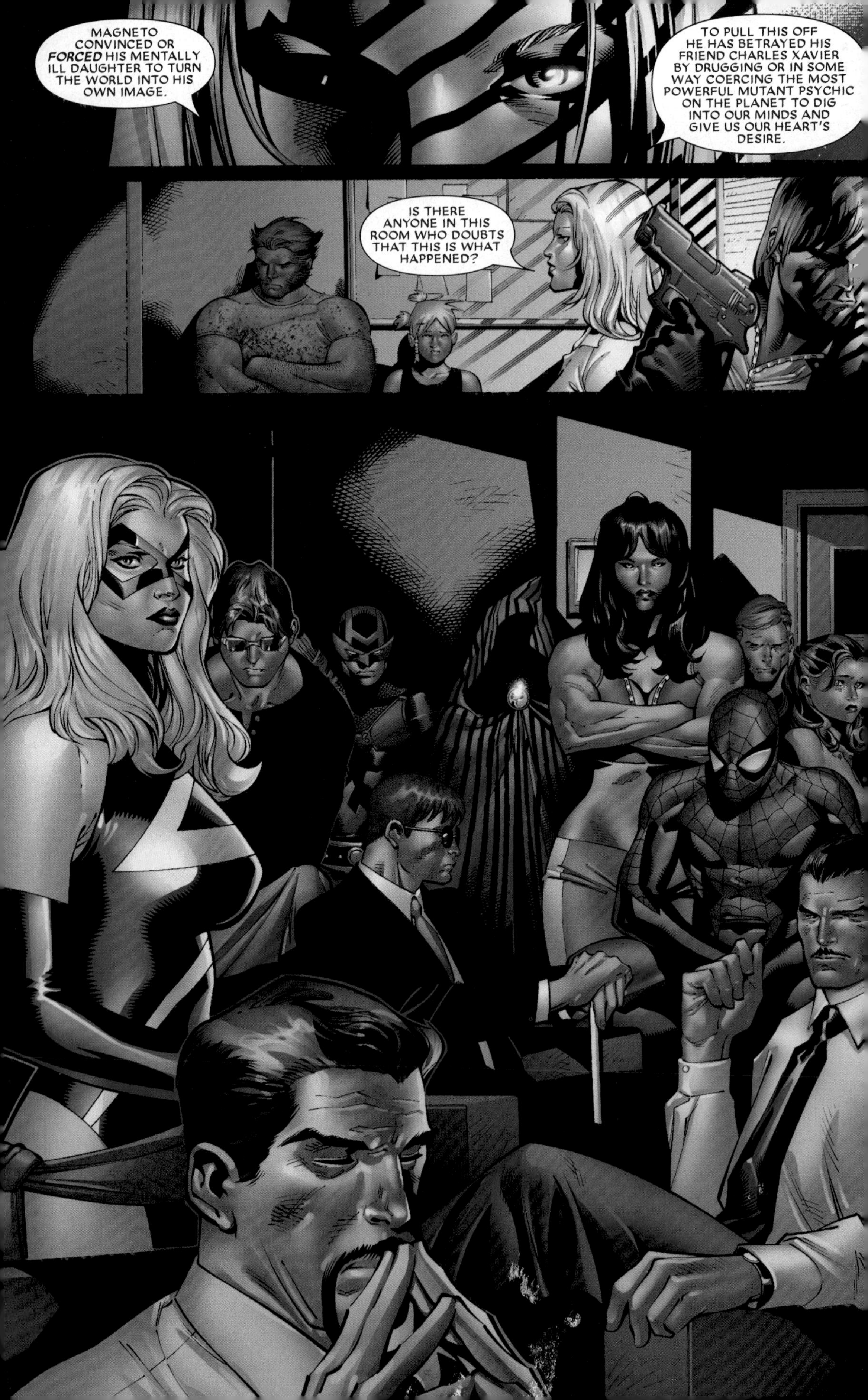
MAGNETO CONVINCED OR FORCED HIS MENTALLY ILL DAUGHTER TO TURN THE WORLD INTO HIS OWN IMAGE.
TO PULL THIS OFF HE HAS BETRAYED HIS FRIEND CHARLES XAVIER BY DRUGGING OR IN SOME WAY COERCING THE MOST POWERFUL MUTANT PSYCHIC ON THE PLANET TO DIG INTO OUR MINDS AND GIVE US OUR HEART'S DESIRE.
IS THERE ANYONE IN THIS ROOM WHO DOUBTS THAT THIS IS WHAT HAPPENED?

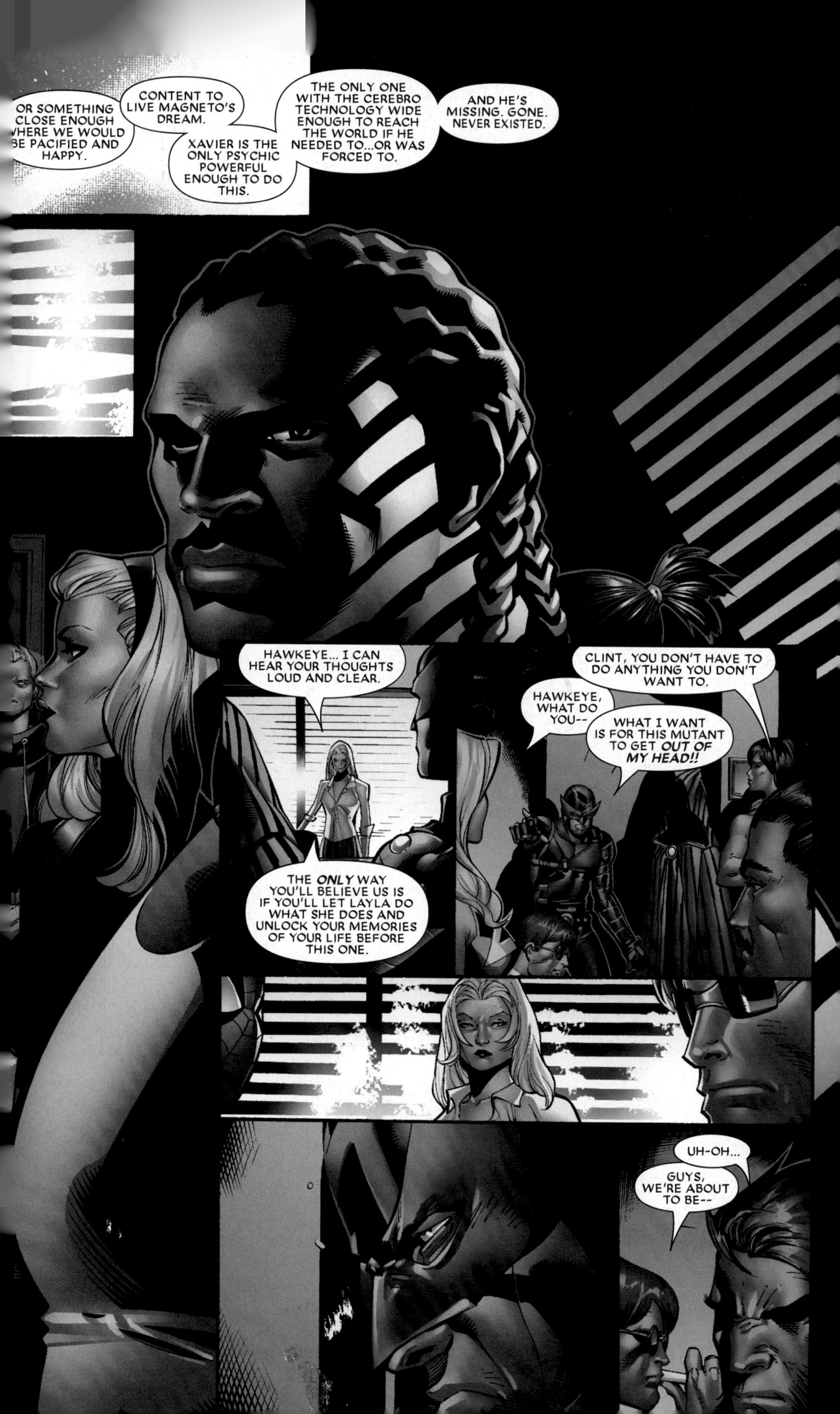
OR SOMETHING CLOSE ENOUGH WHERE WE WOULD BE PACIFIED AND HAPPY.
CONTENT TO LIVE MAGNETO'S DREAM.
XAVIER IS THE ONLY PSYCHIC POWERFUL ENOUGH TO DO THIS.
THE ONLY ONE WITH THE CEREBRO TECHNOLOGY WIDE ENOUGH TO REACH THE WORLD IF HE NEEDED TO...OR WAS FORCED TO.
AND HE'S MISSING. GONE. NEVER EXISTED.
HAWKEYE... I CAN HEAR YOUR THOUGHTS LOUD AND CLEAR.
THE *ONLY* WAY YOU'LL BELIEVE US IS IF YOU'LL LET LAYLA DO WHAT SHE DOES AND UNLOCK YOUR MEMORIES OF YOUR LIFE BEFORE THIS ONE.
CLINT, YOU DON'T HAVE TO DO ANYTHING YOU DON'T WANT TO.
HAWKEYE, WHAT DO YOU--
WHAT I WANT IS FOR THIS MUTANT TO GET ***OUT OF MY HEAD!!***
UH-OH...
GUYS, WE'RE ABOUT TO BE--

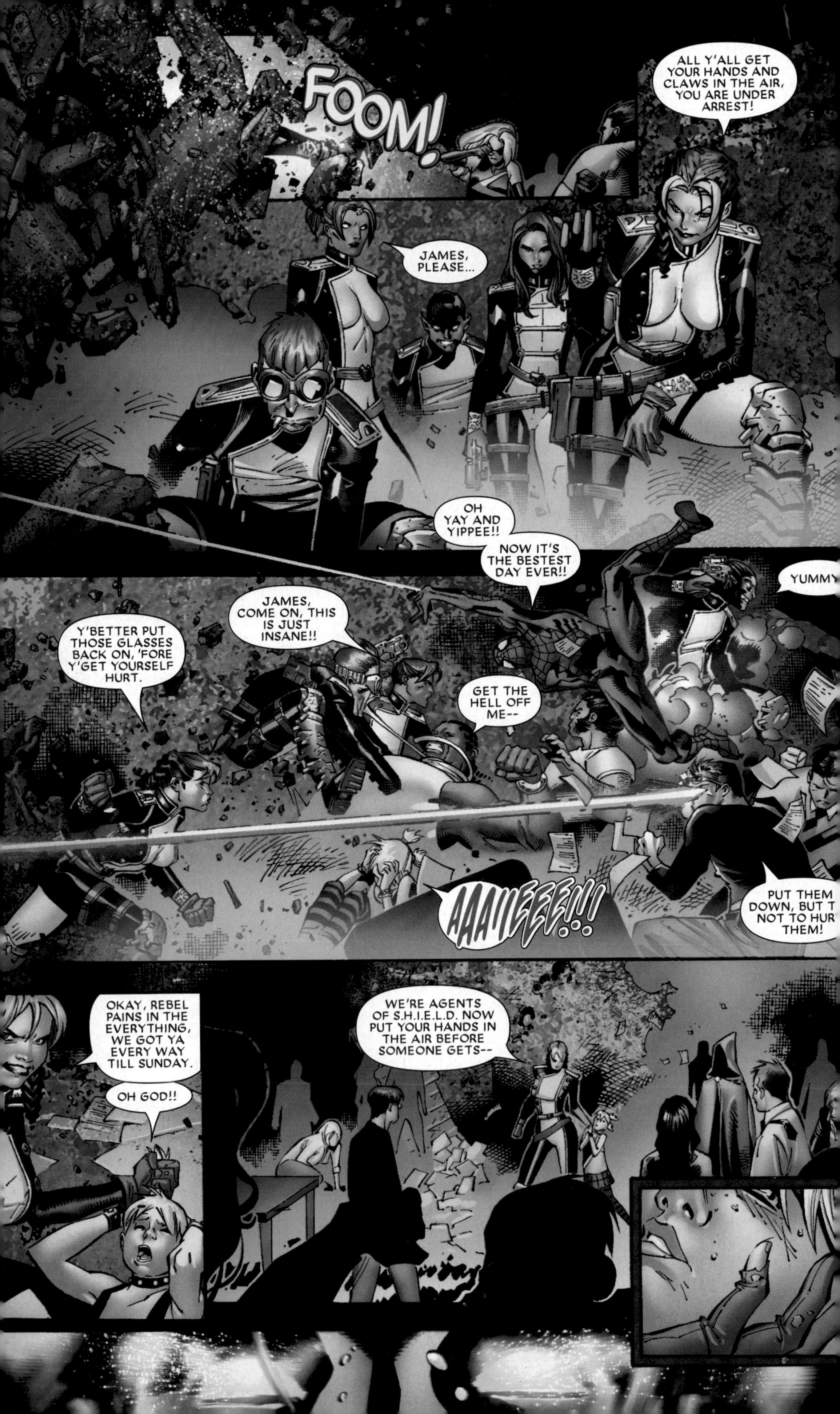
FOOM!
ALL Y'ALL GET YOUR HANDS AND CLAWS IN THE AIR, YOU ARE UNDER ARREST!
JAMES, PLEASE...
OH YAY AND YIPPEE!!
NOW IT'S THE BESTEST DAY EVER!!
YUMMY
JAMES, COME ON, THIS IS JUST INSANE!!
Y'BETTER PUT THOSE GLASSES BACK ON, 'FORE Y'GET YOURSELF HURT.
GET THE HELL OFF ME--
AAAIIEEE!!!
PUT THEM DOWN, BUT T NOT TO HUR THEM!
OKAY, REBEL PAINS IN THE EVERYTHING, WE GOT YA EVERY WAY TILL SUNDAY.
OH GOD!!
WE'RE AGENTS OF S.H.I.E.L.D. NOW PUT YOUR HANDS IN THE AIR BEFORE SOMEONE GETS--

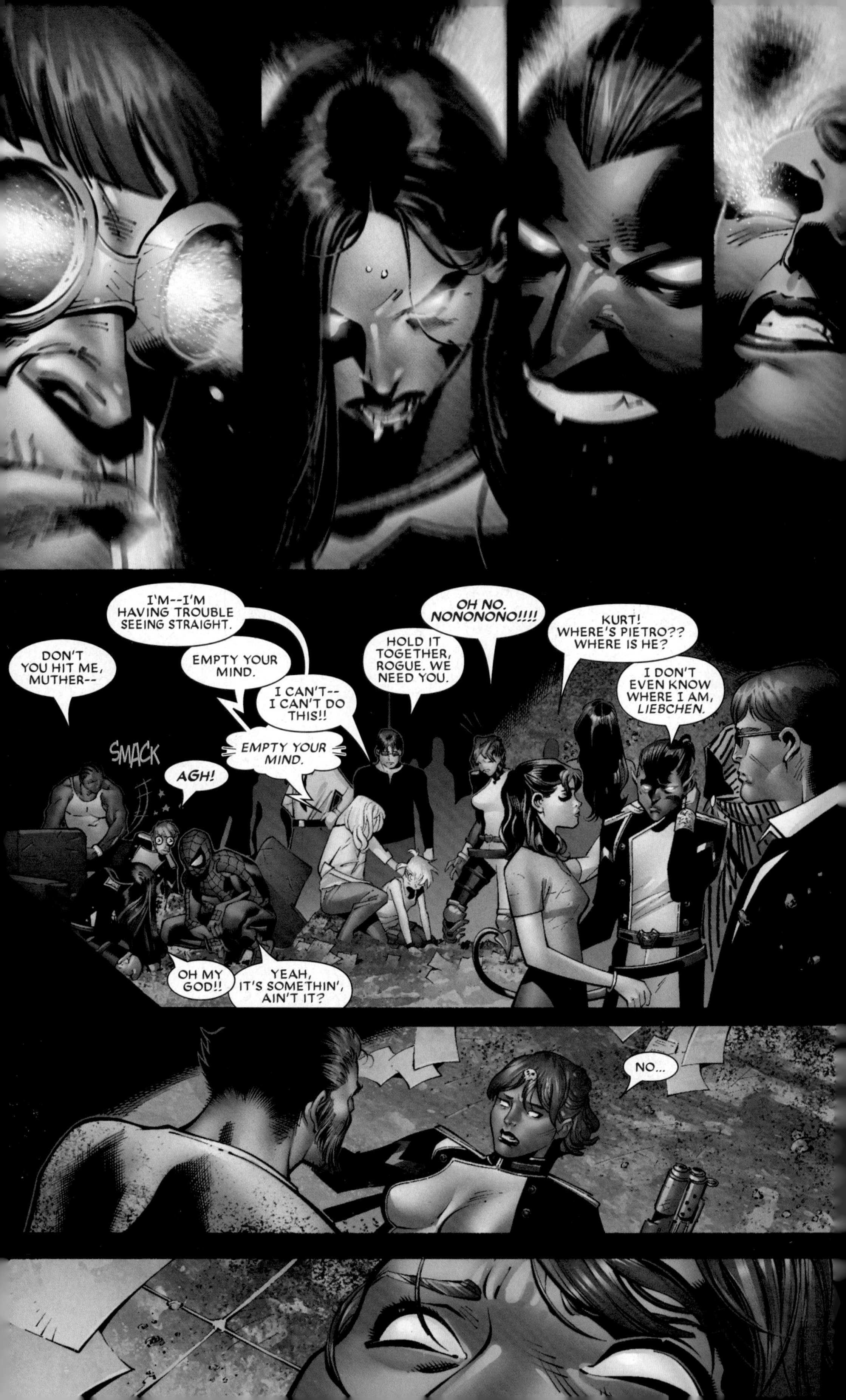
I'M--I'M HAVING TROUBLE SEEING STRAIGHT.
DON'T YOU HIT ME, MUTHER--
EMPTY YOUR MIND.
I CAN'T-- I CAN'T DO THIS!!
EMPTY YOUR MIND.
SMACK
AGH!
HOLD IT TOGETHER, ROGUE. WE NEED YOU.
OH NO. NONONONO!!!!
KURT! WHERE'S PIETRO?? WHERE IS HE?
I DON'T EVEN KNOW WHERE I AM, LIEBCHEN.
OH MY GOD!!
YEAH, IT'S SOMETHIN', AIN'T IT?
NO...

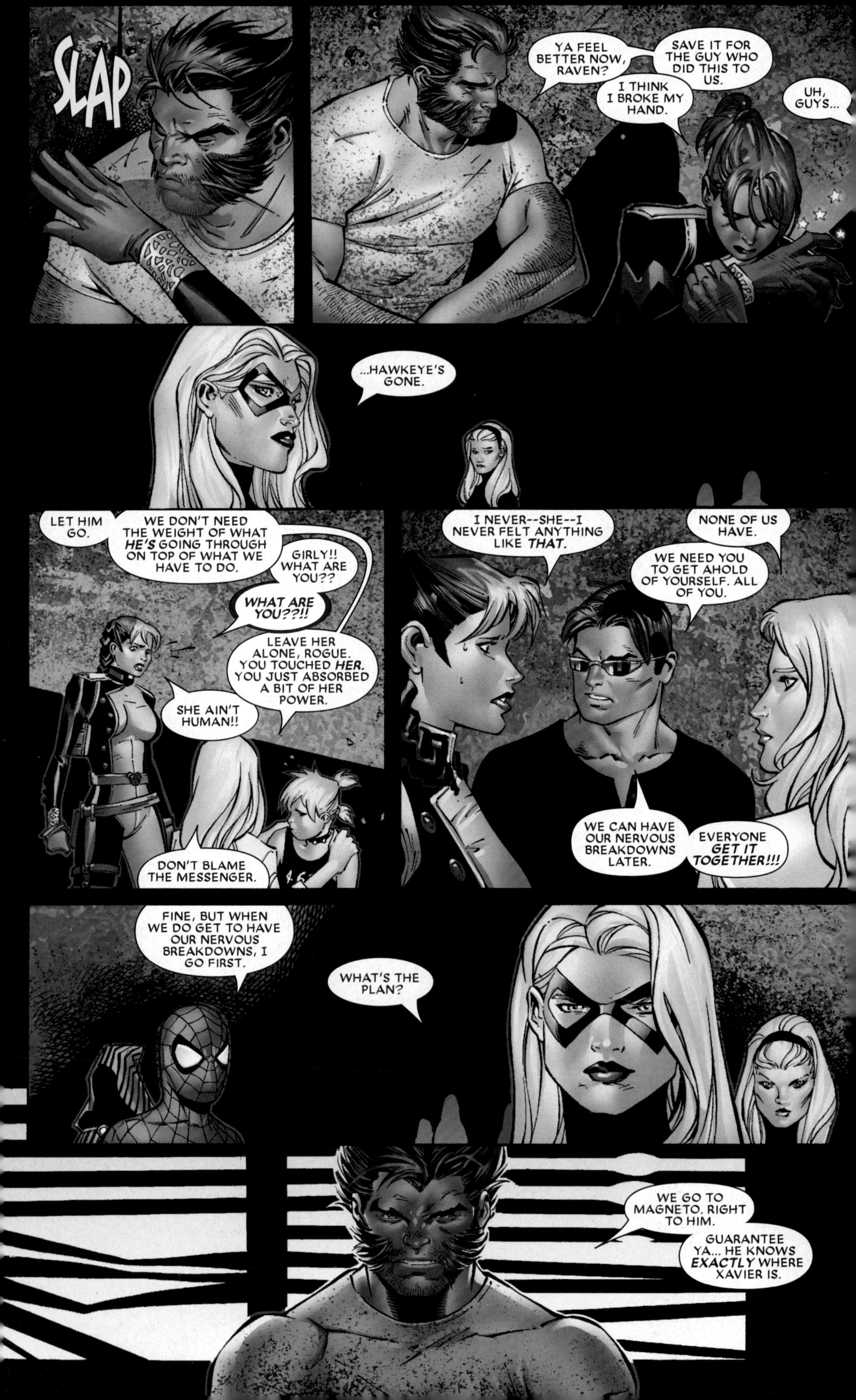
SLAP
YA FEEL BETTER NOW, RAVEN?
SAVE IT FOR THE GUY WHO DID THIS TO US.
I THINK I BROKE MY HAND.
UH, GUYS...
...HAWKEYE'S GONE.
LET HIM GO.
WE DON'T NEED THE WEIGHT OF WHAT HE'S GOING THROUGH ON TOP OF WHAT WE HAVE TO DO.
GIRLY!! WHAT ARE YOU??
WHAT ARE YOU??!!
LEAVE HER ALONE, ROGUE. YOU TOUCHED HER. YOU JUST ABSORBED A BIT OF HER POWER.
SHE AIN'T HUMAN!!
DON'T BLAME THE MESSENGER.
I NEVER--SHE--I NEVER FELT ANYTHING LIKE THAT.
NONE OF US HAVE.
WE NEED YOU TO GET AHOLD OF YOURSELF. ALL OF YOU.
WE CAN HAVE OUR NERVOUS BREAKDOWNS LATER.
EVERYONE GET IT TOGETHER!!!
FINE, BUT WHEN WE DO GET TO HAVE OUR NERVOUS BREAKDOWNS, I GO FIRST.
WHAT'S THE PLAN?
WE GO TO MAGNETO. RIGHT TO HIM.
GUARANTEE YA... HE KNOWS EXACTLY WHERE XAVIER IS.

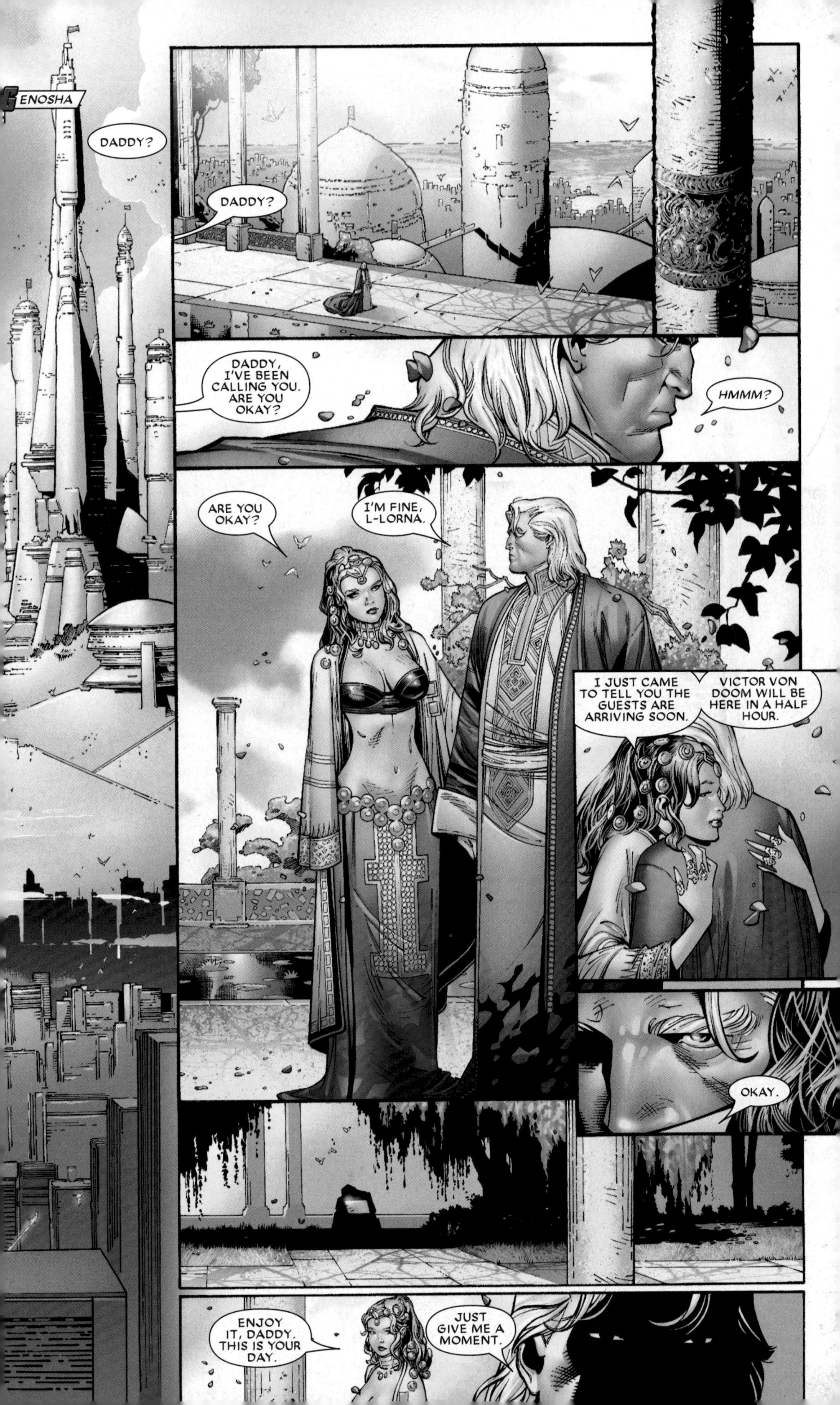

GENOSHA
DADDY?
DADDY?
DADDY, I'VE BEEN CALLING YOU. ARE YOU OKAY?
HMMM?
ARE YOU OKAY?
I'M FINE, L-LORNA.
I JUST CAME TO TELL YOU THE GUESTS ARE ARRIVING SOON.
VICTOR VON DOOM WILL BE HERE IN A HALF HOUR.
OKAY.
ENJOY IT, DADDY. THIS IS YOUR DAY.
JUST GIVE ME A MOMENT.

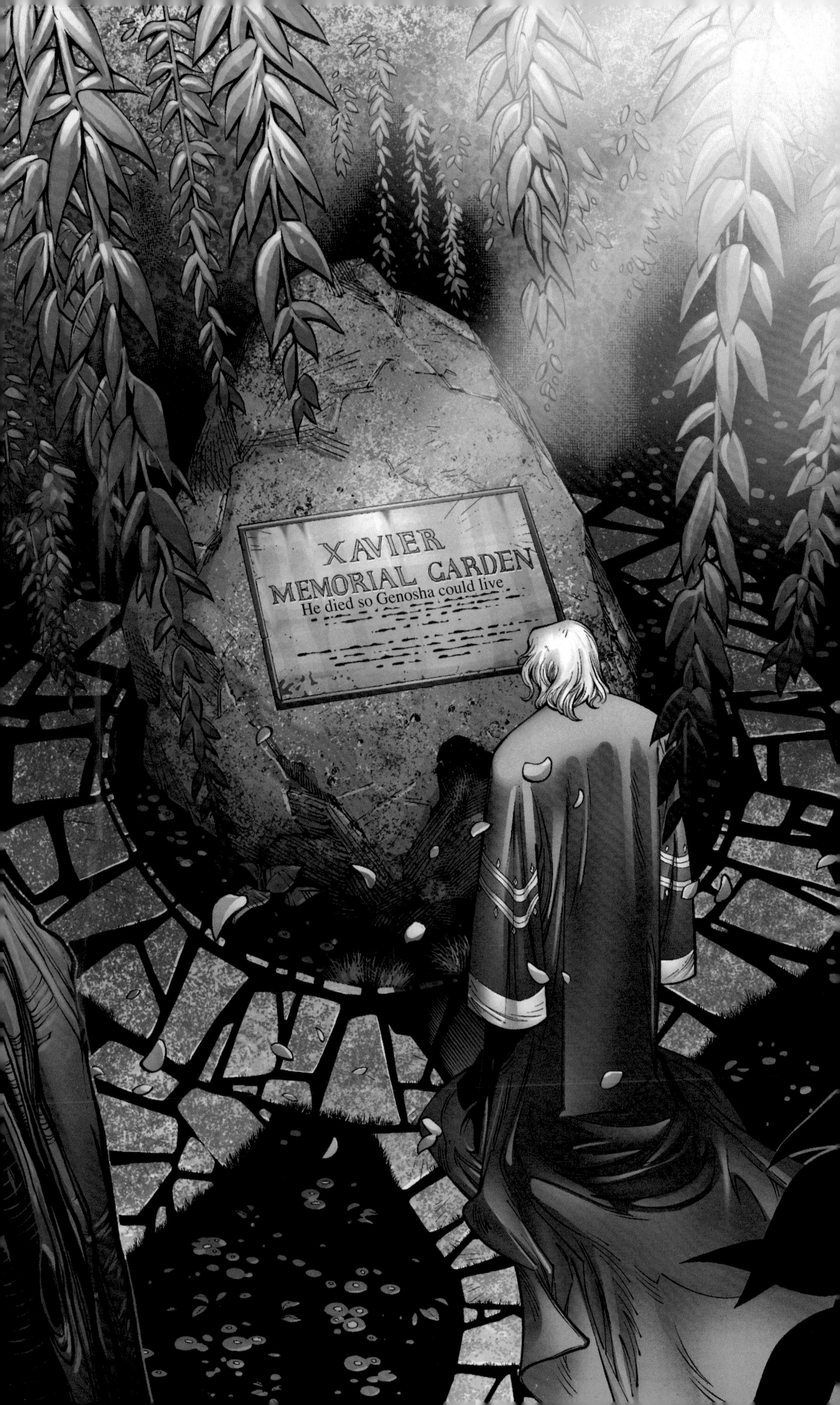
XAVIER
MEMORIAL GARDEN
He died so Genosha could live

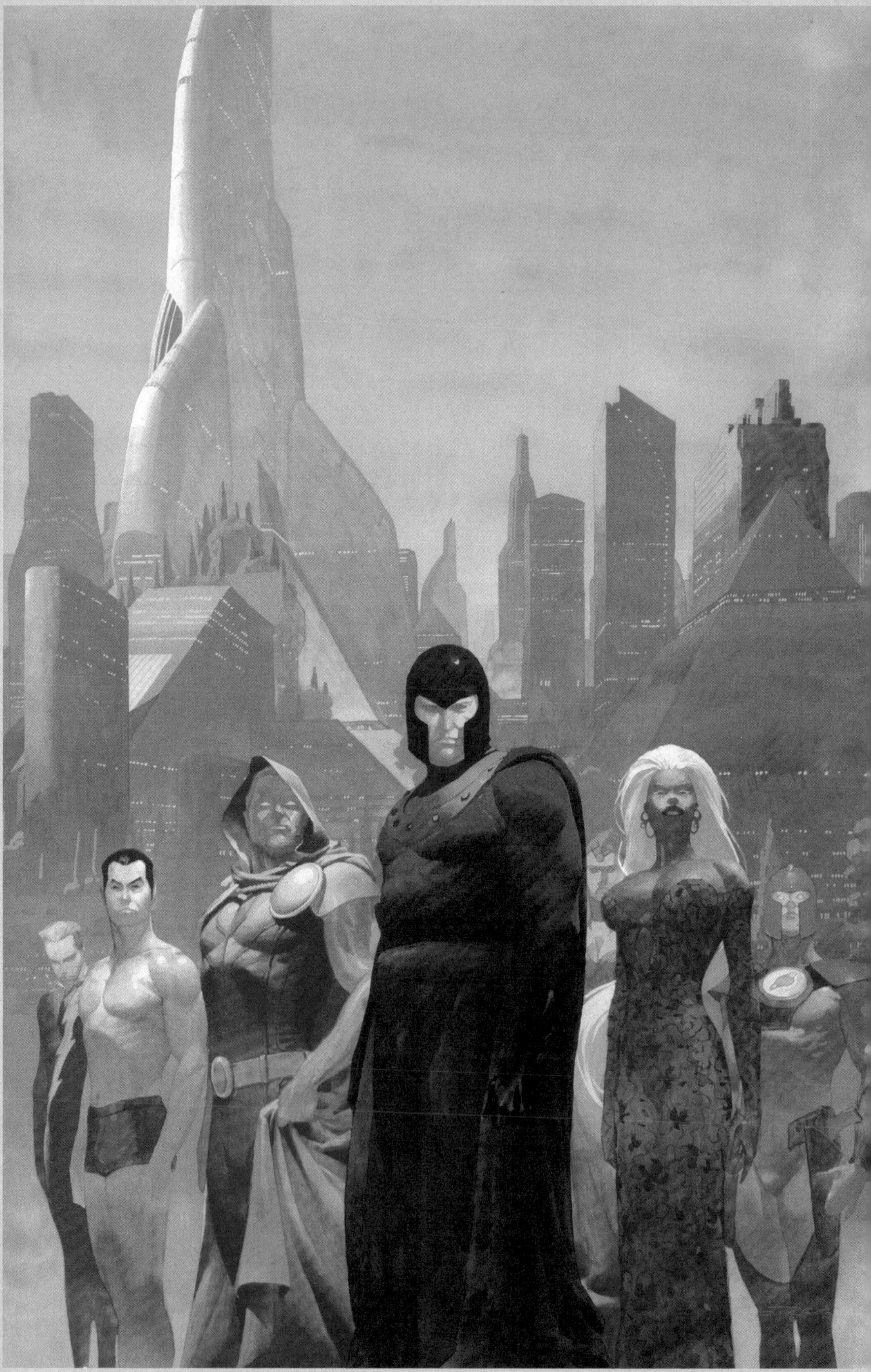

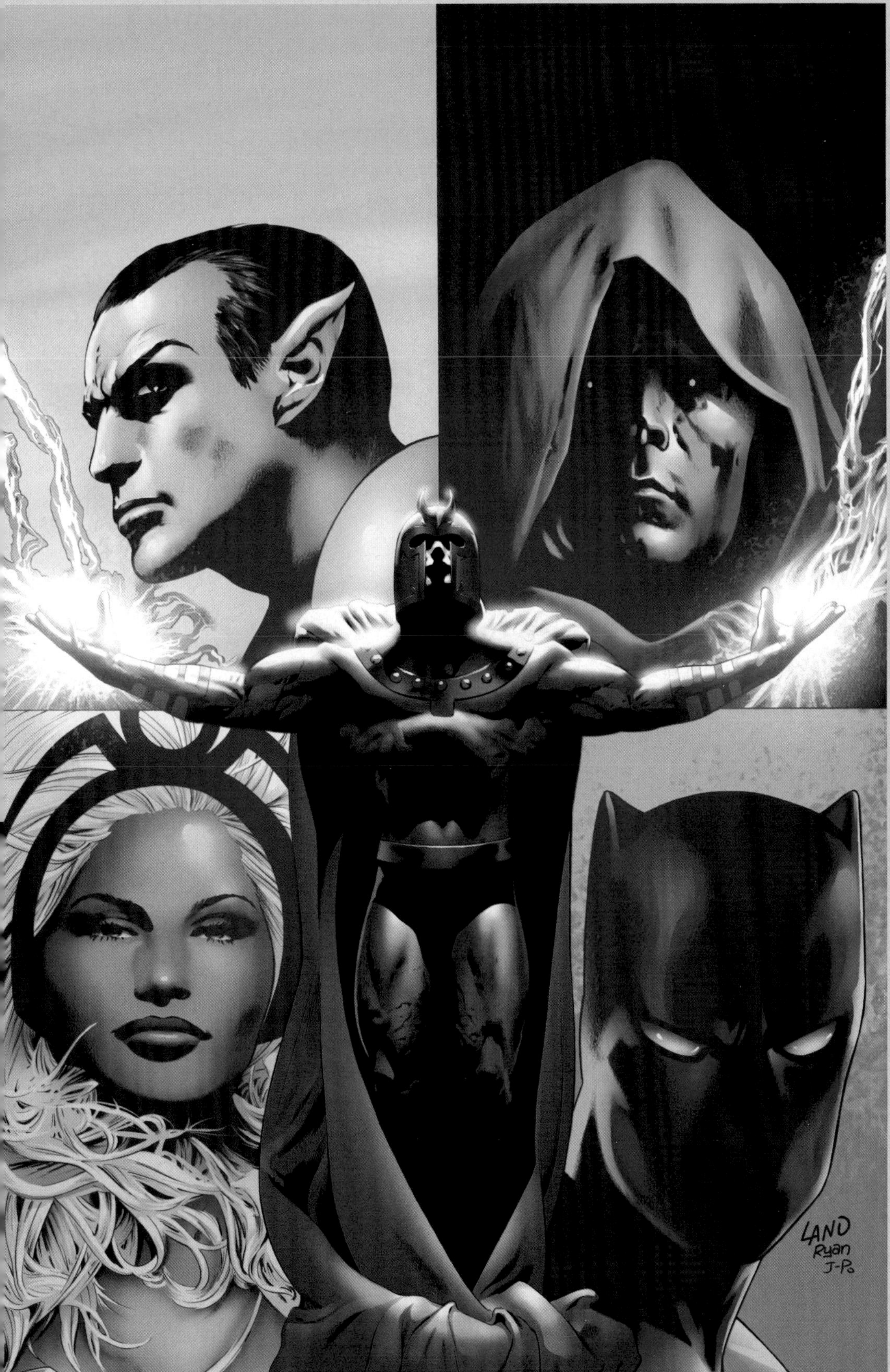
LAND
Ryan
J-Po

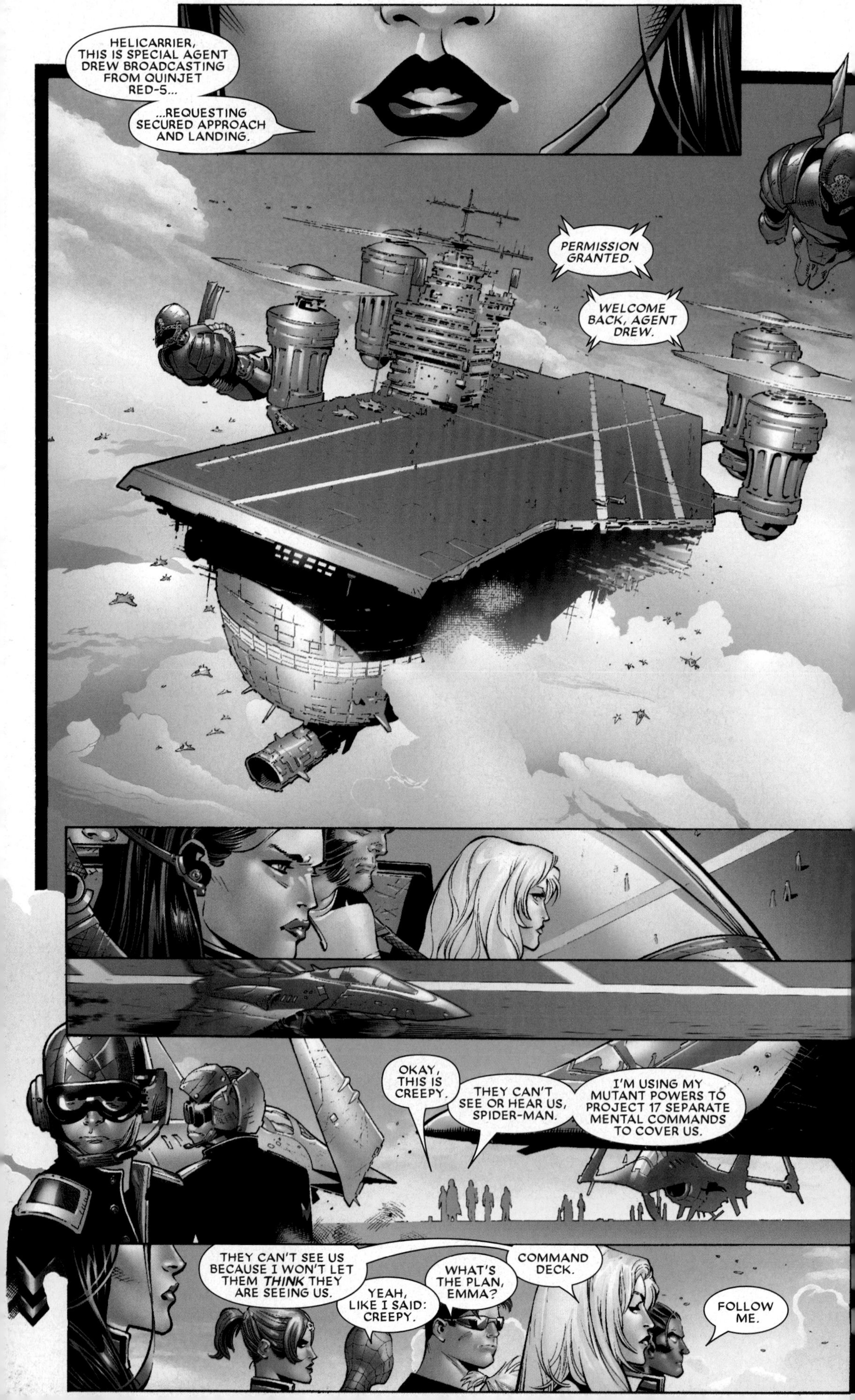
HELICARRIER, THIS IS SPECIAL AGENT DREW BROADCASTING FROM QUINJET RED-5...
...REQUESTING SECURED APPROACH AND LANDING.
PERMISSION GRANTED.
WELCOME BACK, AGENT DREW.
OKAY, THIS IS CREEPY.
THEY CAN'T SEE OR HEAR US, SPIDER-MAN.
I'M USING MY MUTANT POWERS TO PROJECT 17 SEPARATE MENTAL COMMANDS TO COVER US.
THEY CAN'T SEE US BECAUSE I WON'T LET THEM *THINK* THEY ARE SEEING US.
YEAH, LIKE I SAID: CREEPY.
WHAT'S THE PLAN, EMMA?
COMMAND DECK.
FOLLOW ME.

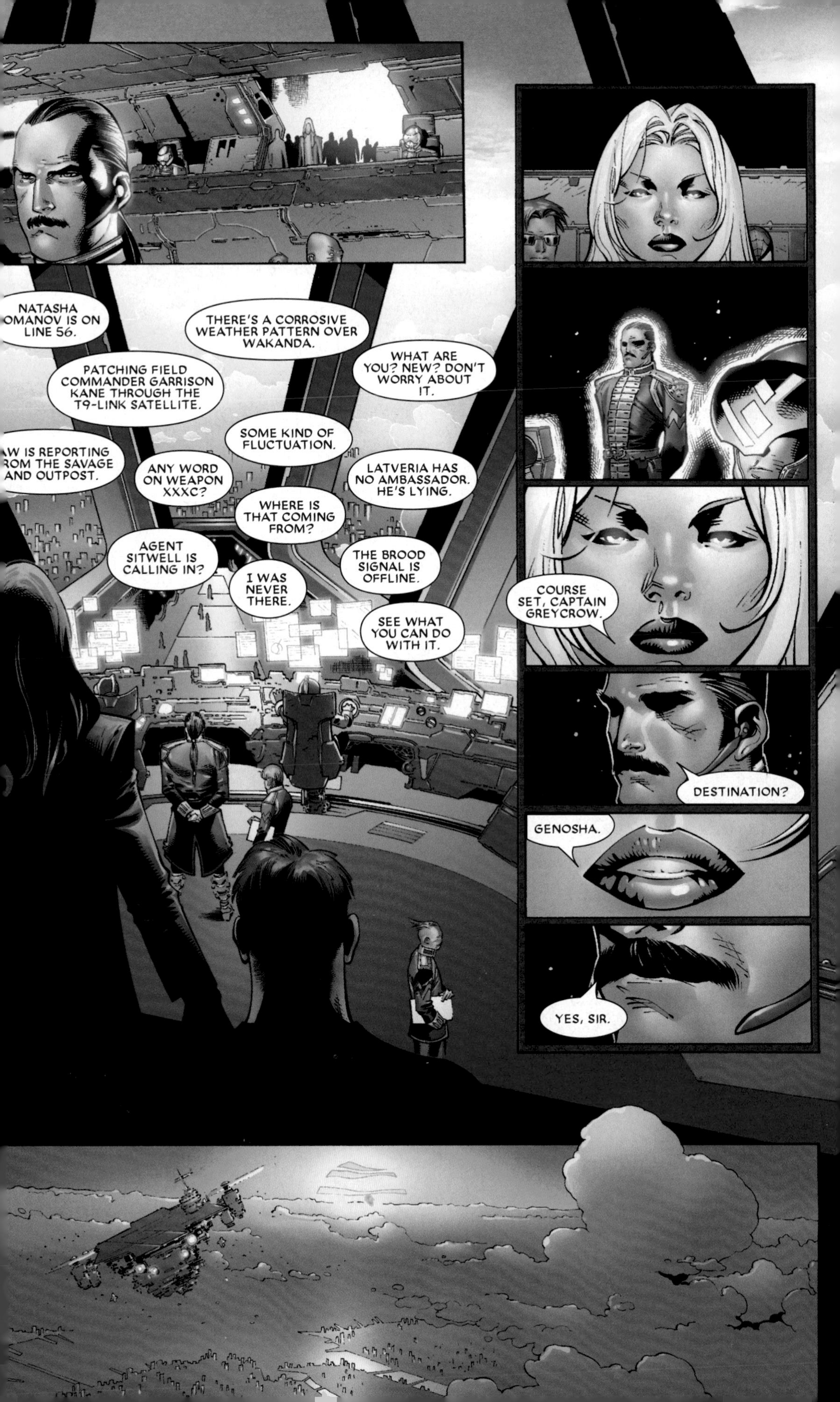

NATASHA
OMANOV IS ON LINE 56.
THERE'S A CORROSIVE WEATHER PATTERN OVER WAKANDA.
PATCHING FIELD COMMANDER GARRISON KANE THROUGH THE T9-LINK SATELLITE.
WHAT ARE YOU? NEW? DON'T WORRY ABOUT IT.
AW IS REPORTING ROM THE SAVAGE AND OUTPOST.
SOME KIND OF FLUCTUATION.
ANY WORD ON WEAPON XXXC?
LATVERIA HAS NO AMBASSADOR. HE'S LYING.
WHERE IS THAT COMING FROM?
AGENT SITWELL IS CALLING IN?
THE BROOD SIGNAL IS OFFLINE.
I WAS NEVER THERE.
SEE WHAT YOU CAN DO WITH IT.
COURSE SET, CAPTAIN GREYCROW.
DESTINATION?
GENOSHA.
YES, SIR.

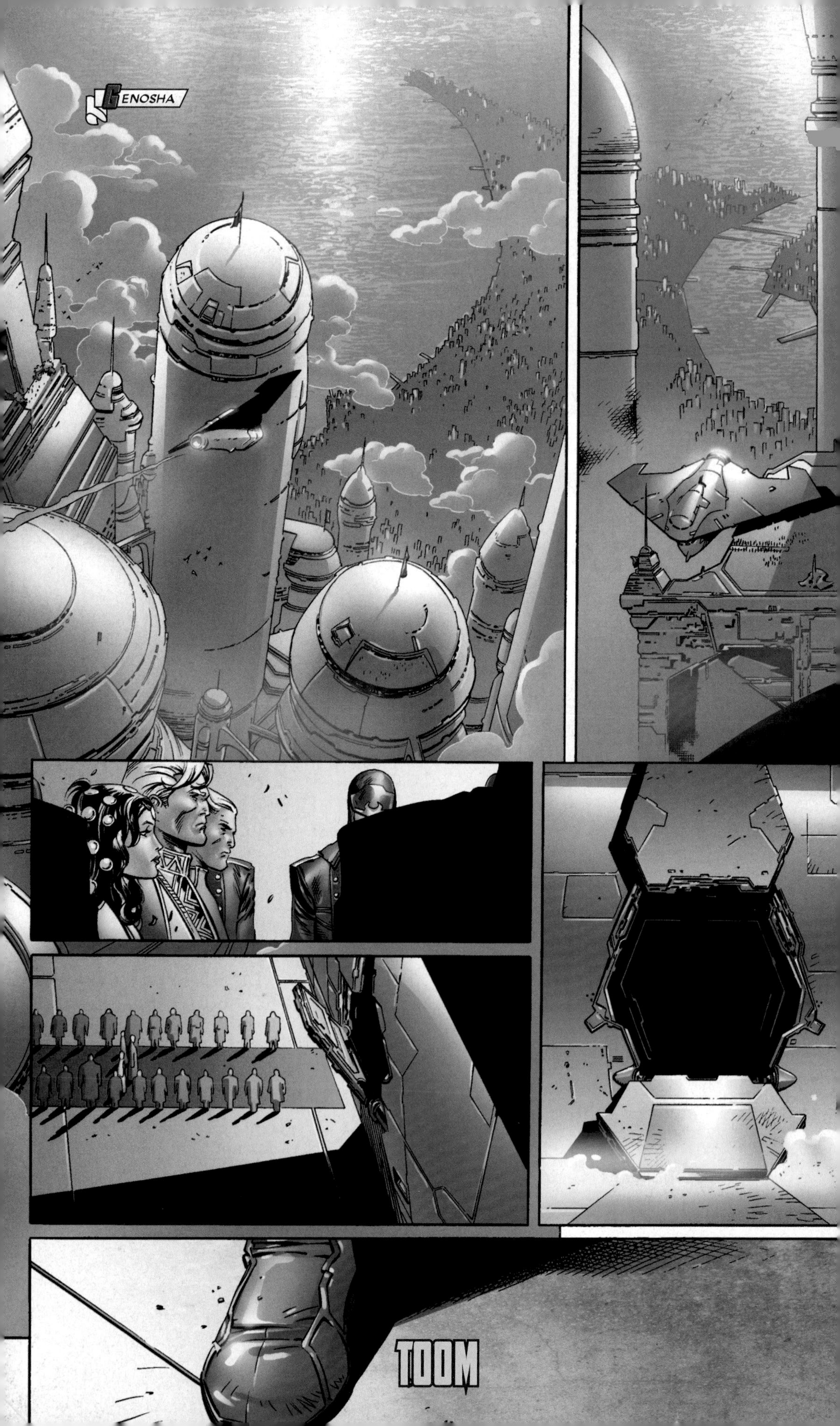
GENOSHA
TOOM

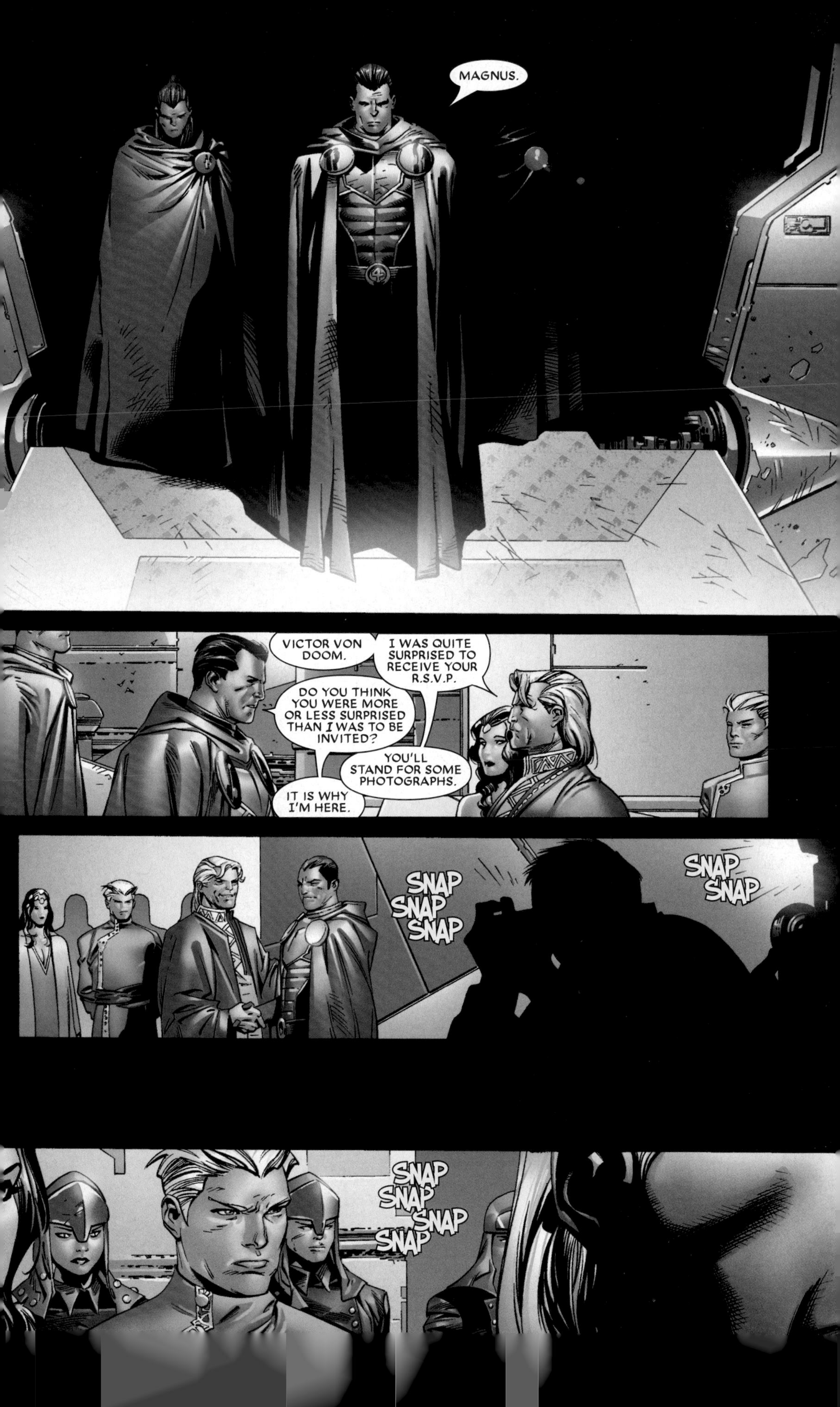

MAGNUS.
VICTOR VON DOOM.
I WAS QUITE SURPRISED TO RECEIVE YOUR R.S.V.P.
DO YOU THINK YOU WERE MORE OR LESS SURPRISED THAN I WAS TO BE INVITED?
YOU'LL STAND FOR SOME PHOTOGRAPHS.
IT IS WHY I'M HERE.
SNAP SNAP SNAP
SNAP SNAP
SNAP SNAP SNAP SNAP

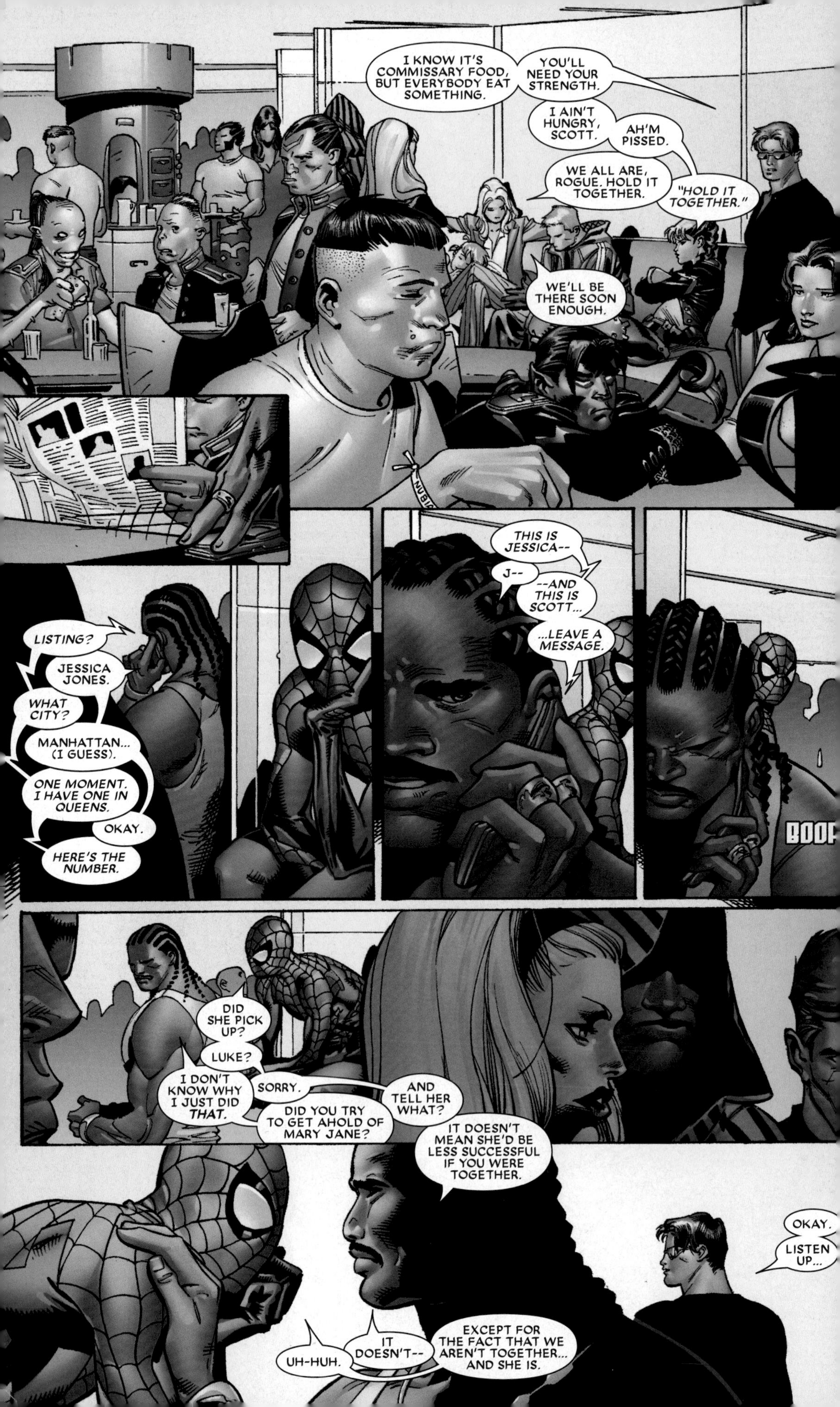

I KNOW IT'S COMMISSARY FOOD, BUT EVERYBODY EAT SOMETHING.
YOU'LL NEED YOUR STRENGTH.
I AIN'T HUNGRY, SCOTT.
AH'M PISSED.
WE ALL ARE, ROGUE. HOLD IT TOGETHER.
"HOLD IT TOGETHER."
WE'LL BE THERE SOON ENOUGH.
LISTING?
JESSICA JONES.
WHAT CITY?
MANHATTAN... (I GUESS).
ONE MOMENT. I HAVE ONE IN QUEENS.
OKAY.
HERE'S THE NUMBER.
THIS IS JESSICA--
J--
--AND THIS IS SCOTT...
...LEAVE A MESSAGE.
BOOP
DID SHE PICK UP?
LUKE?
I DON'T KNOW WHY I JUST DID THAT.
SORRY.
AND TELL HER WHAT?
DID YOU TRY TO GET AHOLD OF MARY JANE?
IT DOESN'T MEAN SHE'D BE LESS SUCCESSFUL IF YOU WERE TOGETHER.
OKAY.
LISTEN UP...
UH-HUH.
IT DOESN'T--
EXCEPT FOR THE FACT THAT WE AREN'T TOGETHER... AND SHE IS.

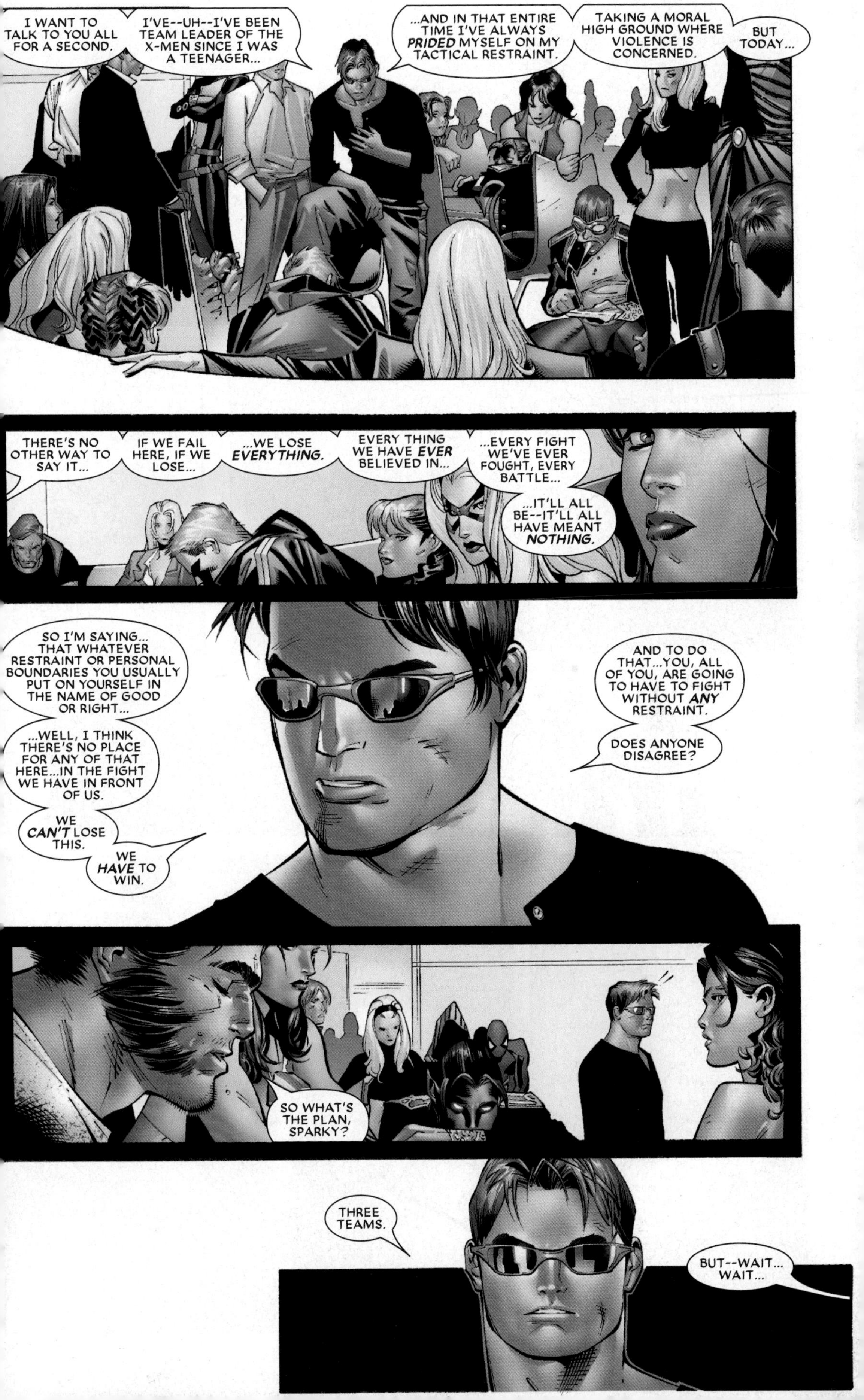

I WANT TO TALK TO YOU ALL FOR A SECOND.
I'VE--UH--I'VE BEEN TEAM LEADER OF THE X-MEN SINCE I WAS A TEENAGER...
...AND IN THAT ENTIRE TIME I'VE ALWAYS *PRIDED* MYSELF ON MY TACTICAL RESTRAINT.
TAKING A MORAL HIGH GROUND WHERE VIOLENCE IS CONCERNED.
BUT TODAY...
THERE'S NO OTHER WAY TO SAY IT...
IF WE FAIL HERE, IF WE LOSE...
...WE LOSE *EVERYTHING.*
EVERY THING WE HAVE *EVER* BELIEVED IN...
...EVERY FIGHT WE'VE EVER FOUGHT, EVERY BATTLE...
...IT'LL ALL BE--IT'LL ALL HAVE MEANT *NOTHING.*
SO I'M SAYING... THAT WHATEVER RESTRAINT OR PERSONAL BOUNDARIES YOU USUALLY PUT ON YOURSELF IN THE NAME OF GOOD OR RIGHT...
...WELL, I THINK THERE'S NO PLACE FOR ANY OF THAT HERE...IN THE FIGHT WE HAVE IN FRONT OF US.
WE *CAN'T* LOSE THIS.
WE *HAVE* TO WIN.
AND TO DO THAT...YOU, ALL OF YOU, ARE GOING TO HAVE TO FIGHT WITHOUT *ANY* RESTRAINT.
DOES ANYONE DISAGREE?
SO WHAT'S THE PLAN, SPARKY?
THREE TEAMS.
BUT--WAIT... WAIT...

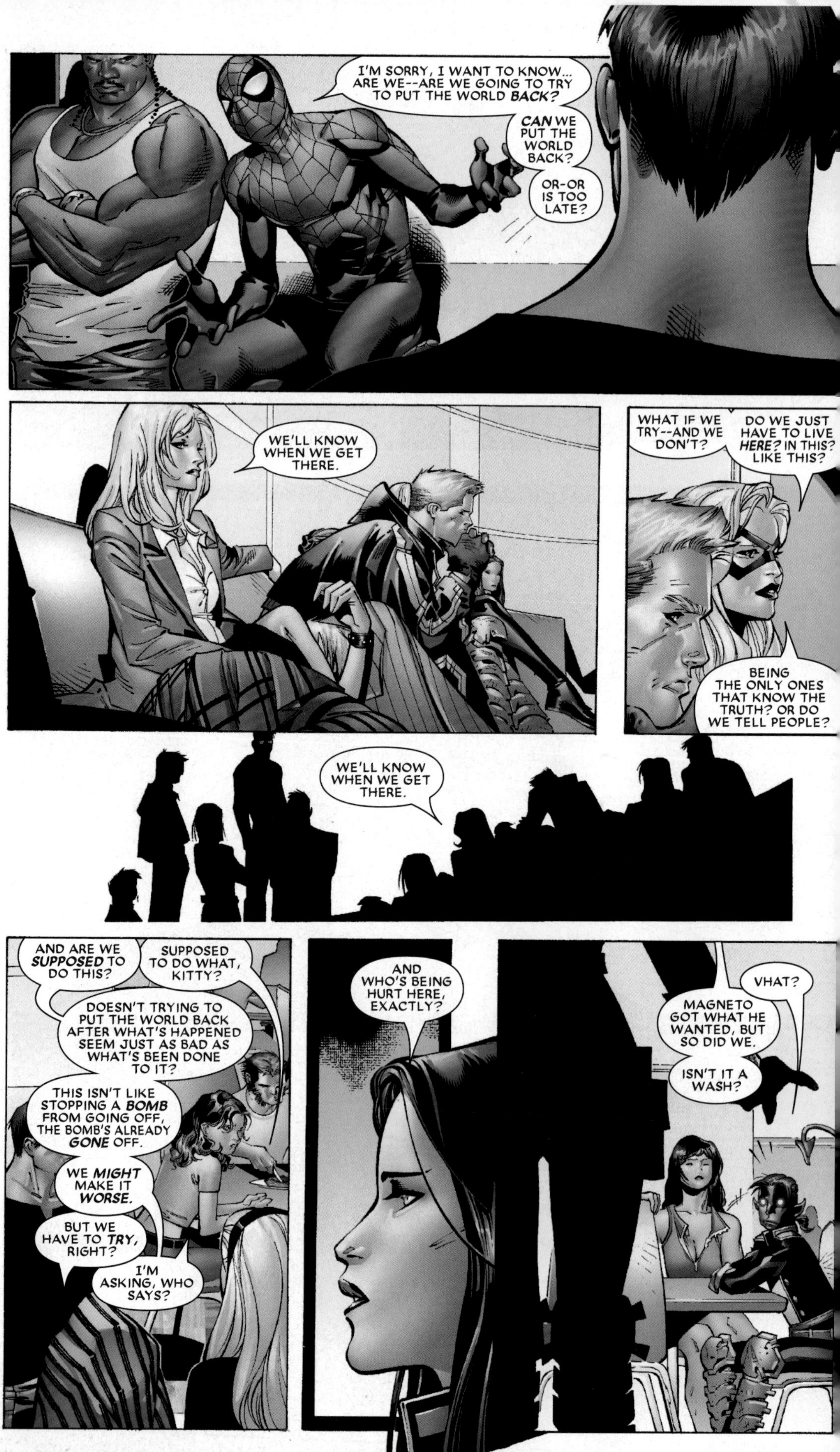
I'M SORRY, I WANT TO KNOW... ARE WE--ARE WE GOING TO TRY TO PUT THE WORLD BACK?
CAN WE PUT THE WORLD BACK?
OR-OR IS TOO LATE?
WE'LL KNOW WHEN WE GET THERE.
WHAT IF WE TRY--AND WE DON'T?
DO WE JUST HAVE TO LIVE HERE? IN THIS? LIKE THIS?
BEING THE ONLY ONES THAT KNOW THE TRUTH? OR DO WE TELL PEOPLE?
WE'LL KNOW WHEN WE GET THERE.
AND ARE WE SUPPOSED TO DO THIS?
SUPPOSED TO DO WHAT, KITTY?
DOESN'T TRYING TO PUT THE WORLD BACK AFTER WHAT'S HAPPENED SEEM JUST AS BAD AS WHAT'S BEEN DONE TO IT?
THIS ISN'T LIKE STOPPING A BOMB FROM GOING OFF, THE BOMB'S ALREADY GONE OFF.
WE MIGHT MAKE IT WORSE.
BUT WE HAVE TO TRY, RIGHT?
I'M ASKING, WHO SAYS?
AND WHO'S BEING HURT HERE, EXACTLY?
VHAT?
MAGNETO GOT WHAT HE WANTED, BUT SO DID WE.
ISN'T IT A WASH?

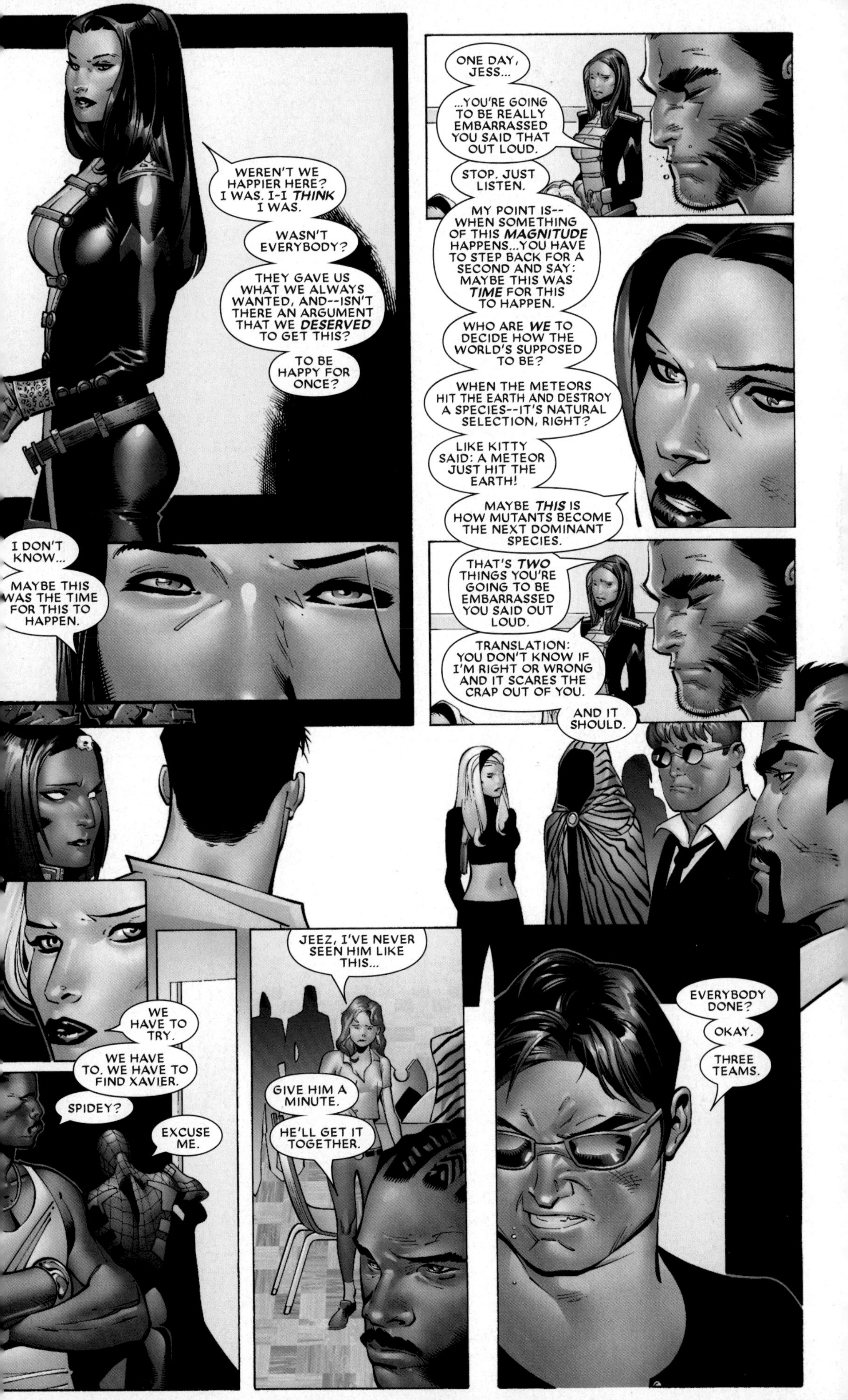
WEREN'T WE HAPPIER HERE? I WAS. I-I THINK I WAS.
WASN'T EVERYBODY?
THEY GAVE US WHAT WE ALWAYS WANTED, AND--ISN'T THERE AN ARGUMENT THAT WE DESERVED TO GET THIS?
TO BE HAPPY FOR ONCE?
ONE DAY, JESS...
...YOU'RE GOING TO BE REALLY EMBARRASSED YOU SAID THAT OUT LOUD.
STOP. JUST LISTEN.
MY POINT IS-- WHEN SOMETHING OF THIS MAGNITUDE HAPPENS...YOU HAVE TO STEP BACK FOR A SECOND AND SAY: MAYBE THIS WAS TIME FOR THIS TO HAPPEN.
WHO ARE WE TO DECIDE HOW THE WORLD'S SUPPOSED TO BE?
WHEN THE METEORS HIT THE EARTH AND DESTROY A SPECIES--IT'S NATURAL SELECTION, RIGHT?
LIKE KITTY SAID: A METEOR JUST HIT THE EARTH!
MAYBE THIS IS HOW MUTANTS BECOME THE NEXT DOMINANT SPECIES.
I DON'T KNOW...
MAYBE THIS WAS THE TIME FOR THIS TO HAPPEN.
THAT'S TWO THINGS YOU'RE GOING TO BE EMBARRASSED YOU SAID OUT LOUD.
TRANSLATION: YOU DON'T KNOW IF I'M RIGHT OR WRONG AND IT SCARES THE CRAP OUT OF YOU.
AND IT SHOULD.
WE HAVE TO TRY.
WE HAVE TO. WE HAVE TO FIND XAVIER.
SPIDEY?
EXCUSE ME.
JEEZ, I'VE NEVER SEEN HIM LIKE THIS...
GIVE HIM A MINUTE.
HE'LL GET IT TOGETHER.
EVERYBODY DONE?
OKAY.
THREE TEAMS.

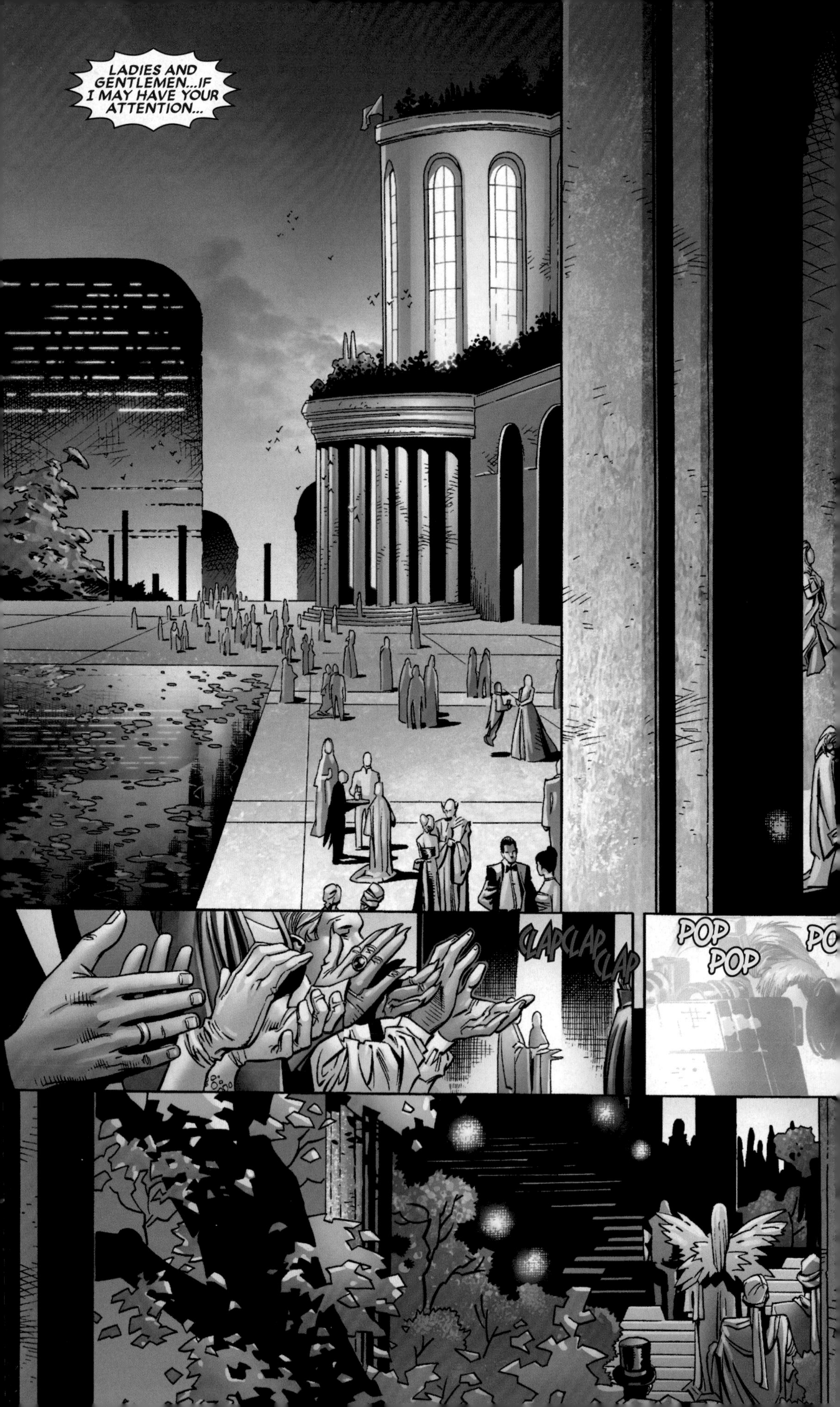
LADIES AND GENTLEMEN...IF I MAY HAVE YOUR ATTENTION...
CLAPCLAPCLAP
POP
POP
POP

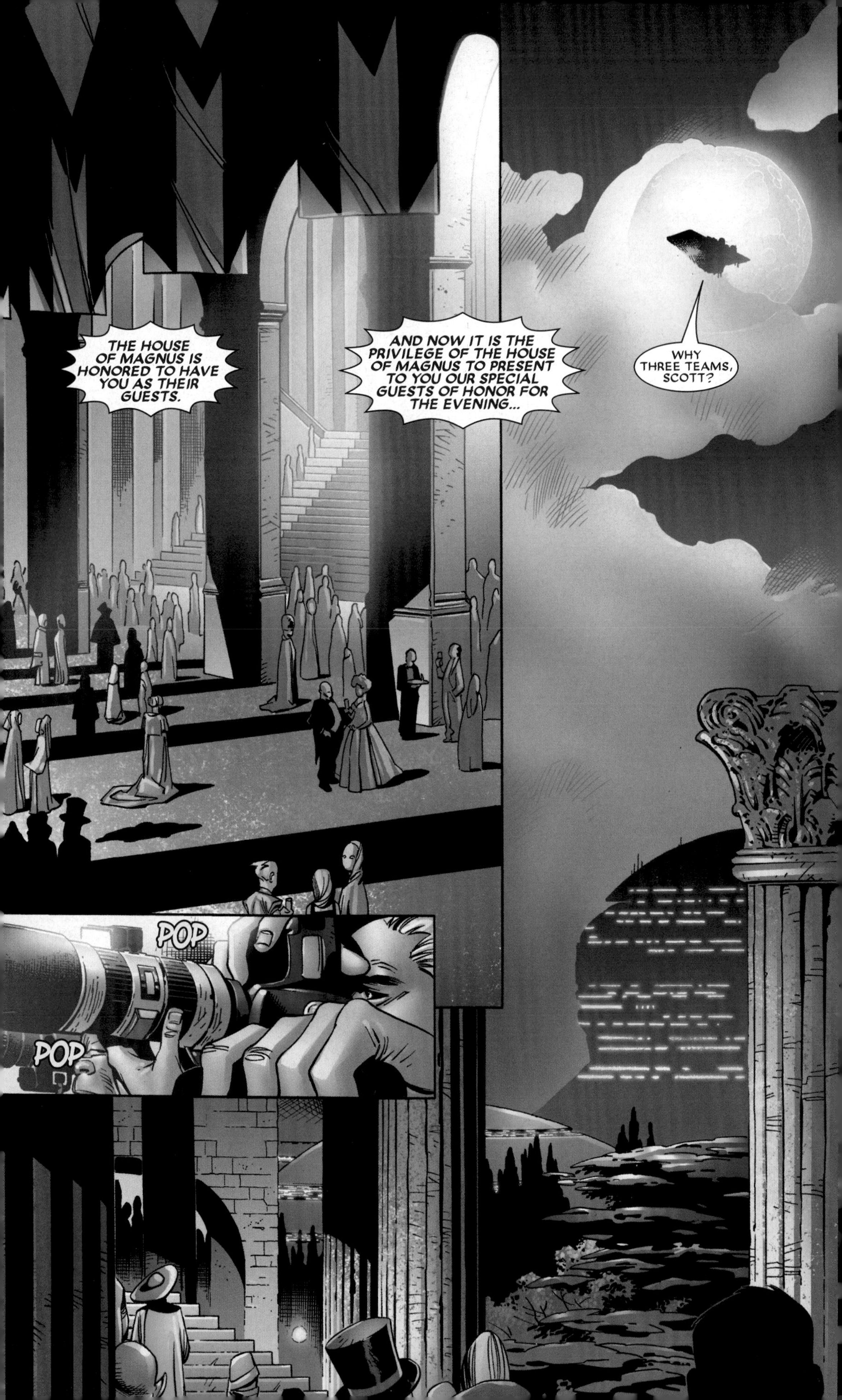
THE HOUSE OF MAGNUS IS HONORED TO HAVE YOU AS THEIR GUESTS.
AND NOW IT IS THE PRIVILEGE OF THE HOUSE OF MAGNUS TO PRESENT TO YOU OUR SPECIAL GUESTS OF HONOR FOR THE EVENING...
WHY THREE TEAMS, SCOTT?
POP
POP

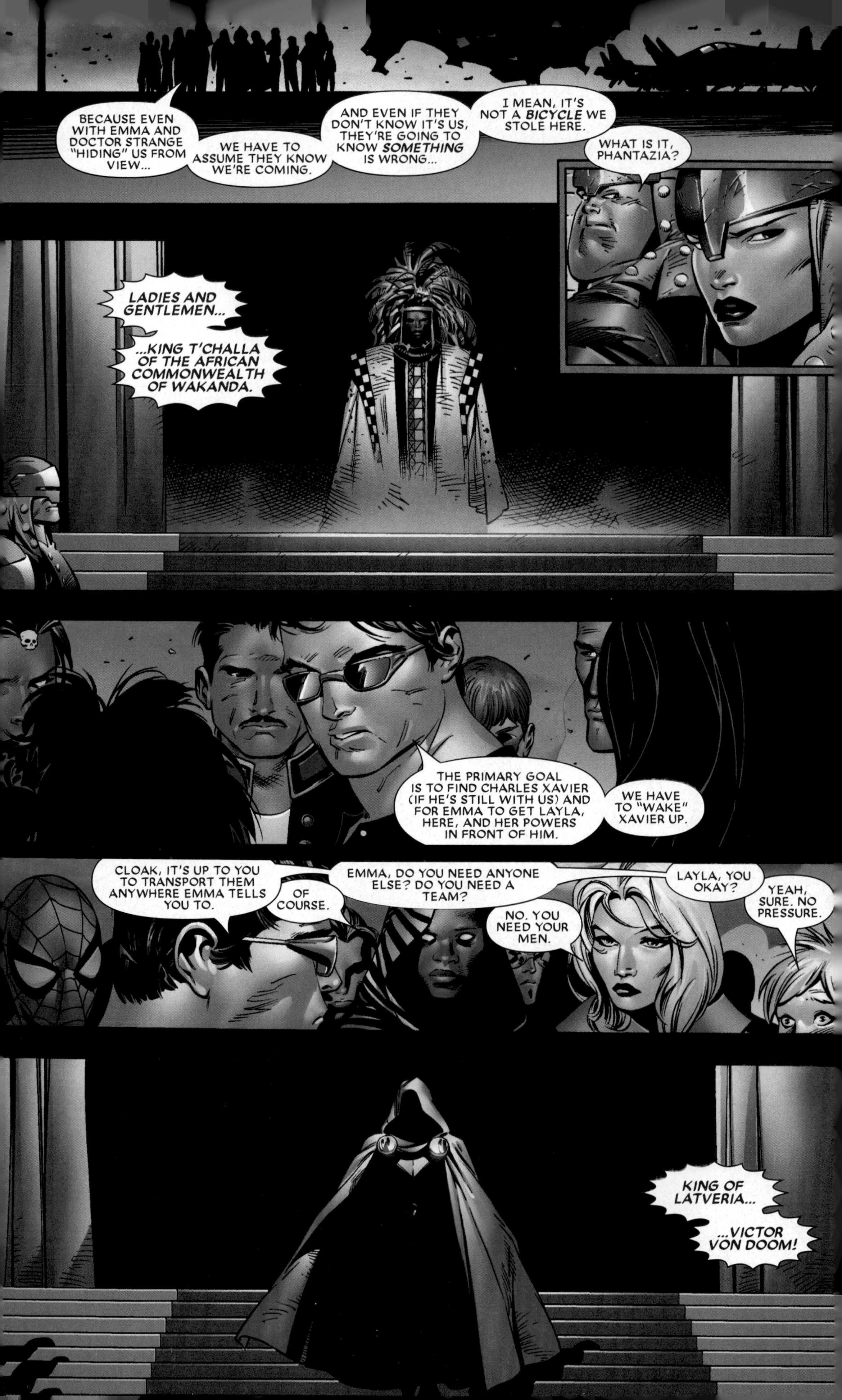

BECAUSE EVEN WITH EMMA AND DOCTOR STRANGE "HIDING" US FROM VIEW...
WE HAVE TO ASSUME THEY KNOW WE'RE COMING.
AND EVEN IF THEY DON'T KNOW IT'S US, THEY'RE GOING TO KNOW *SOMETHING* IS WRONG...
I MEAN, IT'S NOT A *BICYCLE* WE STOLE HERE.
WHAT IS IT, PHANTAZIA?
LADIES AND GENTLEMEN...
...KING T'CHALLA OF THE AFRICAN COMMONWEALTH OF WAKANDA.
THE PRIMARY GOAL IS TO FIND CHARLES XAVIER (IF HE'S STILL WITH US) AND FOR EMMA TO GET LAYLA, HERE, AND HER POWERS IN FRONT OF HIM.
WE HAVE TO "WAKE" XAVIER UP.
CLOAK, IT'S UP TO YOU TO TRANSPORT THEM ANYWHERE EMMA TELLS YOU TO.
OF COURSE.
EMMA, DO YOU NEED ANYONE ELSE? DO YOU NEED A TEAM?
NO. YOU NEED YOUR MEN.
LAYLA, YOU OKAY?
YEAH, SURE. NO PRESSURE.
KING OF LATVERIA...
...VICTOR VON DOOM!

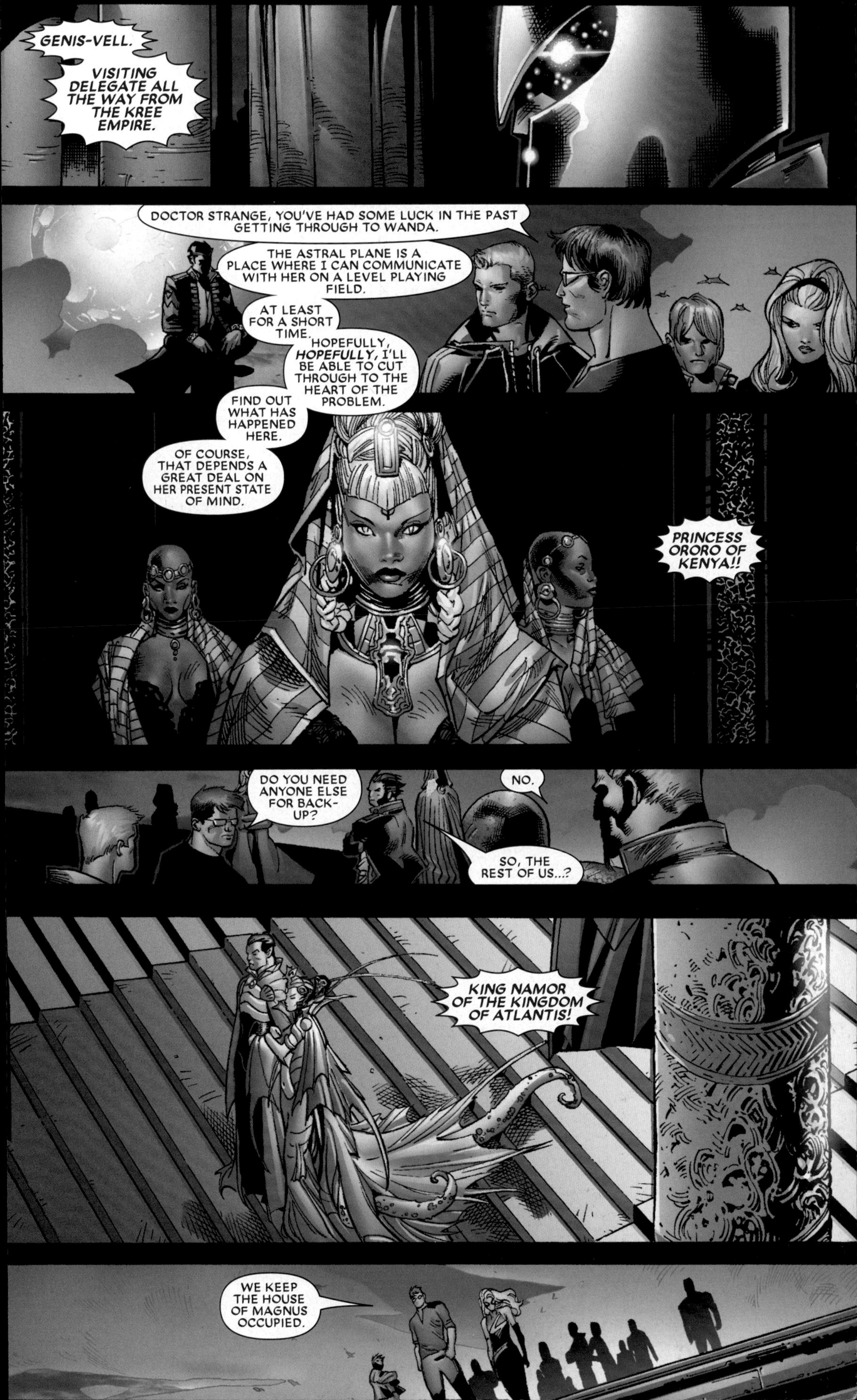
GENIS-VELL.
VISITING DELEGATE ALL THE WAY FROM THE KREE EMPIRE.
DOCTOR STRANGE, YOU'VE HAD SOME LUCK IN THE PAST GETTING THROUGH TO WANDA.
THE ASTRAL PLANE IS A PLACE WHERE I CAN COMMUNICATE WITH HER ON A LEVEL PLAYING FIELD.
AT LEAST FOR A SHORT TIME.
HOPEFULLY, *HOPEFULLY*, I'LL BE ABLE TO CUT THROUGH TO THE HEART OF THE PROBLEM.
FIND OUT WHAT HAS HAPPENED HERE.
OF COURSE, THAT DEPENDS A GREAT DEAL ON HER PRESENT STATE OF MIND.
PRINCESS ORORO OF KENYA!!
DO YOU NEED ANYONE ELSE FOR BACK-UP?
NO.
SO, THE REST OF US...?
KING NAMOR OF THE KINGDOM OF ATLANTIS!
WE KEEP THE HOUSE OF MAGNUS OCCUPIED.

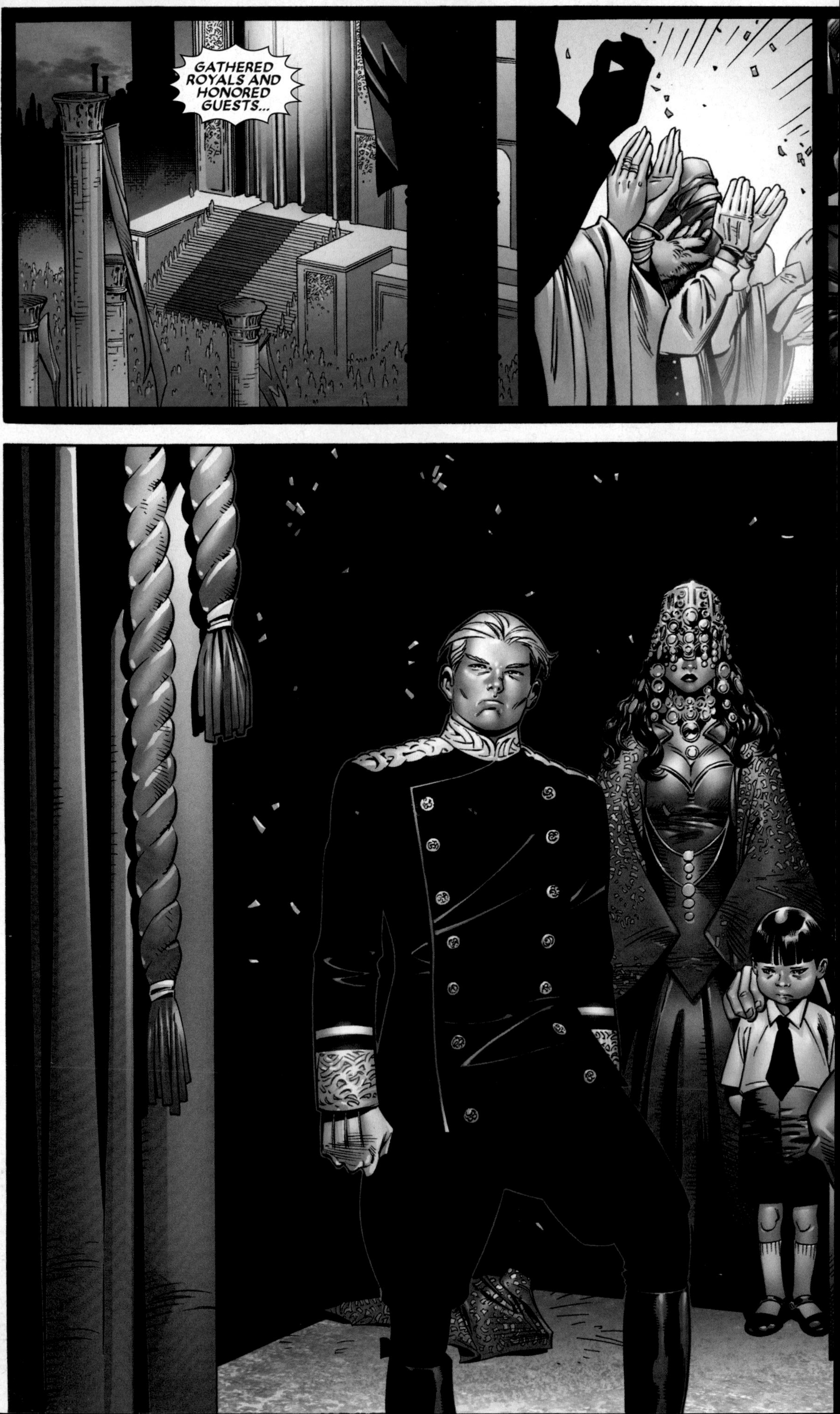
GATHERED ROYALS AND HONORED GUESTS...

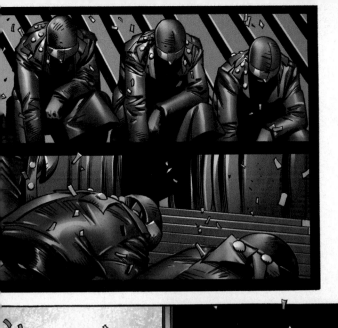

THE HOUSE OF MAGNUS!!!

UH-OH.

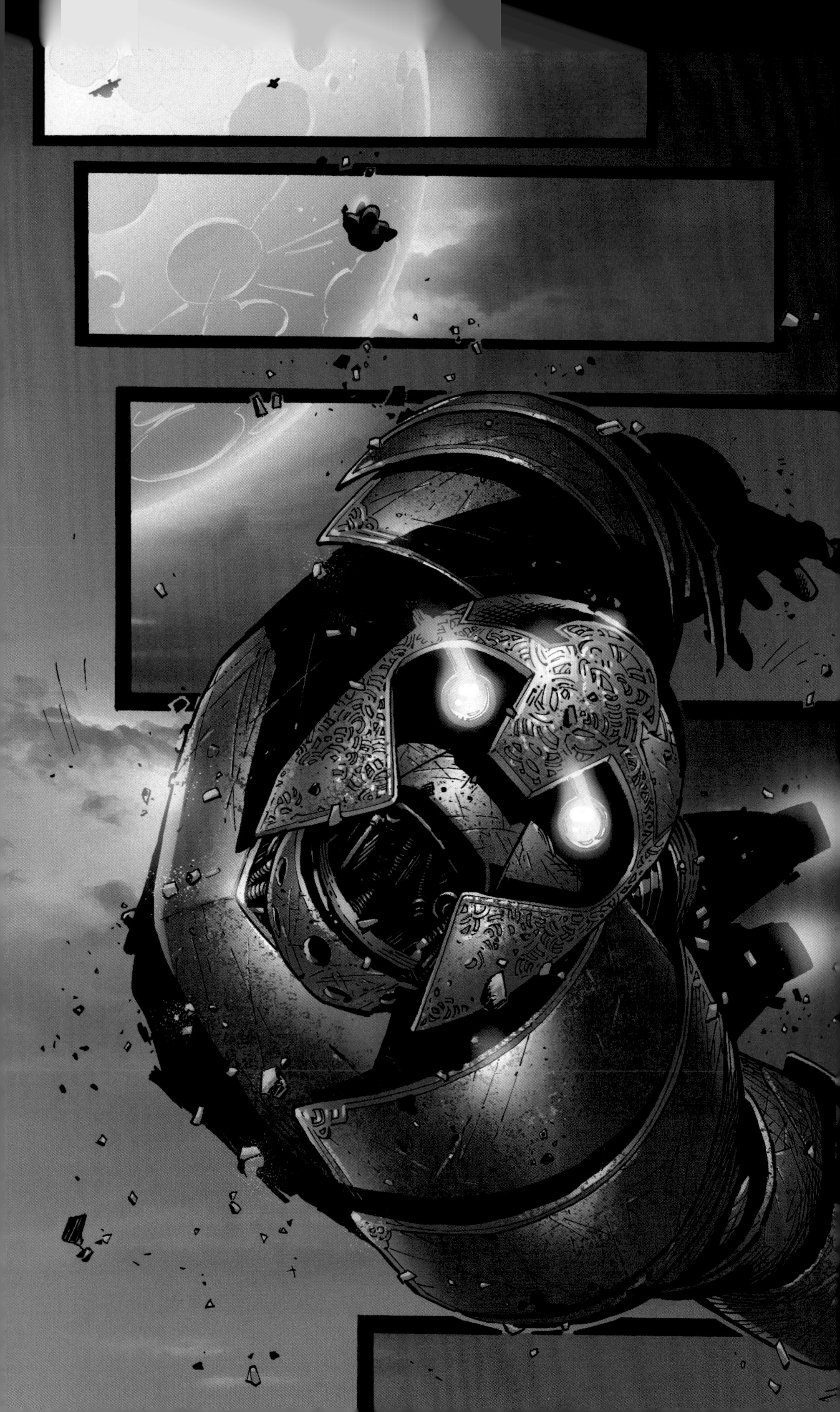

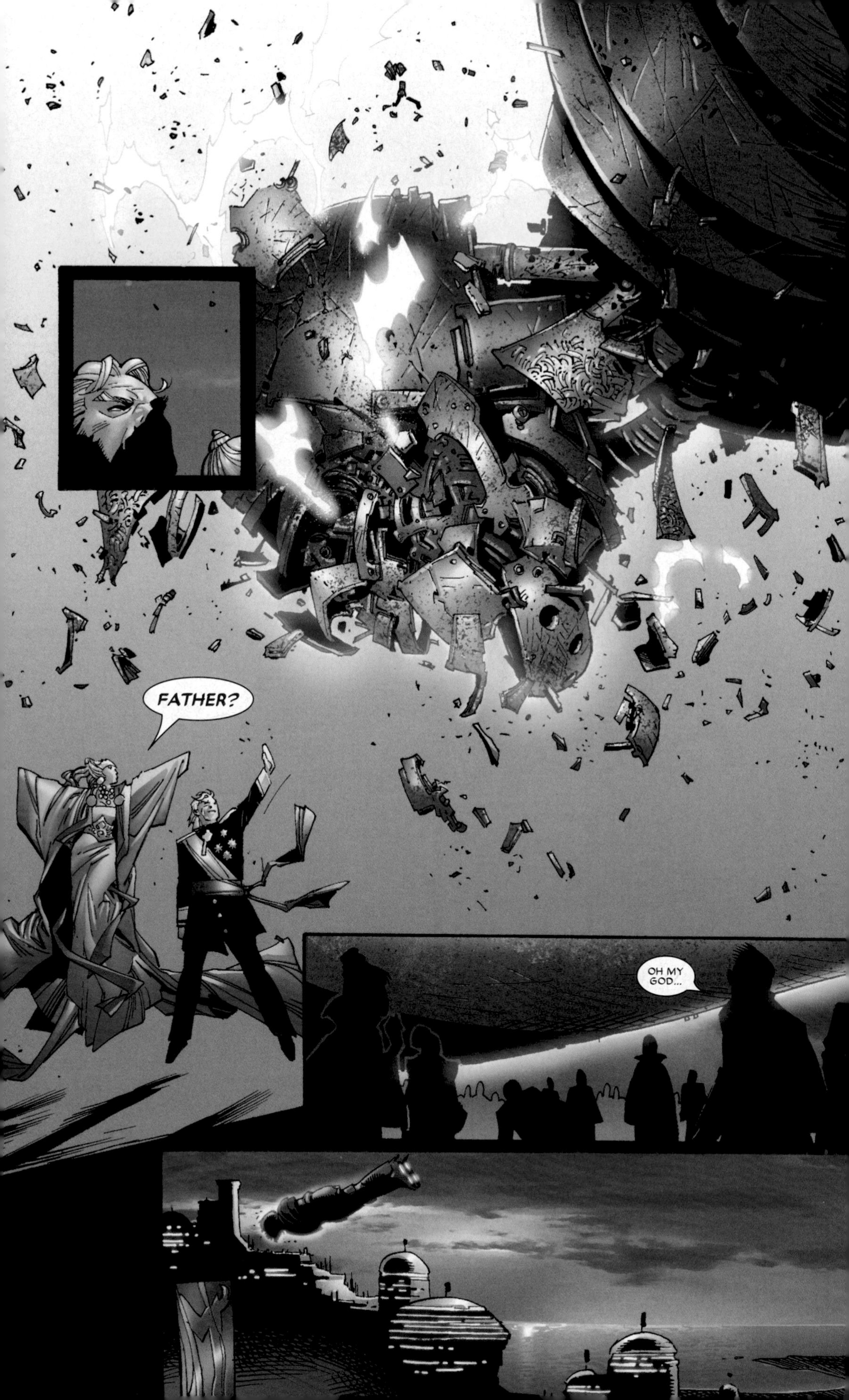
FATHER?
OH MY GOD...

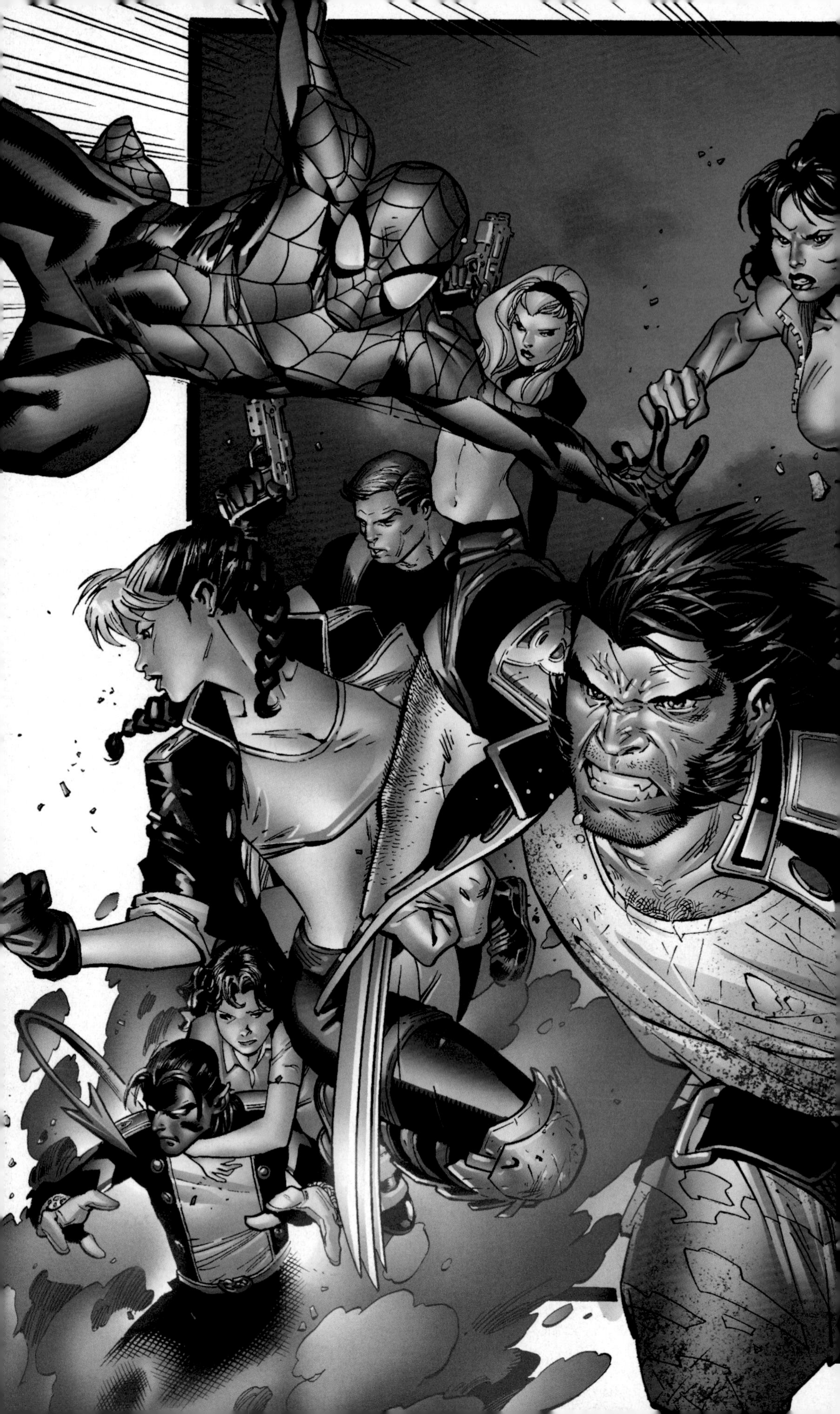

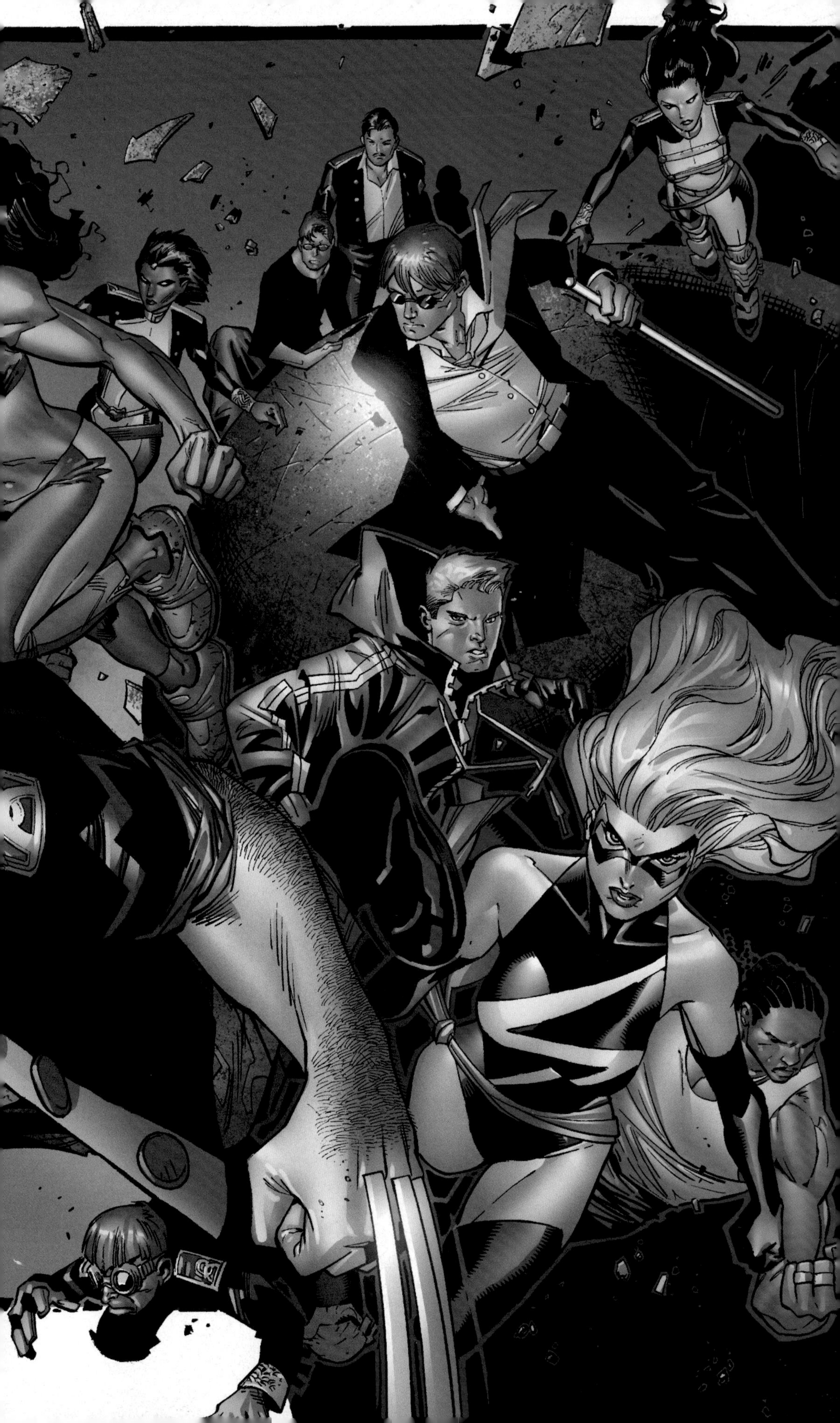

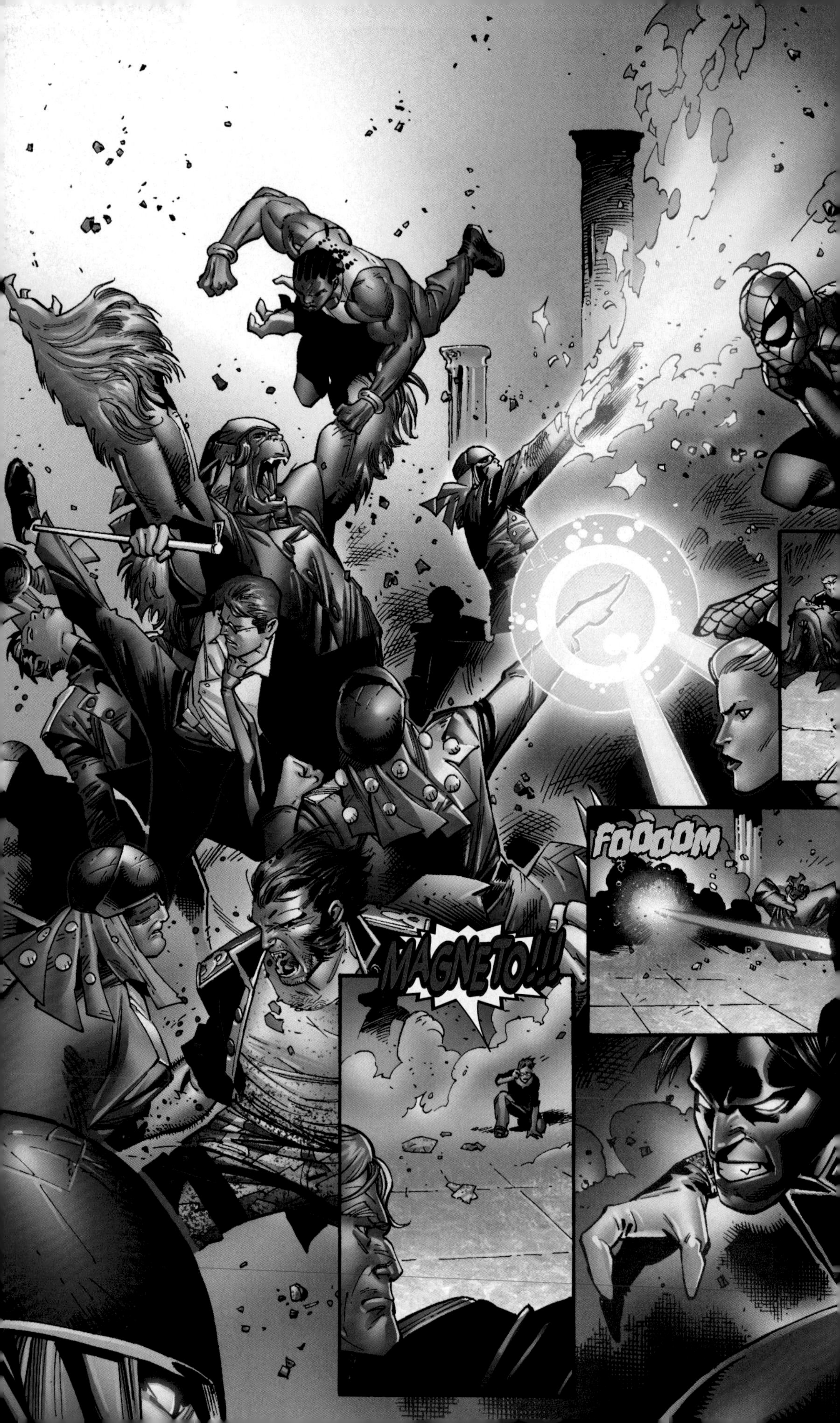

FOOOOM
MAGNETO!!!

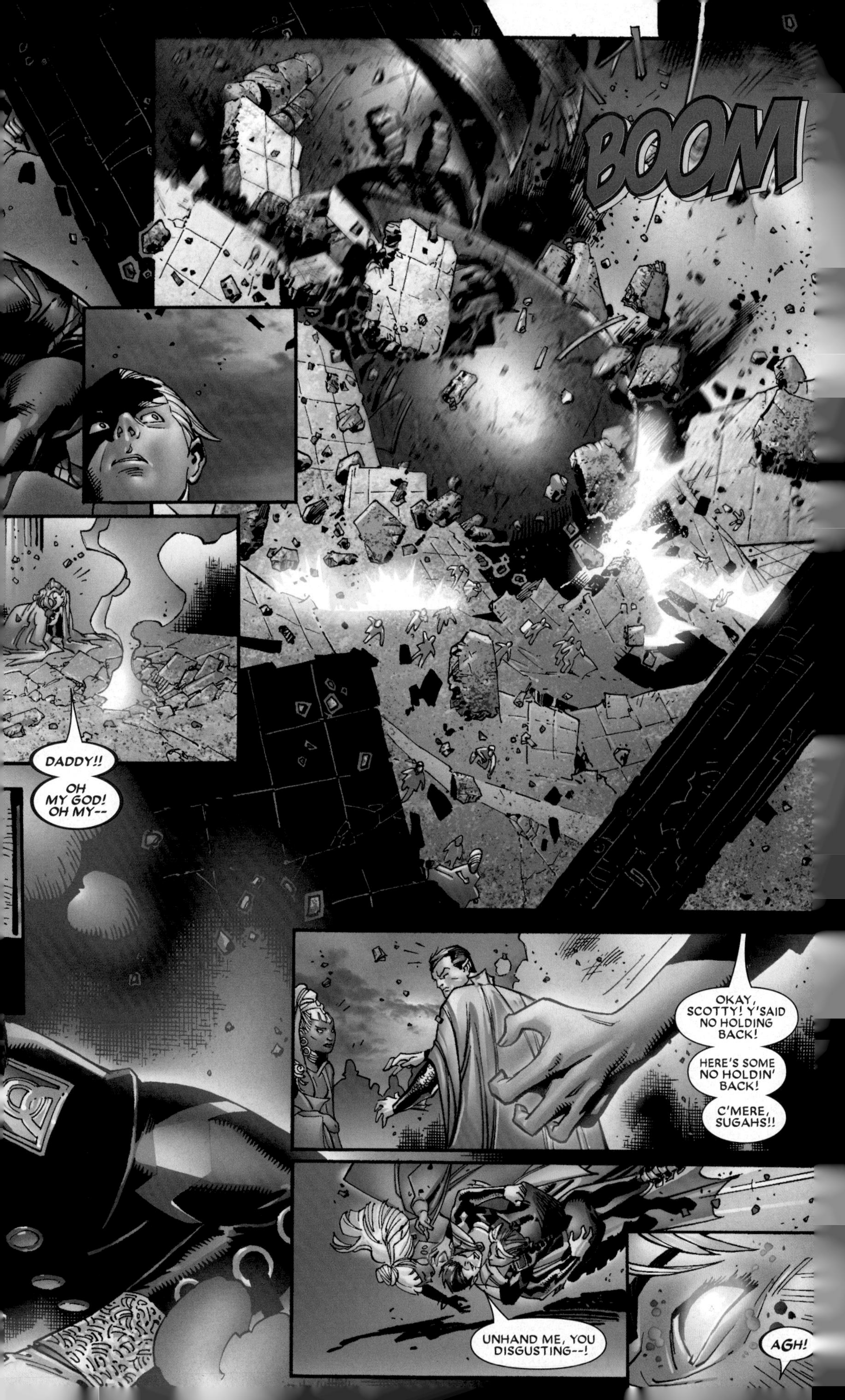
BOOM
DADDY!!
OH MY GOD! OH MY--
OKAY, SCOTTY! Y'SAID NO HOLDING BACK!
HERE'S SOME NO HOLDIN' BACK!
C'MERE, SUGAHS!!
UNHAND ME, YOU DISGUSTING--!
AGH!

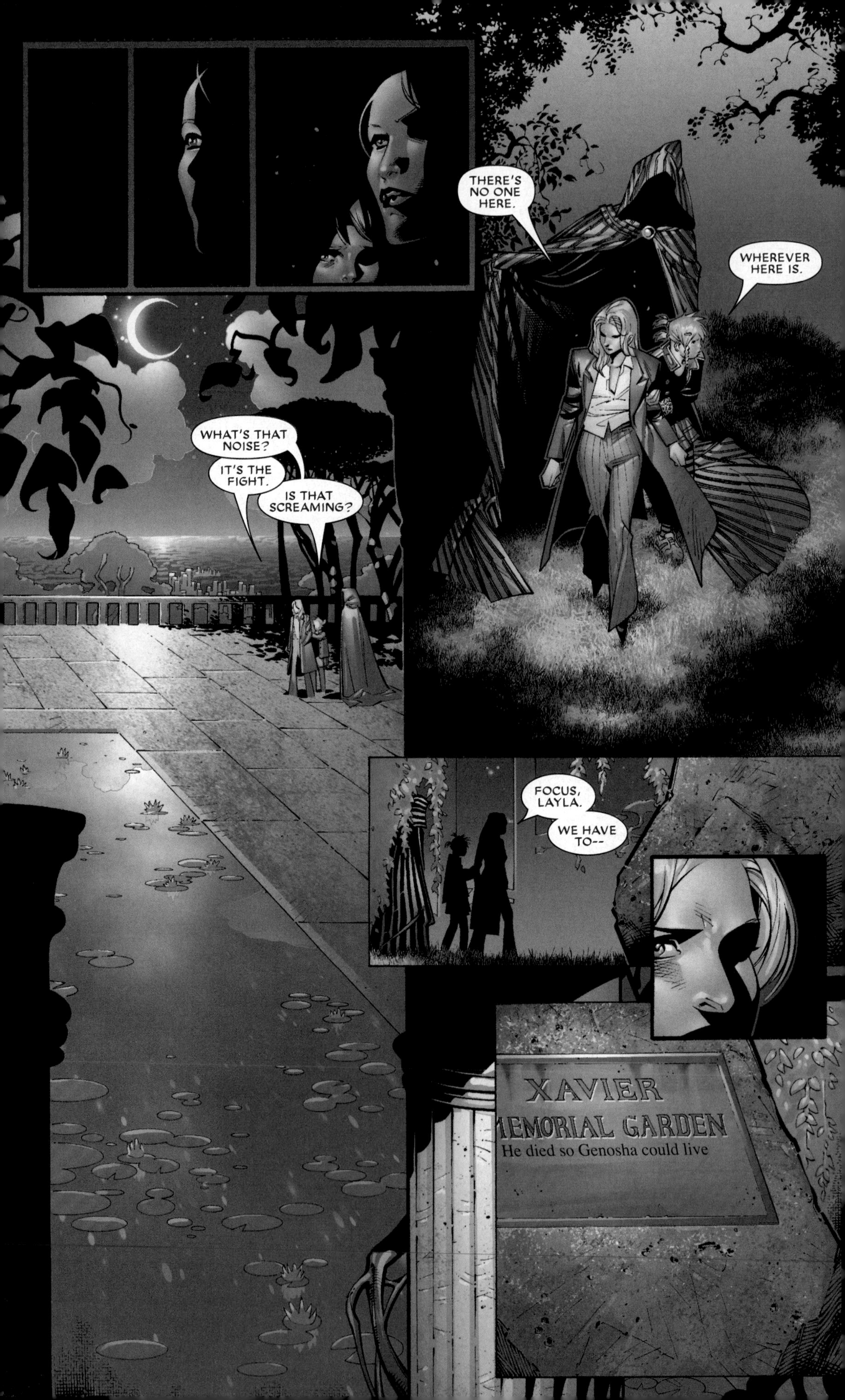

THERE'S NO ONE HERE.
WHEREVER HERE IS.
WHAT'S THAT NOISE?
IT'S THE FIGHT.
IS THAT SCREAMING?
FOCUS, LAYLA.
WE HAVE TO--
XAVIER
MEMORIAL GARDEN
He died so Genosha could live

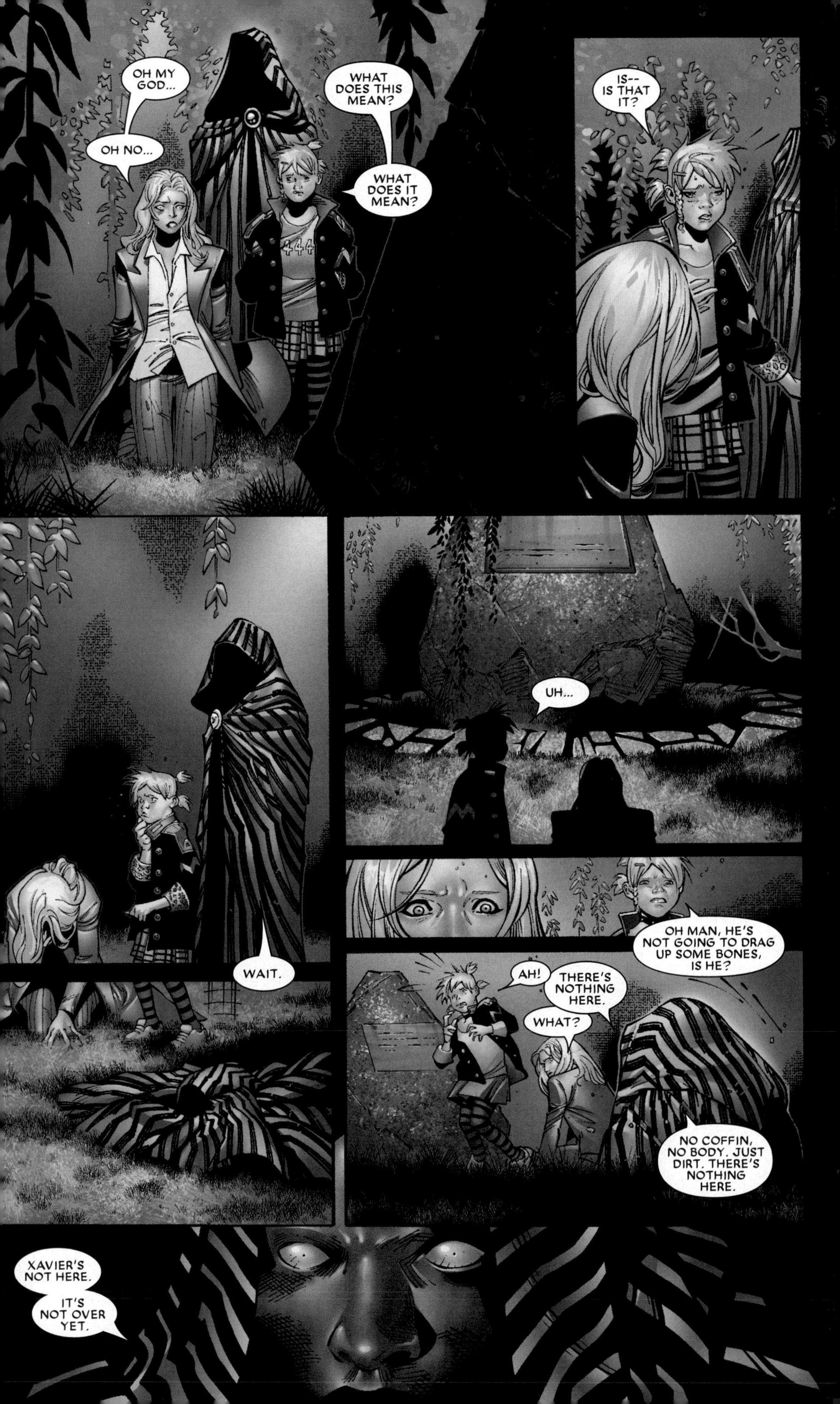

OH MY GOD...
OH NO...
WHAT DOES THIS MEAN?
WHAT DOES IT MEAN?
IS-- IS THAT IT?
WAIT.
UH...
OH MAN, HE'S NOT GOING TO DRAG UP SOME BONES, IS HE?
AH!
THERE'S NOTHING HERE.
WHAT?
NO COFFIN, NO BODY. JUST DIRT. THERE'S NOTHING HERE.
XAVIER'S NOT HERE.
IT'S NOT OVER YET.

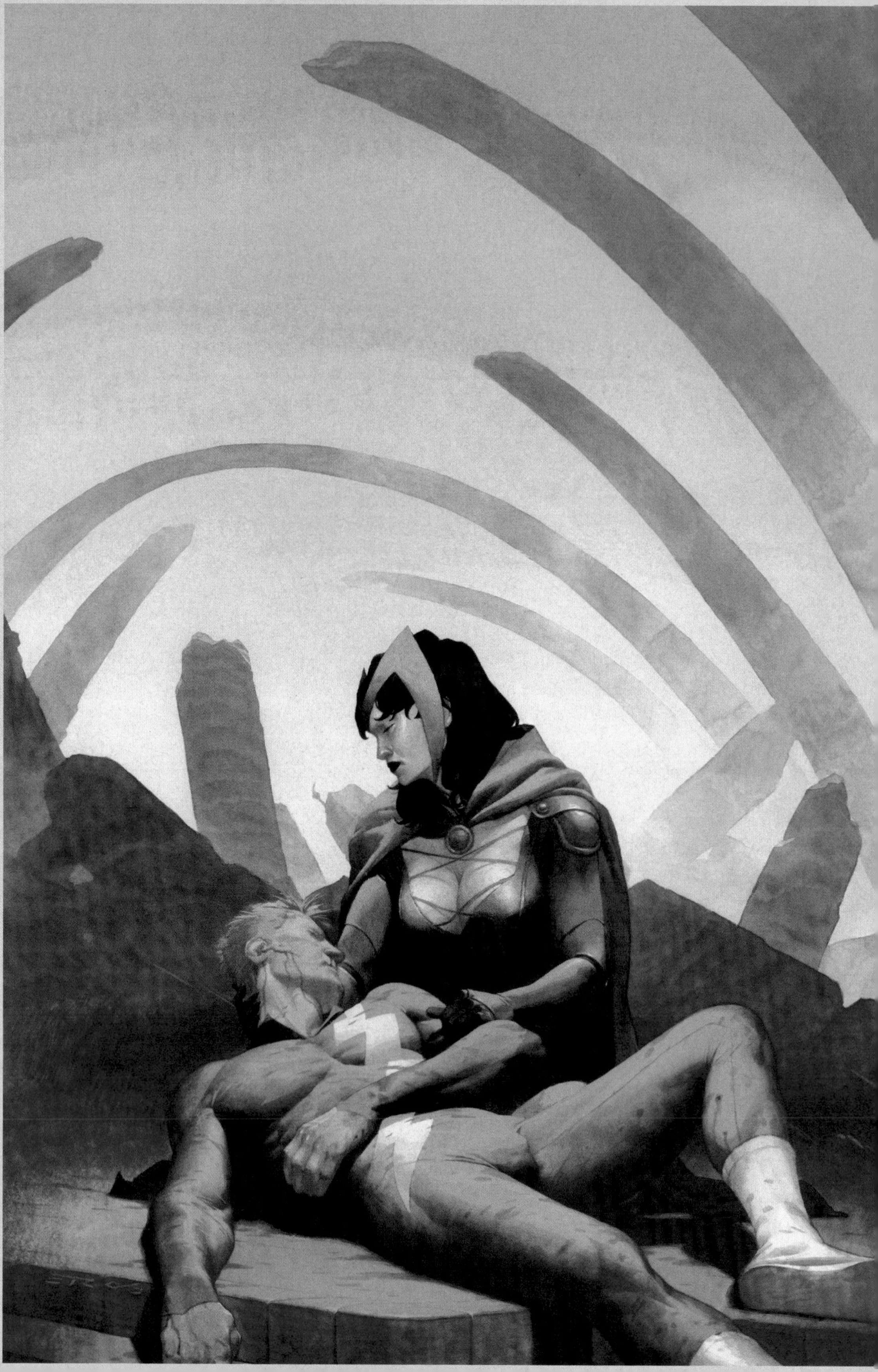

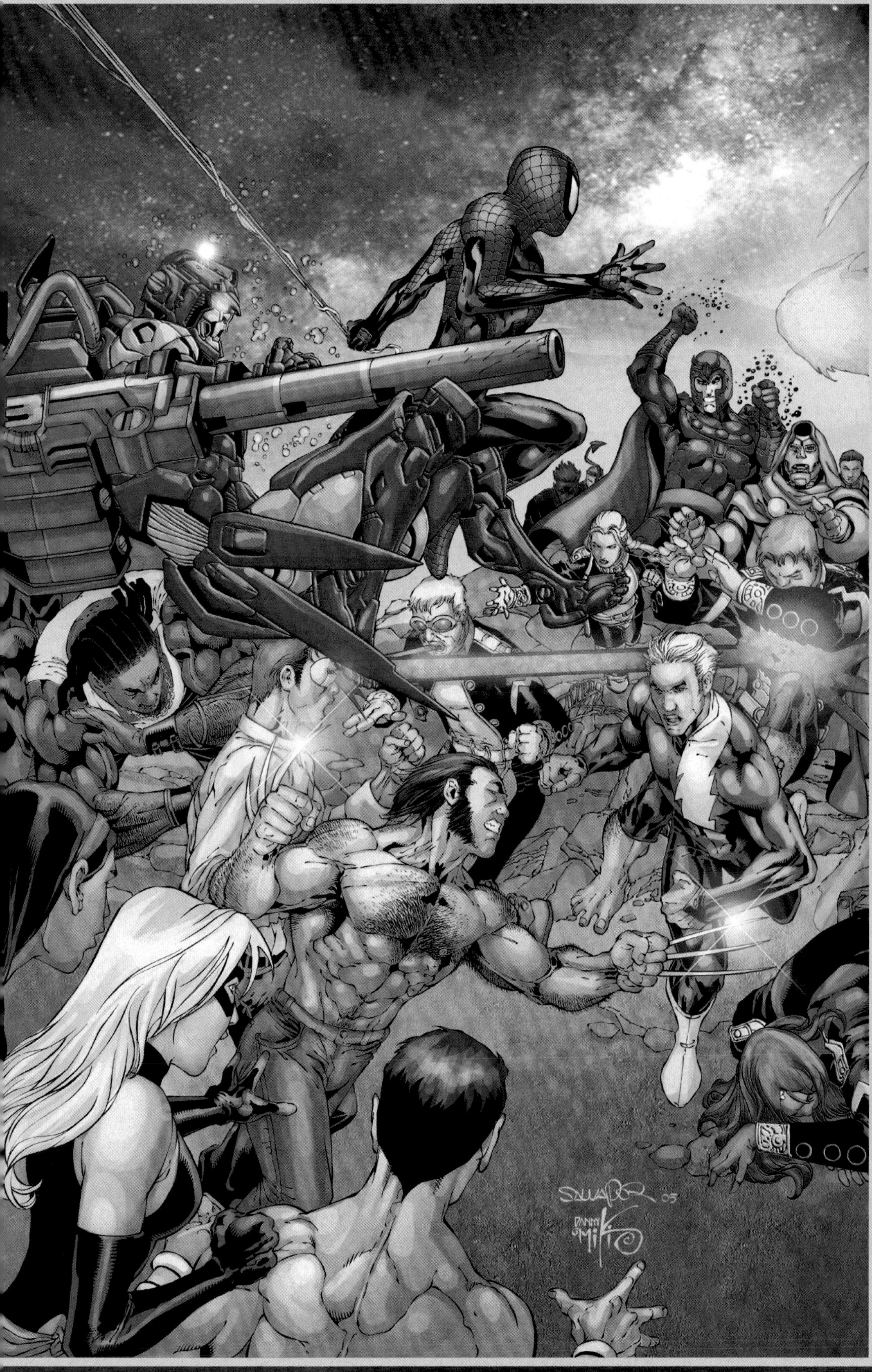

HOUSE OF M #7

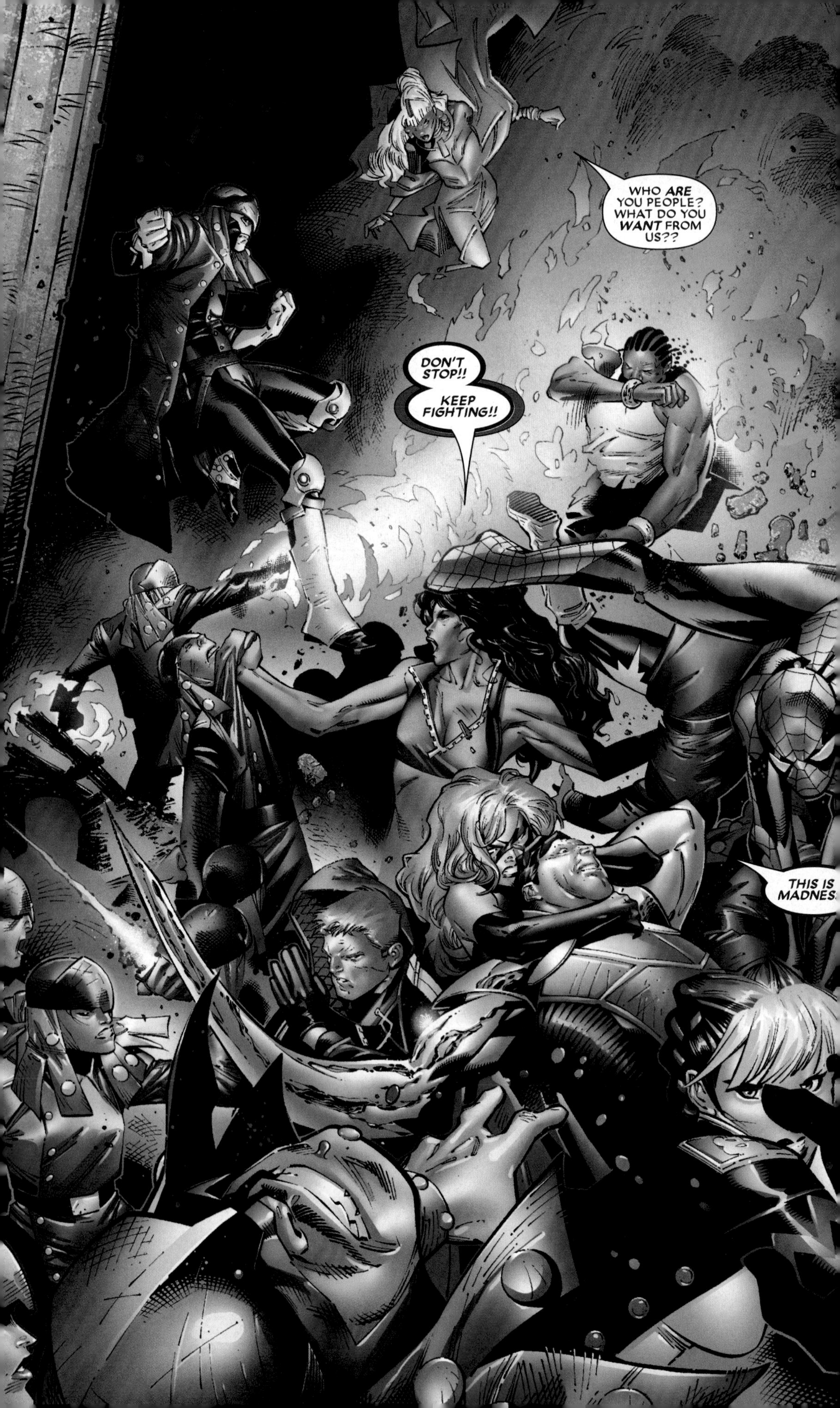

WHO ARE YOU PEOPLE? WHAT DO YOU WANT FROM US??
DON'T STOP!!
KEEP FIGHTING!!
THIS IS MADNES

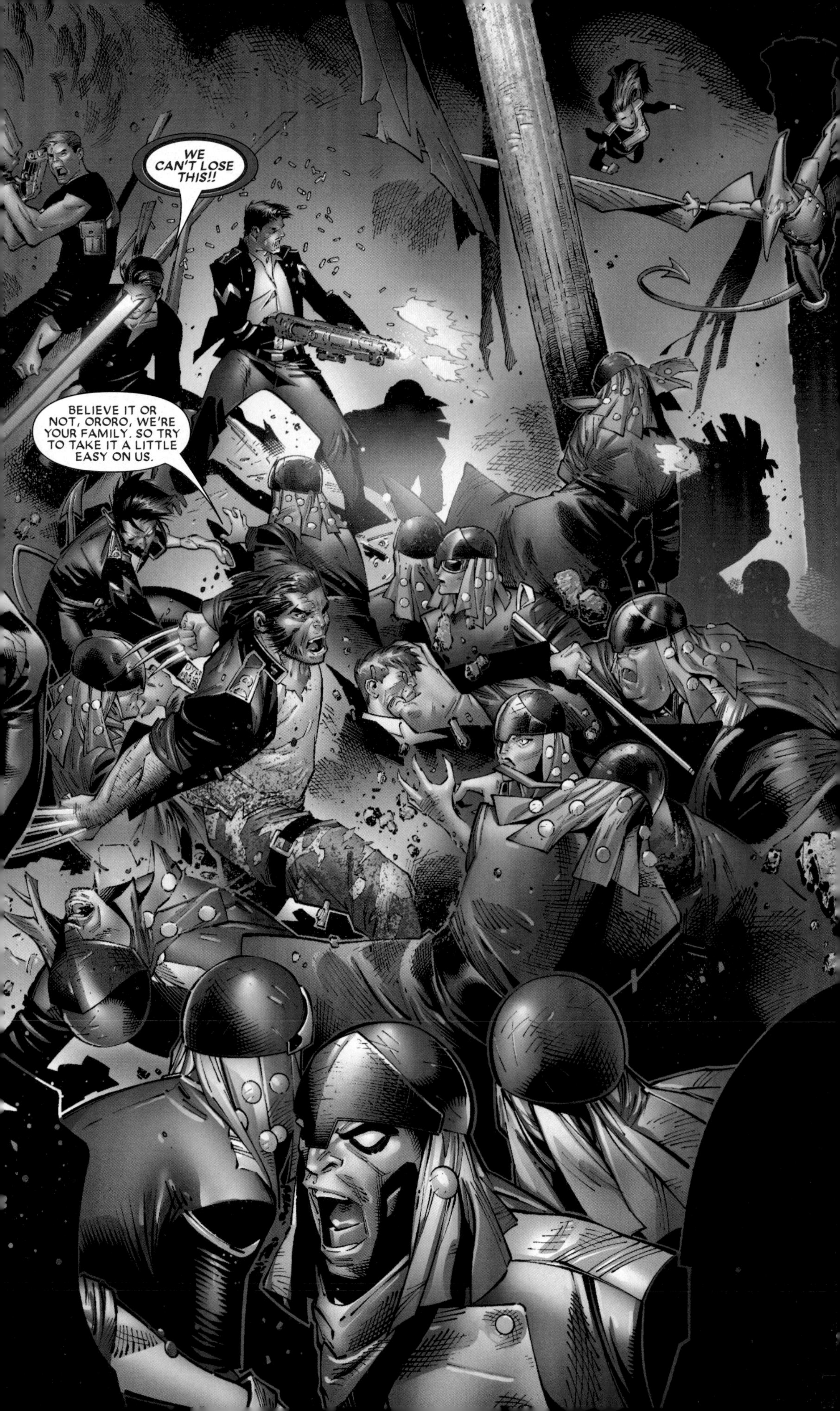
WE CAN'T LOSE THIS!!
BELIEVE IT OR NOT, ORORO, WE'RE YOUR FAMILY. SO TRY TO TAKE IT A LITTLE EASY ON US.

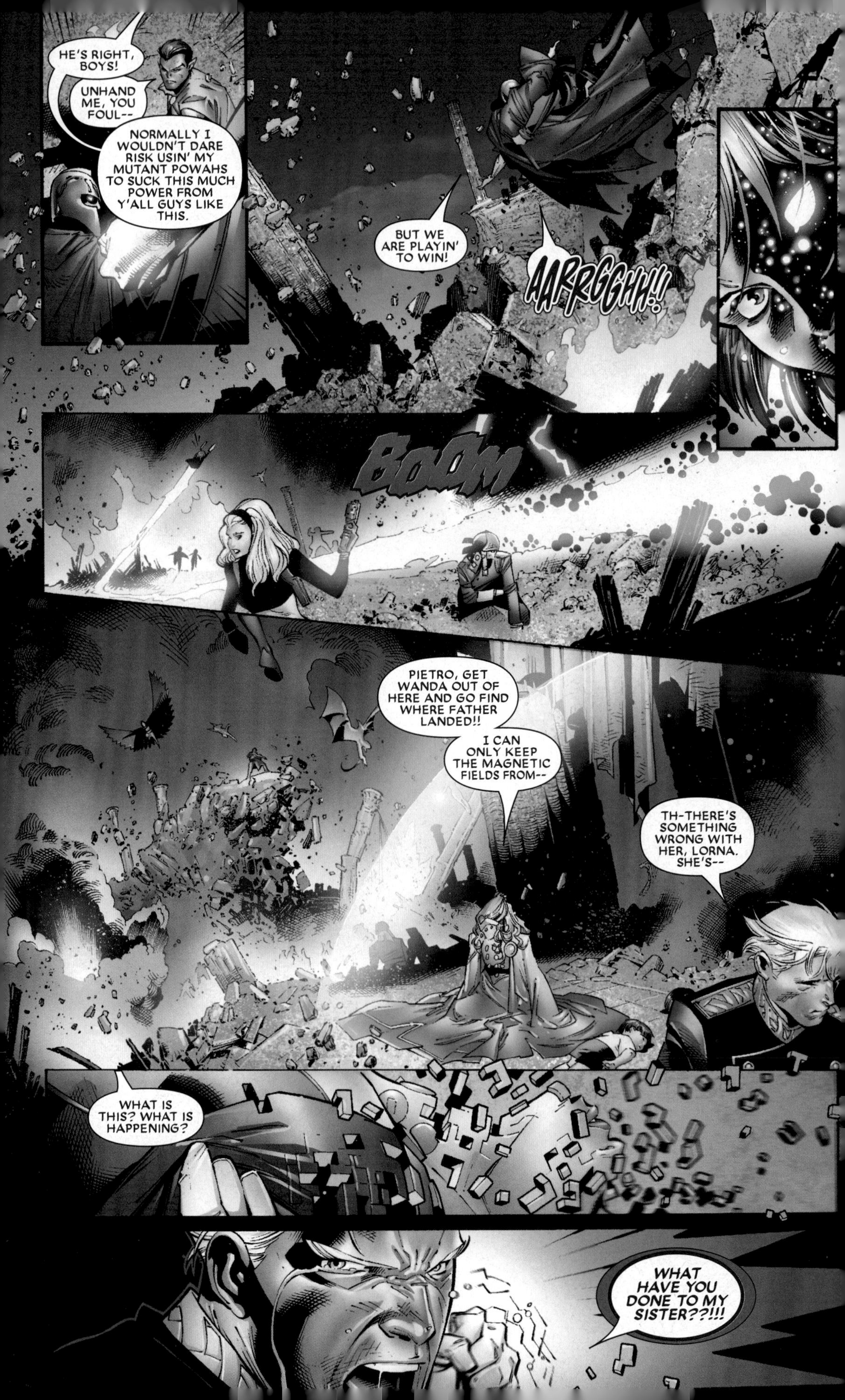
HE'S RIGHT, BOYS!
UNHAND ME, YOU FOUL--
NORMALLY I WOULDN'T DARE RISK USIN' MY MUTANT POWAHS TO SUCK THIS MUCH POWER FROM Y'ALL GUYS LIKE THIS.
BUT WE ARE PLAYIN' TO WIN!
AARRGGHH!!
BOOM
PIETRO, GET WANDA OUT OF HERE AND GO FIND WHERE FATHER LANDED!!
I CAN ONLY KEEP THE MAGNETIC FIELDS FROM--
TH-THERE'S SOMETHING WRONG WITH HER, LORNA. SHE'S--
WHAT IS THIS? WHAT IS HAPPENING?
WHAT HAVE YOU DONE TO MY SISTER??!!!

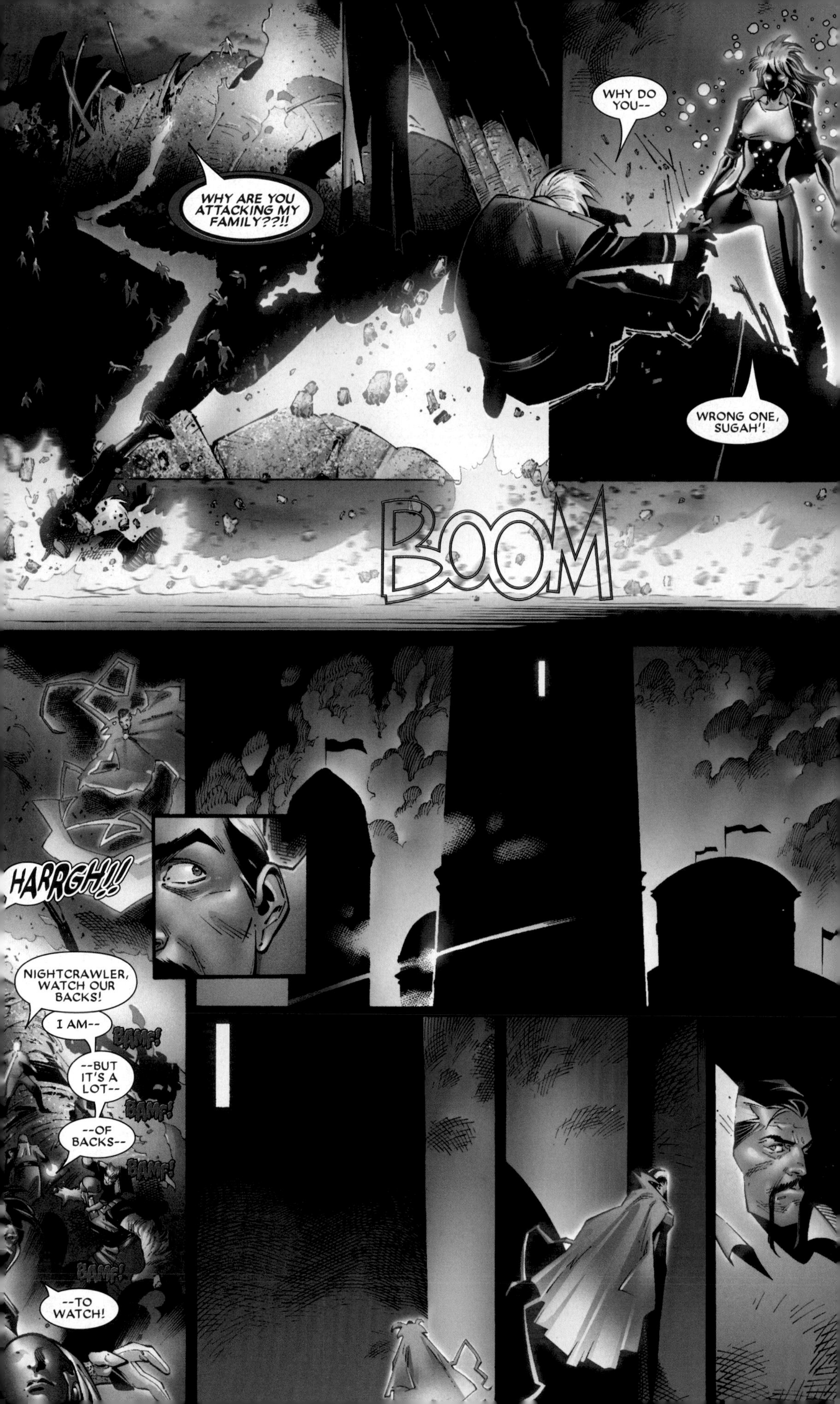
WHY ARE YOU ATTACKING MY FAMILY??!!
WHY DO YOU--
WRONG ONE, SUGAH'!
BOOM
HARRGH!!
NIGHTCRAWLER, WATCH OUR BACKS!
I AM--
BAMF!
--BUT IT'S A LOT--
BAMF!
--OF BACKS--
BAMF!
BAMF!
--TO WATCH!

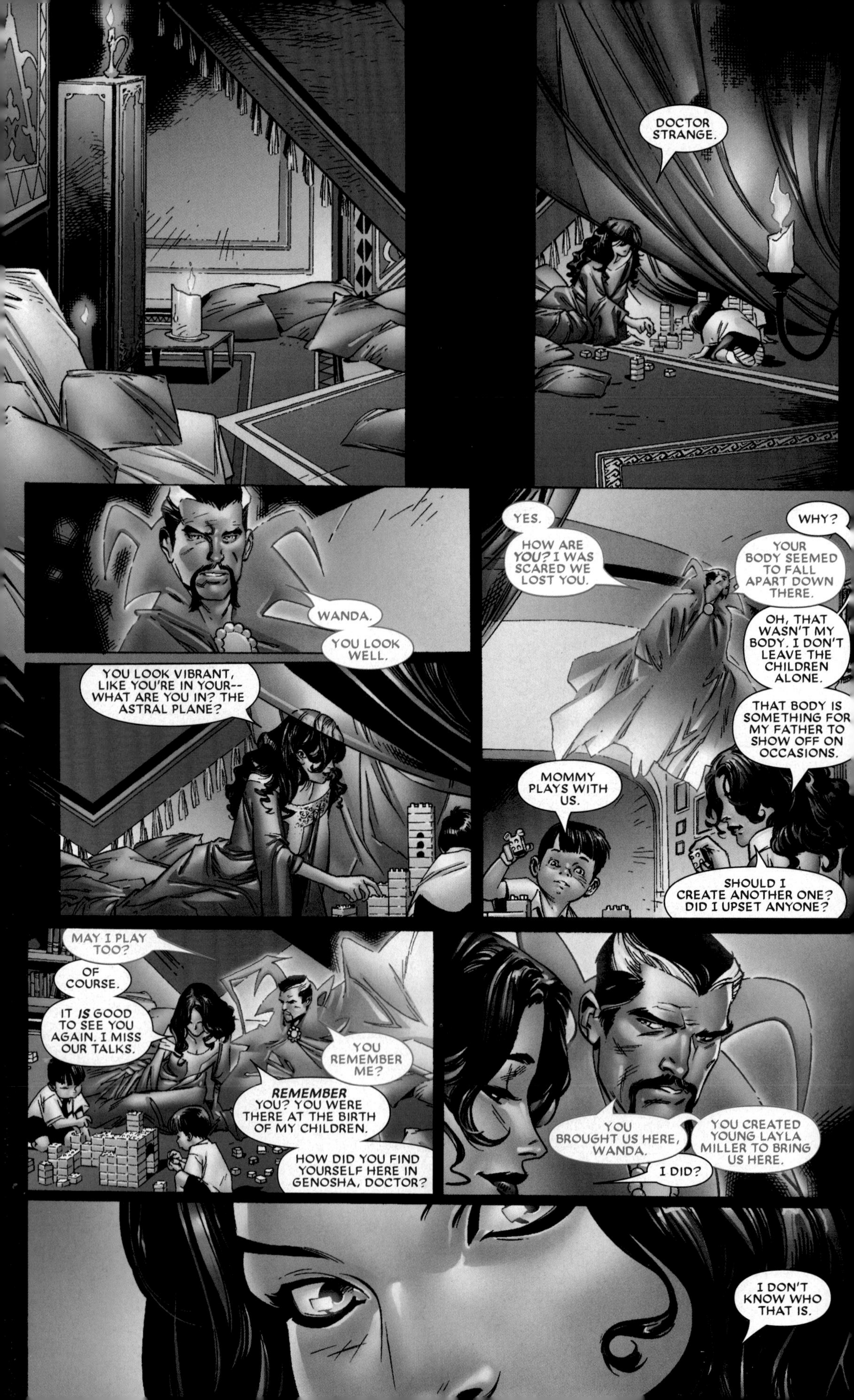
DOCTOR STRANGE.
WANDA.
YOU LOOK WELL.
YOU LOOK VIBRANT, LIKE YOU'RE IN YOUR-- WHAT ARE YOU IN? THE ASTRAL PLANE?
YES.
HOW ARE *YOU?* I WAS SCARED WE LOST YOU.
WHY?
YOUR BODY SEEMED TO FALL APART DOWN THERE.
OH, THAT WASN'T MY BODY. I DON'T LEAVE THE CHILDREN ALONE.
THAT BODY IS SOMETHING FOR MY FATHER TO SHOW OFF ON OCCASIONS.
MOMMY PLAYS WITH US.
SHOULD I CREATE ANOTHER ONE? DID I UPSET ANYONE?
MAY I PLAY TOO?
OF COURSE.
IT ***IS*** GOOD TO SEE YOU AGAIN. I MISS OUR TALKS.
YOU REMEMBER ME?
REMEMBER YOU? YOU WERE THERE AT THE BIRTH OF MY CHILDREN.
HOW DID YOU FIND YOURSELF HERE IN GENOSHA, DOCTOR?
YOU BROUGHT US HERE, WANDA.
YOU CREATED YOUNG LAYLA MILLER TO BRING US HERE.
I DID?
I DON'T KNOW WHO THAT IS.

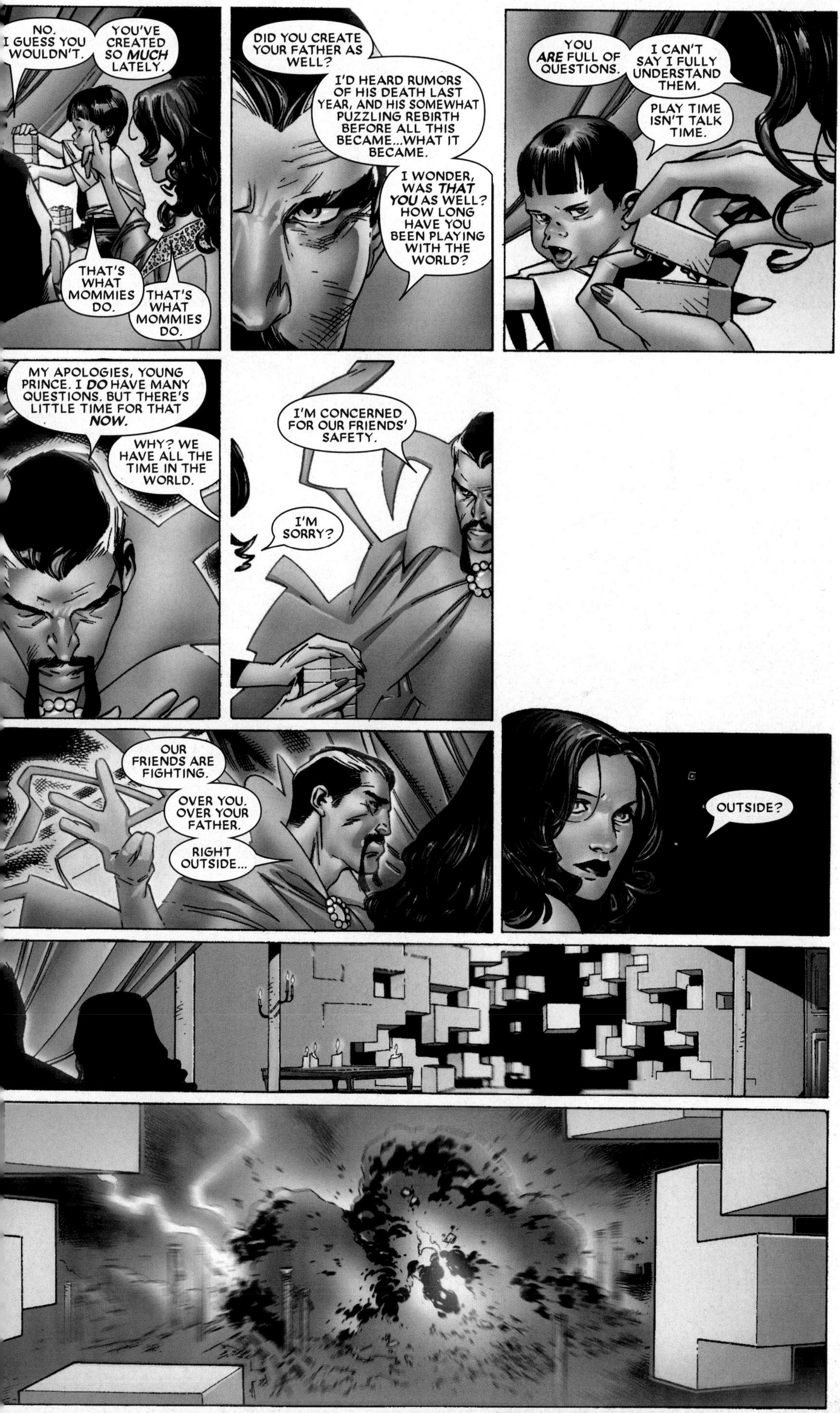

NO. I GUESS YOU WOULDN'T.
YOU'VE CREATED SO *MUCH* LATELY.
THAT'S WHAT MOMMIES DO.
THAT'S WHAT MOMMIES DO.
DID YOU CREATE YOUR FATHER AS WELL?
I'D HEARD RUMORS OF HIS DEATH LAST YEAR, AND HIS SOMEWHAT PUZZLING REBIRTH BEFORE ALL THIS BECAME...WHAT IT BECAME.
I WONDER, WAS *THAT YOU* AS WELL? HOW LONG HAVE YOU BEEN PLAYING WITH THE WORLD?
YOU *ARE* FULL OF QUESTIONS.
I CAN'T SAY I FULLY UNDERSTAND THEM.
PLAY TIME ISN'T TALK TIME.
MY APOLOGIES, YOUNG PRINCE. I *DO* HAVE MANY QUESTIONS. BUT THERE'S LITTLE TIME FOR THAT *NOW.*
WHY? WE HAVE ALL THE TIME IN THE WORLD.
I'M CONCERNED FOR OUR FRIENDS' SAFETY.
I'M SORRY?
OUR FRIENDS ARE FIGHTING.
OVER YOU. OVER YOUR FATHER.
RIGHT OUTSIDE...
OUTSIDE?

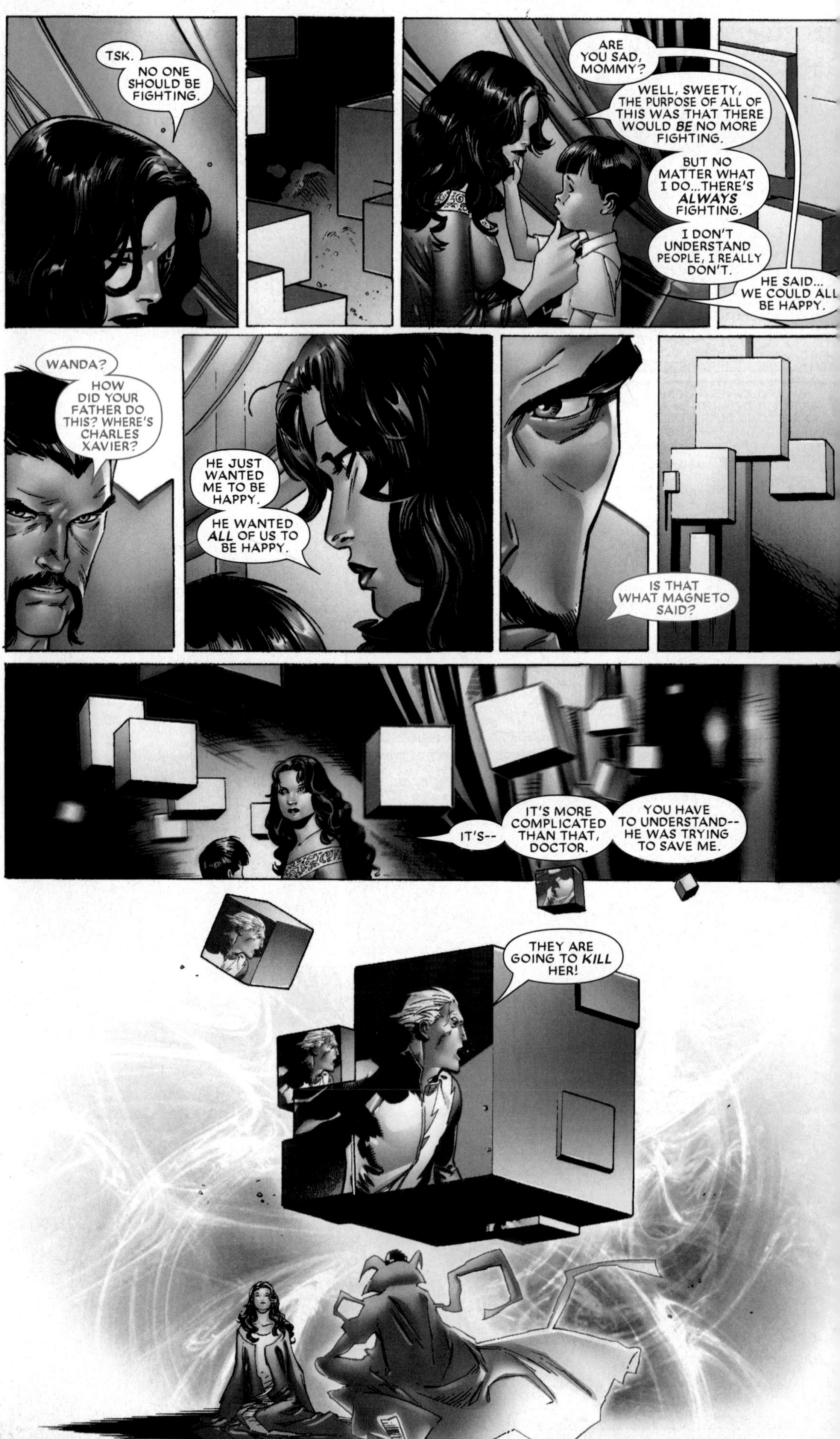
TSK.
NO ONE SHOULD BE FIGHTING.
ARE YOU SAD, MOMMY?
WELL, SWEETY, THE PURPOSE OF ALL OF THIS WAS THAT THERE WOULD BE NO MORE FIGHTING.
BUT NO MATTER WHAT I DO...THERE'S ALWAYS FIGHTING.
I DON'T UNDERSTAND PEOPLE, I REALLY DON'T.
HE SAID... WE COULD ALL BE HAPPY.
WANDA?
HOW DID YOUR FATHER DO THIS? WHERE'S CHARLES XAVIER?
HE JUST WANTED ME TO BE HAPPY.
HE WANTED ALL OF US TO BE HAPPY.
IS THAT WHAT MAGNETO SAID?
IT'S--
IT'S MORE COMPLICATED THAN THAT, DOCTOR.
YOU HAVE TO UNDERSTAND-- HE WAS TRYING TO SAVE ME.
THEY ARE GOING TO KILL HER!

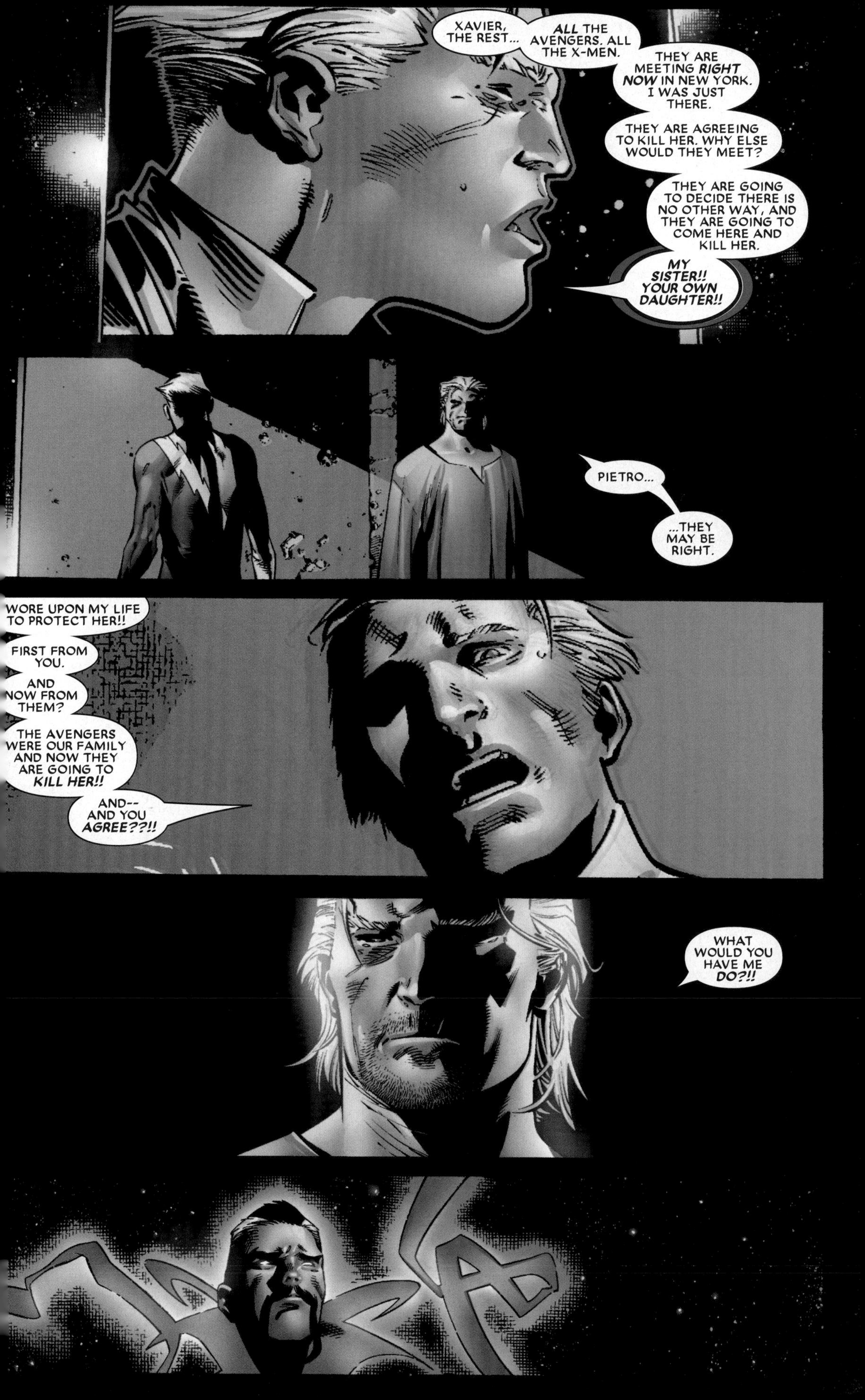

XAVIER, THE REST...
ALL THE AVENGERS. ALL THE X-MEN.
THEY ARE MEETING RIGHT NOW IN NEW YORK. I WAS JUST THERE.
THEY ARE AGREEING TO KILL HER. WHY ELSE WOULD THEY MEET?
THEY ARE GOING TO DECIDE THERE IS NO OTHER WAY, AND THEY ARE GOING TO COME HERE AND KILL HER.
MY SISTER!! YOUR OWN DAUGHTER!!
PIETRO...
...THEY MAY BE RIGHT.
WORE UPON MY LIFE TO PROTECT HER!!
FIRST FROM YOU.
AND NOW FROM THEM?
THE AVENGERS WERE OUR FAMILY AND NOW THEY ARE GOING TO KILL HER!!
AND-- AND YOU AGREE??!!
WHAT WOULD YOU HAVE ME DO?!!

THEY'RE GOING TO *KILL* HER!!

WHAT WOULD YOU HAVE ME *DO??!!*

AGGHHUH!

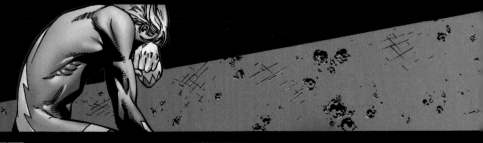

YOU SHOULDN'T YELL AT HIM, PIETRO.

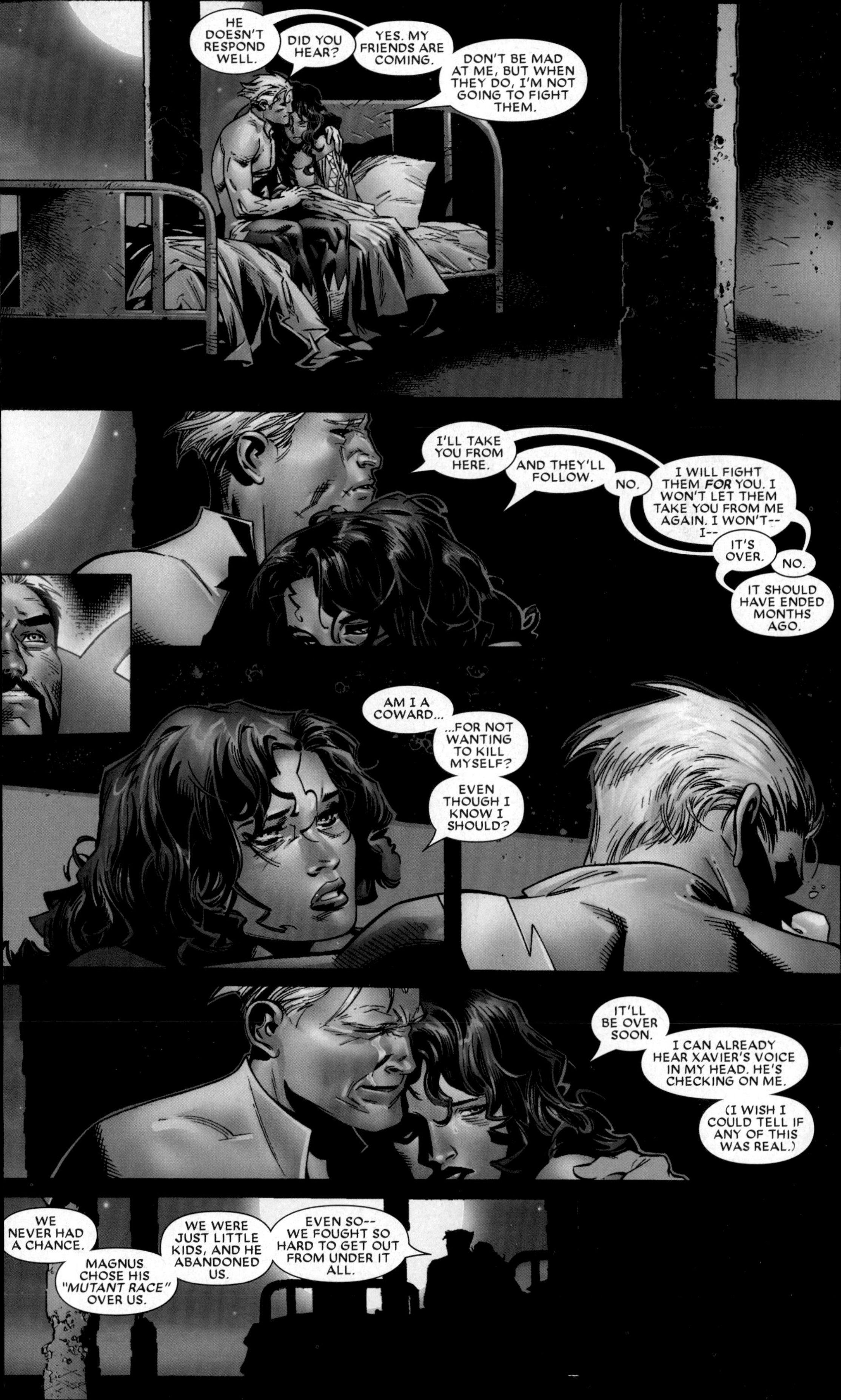
HE DOESN'T RESPOND WELL.
DID YOU HEAR?
YES. MY FRIENDS ARE COMING.
DON'T BE MAD AT ME, BUT WHEN THEY DO, I'M NOT GOING TO FIGHT THEM.
I'LL TAKE YOU FROM HERE.
AND THEY'LL FOLLOW.
NO.
I WILL FIGHT THEM *FOR* YOU. I WON'T LET THEM TAKE YOU FROM ME AGAIN. I WON'T-- I--
IT'S OVER.
NO.
IT SHOULD HAVE ENDED MONTHS AGO.
AM I A COWARD...
...FOR NOT WANTING TO KILL MYSELF?
EVEN THOUGH I KNOW I SHOULD?
IT'LL BE OVER SOON.
I CAN ALREADY HEAR XAVIER'S VOICE IN MY HEAD. HE'S CHECKING ON ME.
(I WISH I COULD TELL IF ANY OF THIS WAS REAL.)
WE NEVER HAD A CHANCE.
MAGNUS CHOSE HIS *"MUTANT RACE"* OVER US.
WE WERE JUST LITTLE KIDS, AND HE ABANDONED US.
EVEN SO-- WE FOUGHT SO HARD TO GET OUT FROM UNDER IT ALL.

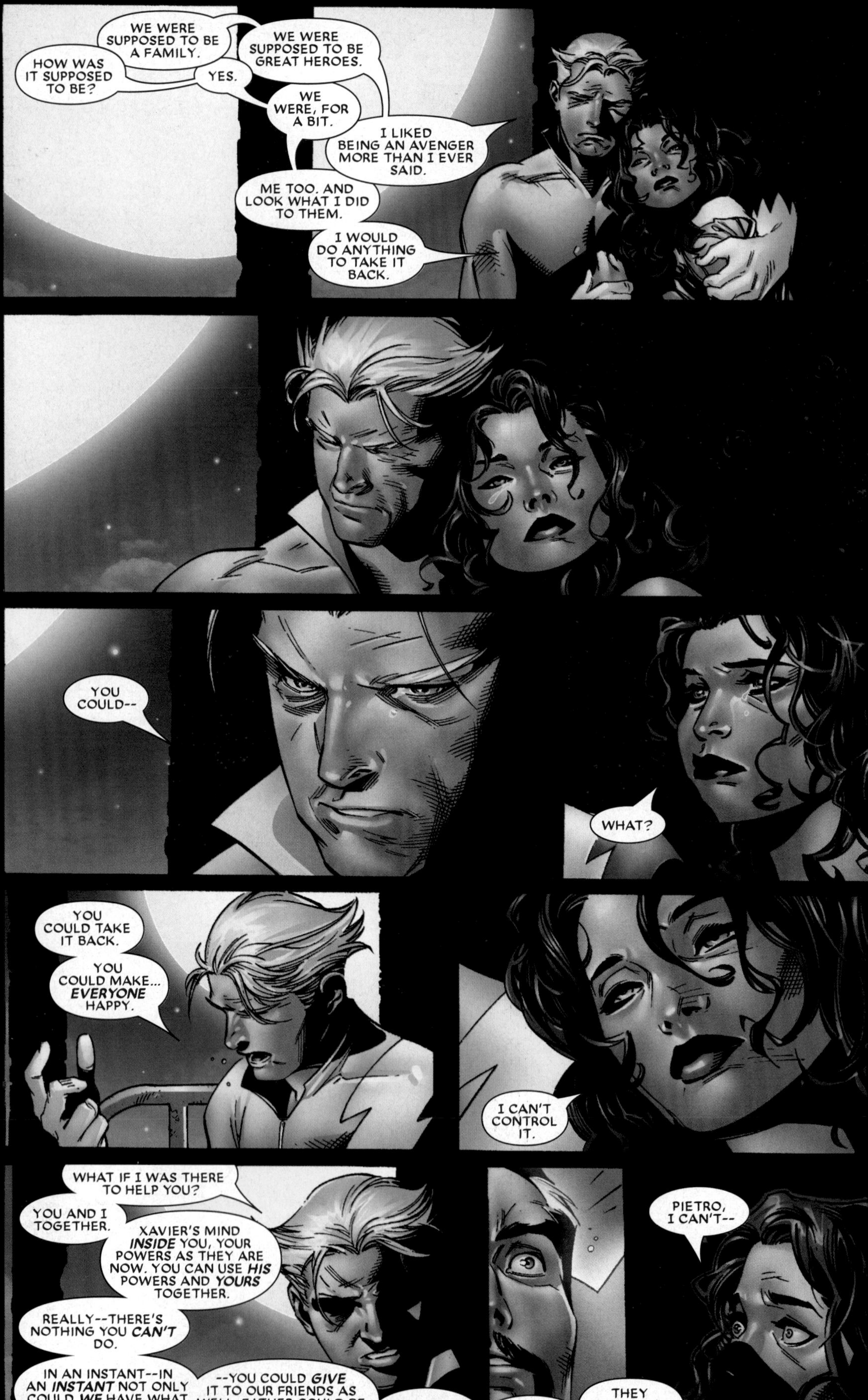
HOW WAS IT SUPPOSED TO BE?
WE WERE SUPPOSED TO BE A FAMILY.
WE WERE SUPPOSED TO BE GREAT HEROES.
YES.
WE WERE, FOR A BIT.
I LIKED BEING AN AVENGER MORE THAN I EVER SAID.
ME TOO. AND LOOK WHAT I DID TO THEM.
I WOULD DO ANYTHING TO TAKE IT BACK.
YOU COULD--
WHAT?
YOU COULD TAKE IT BACK.
YOU COULD MAKE... *EVERYONE* HAPPY.
I CAN'T CONTROL IT.
WHAT IF I WAS THERE TO HELP YOU?
YOU AND I TOGETHER.
XAVIER'S MIND *INSIDE* YOU, YOUR POWERS AS THEY ARE NOW. YOU CAN USE *HIS* POWERS AND *YOURS* TOGETHER.
REALLY--THERE'S NOTHING YOU *CAN'T* DO.
IN AN INSTANT--IN AN *INSTANT* NOT ONLY COULD *WE* HAVE WHAT WE DESERVE--
--YOU COULD *GIVE* IT TO OUR FRIENDS AS WELL. FATHER COULD BE GIVEN EVERYTHING HE DREAMED OF.
WE CAN FINALLY BE A FAMILY.
THEY'D ALL BE HAPPY.
THEY WOULDN'T *BOTHER* US ANYMORE.
PIETRO, I CAN'T--

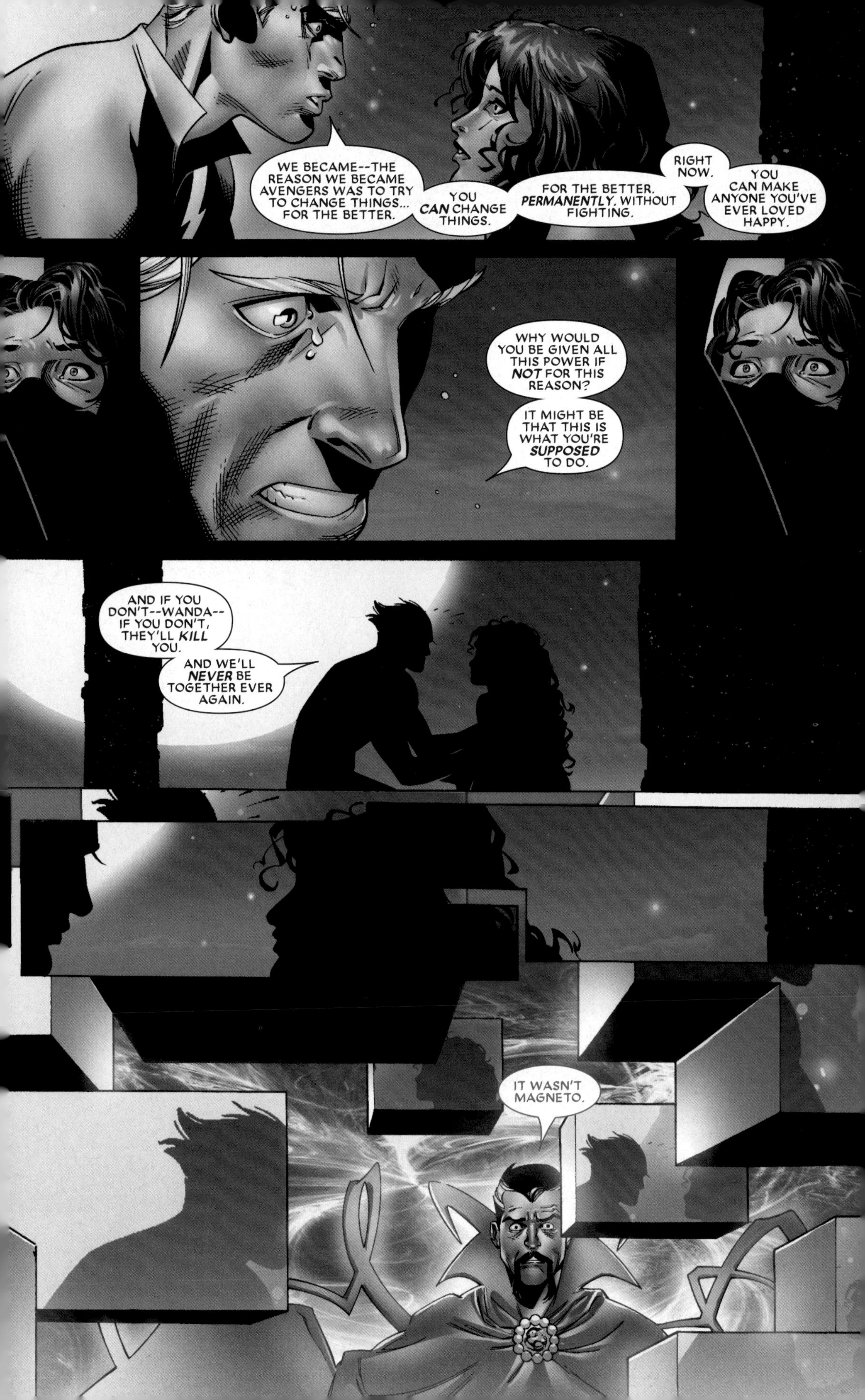
WE BECAME--THE REASON WE BECAME AVENGERS WAS TO TRY TO CHANGE THINGS... FOR THE BETTER.
YOU CAN CHANGE THINGS.
FOR THE BETTER. PERMANENTLY. WITHOUT FIGHTING.
RIGHT NOW.
YOU CAN MAKE ANYONE YOU'VE EVER LOVED HAPPY.
WHY WOULD YOU BE GIVEN ALL THIS POWER IF NOT FOR THIS REASON?
IT MIGHT BE THAT THIS IS WHAT YOU'RE SUPPOSED TO DO.
AND IF YOU DON'T--WANDA--IF YOU DON'T, THEY'LL KILL YOU.
AND WE'LL NEVER BE TOGETHER EVER AGAIN.
IT WASN'T MAGNETO.

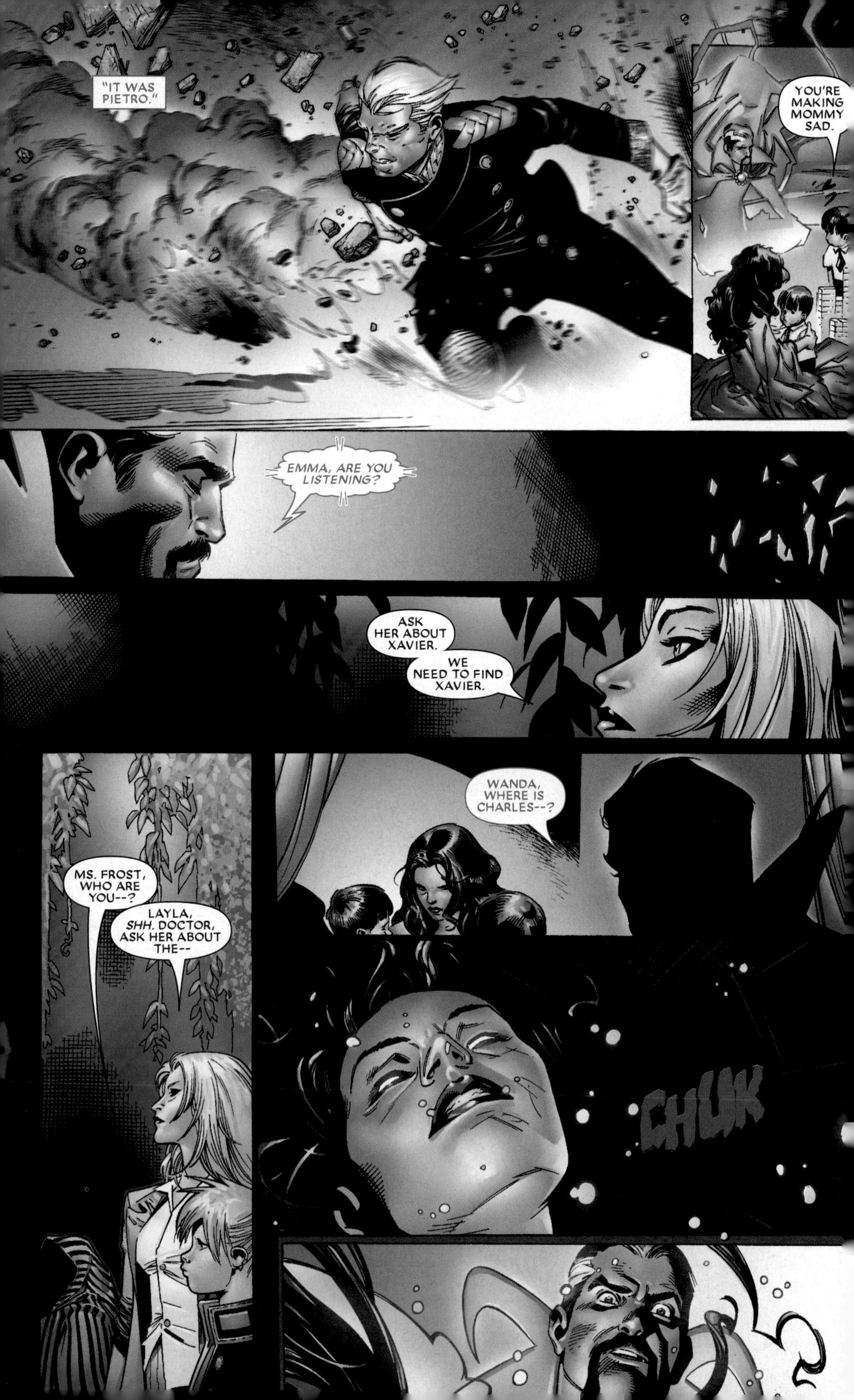
"IT WAS PIETRO."
YOU'RE MAKING MOMMY SAD.
EMMA, ARE YOU LISTENING?
ASK HER ABOUT XAVIER.
WE NEED TO FIND XAVIER.
MS. FROST, WHO ARE YOU--?
LAYLA, SHH. DOCTOR, ASK HER ABOUT THE--
WANDA, WHERE IS CHARLES--?
CHUK

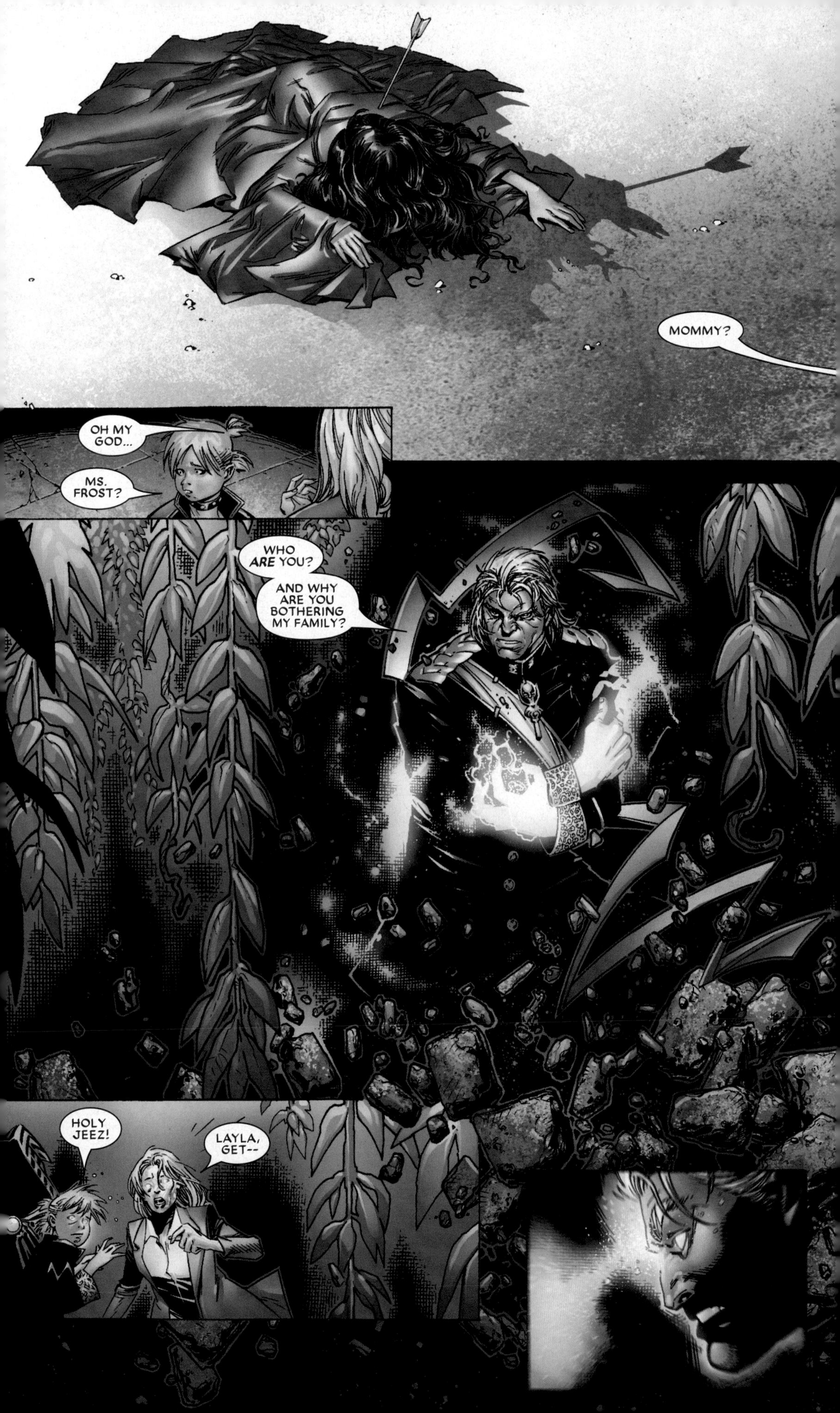
MOMMY?
OH MY GOD...
MS. FROST?
WHO ARE YOU?
AND WHY ARE YOU BOTHERING MY FAMILY?
HOLY JEEZ!
LAYLA, GET--

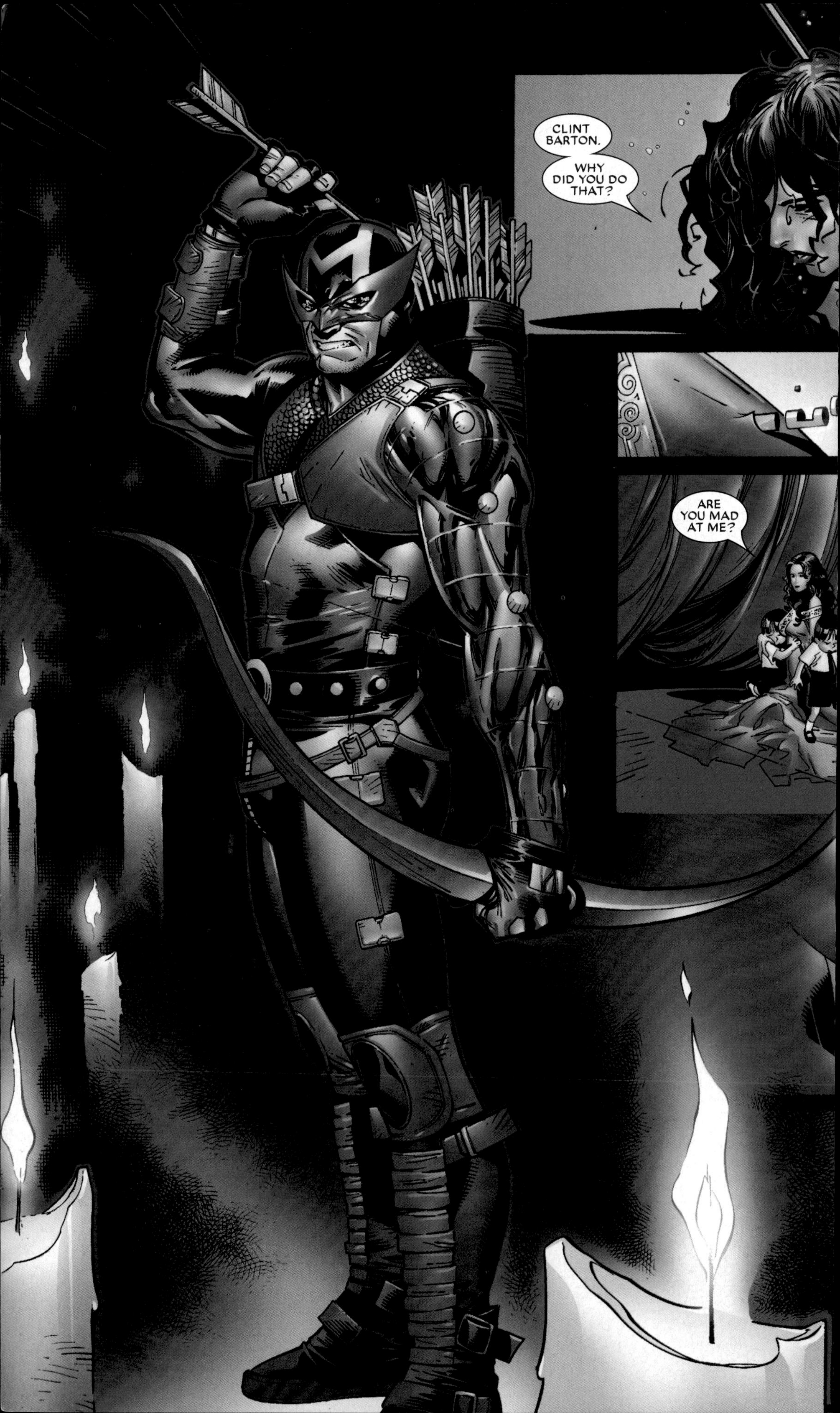
CLINT BARTON.
WHY DID YOU DO THAT?
ARE YOU MAD AT ME?

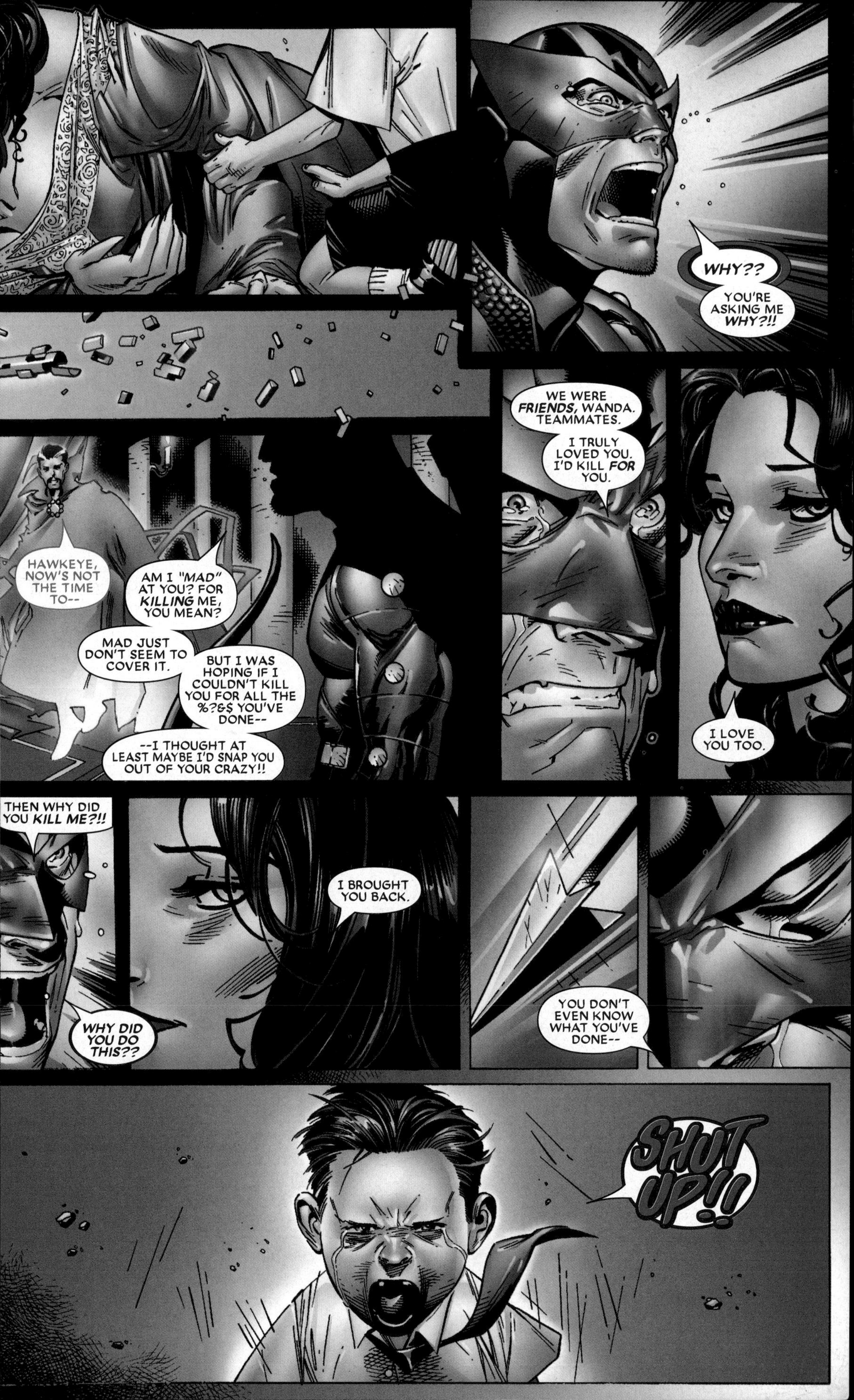
WHY??
YOU'RE ASKING ME WHY?!!
WE WERE FRIENDS, WANDA. TEAMMATES.
I TRULY LOVED YOU. I'D KILL FOR YOU.
I LOVE YOU TOO.
HAWKEYE, NOW'S NOT THE TIME TO--
AM I "MAD" AT YOU? FOR KILLING ME, YOU MEAN?
MAD JUST DON'T SEEM TO COVER IT.
BUT I WAS HOPING IF I COULDN'T KILL YOU FOR ALL THE %?&$ YOU'VE DONE--
--I THOUGHT AT LEAST MAYBE I'D SNAP YOU OUT OF YOUR CRAZY!!
THEN WHY DID YOU KILL ME?!!
WHY DID YOU DO THIS??
I BROUGHT YOU BACK.
YOU DON'T EVEN KNOW WHAT YOU'VE DONE--
SHUT UP!!

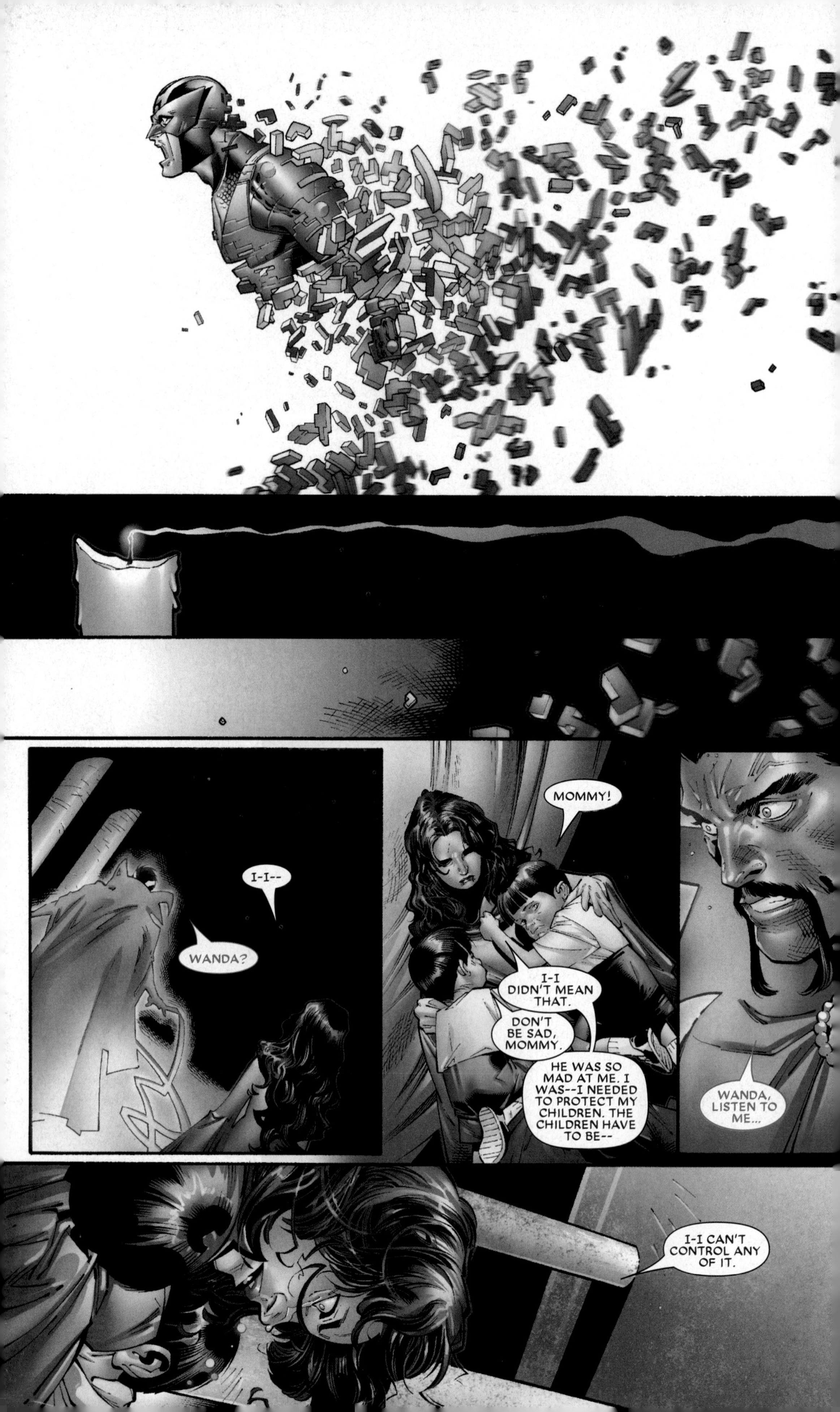
I-I--
WANDA?
MOMMY!
I-I DIDN'T MEAN THAT.
DON'T BE SAD, MOMMY.
HE WAS SO MAD AT ME. I WAS--I NEEDED TO PROTECT MY CHILDREN. THE CHILDREN HAVE TO BE--
WANDA, LISTEN TO ME...
I-I CAN'T CONTROL ANY OF IT.

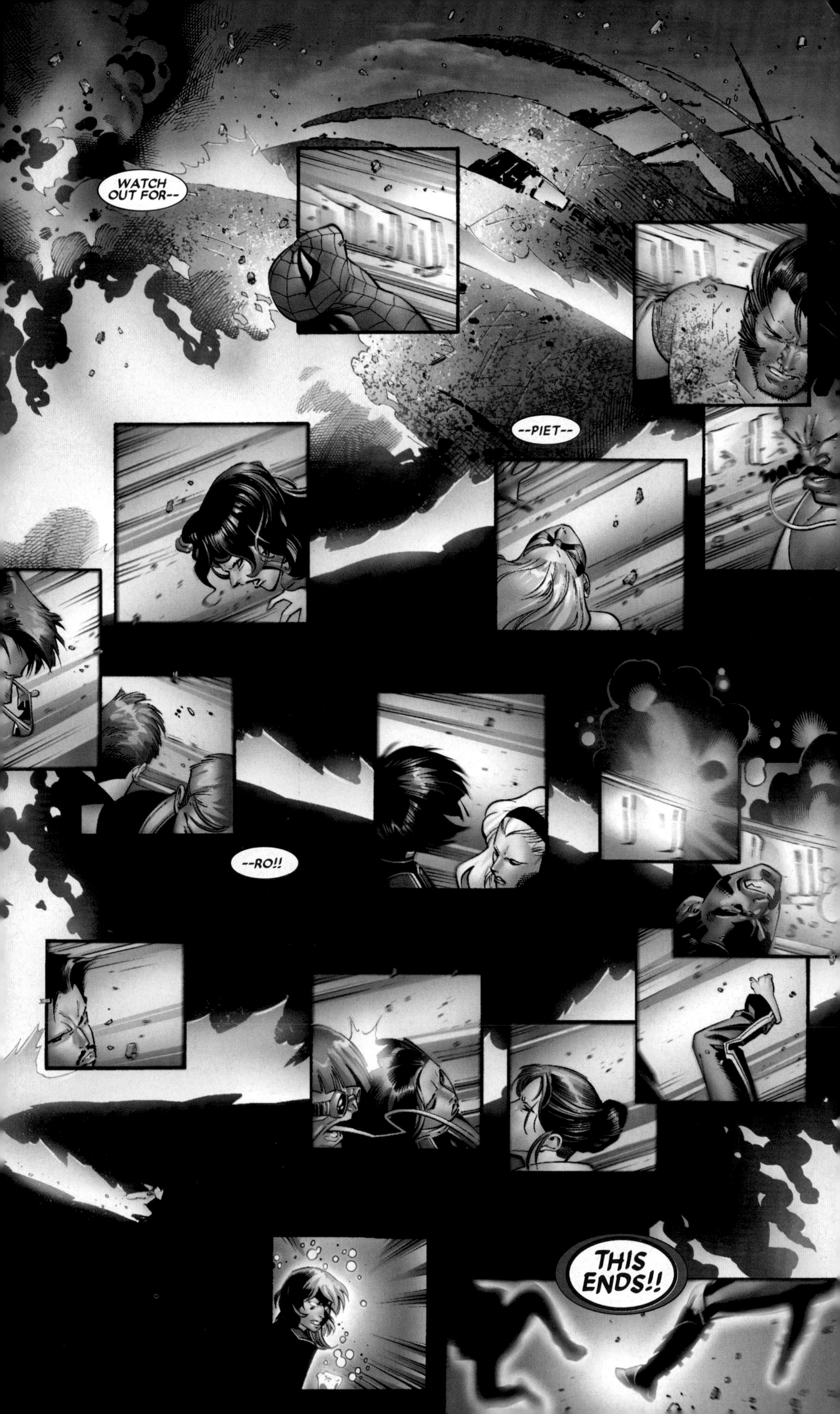
WATCH OUT FOR--
--PIET--
--RO!!
THIS ENDS!!

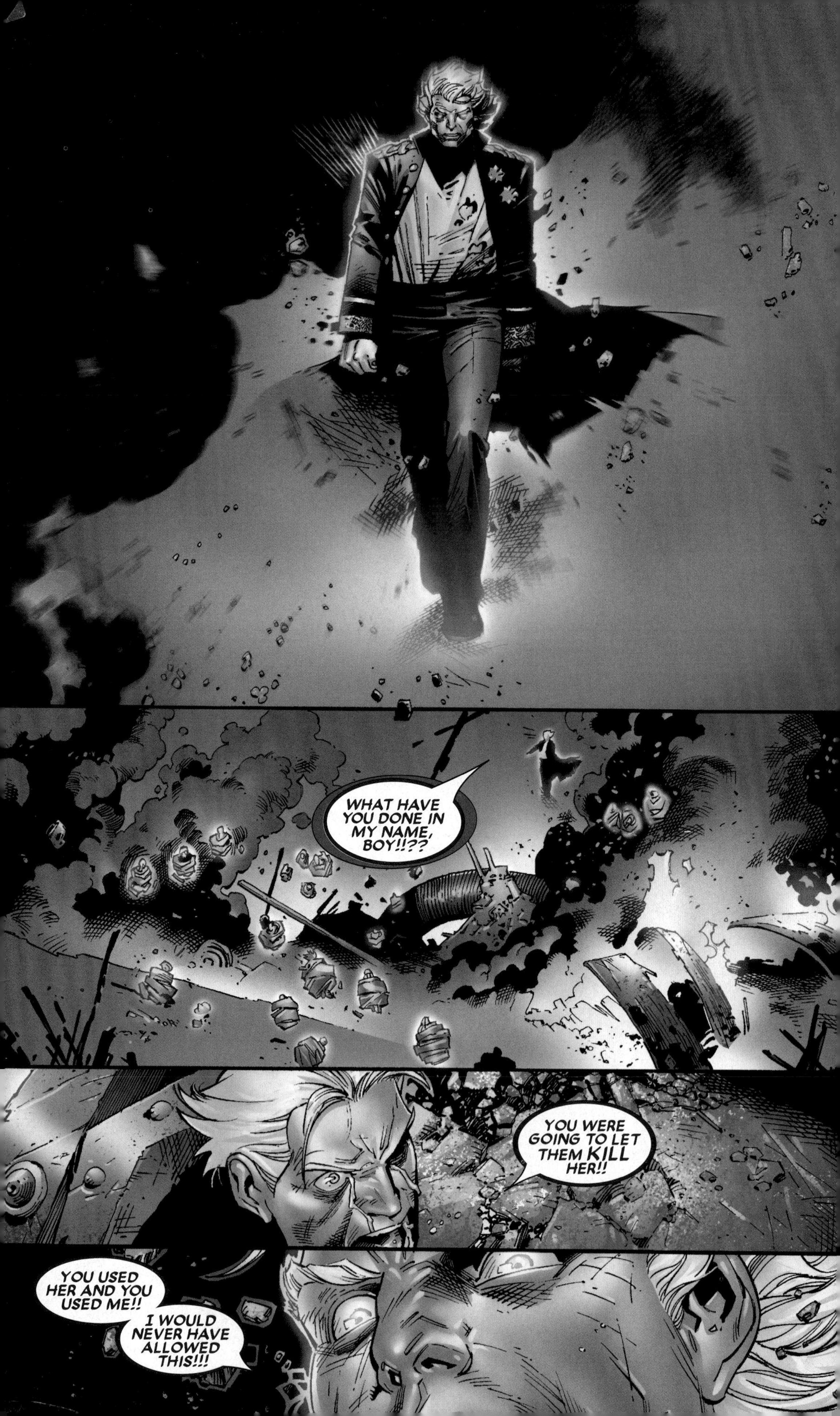
WHAT HAVE YOU DONE IN MY NAME, BOY!!??
YOU WERE GOING TO LET THEM KILL HER!!
YOU USED HER AND YOU USED ME!!
I WOULD NEVER HAVE ALLOWED THIS!!!

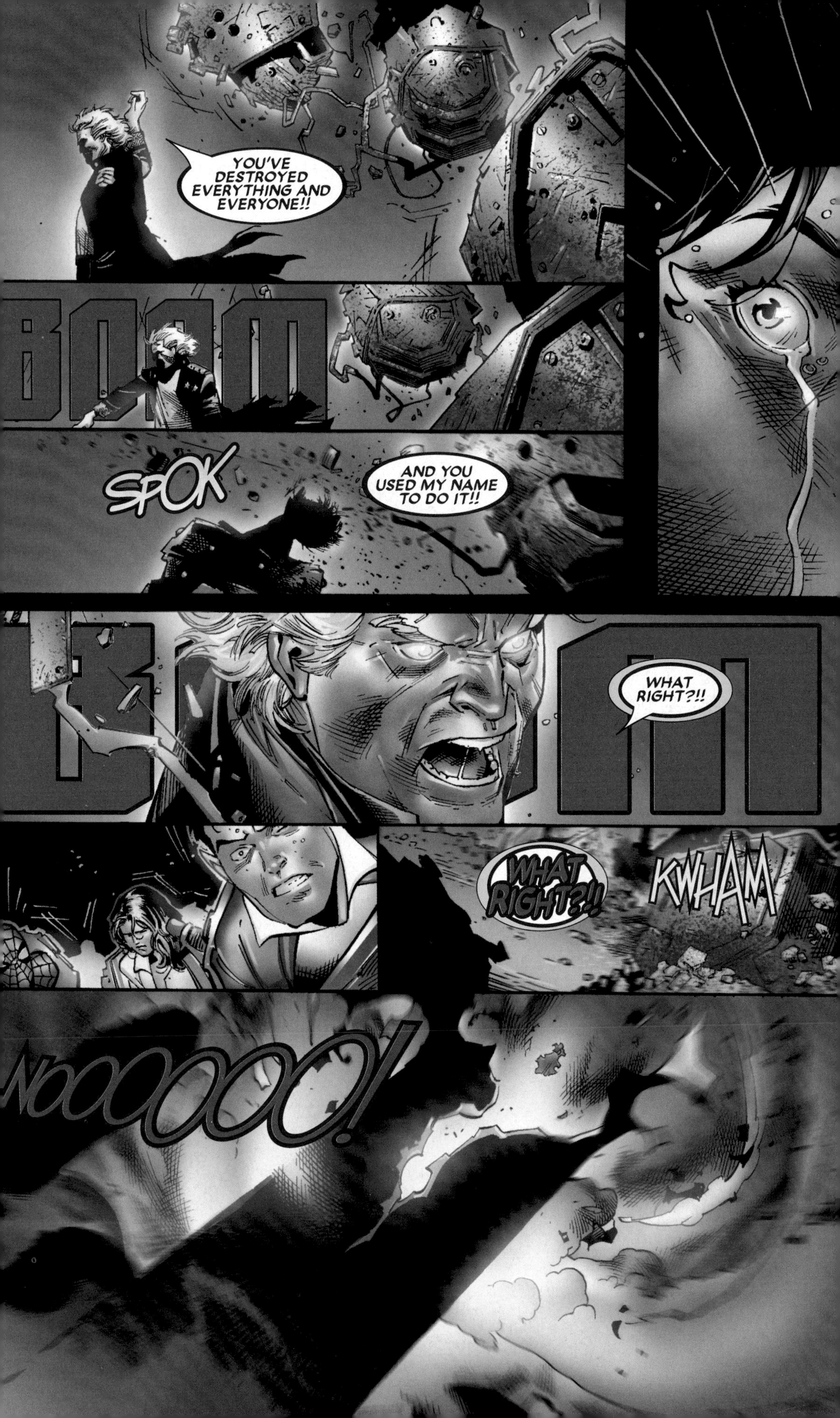
YOU'VE DESTROYED EVERYTHING AND EVERYONE!!
BOOM
SPOK
AND YOU USED MY NAME TO DO IT!!
WHAT RIGHT?!!
WHAT RIGHT?!!
KWHAM
NOOOOOO!

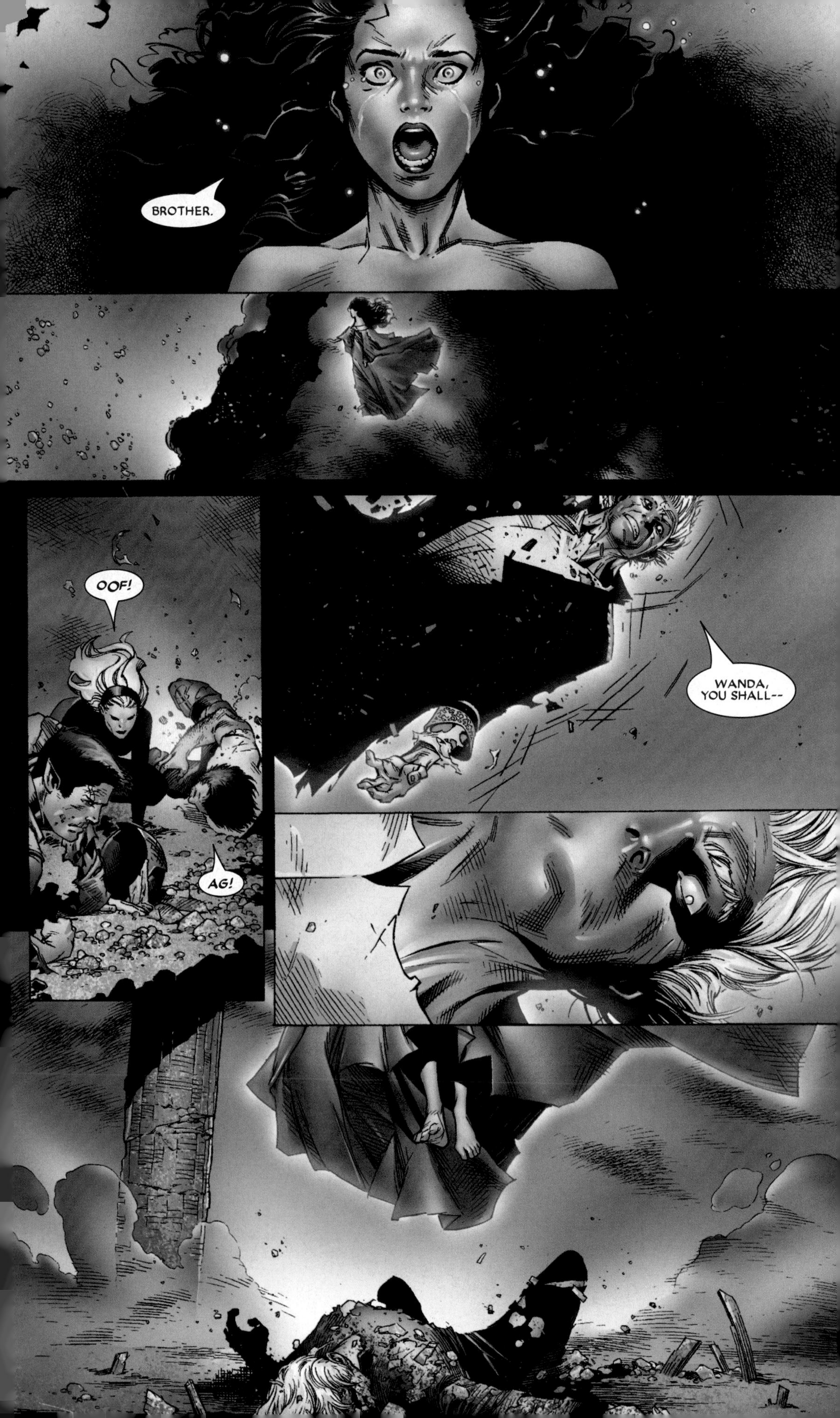
BROTHER.
OOF!
AG!
WANDA, YOU SHALL--

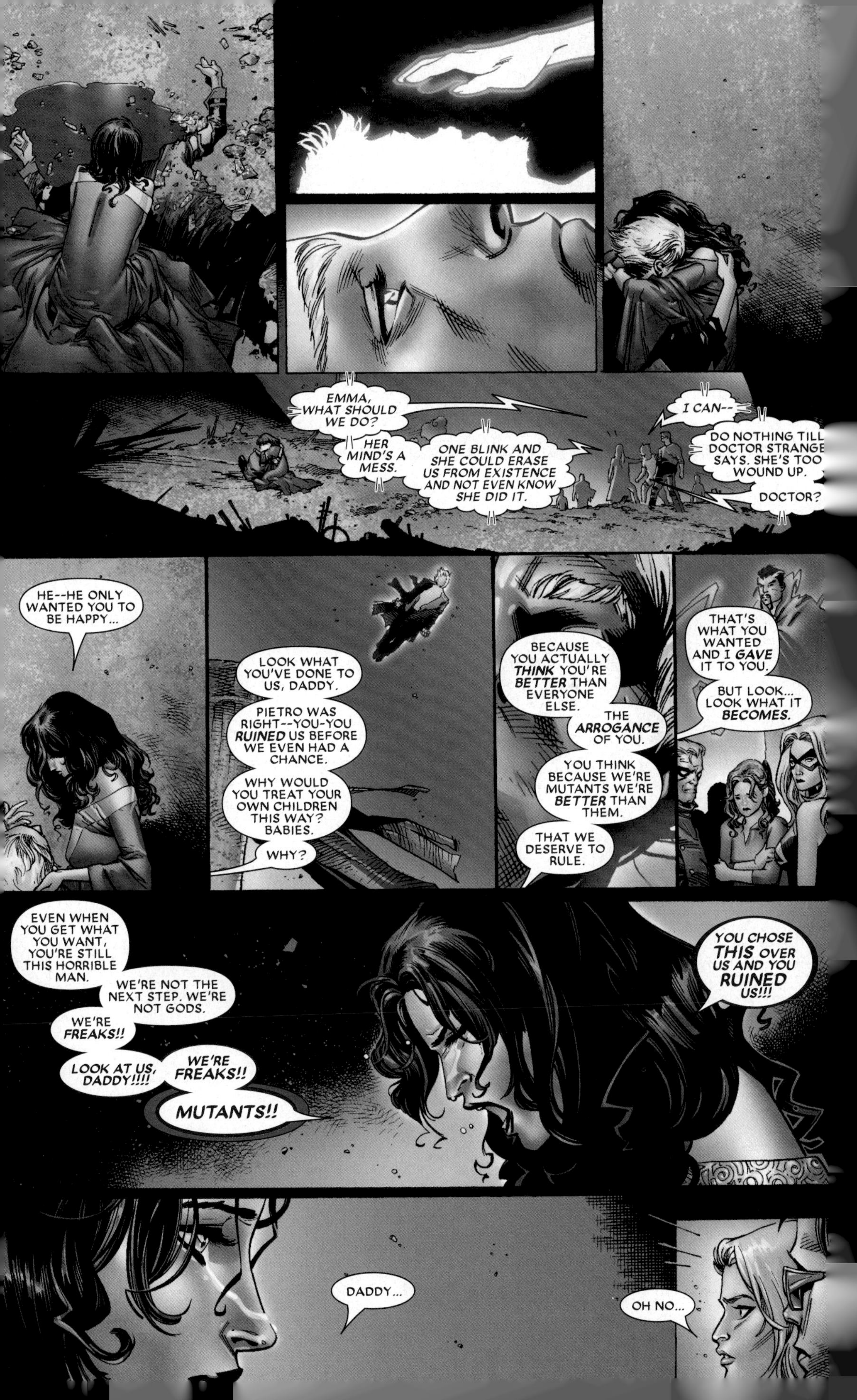
EMMA, WHAT SHOULD WE DO?
HER MIND'S A MESS.
ONE BLINK AND SHE COULD ERASE US FROM EXISTENCE AND NOT EVEN KNOW SHE DID IT.
I CAN--
DO NOTHING TILL DOCTOR STRANGE SAYS. SHE'S TOO WOUND UP.
DOCTOR?
HE--HE ONLY WANTED YOU TO BE HAPPY...
LOOK WHAT YOU'VE DONE TO US, DADDY.
PIETRO WAS RIGHT--YOU-YOU RUINED US BEFORE WE EVEN HAD A CHANCE.
WHY WOULD YOU TREAT YOUR OWN CHILDREN THIS WAY? BABIES.
WHY?
BECAUSE YOU ACTUALLY THINK YOU'RE BETTER THAN EVERYONE ELSE.
THE ARROGANCE OF YOU.
YOU THINK BECAUSE WE'RE MUTANTS WE'RE BETTER THAN THEM.
THAT WE DESERVE TO RULE.
THAT'S WHAT YOU WANTED AND I GAVE IT TO YOU.
BUT LOOK... LOOK WHAT IT BECOMES.
EVEN WHEN YOU GET WHAT YOU WANT, YOU'RE STILL THIS HORRIBLE MAN.
WE'RE NOT THE NEXT STEP. WE'RE NOT GODS.
WE'RE FREAKS!!
LOOK AT US, DADDY!!!!
WE'RE FREAKS!!
MUTANTS!!
YOU CHOSE THIS OVER US AND YOU RUINED US!!!
DADDY...
OH NO...

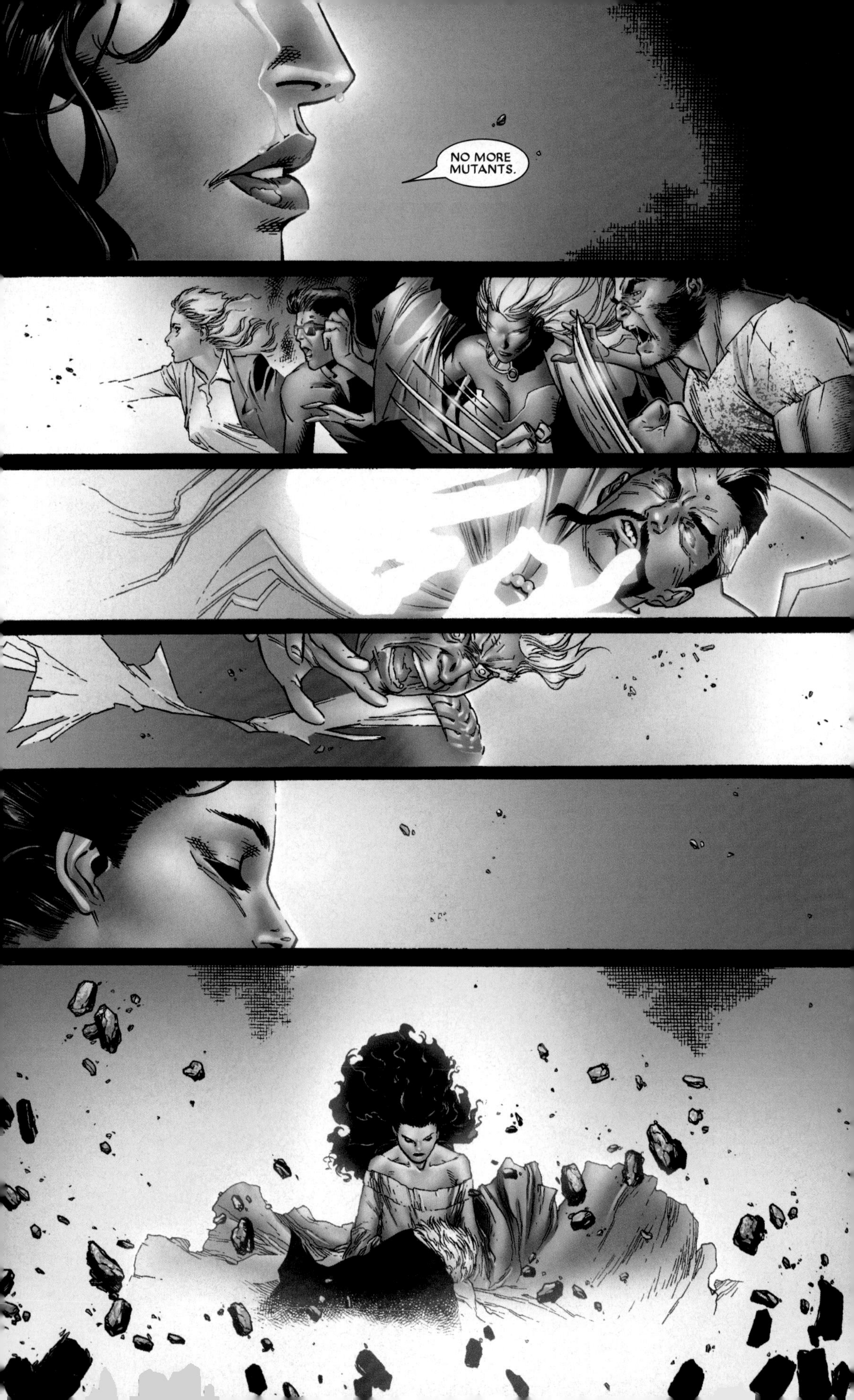
NO MORE MUTANTS.

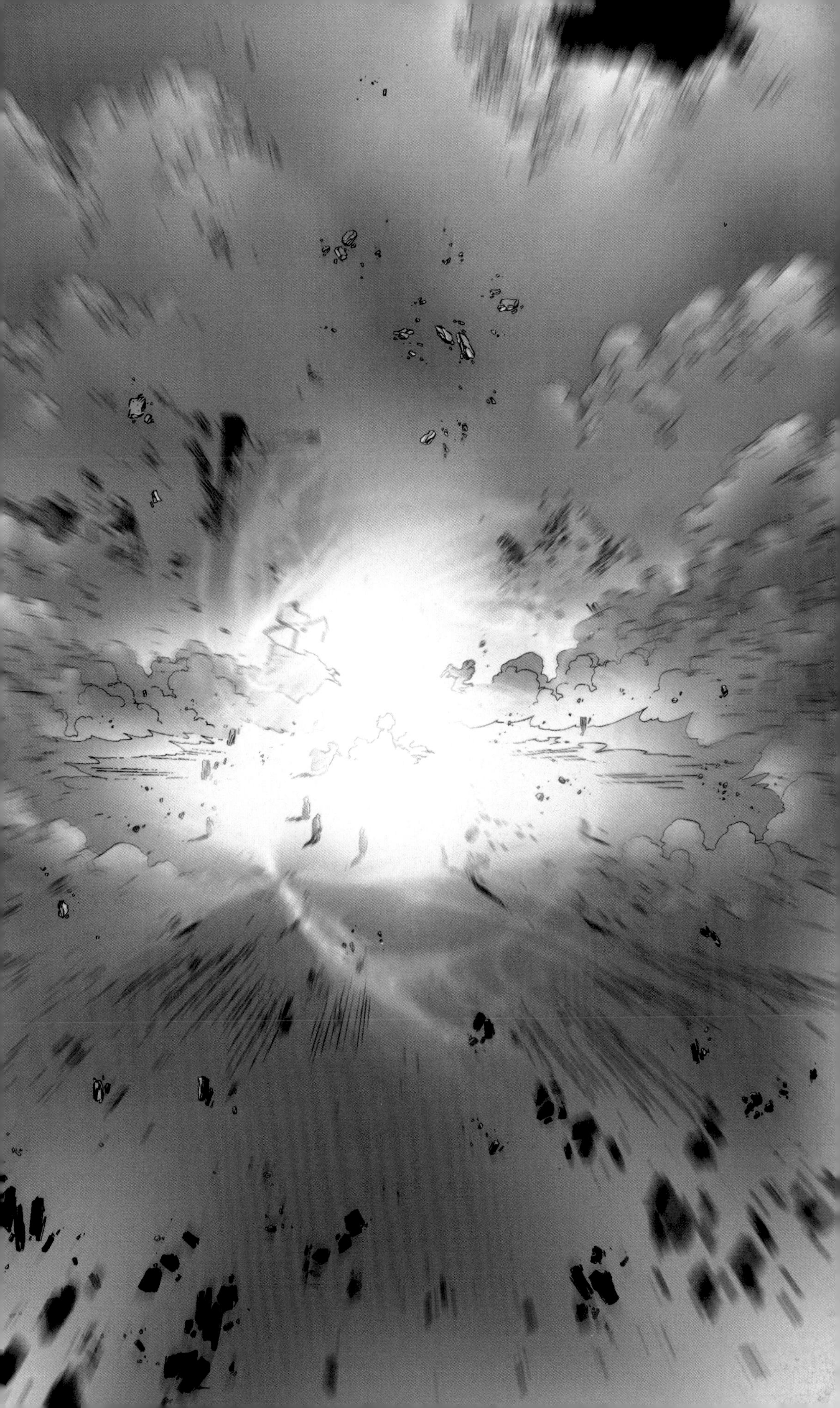

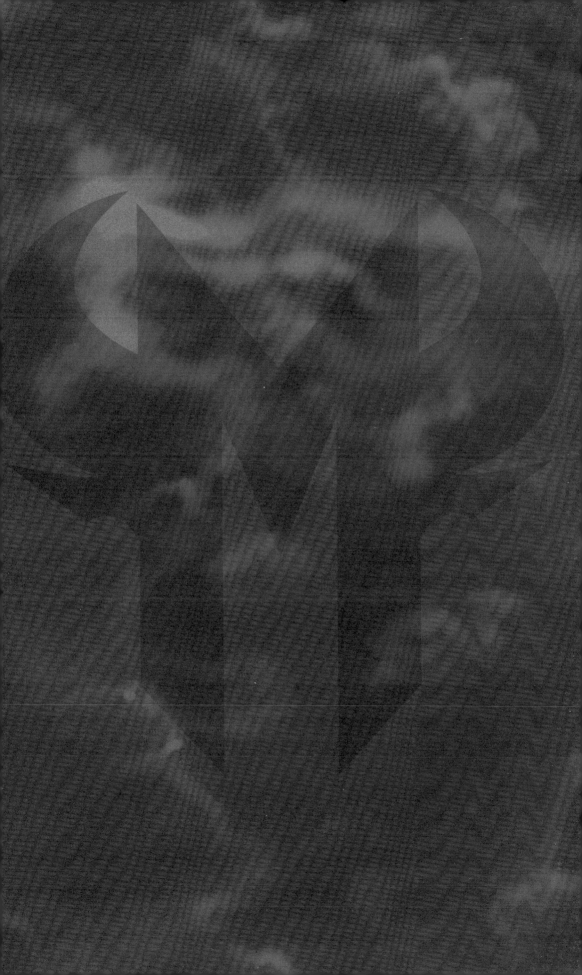

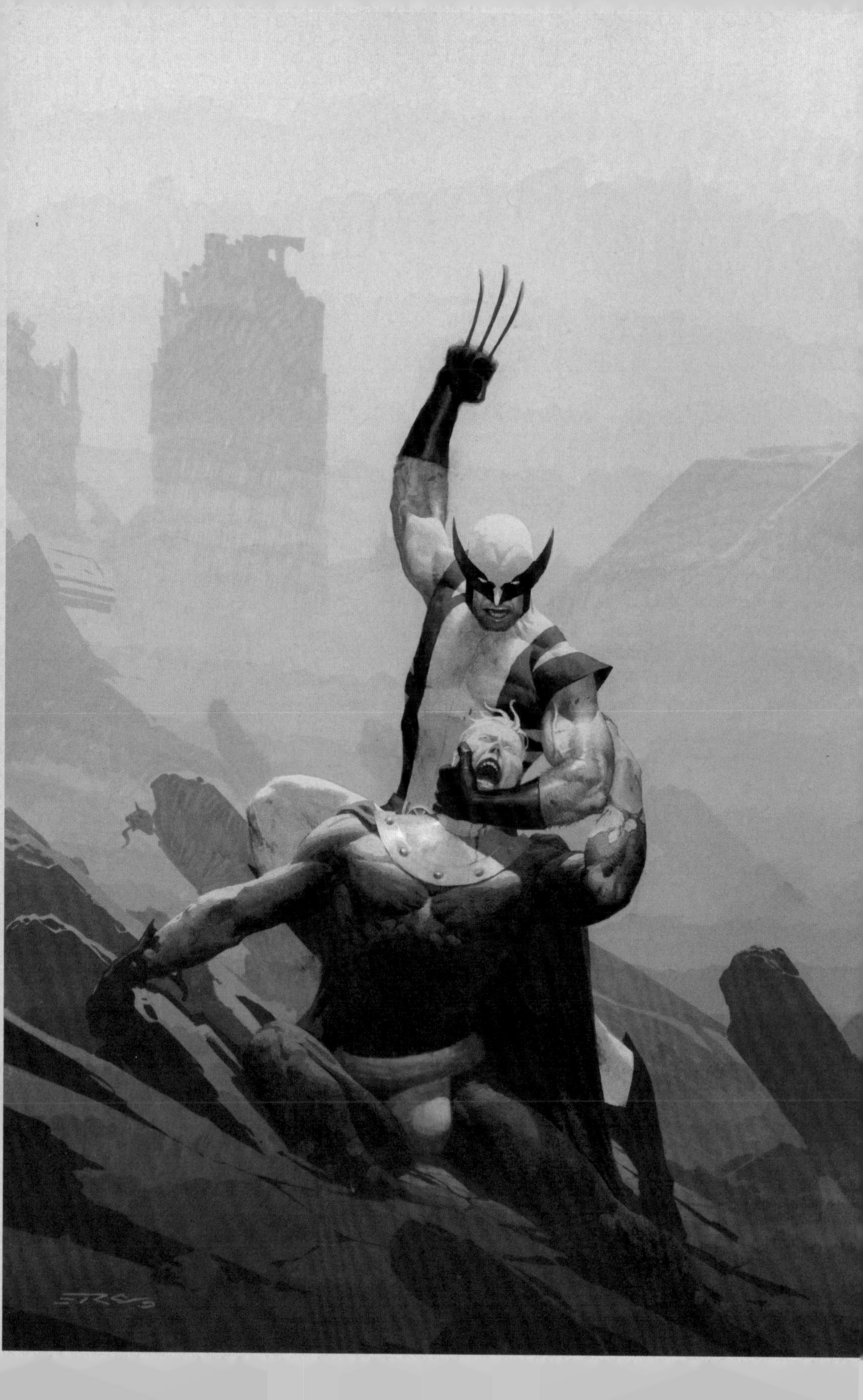

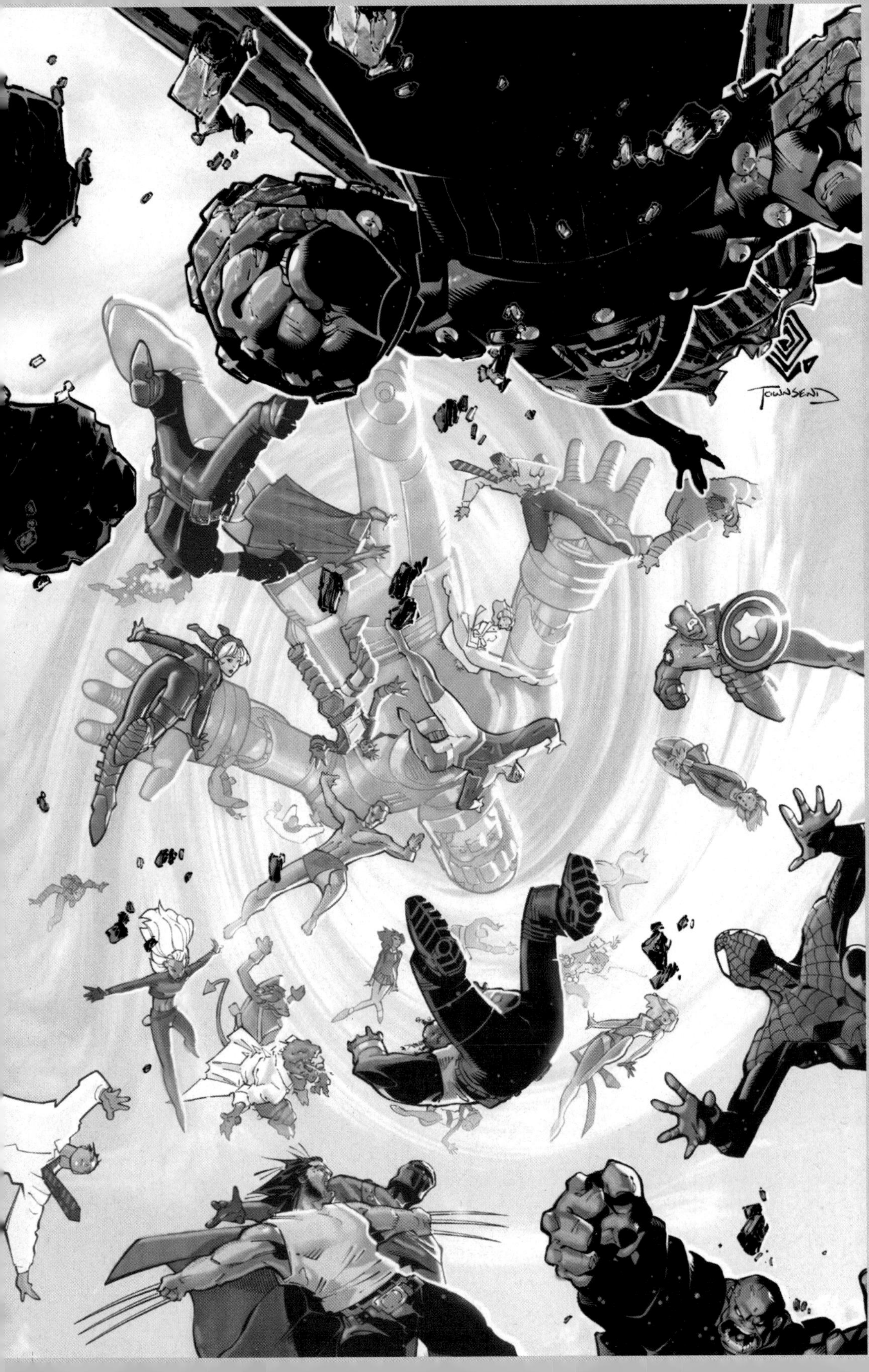
TOWNSEND

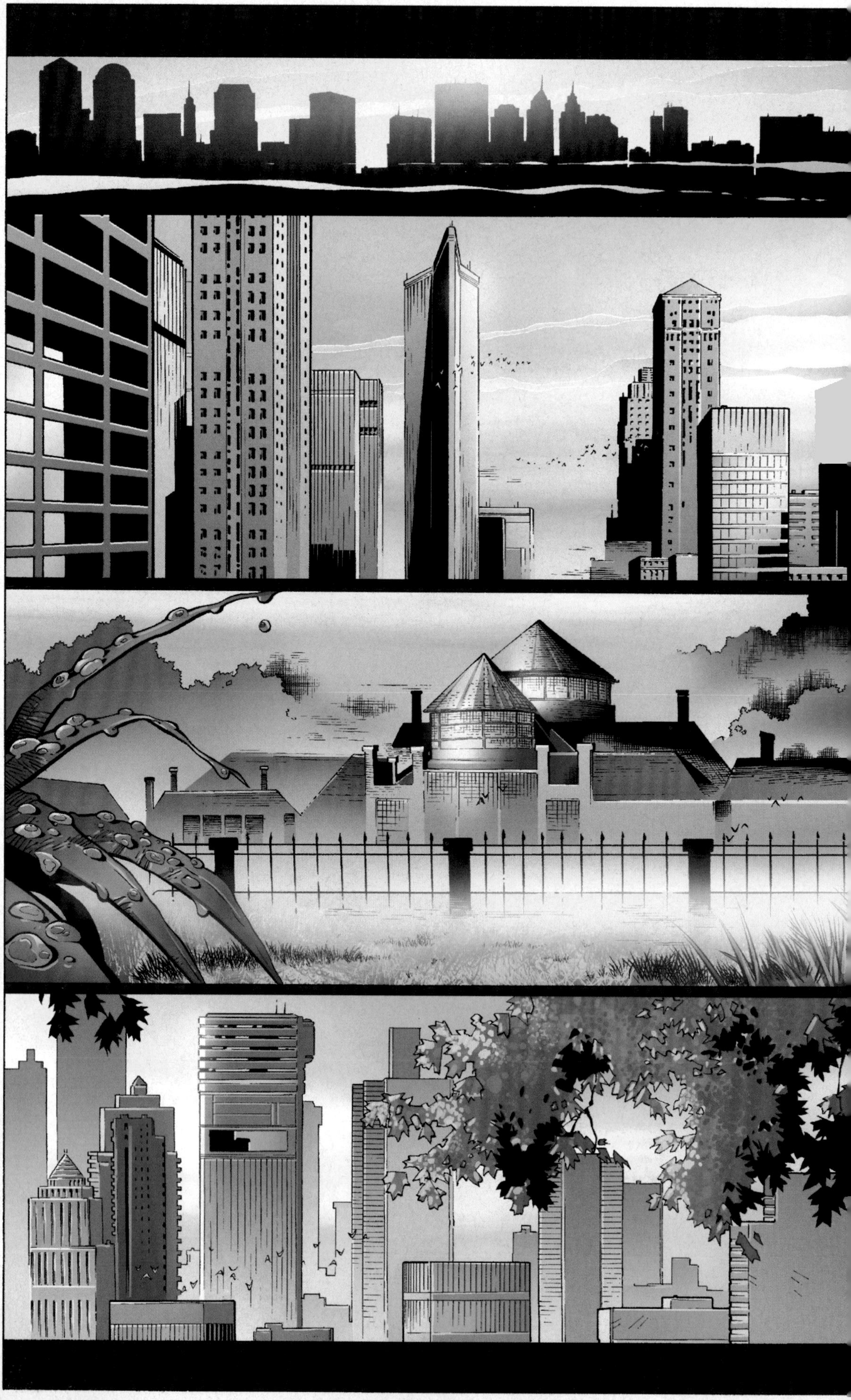

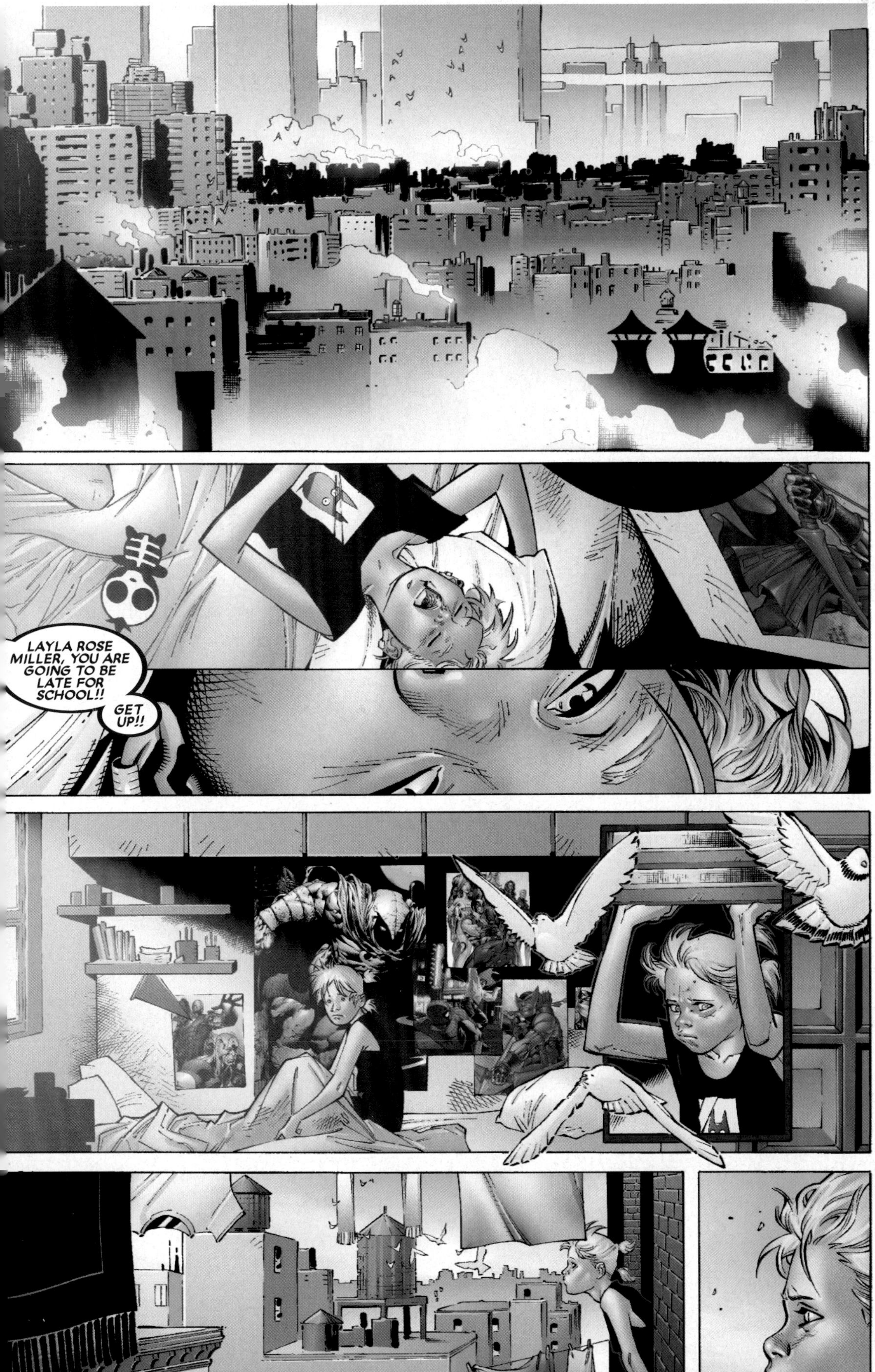
LAYLA ROSE MILLER, YOU ARE GOING TO BE LATE FOR SCHOOL!!
GET UP!!

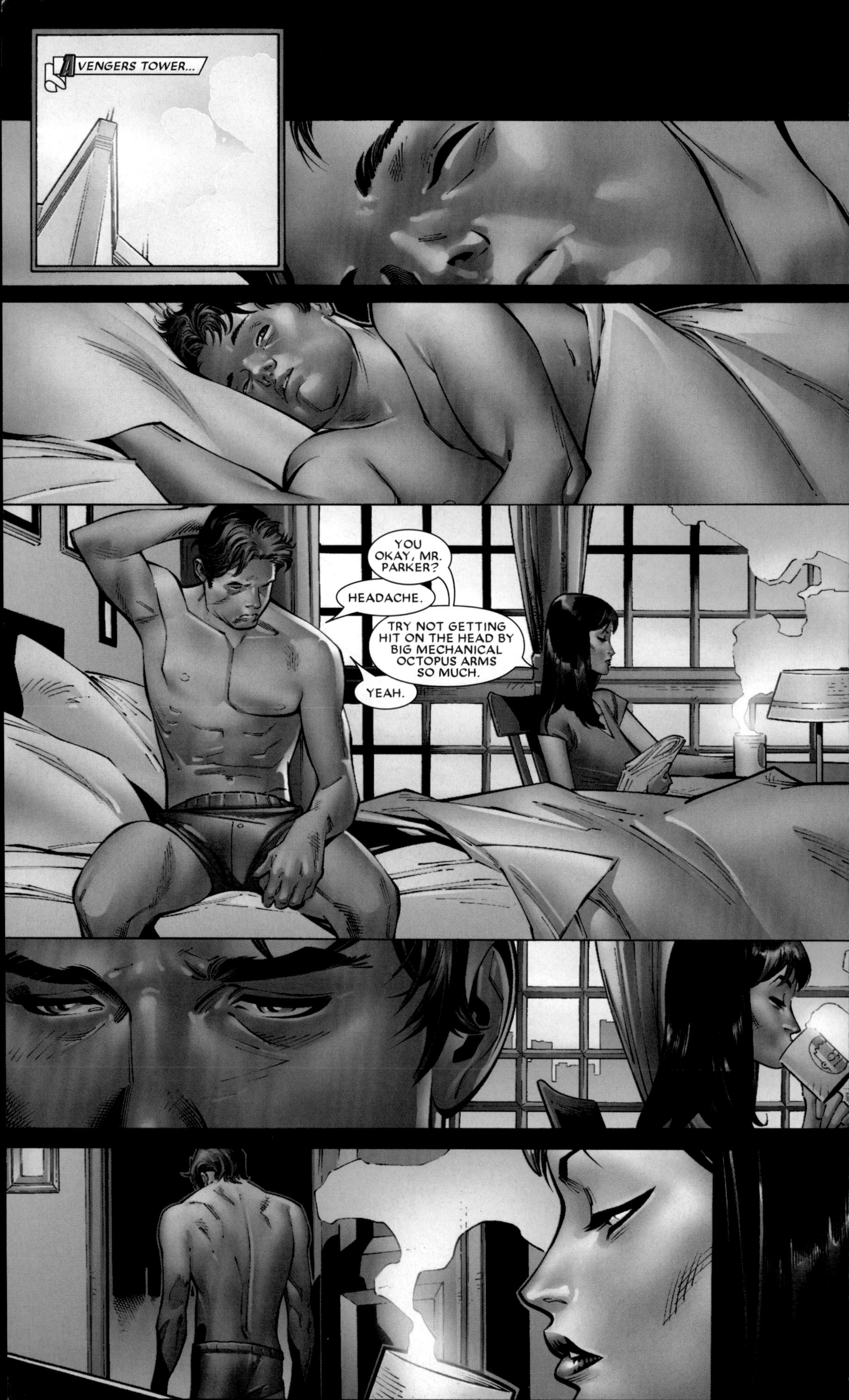
AVENGERS TOWER...
YOU OKAY, MR. PARKER?
HEADACHE.
TRY NOT GETTING HIT ON THE HEAD BY BIG MECHANICAL OCTOPUS ARMS SO MUCH.
YEAH.

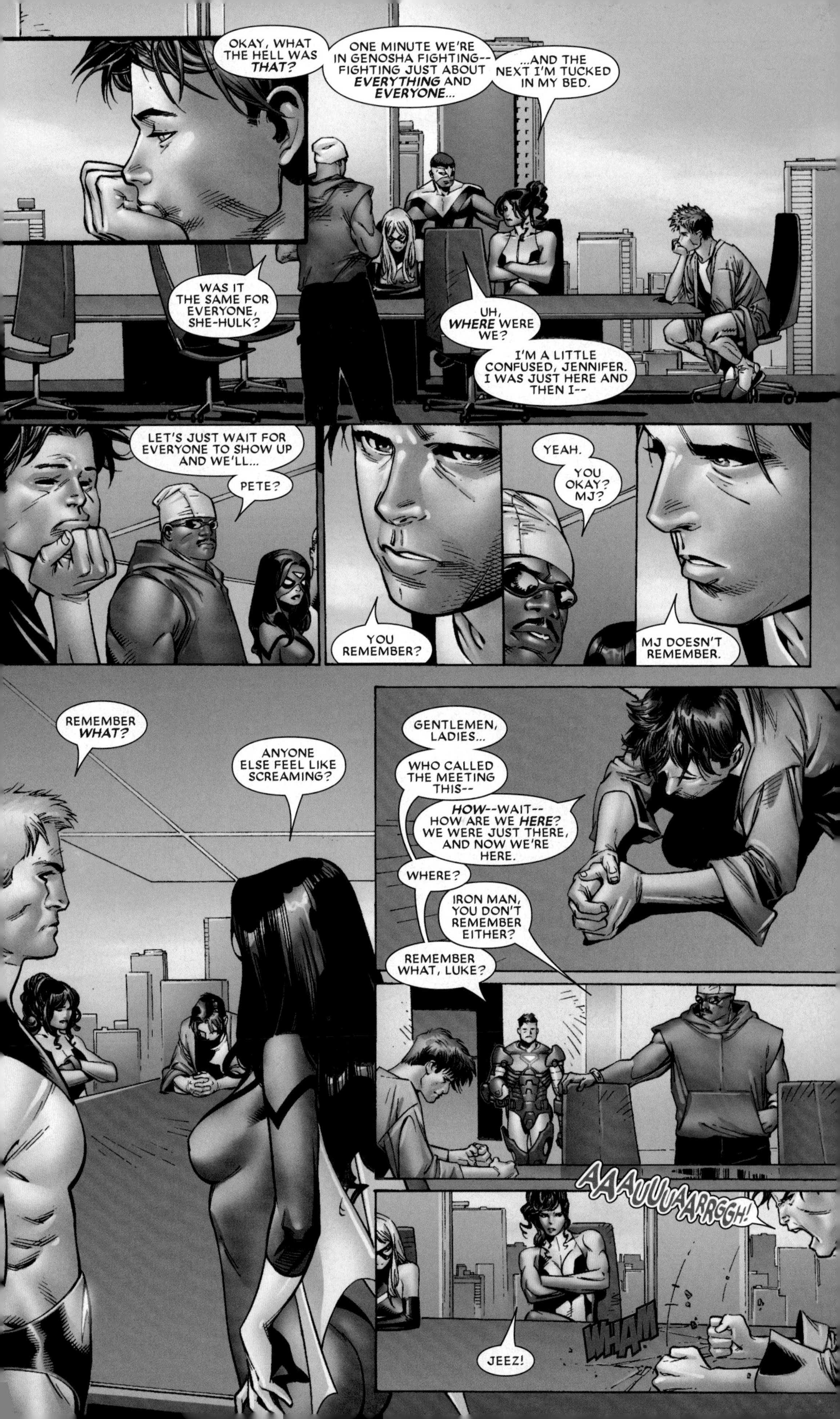
OKAY, WHAT THE HELL WAS *THAT?*
ONE MINUTE WE'RE IN GENOSHA FIGHTING-- FIGHTING JUST ABOUT *EVERYTHING* AND *EVERYONE*...
...AND THE NEXT I'M TUCKED IN MY BED.
WAS IT THE SAME FOR EVERYONE, SHE-HULK?
UH, *WHERE* WERE WE?
I'M A LITTLE CONFUSED, JENNIFER. I WAS JUST HERE AND THEN I--
LET'S JUST WAIT FOR EVERYONE TO SHOW UP AND WE'LL...
PETE?
YOU REMEMBER?
YEAH.
YOU OKAY? MJ?
MJ DOESN'T REMEMBER.
REMEMBER *WHAT?*
ANYONE ELSE FEEL LIKE SCREAMING?
GENTLEMEN, LADIES...
WHO CALLED THE MEETING THIS--
HOW--WAIT-- HOW ARE WE *HERE?* WE WERE JUST THERE, AND NOW WE'RE HERE.
WHERE?
IRON MAN, YOU DON'T REMEMBER EITHER?
REMEMBER WHAT, LUKE?
AAAUUUAARRGGH!
WHAM
JEEZ!

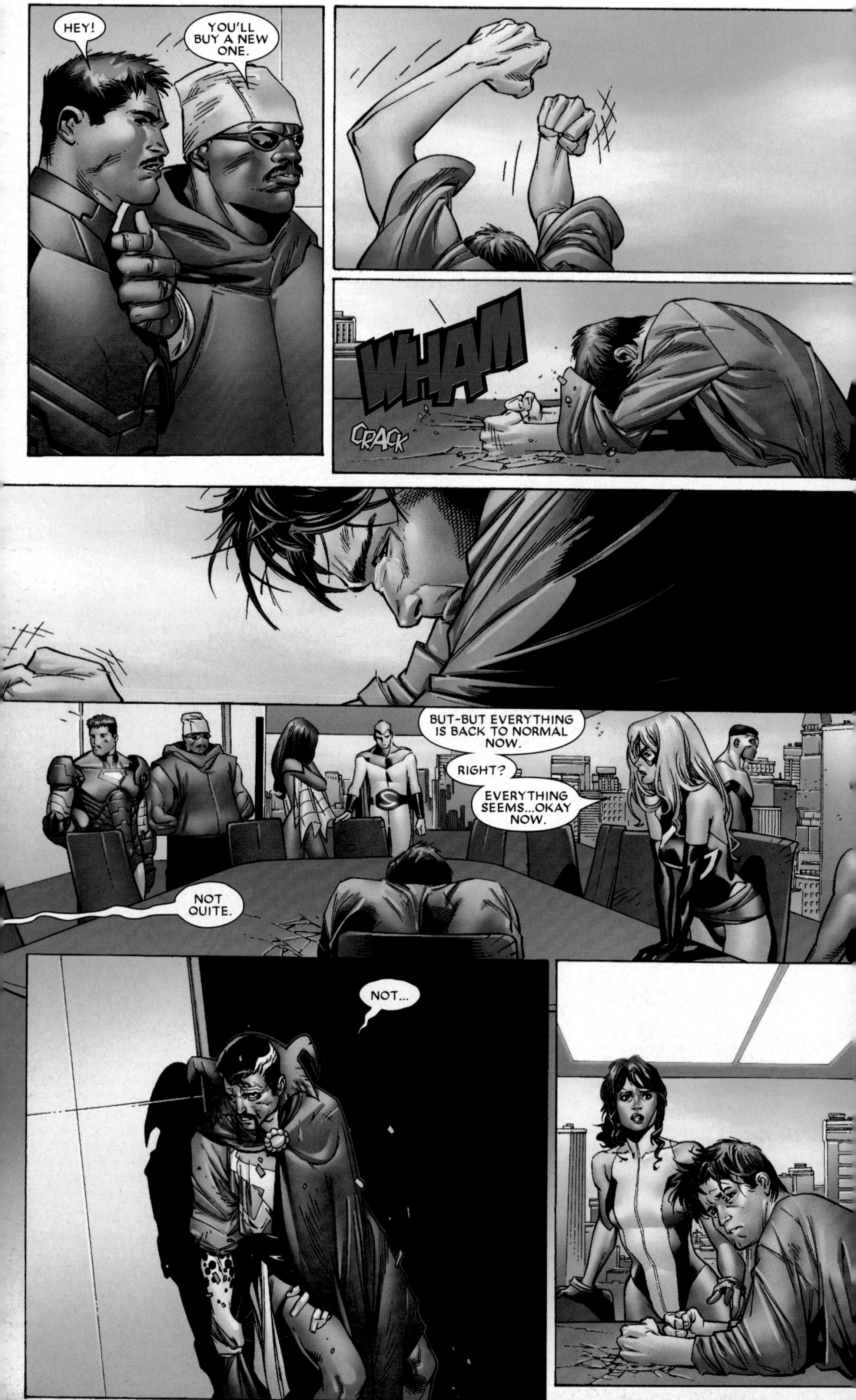

HEY!
YOU'LL BUY A NEW ONE.
WHAM
CRACK
BUT-BUT EVERYTHING IS BACK TO NORMAL NOW.
RIGHT?
EVERYTHING SEEMS...OKAY NOW.
NOT QUITE.
NOT...

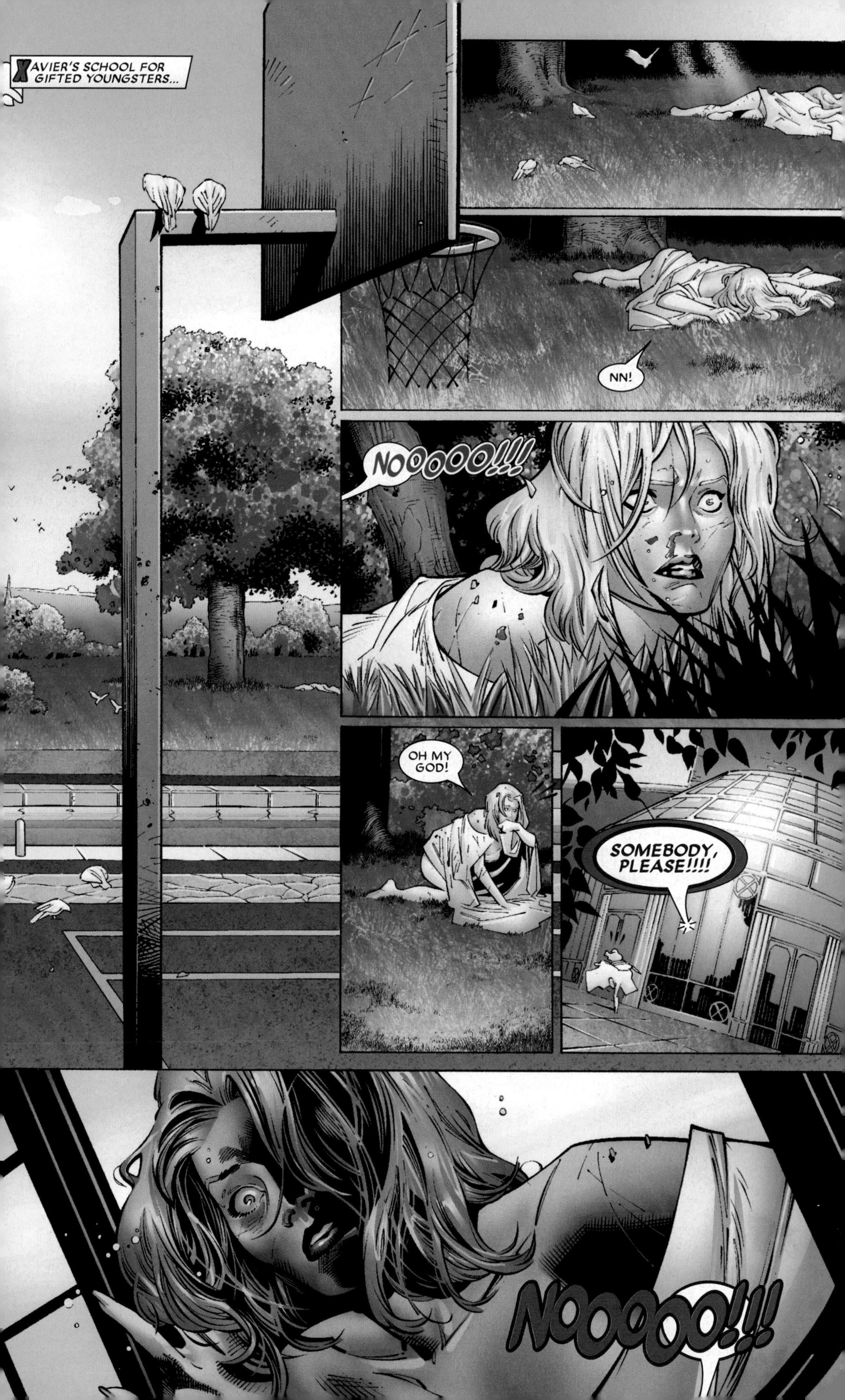
XAVIER'S SCHOOL FOR GIFTED YOUNGSTERS...
NN!
NOOOOO!!!
OH MY GOD!
SOMEBODY, PLEASE!!!!
NOOOOO!!!

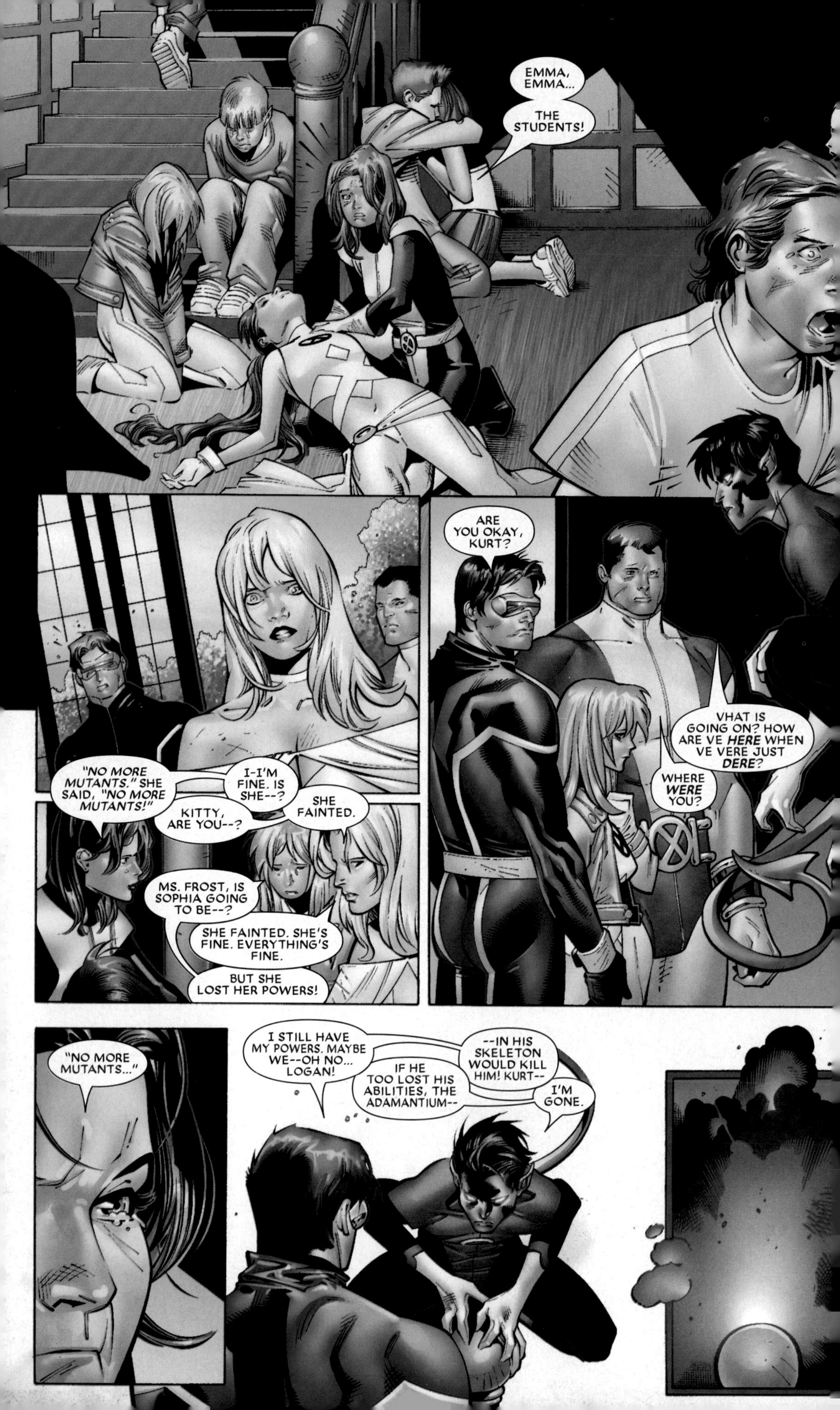

EMMA, EMMA...
THE STUDENTS!
ARE YOU OKAY, KURT?
VHAT IS GOING ON? HOW ARE VE HERE WHEN VE VERE JUST DERE?
WHERE WERE YOU?
"NO MORE MUTANTS." SHE SAID, "NO MORE MUTANTS!"
I-I'M FINE. IS SHE--?
KITTY, ARE YOU--?
SHE FAINTED.
MS. FROST, IS SOPHIA GOING TO BE--?
SHE FAINTED. SHE'S FINE. EVERYTHING'S FINE.
BUT SHE LOST HER POWERS!
"NO MORE MUTANTS..."
I STILL HAVE MY POWERS. MAYBE WE--OH NO... LOGAN!
IF HE TOO LOST HIS ABILITIES, THE ADAMANTIUM--
--IN HIS SKELETON WOULD KILL HIM! KURT--
I'M GONE.

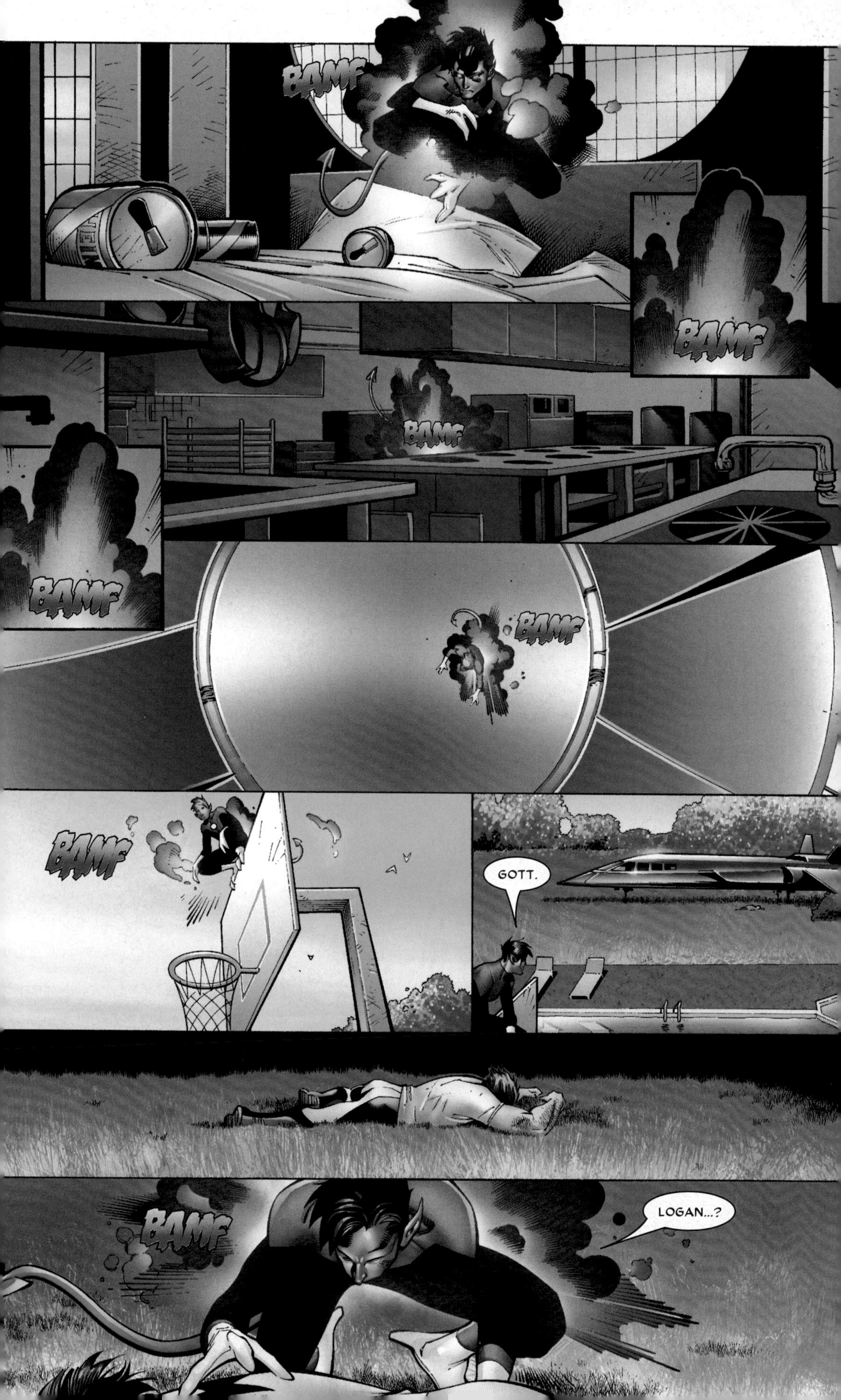

BAMF
BAMF
BAMF
BAMF
BAMF
BAMF
GOTT.
BAMF
LOGAN...?

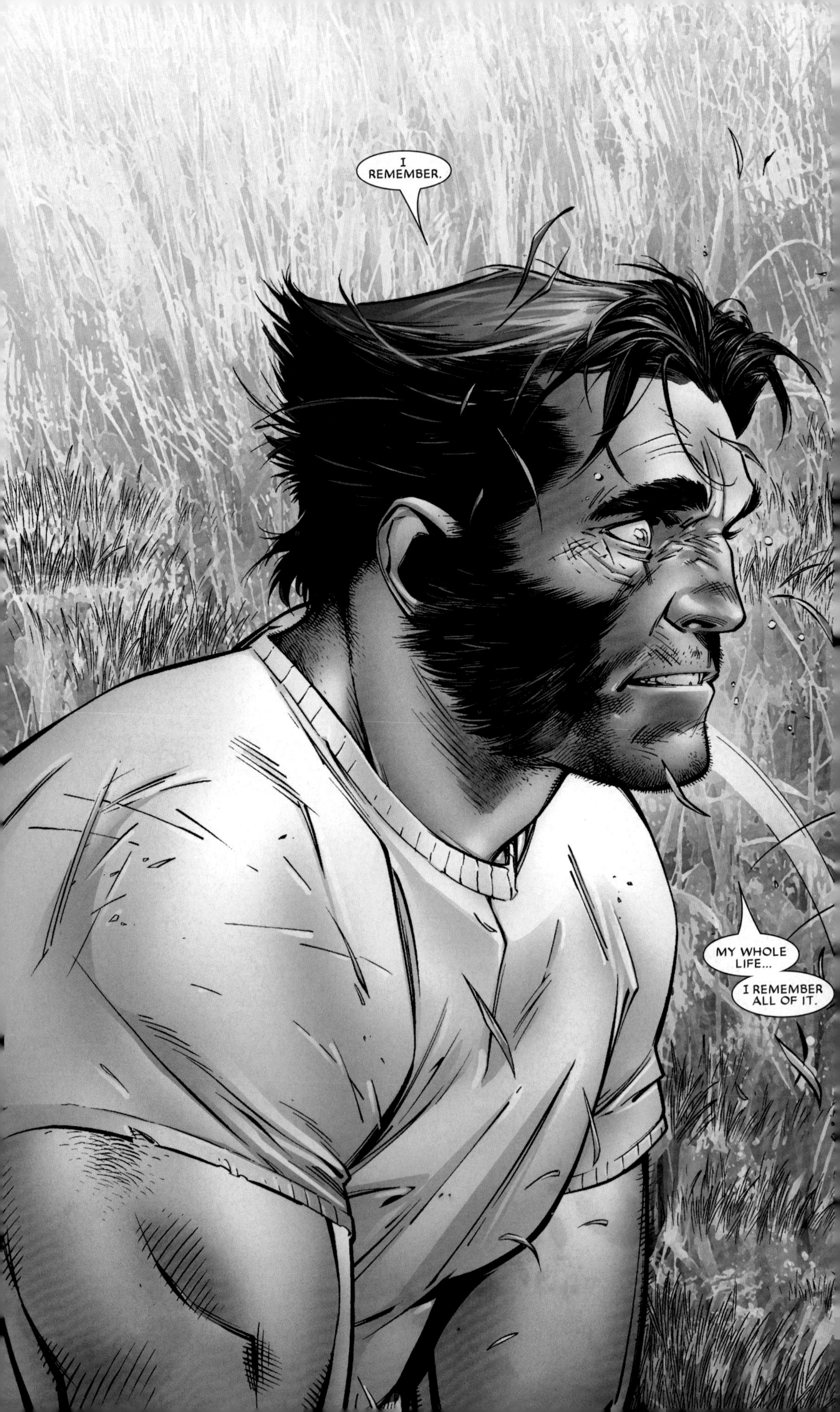
I REMEMBER.
MY WHOLE LIFE...
I REMEMBER ALL OF IT.

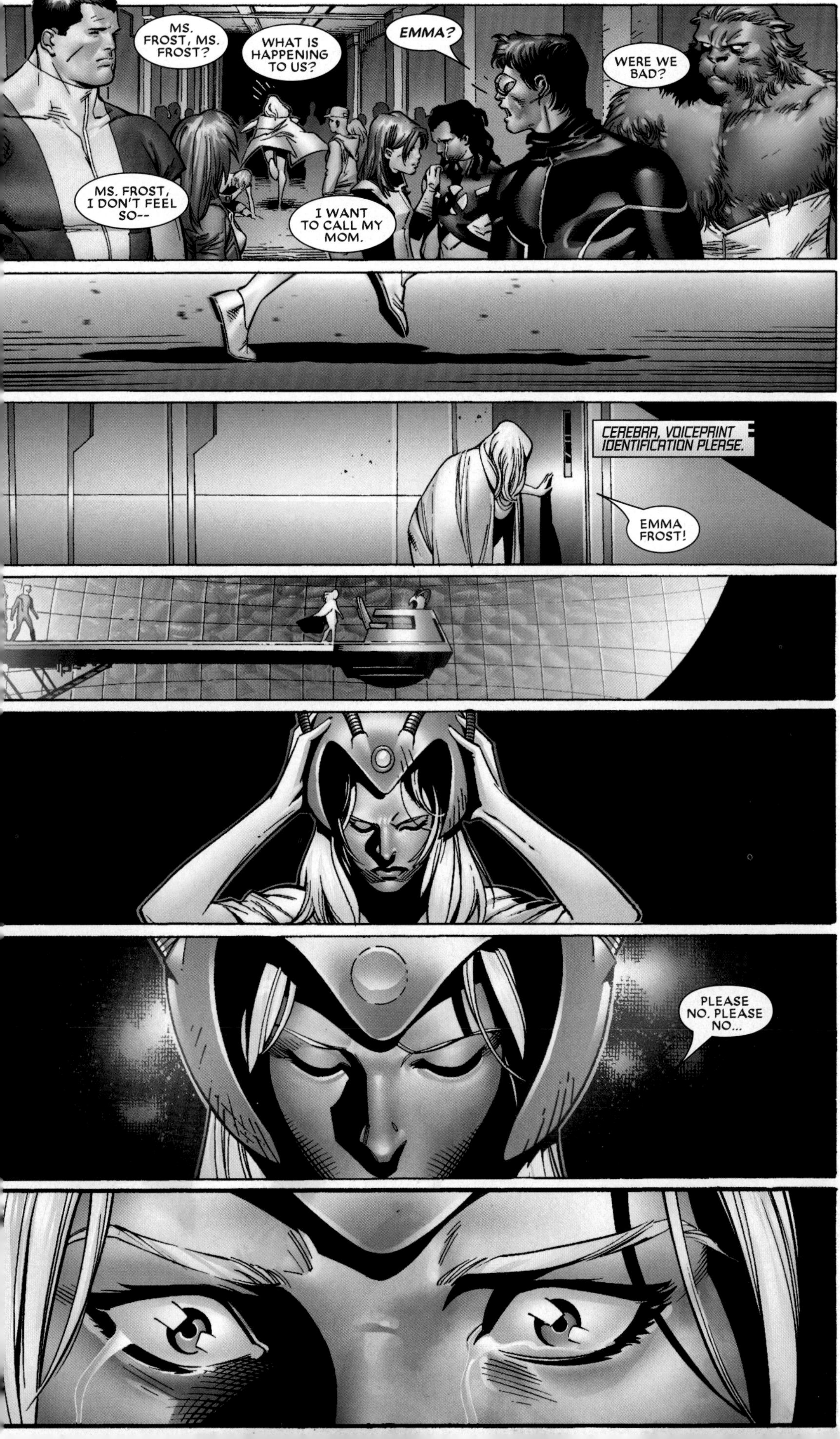
MS. FROST, MS. FROST?
WHAT IS HAPPENING TO US?
EMMA?
WERE WE BAD?
MS. FROST, I DON'T FEEL SO--
I WANT TO CALL MY MOM.
CEREBRA, VOICEPRINT IDENTIFICATION PLEASE.
EMMA FROST!
PLEASE NO. PLEASE NO...

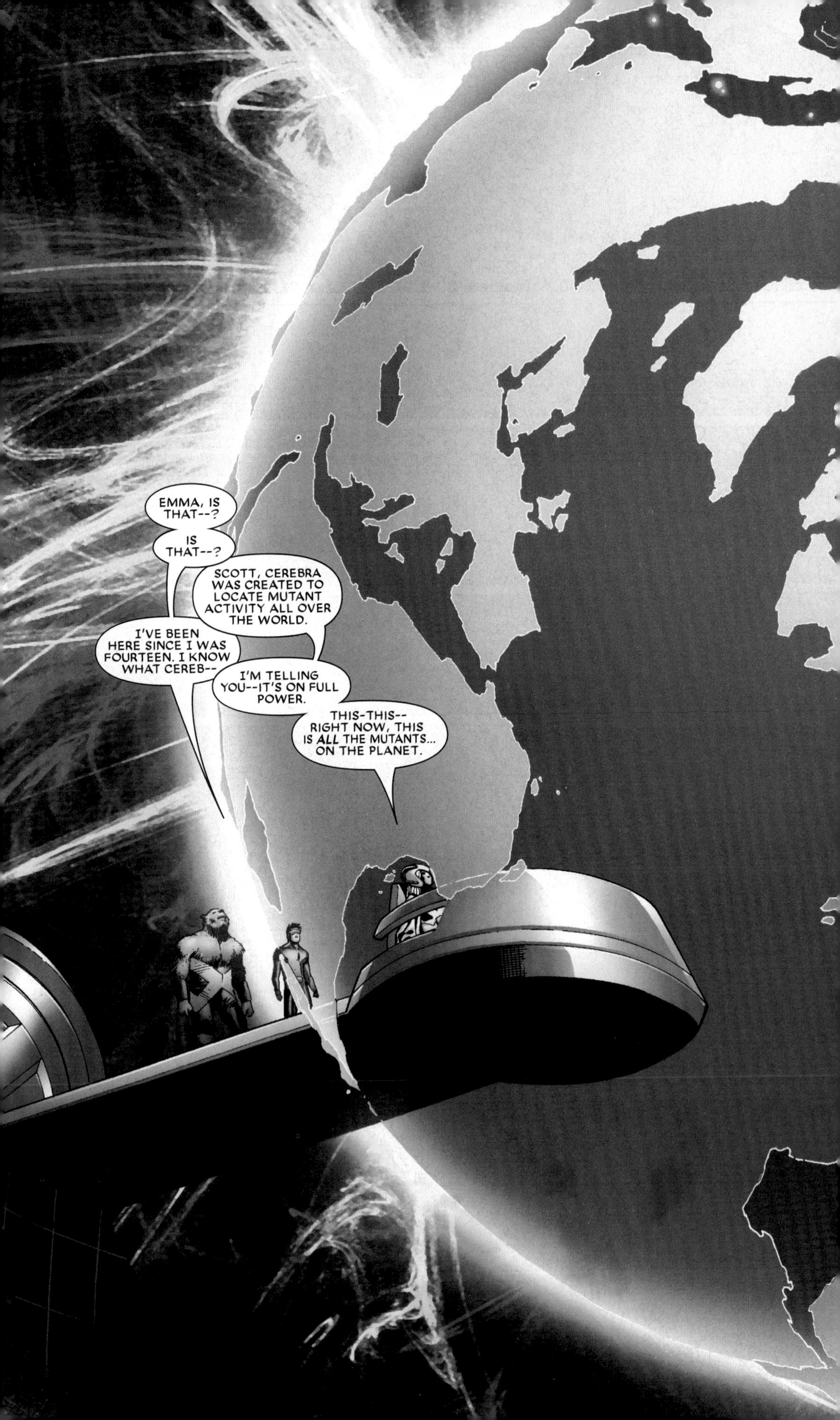
EMMA, IS THAT--?
IS THAT--?
SCOTT, CEREBRA WAS CREATED TO LOCATE MUTANT ACTIVITY ALL OVER THE WORLD.
I'VE BEEN HERE SINCE I WAS FOURTEEN. I KNOW WHAT CEREB--
I'M TELLING YOU--IT'S ON FULL POWER.
THIS-THIS-- RIGHT NOW, THIS IS ALL THE MUTANTS... ON THE PLANET.

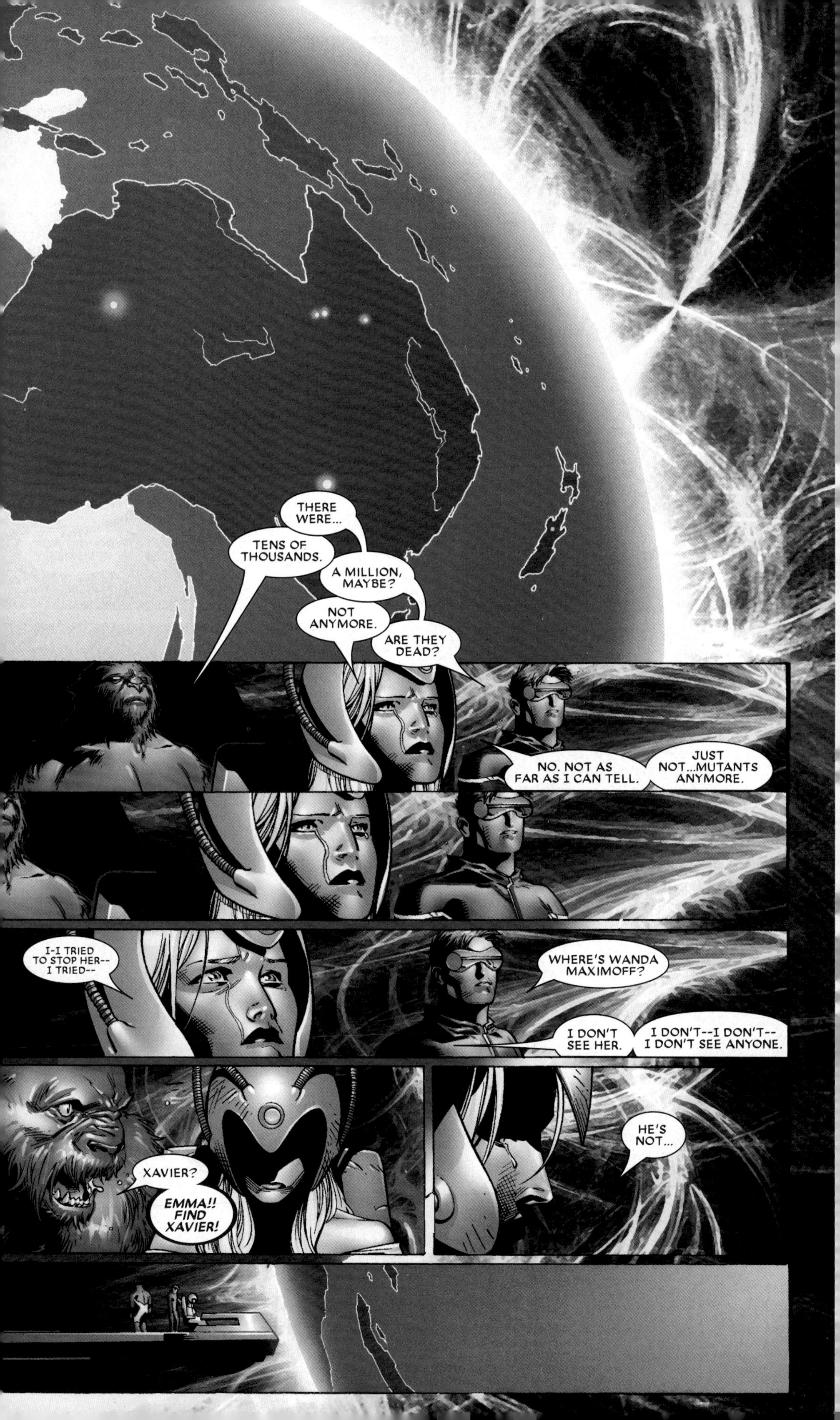
THERE WERE...
TENS OF THOUSANDS.
A MILLION, MAYBE?
NOT ANYMORE.
ARE THEY DEAD?
NO. NOT AS FAR AS I CAN TELL.
JUST NOT...MUTANTS ANYMORE.
I-I TRIED TO STOP HER-- I TRIED--
WHERE'S WANDA MAXIMOFF?
I DON'T SEE HER.
I DON'T--I DON'T-- I DON'T SEE ANYONE.
XAVIER?
EMMA!! FIND XAVIER!
HE'S NOT...

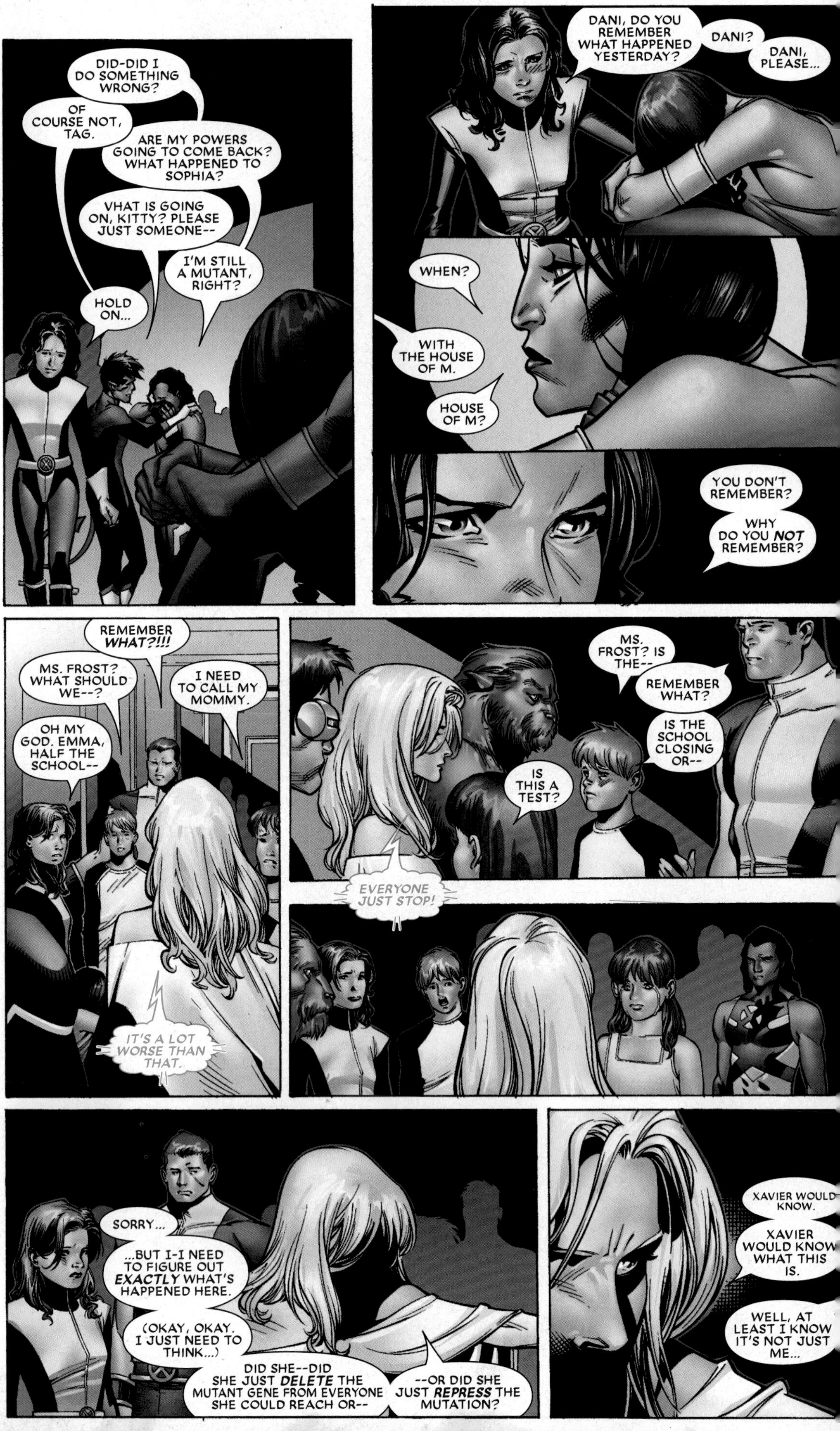
DID-DID I DO SOMETHING WRONG?
OF COURSE NOT, TAG.
ARE MY POWERS GOING TO COME BACK? WHAT HAPPENED TO SOPHIA?
VHAT IS GOING ON, KITTY? PLEASE JUST SOMEONE--
I'M STILL A MUTANT, RIGHT?
HOLD ON...
DANI, DO YOU REMEMBER WHAT HAPPENED YESTERDAY?
DANI?
DANI, PLEASE...
WHEN?
WITH THE HOUSE OF M.
HOUSE OF M?
YOU DON'T REMEMBER?
WHY DO YOU NOT REMEMBER?
REMEMBER WHAT?!!!
MS. FROST? WHAT SHOULD WE--?
I NEED TO CALL MY MOMMY.
OH MY GOD. EMMA, HALF THE SCHOOL--
IT'S A LOT WORSE THAN THAT.
MS. FROST? IS THE--
REMEMBER WHAT?
IS THE SCHOOL CLOSING OR--
IS THIS A TEST?
EVERYONE JUST STOP!
SORRY...
...BUT I-I NEED TO FIGURE OUT EXACTLY WHAT'S HAPPENED HERE.
(OKAY, OKAY. I JUST NEED TO THINK...)
DID SHE--DID SHE JUST DELETE THE MUTANT GENE FROM EVERYONE SHE COULD REACH OR--
--OR DID SHE JUST REPRESS THE MUTATION?
XAVIER WOULD KNOW.
XAVIER WOULD KNOW WHAT THIS IS.
WELL, AT LEAST I KNOW IT'S NOT JUST ME...

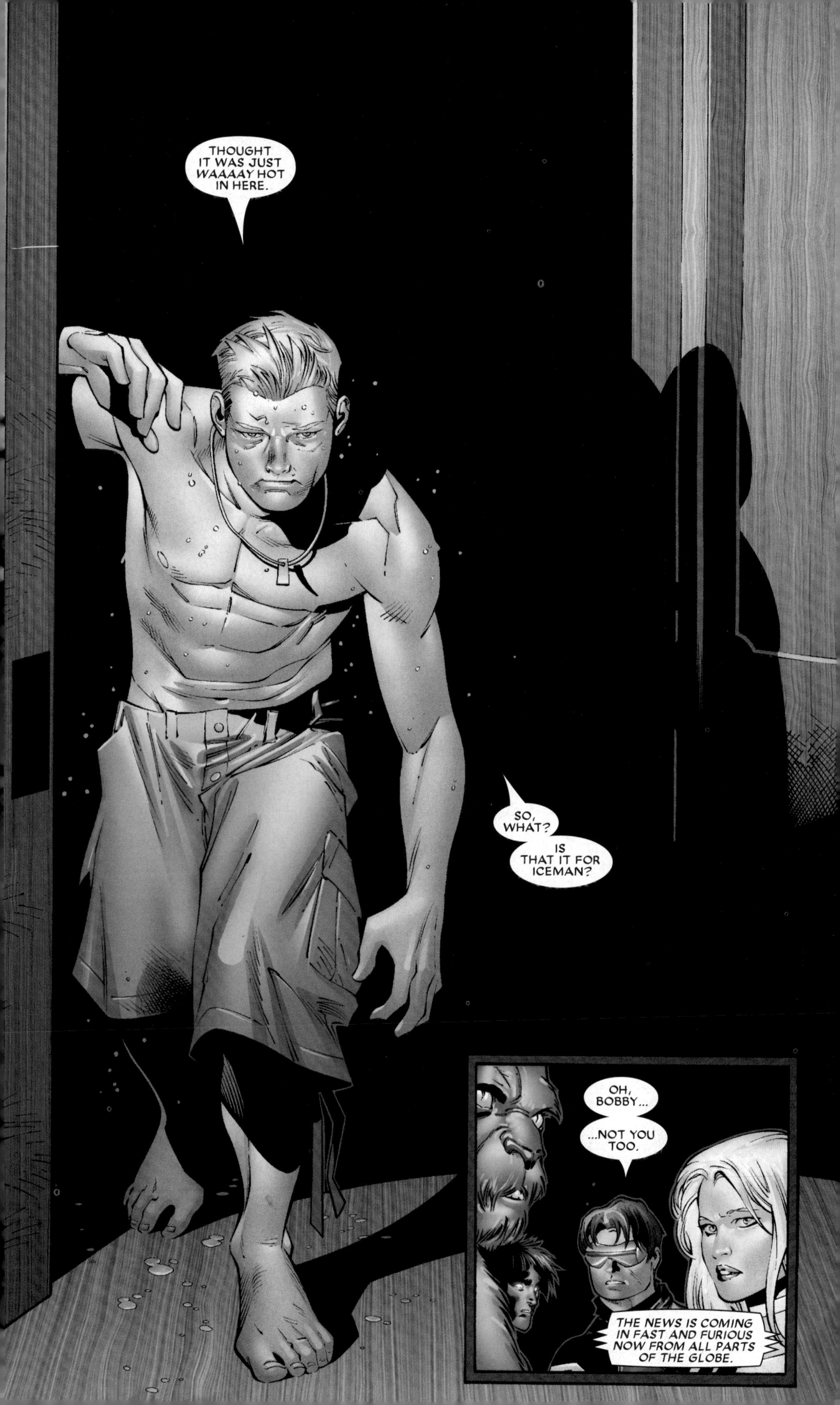
THOUGHT IT WAS JUST WAAAAY HOT IN HERE.
SO, WHAT?
IS THAT IT FOR ICEMAN?
OH, BOBBY...
...NOT YOU TOO.
THE NEWS IS COMING IN FAST AND FURIOUS NOW FROM ALL PARTS OF THE GLOBE.

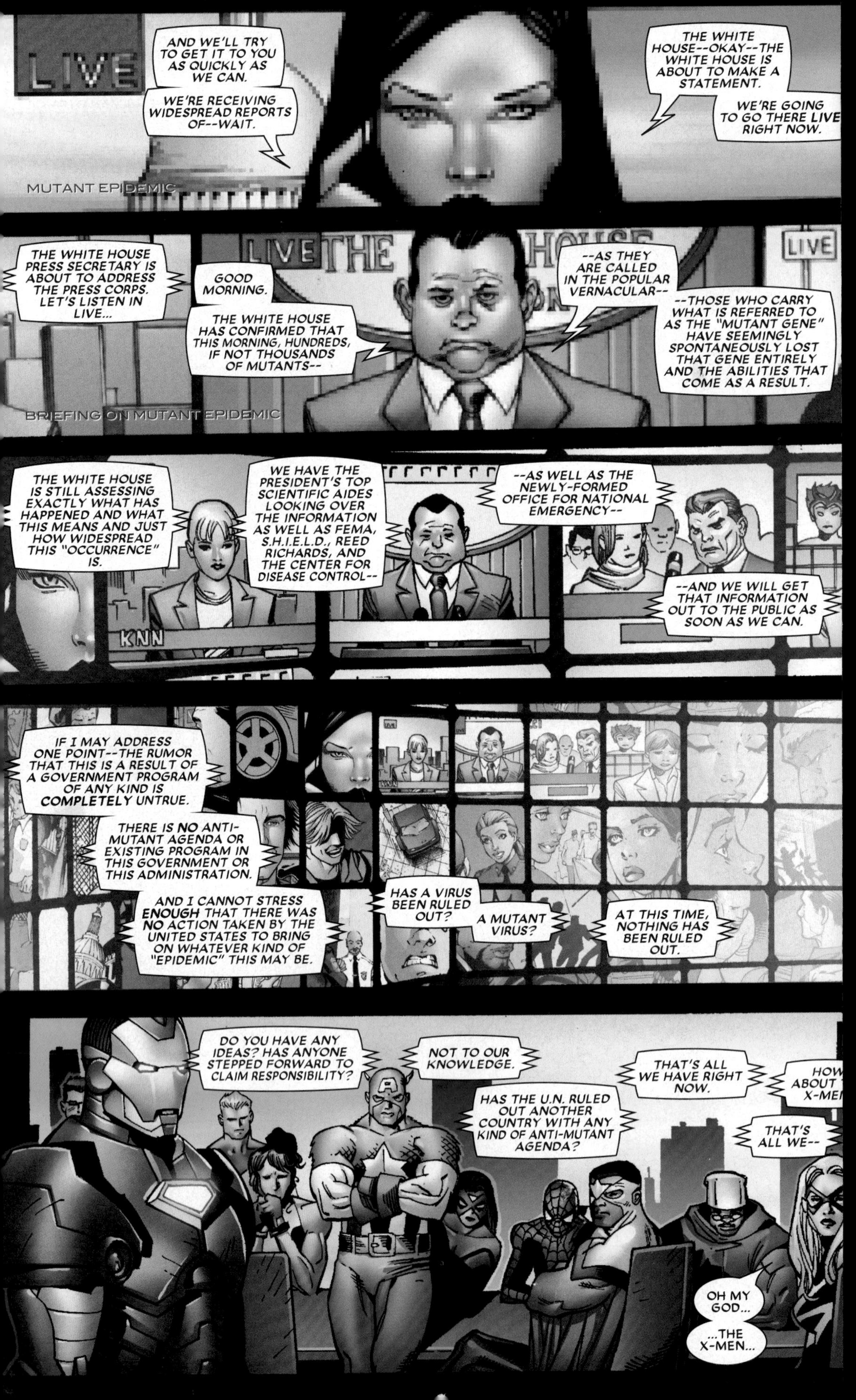

LIVE
AND WE'LL TRY TO GET IT TO YOU AS QUICKLY AS WE CAN.
WE'RE RECEIVING WIDESPREAD REPORTS OF--WAIT.
MUTANT EPIDEMIC
THE WHITE HOUSE--OKAY--THE WHITE HOUSE IS ABOUT TO MAKE A STATEMENT.
WE'RE GOING TO GO THERE LIVE RIGHT NOW.
THE WHITE HOUSE PRESS SECRETARY IS ABOUT TO ADDRESS THE PRESS CORPS. LET'S LISTEN IN LIVE...
GOOD MORNING.
THE WHITE HOUSE HAS CONFIRMED THAT THIS MORNING, HUNDREDS, IF NOT THOUSANDS OF MUTANTS--
--AS THEY ARE CALLED IN THE POPULAR VERNACULAR--
--THOSE WHO CARRY WHAT IS REFERRED TO AS THE "MUTANT GENE" HAVE SEEMINGLY SPONTANEOUSLY LOST THAT GENE ENTIRELY AND THE ABILITIES THAT COME AS A RESULT.
BRIEFING ON MUTANT EPIDEMIC
THE WHITE HOUSE IS STILL ASSESSING EXACTLY WHAT HAS HAPPENED AND WHAT THIS MEANS AND JUST HOW WIDESPREAD THIS "OCCURRENCE" IS.
WE HAVE THE PRESIDENT'S TOP SCIENTIFIC AIDES LOOKING OVER THE INFORMATION AS WELL AS FEMA, S.H.I.E.L.D., REED RICHARDS, AND THE CENTER FOR DISEASE CONTROL--
--AS WELL AS THE NEWLY-FORMED OFFICE FOR NATIONAL EMERGENCY--
--AND WE WILL GET THAT INFORMATION OUT TO THE PUBLIC AS SOON AS WE CAN.
KNN
IF I MAY ADDRESS ONE POINT--THE RUMOR THAT THIS IS A RESULT OF A GOVERNMENT PROGRAM OF ANY KIND IS COMPLETELY UNTRUE.
THERE IS NO ANTI-MUTANT AGENDA OR EXISTING PROGRAM IN THIS GOVERNMENT OR THIS ADMINISTRATION.
AND I CANNOT STRESS ENOUGH THAT THERE WAS NO ACTION TAKEN BY THE UNITED STATES TO BRING ON WHATEVER KIND OF "EPIDEMIC" THIS MAY BE.
HAS A VIRUS BEEN RULED OUT?
A MUTANT VIRUS?
AT THIS TIME, NOTHING HAS BEEN RULED OUT.
DO YOU HAVE ANY IDEAS? HAS ANYONE STEPPED FORWARD TO CLAIM RESPONSIBILITY?
NOT TO OUR KNOWLEDGE.
HAS THE U.N. RULED OUT ANOTHER COUNTRY WITH ANY KIND OF ANTI-MUTANT AGENDA?
THAT'S ALL WE HAVE RIGHT NOW.
HOW ABOUT T X-ME
THAT'S ALL WE--
OH MY GOD...
...THE X-MEN...

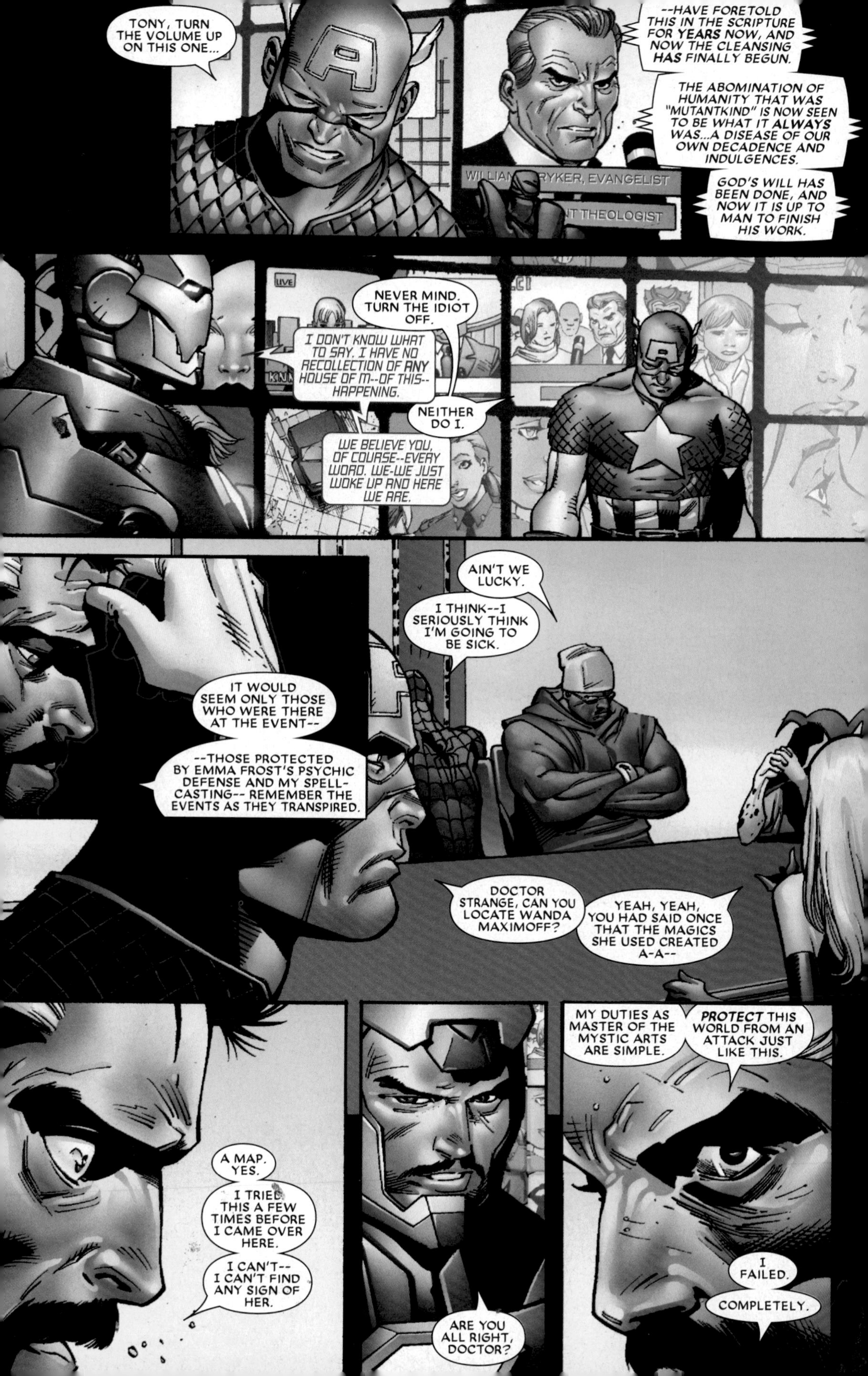

TONY, TURN THE VOLUME UP ON THIS ONE...
--HAVE FORETOLD THIS IN THE SCRIPTURE FOR YEARS NOW, AND NOW THE CLEANSING HAS FINALLY BEGUN.
THE ABOMINATION OF HUMANITY THAT WAS "MUTANTKIND" IS NOW SEEN TO BE WHAT IT ALWAYS WAS...A DISEASE OF OUR OWN DECADENCE AND INDULGENCES.
GOD'S WILL HAS BEEN DONE, AND NOW IT IS UP TO MAN TO FINISH HIS WORK.
RYKER, EVANGELIST
THEOLOGIST
LIVE
I DON'T KNOW WHAT TO SAY. I HAVE NO RECOLLECTION OF ANY HOUSE OF M--OF THIS--HAPPENING.
NEVER MIND. TURN THE IDIOT OFF.
NEITHER DO I.
WE BELIEVE YOU, OF COURSE--EVERY WORD. WE-WE JUST WOKE UP AND HERE WE ARE.
AIN'T WE LUCKY.
I THINK--I SERIOUSLY THINK I'M GOING TO BE SICK.
IT WOULD SEEM ONLY THOSE WHO WERE THERE AT THE EVENT--
--THOSE PROTECTED BY EMMA FROST'S PSYCHIC DEFENSE AND MY SPELL-CASTING-- REMEMBER THE EVENTS AS THEY TRANSPIRED.
DOCTOR STRANGE, CAN YOU LOCATE WANDA MAXIMOFF?
YEAH, YEAH, YOU HAD SAID ONCE THAT THE MAGICS SHE USED CREATED A-A--
A MAP. YES.
I TRIED THIS A FEW TIMES BEFORE I CAME OVER HERE.
I CAN'T--I CAN'T FIND ANY SIGN OF HER.
ARE YOU ALL RIGHT, DOCTOR?
MY DUTIES AS MASTER OF THE MYSTIC ARTS ARE SIMPLE.
PROTECT THIS WORLD FROM AN ATTACK JUST LIKE THIS.
I FAILED.
COMPLETELY.

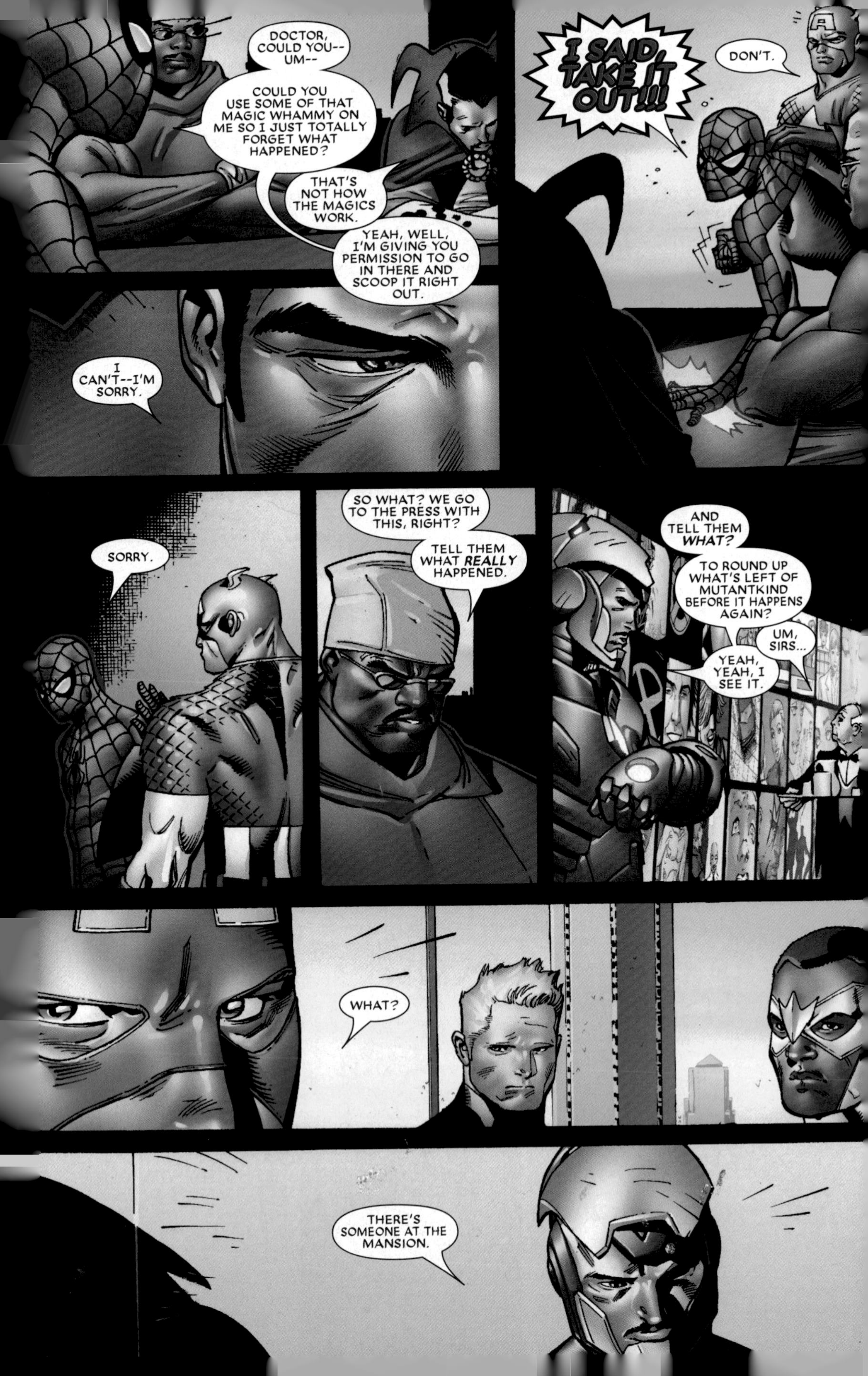
DOCTOR, COULD YOU-- UM--
COULD YOU USE SOME OF THAT MAGIC WHAMMY ON ME SO I JUST TOTALLY FORGET WHAT HAPPENED?
THAT'S NOT HOW THE MAGICS WORK.
YEAH, WELL, I'M GIVING YOU PERMISSION TO GO IN THERE AND SCOOP IT RIGHT OUT.
I CAN'T--I'M SORRY.
I SAID, TAKE IT OUT!!!
DON'T.
SORRY.
SO WHAT? WE GO TO THE PRESS WITH THIS, RIGHT?
TELL THEM WHAT *REALLY* HAPPENED.
AND TELL THEM *WHAT?*
TO ROUND UP WHAT'S LEFT OF MUTANTKIND BEFORE IT HAPPENS AGAIN?
UM, SIRS...
YEAH, YEAH, I SEE IT.
WHAT?
THERE'S SOMEONE AT THE MANSION.

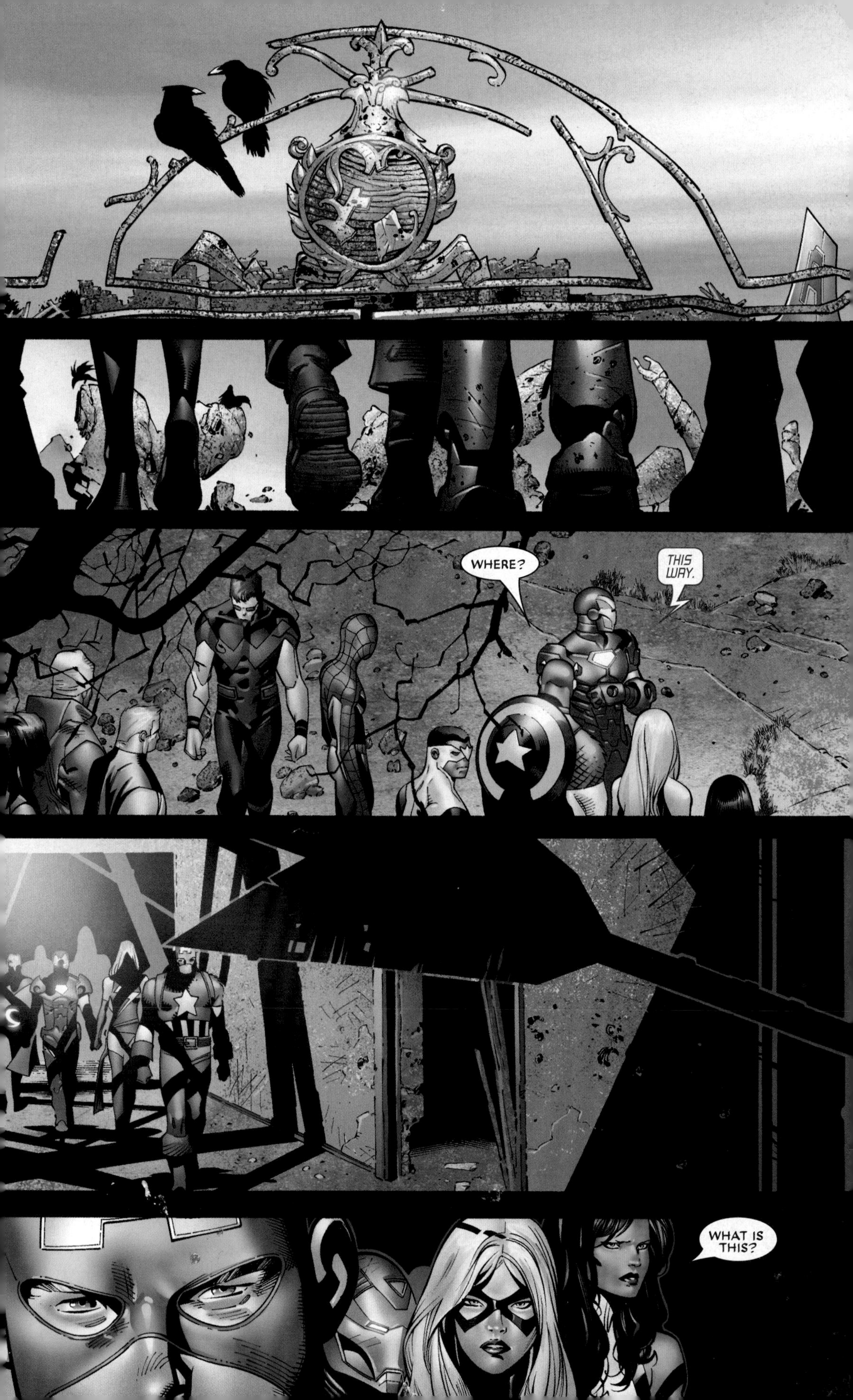
WHERE?
THIS WAY.
WHAT IS THIS?

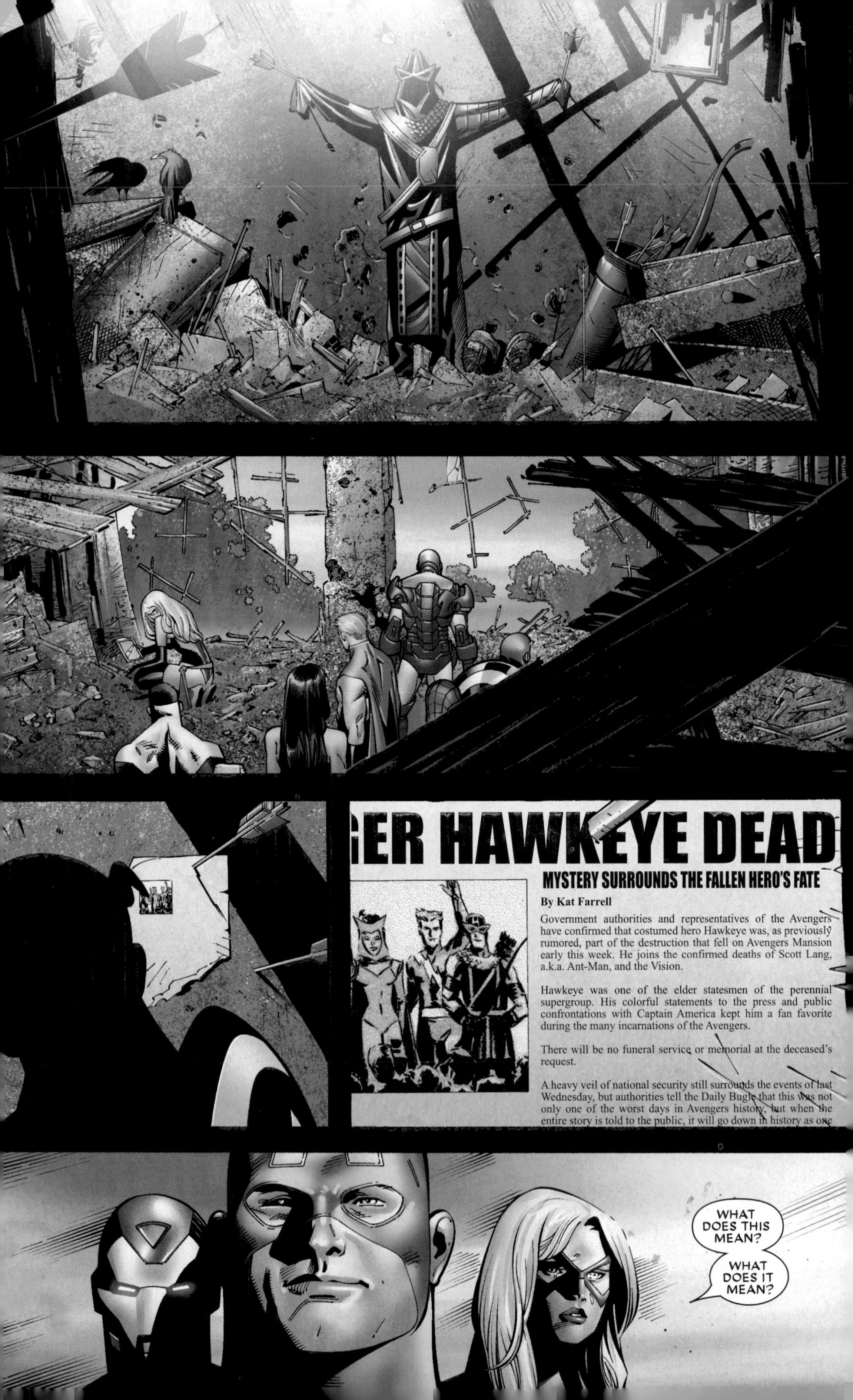

GER HAWKEYE DEAD
MYSTERY SURROUNDS THE FALLEN HERO'S FATE
By Kat Farrell
Government authorities and representatives of the Avengers have confirmed that costumed hero Hawkeye was, as previously rumored, part of the destruction that fell on Avengers Mansion early this week. He joins the confirmed deaths of Scott Lang, a.k.a. Ant-Man, and the Vision.
Hawkeye was one of the elder statesmen of the perennial supergroup. His colorful statements to the press and public confrontations with Captain America kept him a fan favorite during the many incarnations of the Avengers.
There will be no funeral service or memorial at the deceased's request.
A heavy veil of national security still surrounds the events of last Wednesday, but authorities tell the Daily Bugle that this was not only one of the worst days in Avengers history, but when the entire story is told to the public, it will go down in history as one
WHAT DOES THIS MEAN?
WHAT DOES IT MEAN?

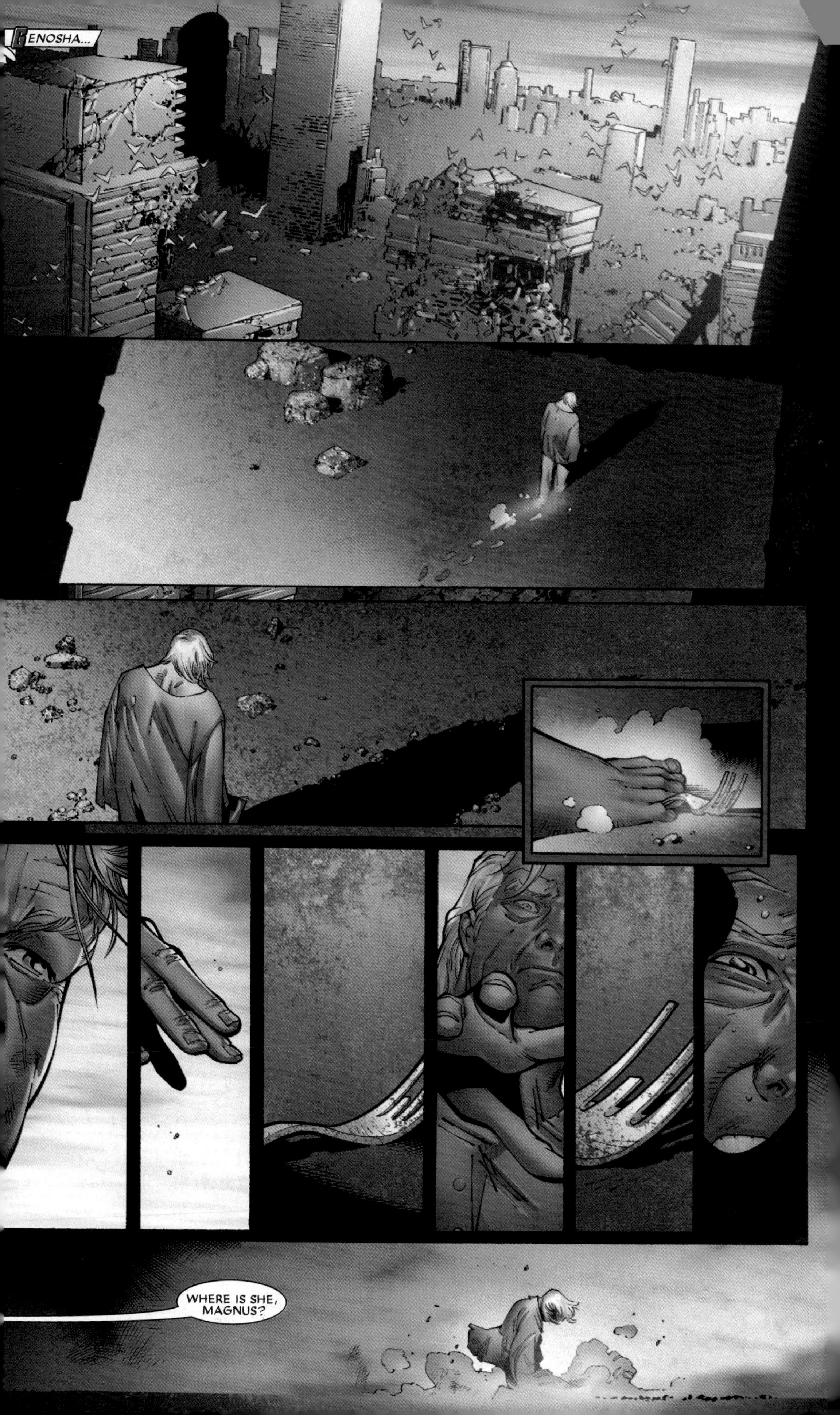
GENOSHA...
WHERE IS SHE, MAGNUS?

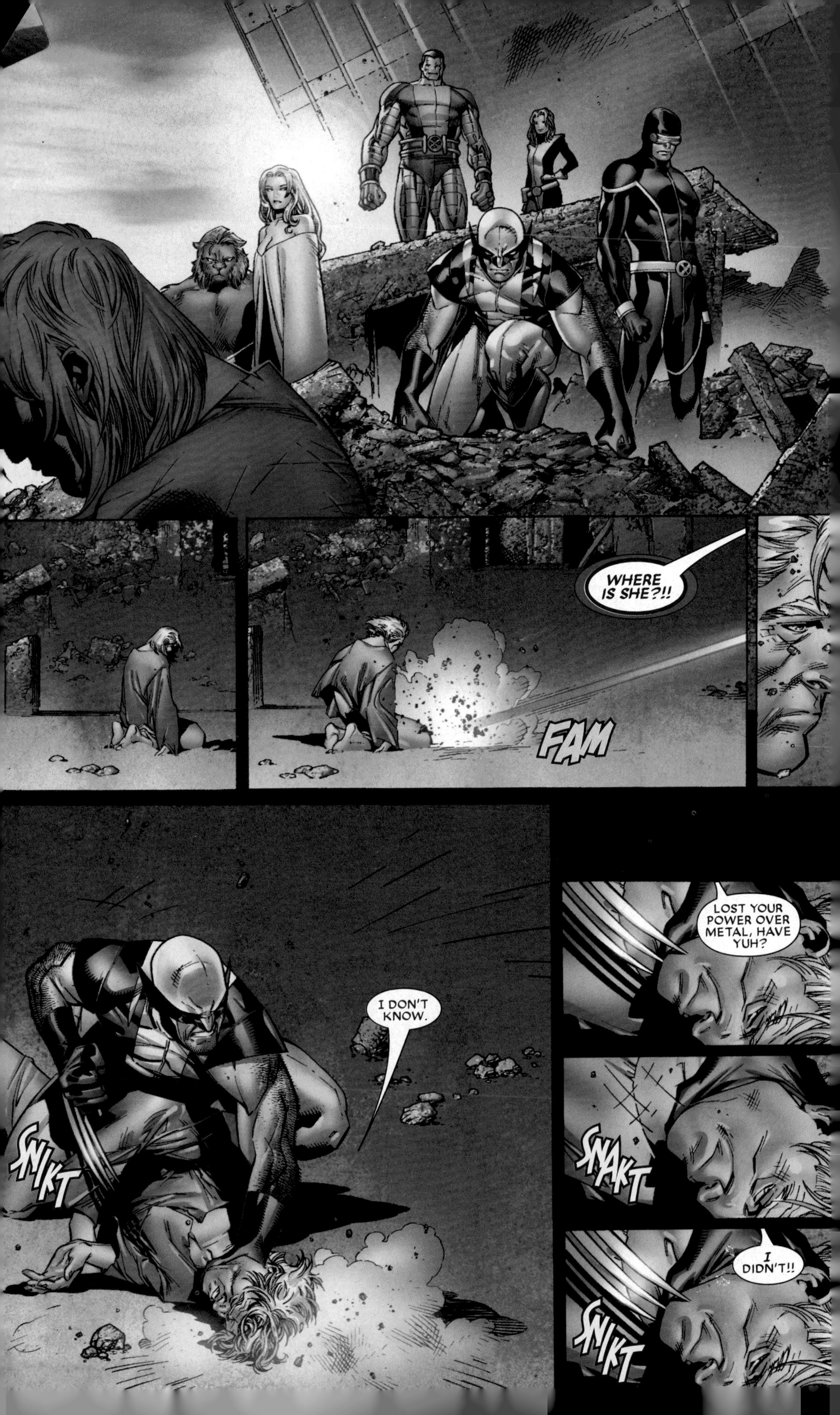
WHERE IS SHE?!!
FAM
I DON'T KNOW.
SNIKT
LOST YOUR POWER OVER METAL, HAVE YUH?
SNAKT
I DIDN'T!!
SNIKT

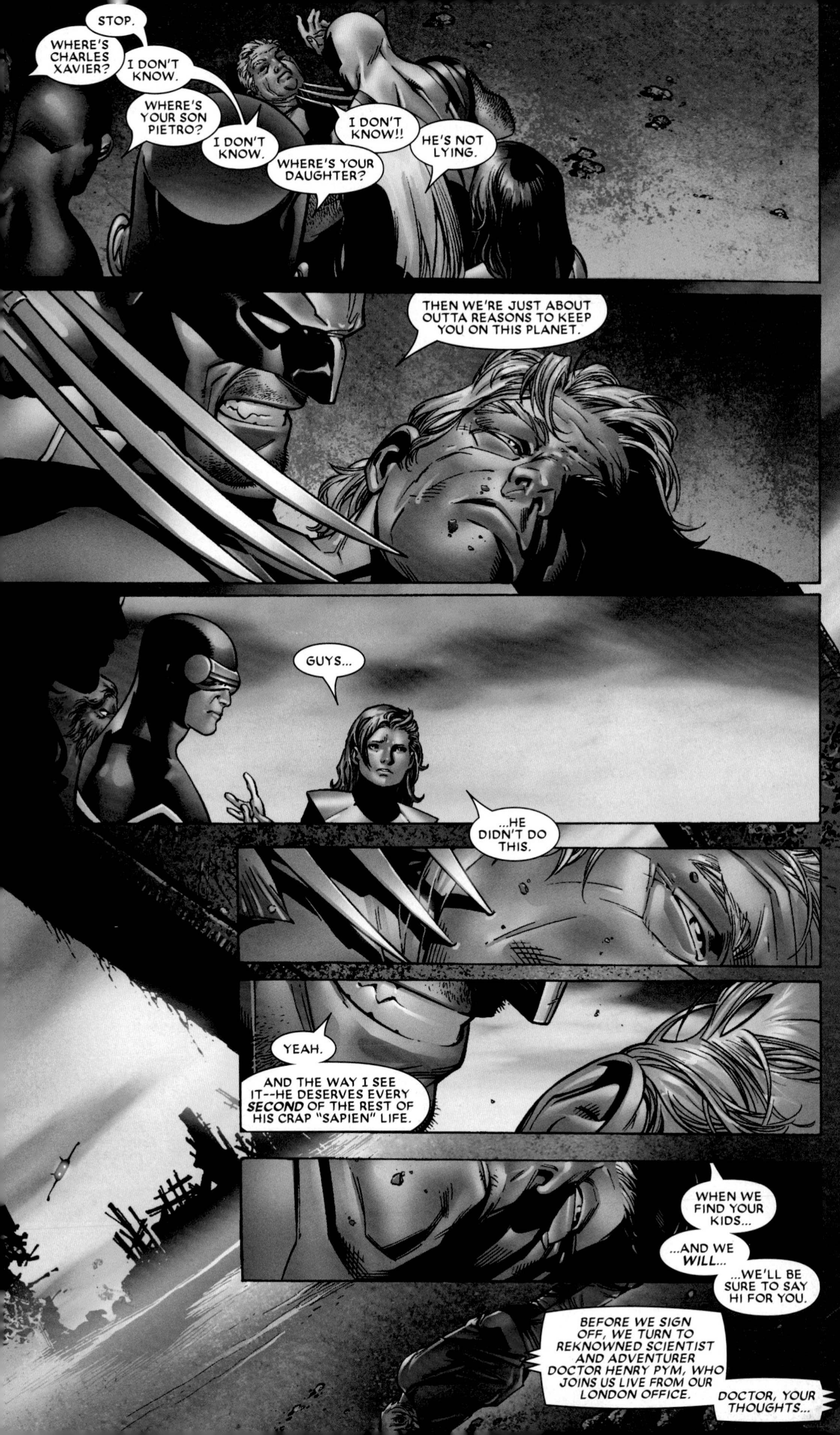

STOP.
WHERE'S CHARLES XAVIER?
I DON'T KNOW.
WHERE'S YOUR SON PIETRO?
I DON'T KNOW.
WHERE'S YOUR DAUGHTER?
I DON'T KNOW!!
HE'S NOT LYING.
THEN WE'RE JUST ABOUT OUTTA REASONS TO KEEP YOU ON THIS PLANET.
GUYS...
...HE DIDN'T DO THIS.
YEAH.
AND THE WAY I SEE IT--HE DESERVES EVERY *SECOND* OF THE REST OF HIS CRAP "SAPIEN" LIFE.
WHEN WE FIND YOUR KIDS...
...AND WE *WILL*...
...WE'LL BE SURE TO SAY HI FOR YOU.
BEFORE WE SIGN OFF, WE TURN TO REKNOWNED SCIENTIST AND ADVENTURER DOCTOR HENRY PYM, WHO JOINS US LIVE FROM OUR LONDON OFFICE.
DOCTOR, YOUR THOUGHTS...

AND I DON'T THINK THAT ANY PERSON C SCIENCE CAN REST UN WE FIND OUT EXACT WHAT HAS HAPPENE AND WHO OR WHAT RESPONSIBLE.

BECAUSE NOT ONLY HAS THE MUTA POPULATION BEEN DEVASTATED...

...AND MY HEART BREAKS FOR ALL MY MUTANT BROTHERS AND SISTERS...

...BUT THINK O HOW THIS EFFEC OUR ENTIRE ECOSYSTEM!

THE NATURAL ORDER OF OUR EVOLUTION AS A SPECIES HAS BEEN ALTERED.

'MORNING.

'MORNING.

THE ENTIRE WAY OUR PLANET REACTS TO OUR EXISTENCE HAS NOW CHANGED.

OUR PLANET MAY NOT BE READY TO HANDLE THE SUDDEN CHANGES THAT HAVE BEEN PUT UPON US AND IT.

AND THINK ABOUT THIS...

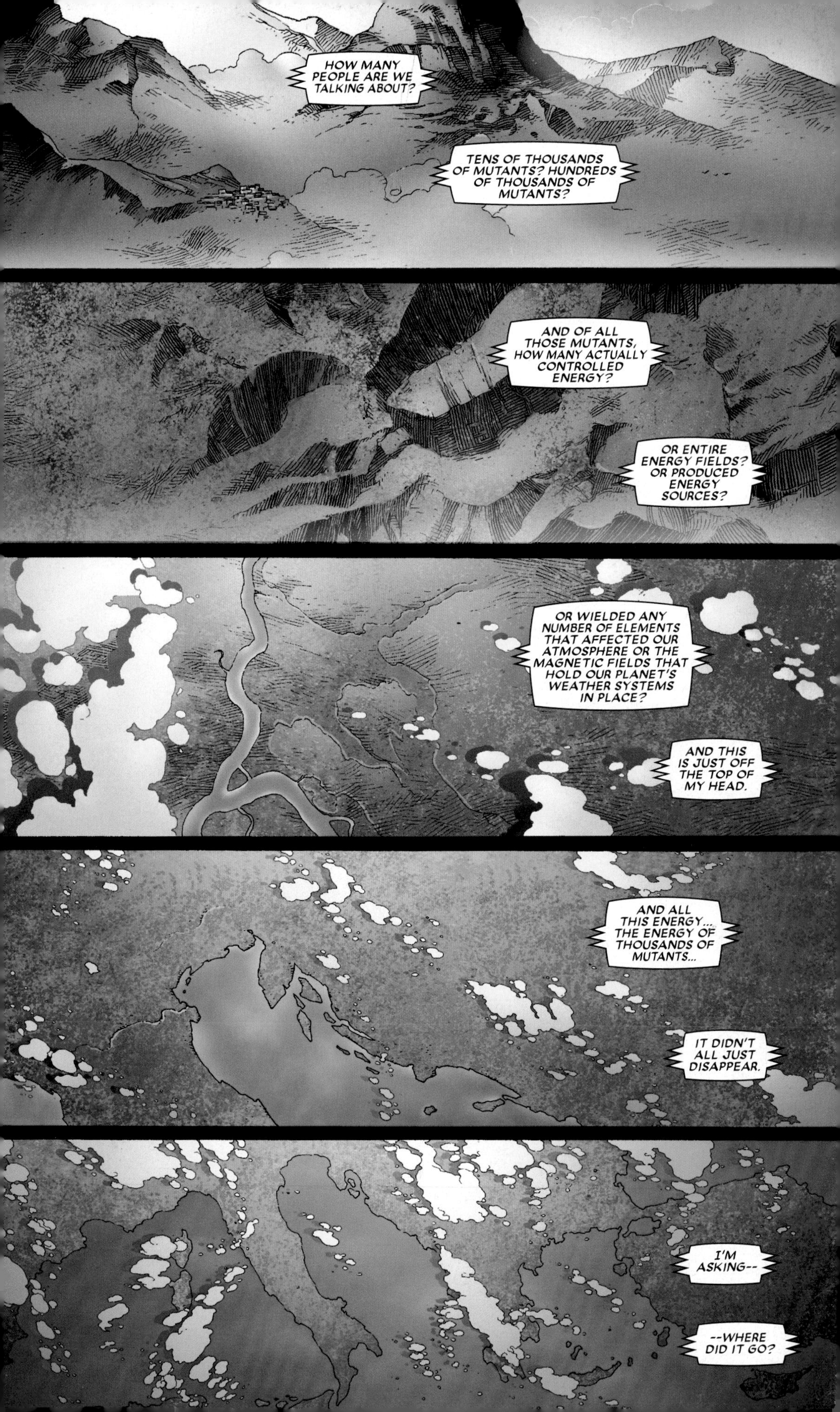
HOW MANY PEOPLE ARE WE TALKING ABOUT?
TENS OF THOUSANDS OF MUTANTS? HUNDREDS OF THOUSANDS OF MUTANTS?
AND OF ALL THOSE MUTANTS, HOW MANY ACTUALLY CONTROLLED ENERGY?
OR ENTIRE ENERGY FIELDS? OR PRODUCED ENERGY SOURCES?
OR WIELDED ANY NUMBER OF ELEMENTS THAT AFFECTED OUR ATMOSPHERE OR THE MAGNETIC FIELDS THAT HOLD OUR PLANET'S WEATHER SYSTEMS IN PLACE?
AND THIS IS JUST OFF THE TOP OF MY HEAD.
AND ALL THIS ENERGY... THE ENERGY OF THOUSANDS OF MUTANTS...
IT DIDN'T ALL JUST DISAPPEAR.
I'M ASKING--
--WHERE DID IT GO?

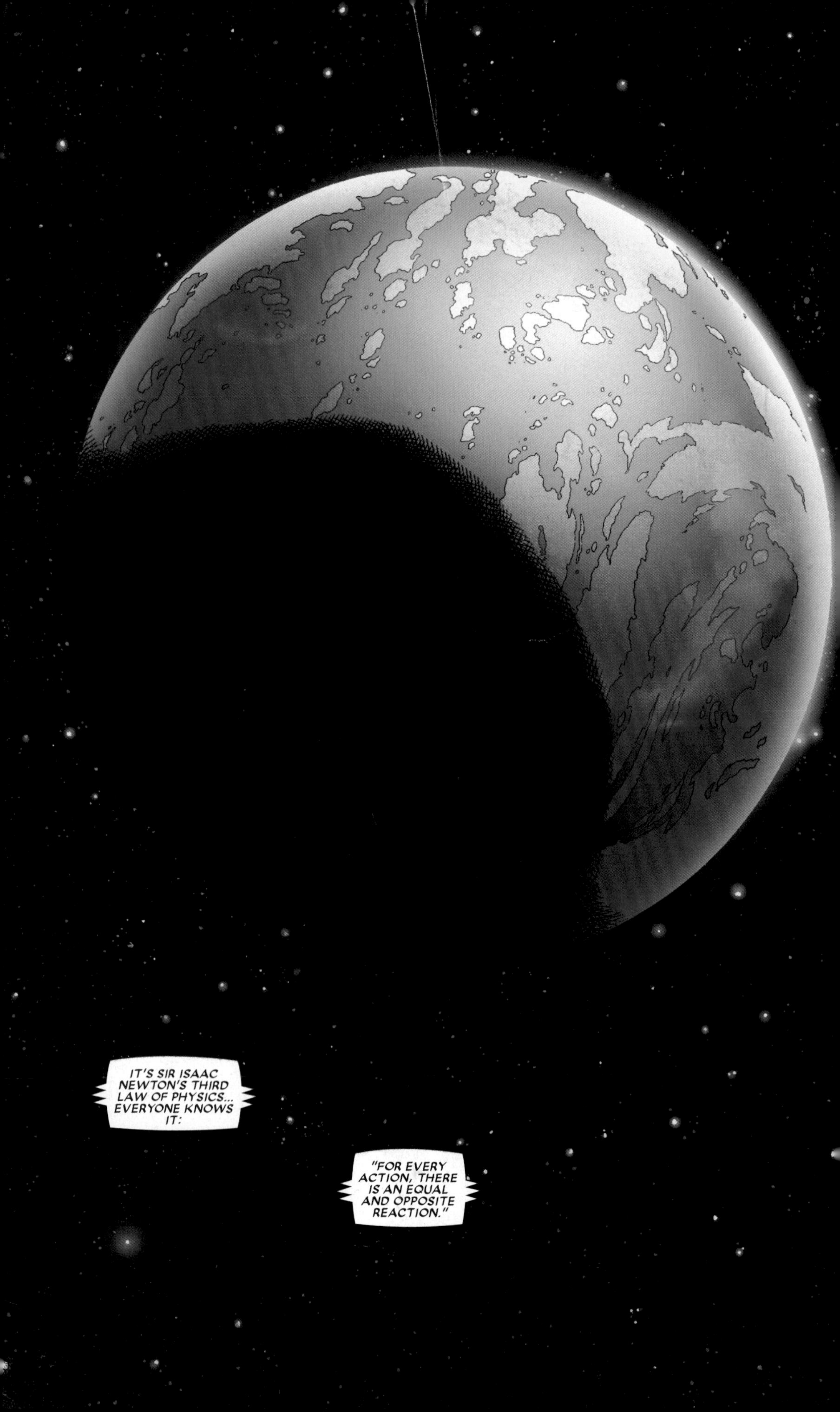
IT'S SIR ISAAC NEWTON'S THIRD LAW OF PHYSICS... EVERYONE KNOWS IT:
"FOR EVERY ACTION, THERE IS AN EQUAL AND OPPOSITE REACTION."

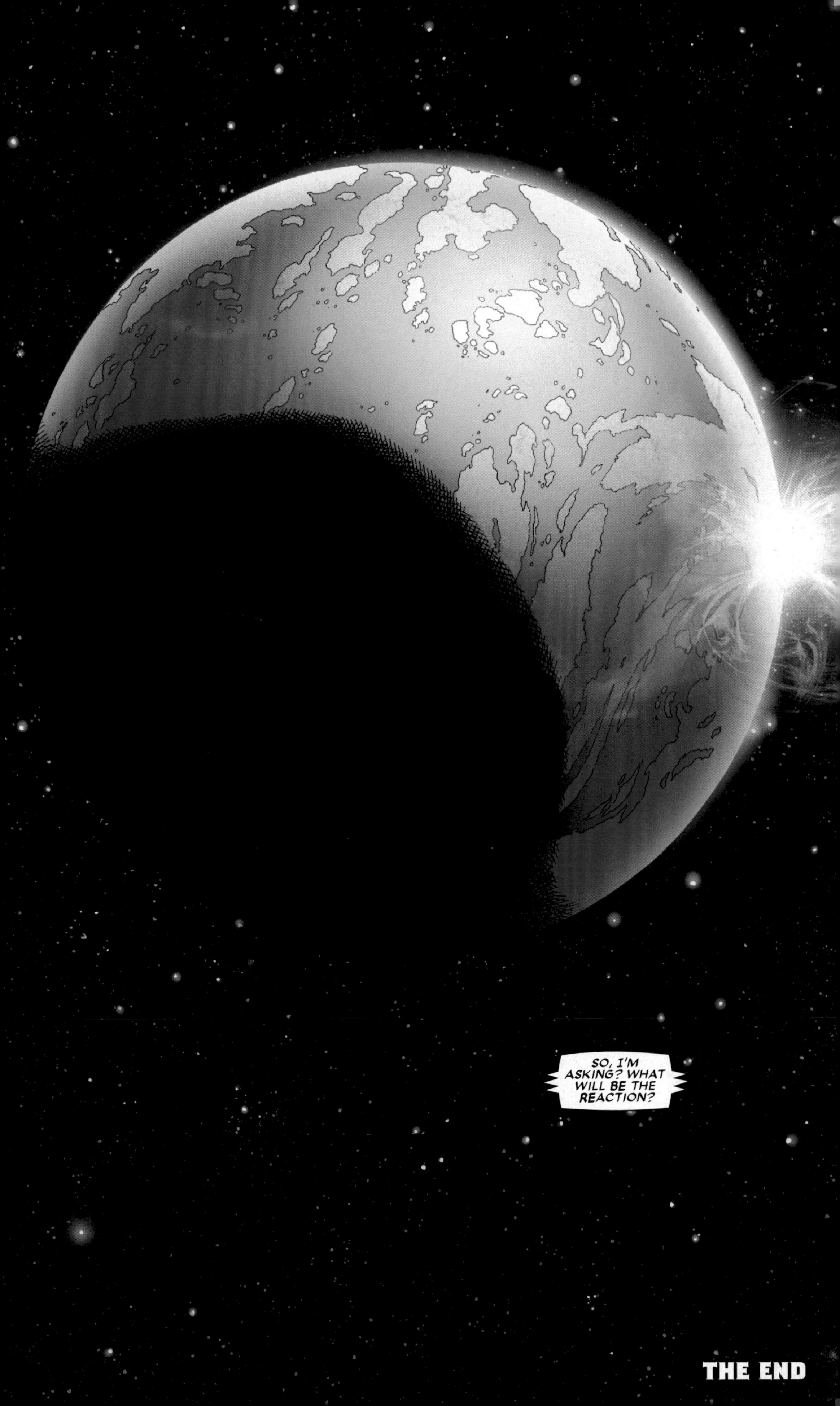
SO, I'M ASKING? WHAT WILL BE THE REACTION?
THE END

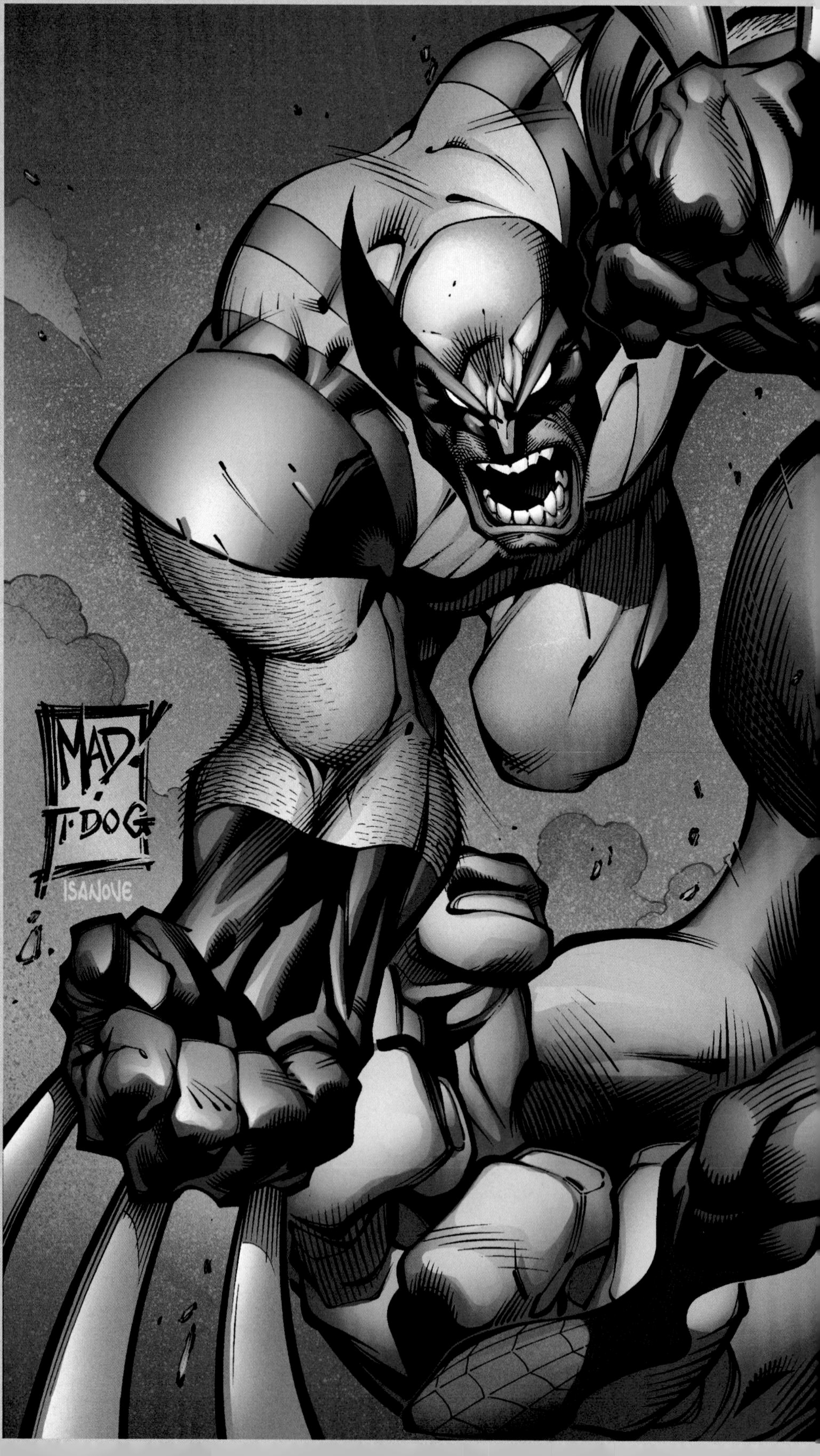
MAD
T·DOG
ISANOVE

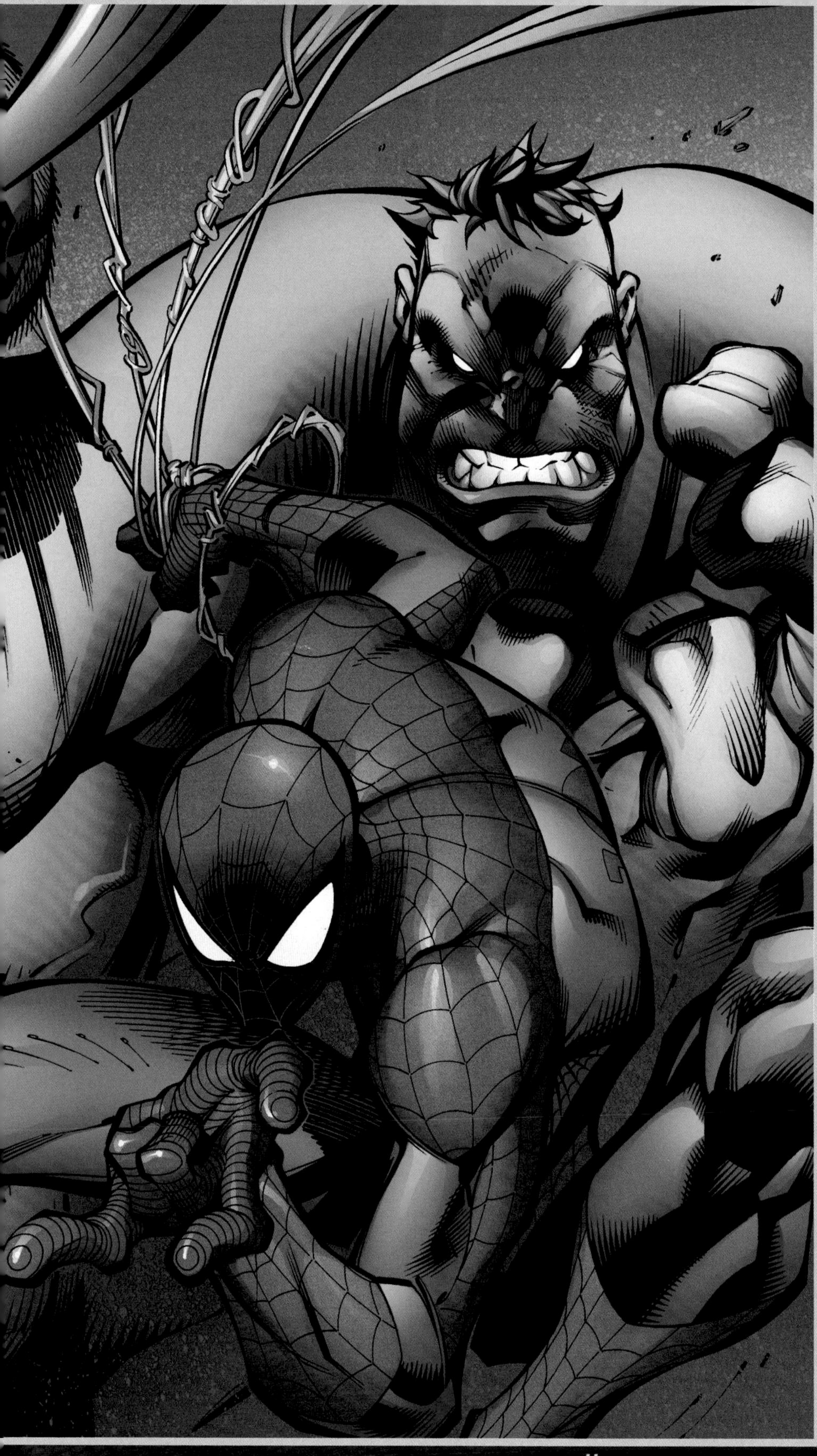

HOUSE OF M #1

Variant cover by Joe Madureira, Tim Townsend & Richard Isanove

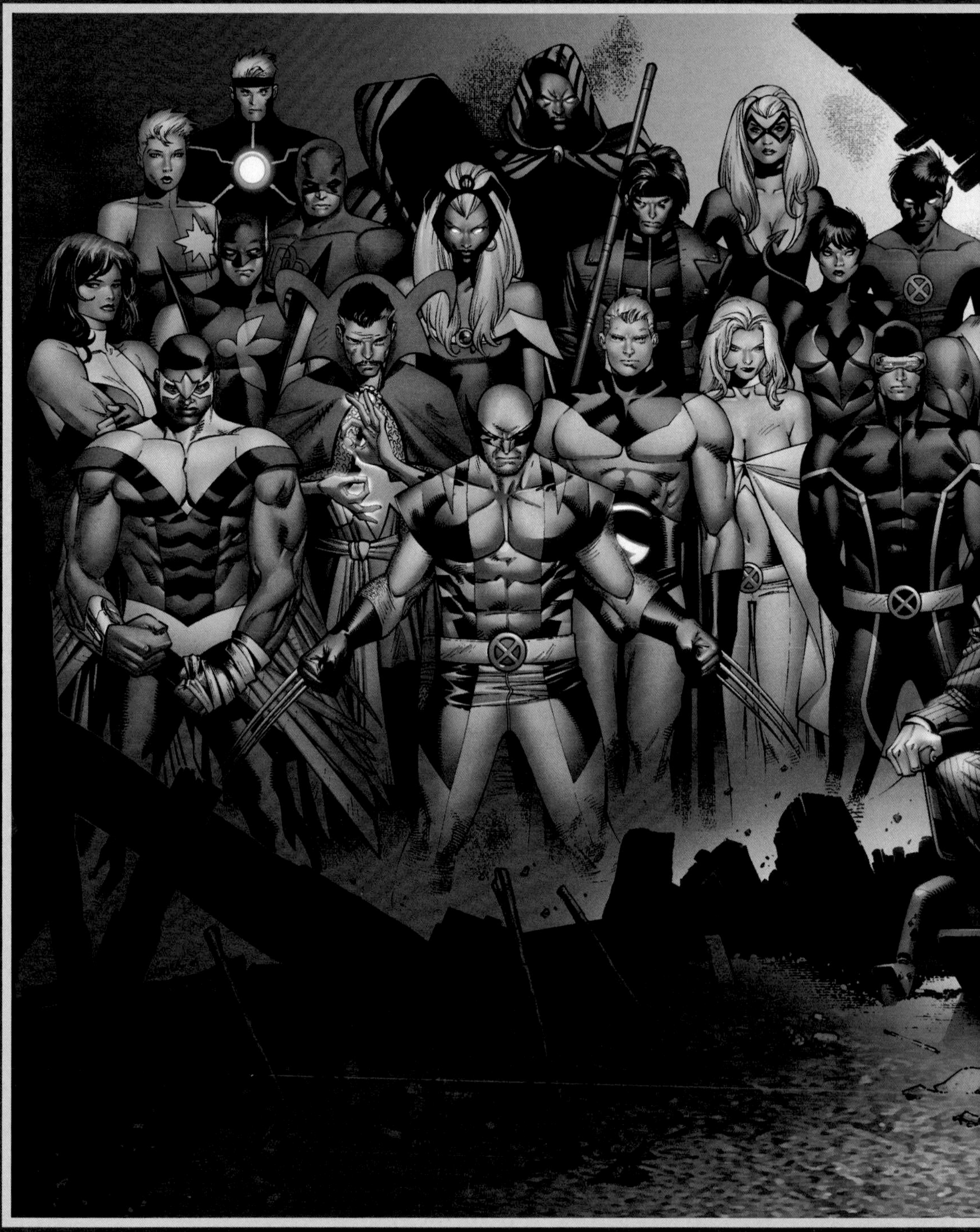

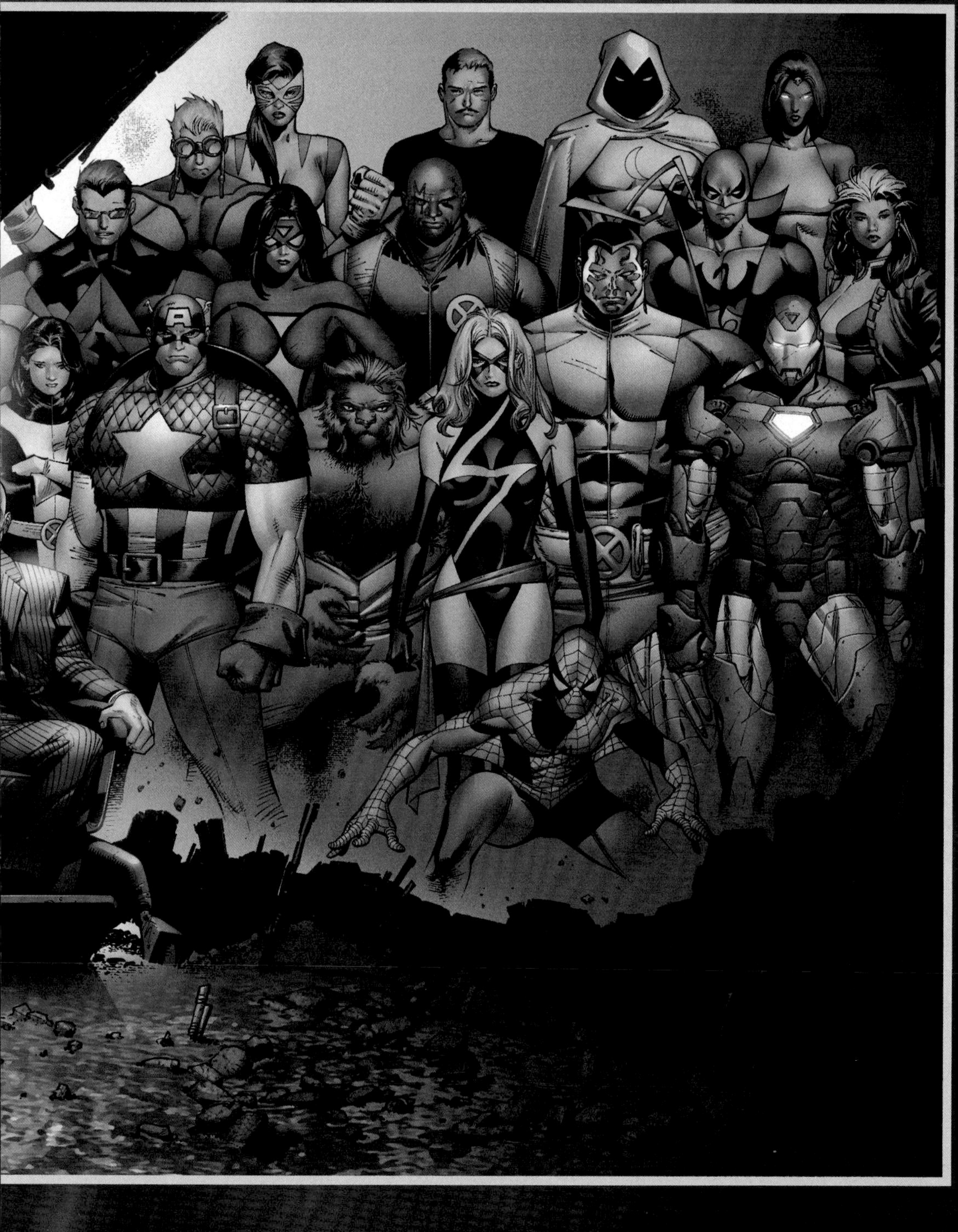

HOUSE OF M #1

Variant cover by Olivier Coipel, Tim Townsend & Frank D'Armata

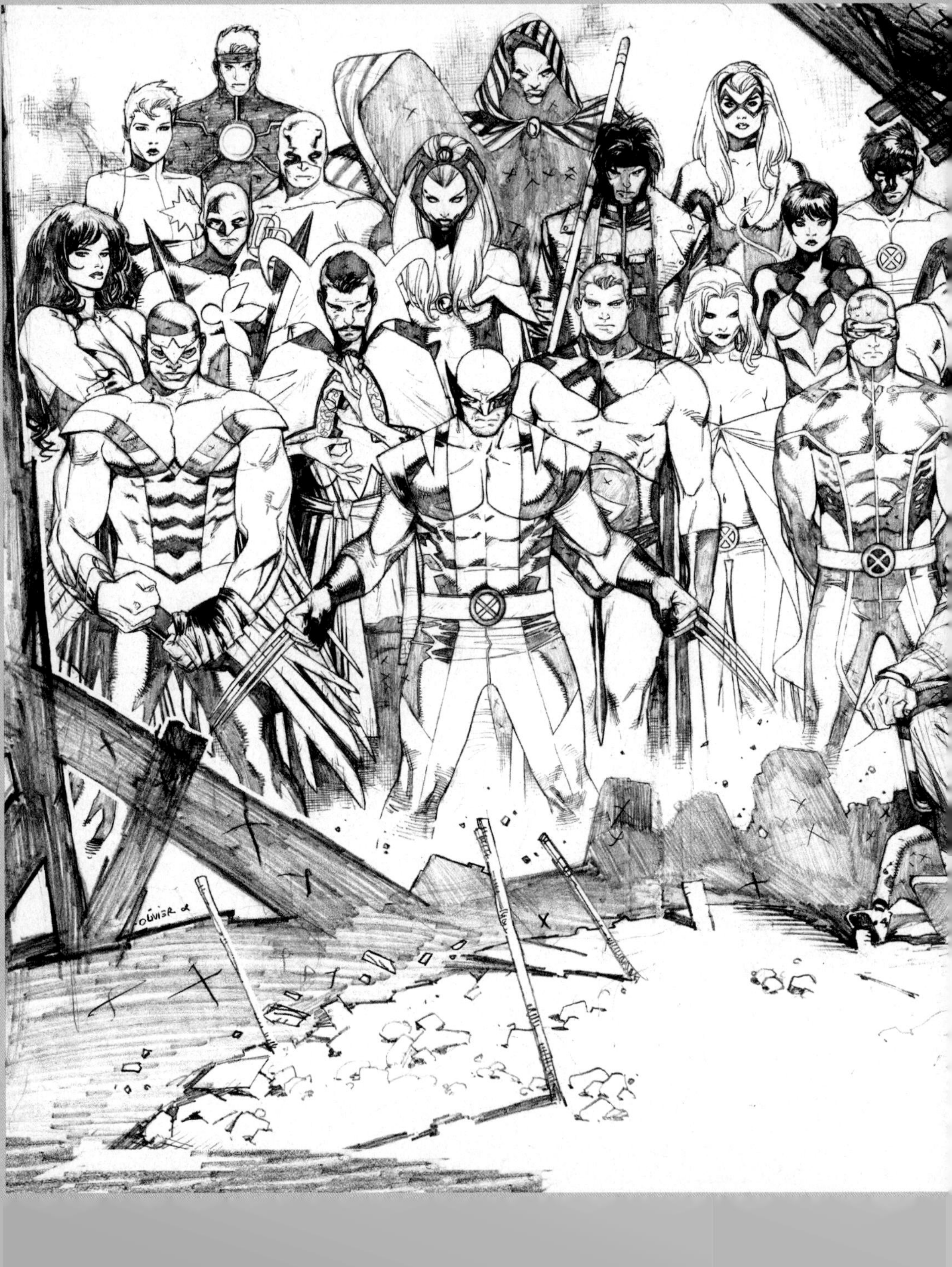

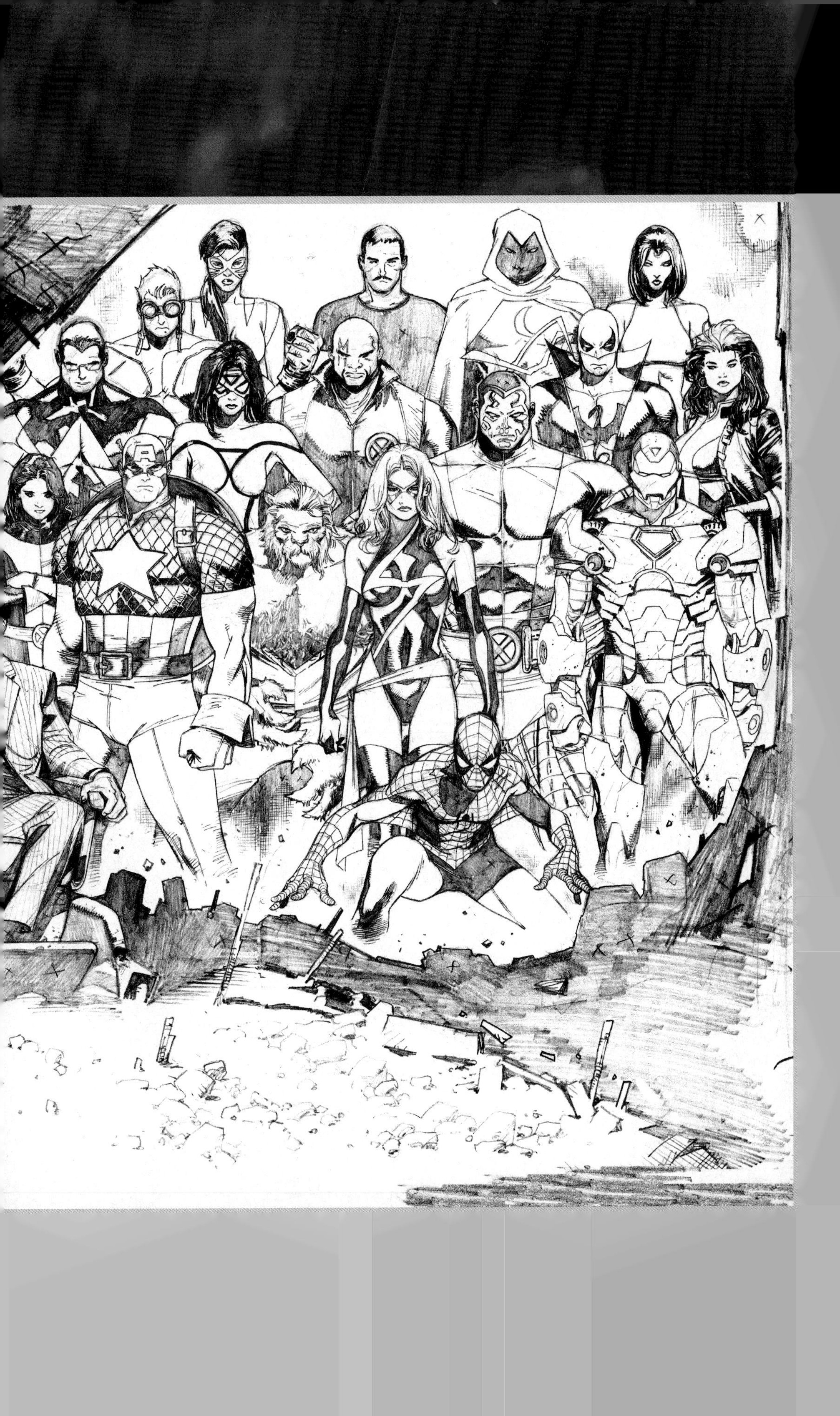

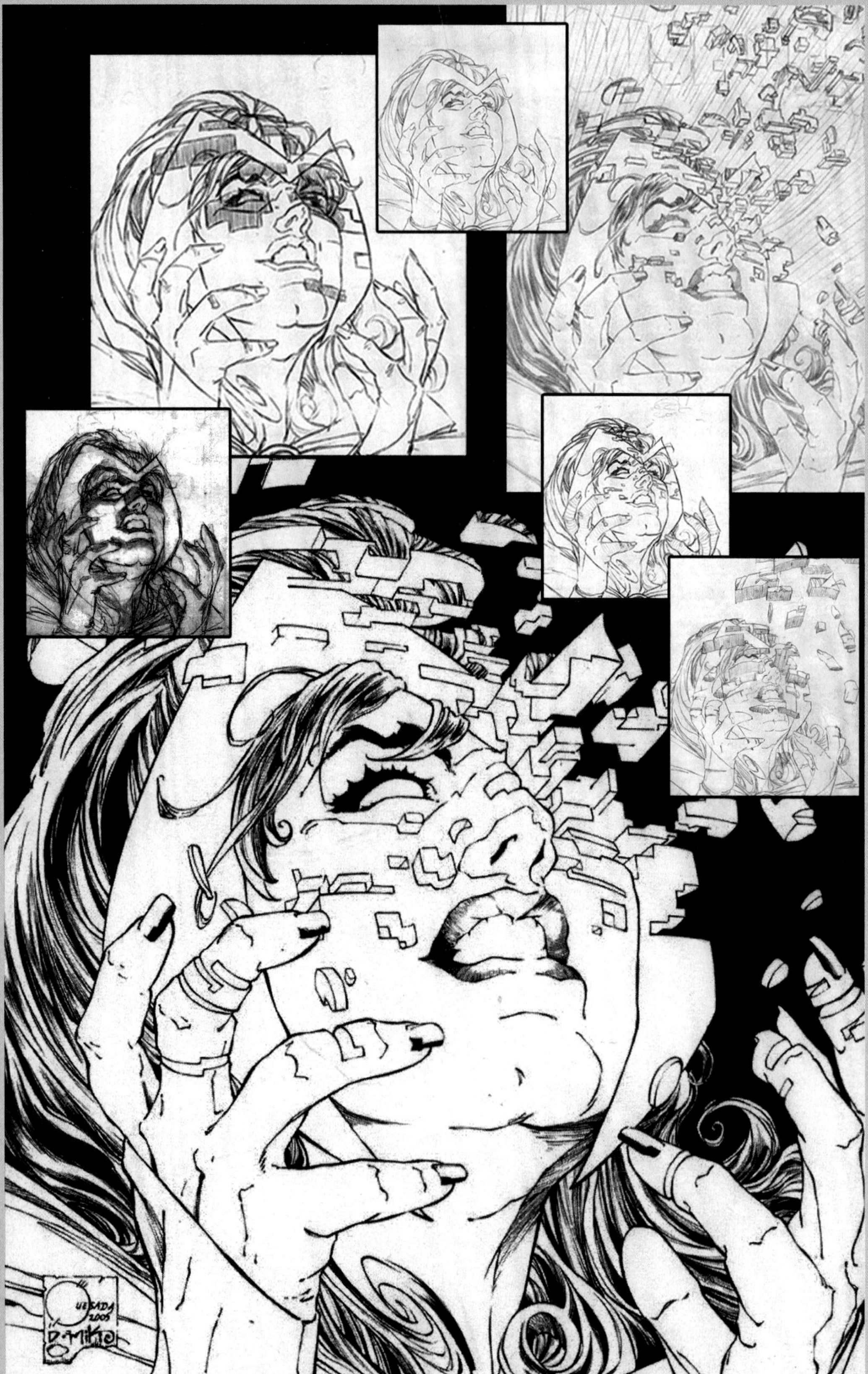

HOUSE OF M #1

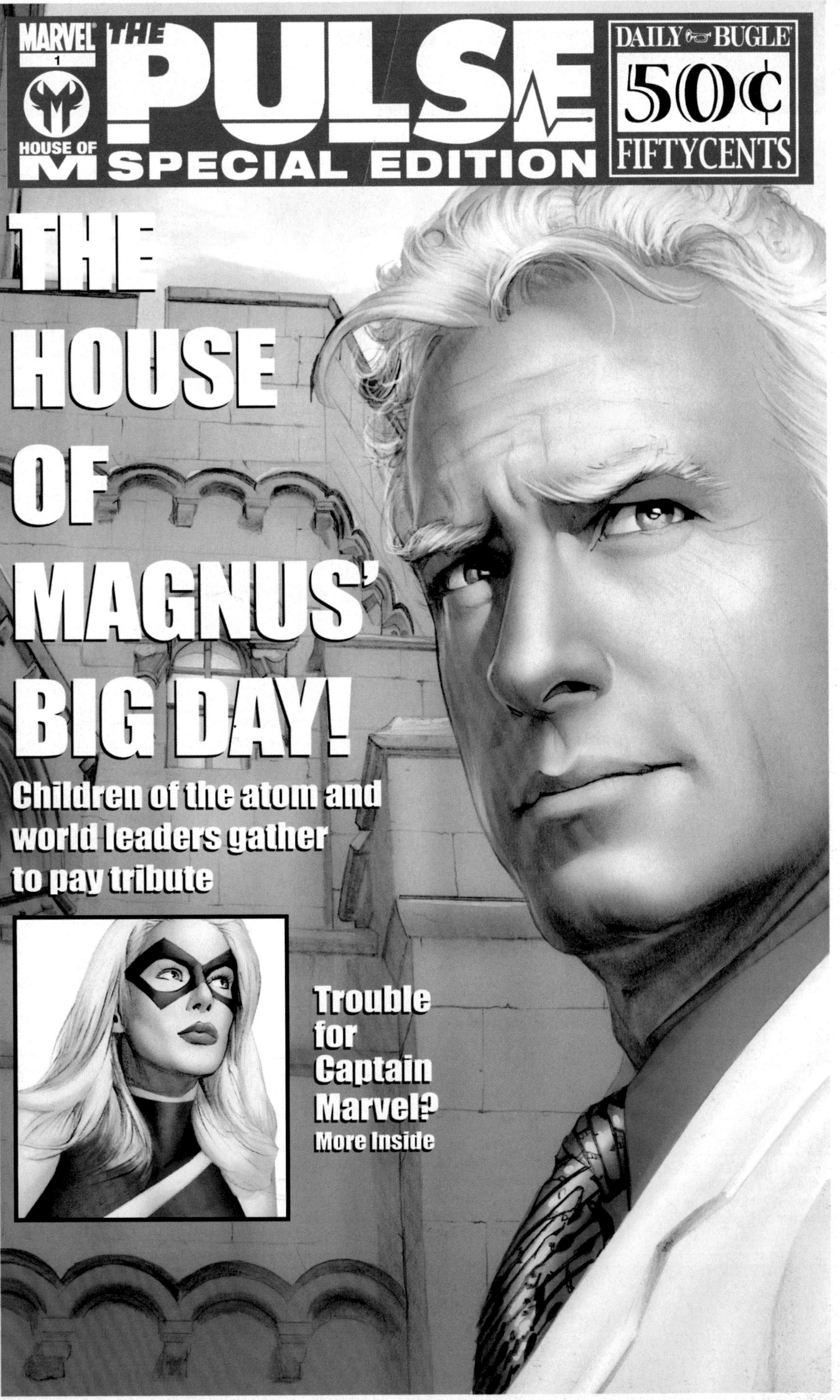
MARVEL 1
HOUSE OF M
THE PULSE
SPECIAL EDITION
DAILY BUGLE
50¢
FIFTYCENTS
THE HOUSE OF MAGNUS' BIG DAY!
Children of the atom and world leaders gather to pay tribute
Trouble for Captain Marvel?
More Inside

DAILY BUGLE

THE PULSE

SPECIAL EDITION

50¢ FIFTY CENTS

HOUSE OF MAGNUS

HOUSE OF MAGNUS
GALA THIS WEEKEND

BETTY BRANT

Eric Magnus will be the center of attention, once again! This time at a charity gala in his honor hosted by the British Royal family.

Prince Namor, King T'Challa, Sir Victor Von Doom, Genis-Vell, Princess Ororo of Kenya and a smorgasbord of international glitterati are expected to pay tribute to the man in a once-in-a-lifetime event commemorating the anniversary of the rebellion against homo sapien oppressors that held the world captive for decades.

The event has been put together by Magnus's children, all of whom will be in attendance.

Security will be tight as a highly publicized event like this makes a prime target for sapien relation sympathizers. Rumors of several underground movements using this event to make a statement of violence against the house of Magnus have been circulating for weeks, but sources close to the event say that no such threats have surfaced and that "we do not live in fear."

Born in the Nazi death camp in Auschwitz, Poland and the only member of his family to survive the camp, Magnus discovered himself to be one of the earliest reported mutants. With his all-encompassing powers over Earth's magnetic fields, Magnus became an early target in anti-mutant propaganda, where he was given the mocking name Magneto.

Magnus struggled through a number of sapien attacks over the years with various world governments and the media branding him a mutant terrorist. As New Yorkers know, on August 18, 1979, Eric Magnus came under attack by the original and highly

PRINCE NAMOR, ruler of Atlantis, will be attending.

controversial mutant-hunting Sentinels. This spectacular fight over the skies of New York City ended with Magnus unveiling proof of a worldwide multi-governmental anti-mutant conspiracy that funneled all the way up to our elected world leaders of the time, including American President Richard Nixon.

It was soon after the famed Sentinel takedown that the U.N. granted Magneto sovereignty over the newly established island of Genosha as the world capital of the mutant population.

Since then, with the homo superior population growing so quickly it is believed it will overtake the sapien population by the year 2013, Magneto's power base has restructured the world governments to include the pro-mutant life agenda into any and all law-making.

Look for full coverage of the event in the weekend edition of The Pulse along with an exclusive full color photo-essay of the red carpet arrivals.

House of Magnus' **ERIC MAGNUS** and **PRINCESS ORORO** of Kenya will be among the dignitaries celebrating thirty years of freedom from oppression by Sapiens.

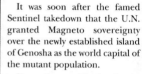

TABLE OF CONTENTS:

Headline News........ pages 2 & 3

Global News........... pages 4 & 5

Politics............................. page 6

History Today.................. page 7

Science............................ page 8

Sports .... page 9

Arts & Leisure .... page 10

Personal Growth........... page 11

HOT AS HELL!

TONY STARK
Hostile takeover averted. Industrialist Iron Man pulls a rabbit out of his hat and gets to keep his name on the door.

ALISON BLAIRE
Talk show picked up for three years for a reported 50 million dollar payday.

RALPH MACCHIO
Comics guru makes the House of Ideas the largest print publisher on the planet.

JASON WYNGARDE
Goes head to head with Tony Stark and has nothing to show for it.

WARREN WORTHINGTON III
Sex scandal threatens to bring down family empire.

HELLFIRE CLUB
Closes its doors for the first time since 1760.

COLD AS ICE!

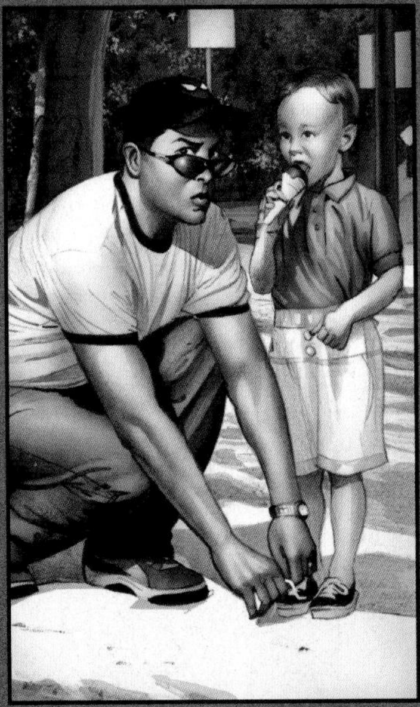

SPIDEY AND SON: **PETER PARKER and son RICHIE spend quality time in Central Park.**

BLIND ITEMS

GREEN WITH...

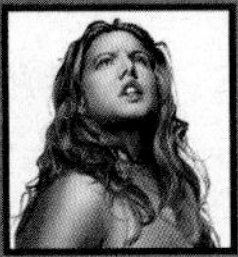

Word around City Hall is that a certain green-skinned, purple suited She-lawyer, who tends to overbill her sapien clients and then bully them into paying the tab, has been pressing green to flesh with a sight-impaired peer in the back halls of the courthouse. Though green isn't this man-about-town's favorite color, I certainly think she can do a little better. But hey, they say love is blind. They also say it isn't easy being green. And they also say: get a room, girl!!

WHEN IS IT TIME...

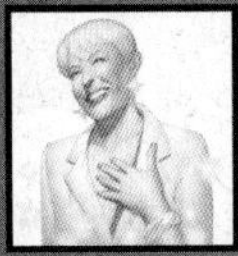

Poor national TV talk show host, Alison Blaire, whose bright shining smile brightens every dreary drone's mediocre life. With her big contract negotiation out of the way, when will she break the news to her daytime audience that her mutant days are numbered due to a rare blood disorder that has all but pulled the plug on her signature light show?

BUN IN THE IRON OVEN?

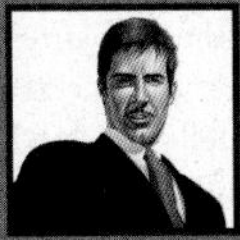

Like he didn't have enough trouble, now we hear that a once truly super super model is six months preggers and three months away from what's gotta be one of the biggest paydays in palimony history. And if the mustached one doesn't start returning her phone calls, it could get mighty ugly, mighty fast. Book and TV offers are flooding in. Tony, phone call on line one.

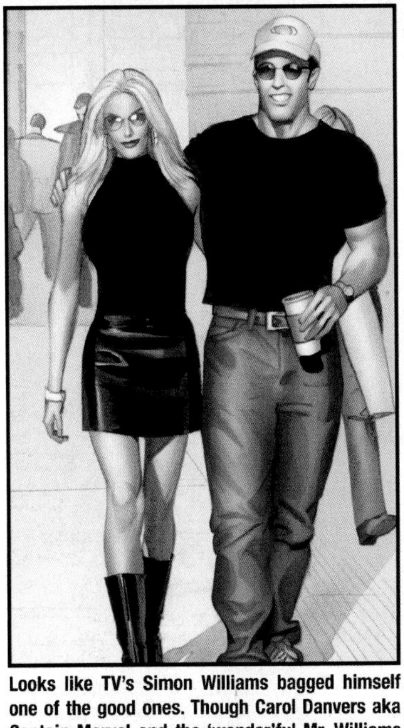

Looks like TV's Simon Williams bagged himself one of the good ones. Though Carol Danvers aka Captain Marvel and the 'wonder'ful Mr. Williams won't go on record, here's proof positive that they ARE just friends... with benefits.

NEW TECHNIQUE EYED IN MUTANT STEM-CELL DEBATE

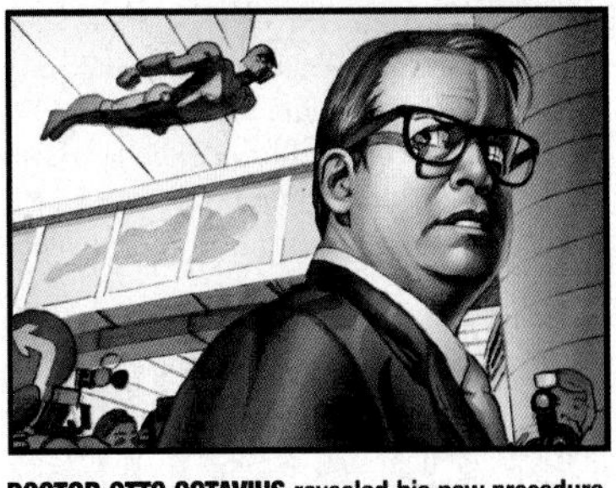

DOCTOR OTTO OCTAVIUS revealed his new procedure, known as "Altered."

With the nation deadlocked over the questionable morality of using mutated homo superior embryos for research for human medical treatments, a high ranking member of the President's Council on Nu-Bioethics is developing a proposal that might allow scientists to create the equivalent of homo superior embryonic stem cells without destroying mutant embryos, offering a potential path out of the controversy.

Dr. Otto Octavius, a bioethicist and staunch opponent of research on mutant embryos, has developed a procedure called Altered (Continued 15-B)

HYDRA SPLINTER GROUP CLAIMS RESPONSIBILITY FOR KIDNAPPING

A woman who goes by the name Madame Hydra released a statement to the press via a web site claiming responsibility for the abduction of Mariko Harada, daughter of Japanese businessman Keniuchio Harada. The statement claims that Harada is actually the leader of the Japanese crime cartel Clan Yashida. Harada has denied these claims on numerous occasion and points to his legitimate business ventures both here in America and abroad.

Mariko Harada, 11, was last seen being dragged into a red van containing at least five masked males right outside the Baxter Building, NYPD Sgt. Jasper Sitwell said that the girl is believed to be in imminent danger. Madame Hydra's statement included the words: "This girl's mutant blood will spill in the streets if the Harada family does not forfeit their profits in the Indonesian MGH drug trade."

The Harada family, through a statement, said: "This devastating turn of events is nothing short of blackmail. The Harada family does not profit from the international drug trade. This is the work of psychotics. Please, we beg you, give us our innocent daughter back. If she is not returned unharmed, there will be no end to the retaliation."

Mariko is described as 4 feet tall, weighing 65 pounds, with black hair and black eyes, and wearing a white sweater and black jeans.

Anyone with information is asked to contact the nearest law-enforcement agency.

MARIKO HARADA, AGE 11. If you have any information regarding her whereabouts, please contact the F.B.I.

LORD KEVIN PLUNDER GETS ASYLUM IN THE UNITED STATES

LORD PLUNDER seen here with constant companion **ZABU.**

Human rights activist Lord Kevin Reginald Plunder has obtained political asylum in the United States after fleeing Pangea, where he had been serving a prison sentence for speaking out against the established government.

Plunder, 26, was originally given a four-year prison sentence on appeal on September 25th. In the last of a series of secret hearings, the Seventh District Court of Pandor sentenced Lord Plunder to (Continued 6-B)

SUSPECTED SAPIEN GANG MEMBERS ARRESTED IN HELL'S KITCHEN

NYPD AJ15279
RAPHAEL VEGA
DOB 05 27 87 MALE
NYPD SHANG-CHI AJ15310
DOB 03 24 84 MALE

SUSPECTS RAPHAEL VEGA AND SHANG-CH
Suspects in custody.

HELL'S KITCHEN (Reuters) Fifty-on people believed to be members of tw powerful organized sapien crime gang in New York were rounded up in pre dawn raids and indicted on Tuesday authorities said.

In three separate indictments filed in Manhattan Federal Court, the gang members faced charges including mur der, attempted murder, racketeering extortion, money laundering and opera tion of illegal gambling businesses.

Federal agents and New York police arrested members of the Dragon and Wolfpack crime organizations after investigations spanning two years, authorities said.

The Dragon group, led by Shang-Chi, and the Wolfpack group, headed by Raphael Vega, used violence and threats to protect their turf and profits, the U.S Attorney General's office said.

A third indictment charged five defen dants with smuggling illegal sapiens from Europe to the United States for fees of up to $44,000 each, and holding them hostage pending payment.

It is expected to take several weeks for the trial to begin due to the defense arguing that no mutant should be on the jury. This would set a danger ous precedent if the judge rules in favor of the defense on this point.

THUNDER DOWN UNDER

NOT-SO-JOLLY GREEN GIANT — The Hulk in the Australian Outback.

THE PULSE:
SPECIAL EDITION NEWSPAPER

THE PULSE Created by **BRIAN MICHAEL BENDIS**
Photography by **MIKE MAYHEW** with color stock
from **AVALON STUDIOS**
Contributing Writers:
BRIAN MICHAEL BENDIS
ED BRUBAKER
CHRIS CLAREMONT
PETER DAVID
NUNZIO DEFILLIPIS
DAVID HINE
REGINALD HUDLIN
JOHN LAYMAN
FABIAN NICIEZA
GREG PAK
TOM PEYER
DANIEL WAY
CHRISTINA WEIR
Designed by **PATRICK MCGRATH**
Creative Director: **TOM MARVELLI**
Assistant Editor: **AUBREY SITTERSON**
Editor: **ANDY SCHMIDT**
Editor in Chief: **JOE QUESADA**
Publisher: **DAN BUCKLEY**

by Jacob Gunterson

The potential threat to the Australian government, run by the individual known simply as "Exodus," was first revealed when government forces stationed in Darwin made an aerial and ground assault on illegally massing humans at the border of the Tanami Desert. Australian laws regarding norm gatherings are the strictest in the world, since illegal immigration by norms has been a consistent problem in Australia for some time now. Consequently, the norm population is closely monitored, and illegals are subject to immediate arrest and deportation.

"The Tanami Desert has become a major problem for us," said one mutant official, speaking on condition of anonymity. "Norms have been flooding in from all over and putting down stakes there. Maybe they thought that no one would care about it, them being in the desert and all."

If that was indeed their reasoning, then it was incorrect. Government forces, under the command of "Unus the Untouchable," mounted an assault against the Tanami refugees with the intention of arrest, trial, and deportation. Either that or, according to sources, the most physically able would be put to work in labor camps where they would be retrained to be of benefit to the government.

The surprising appearance of the Hulk, however, turned what was expected to be a simple operation into a terrifying rout for the government forces.

"He came out of nowhere!" stated John Hoffman, 34, one of the government soldiers. "He had to be, like, fifteen feet tall! And he had laser beams shooting out his eyes, and giant claws out to here!"

Other witnesses claimed additional powers for the Hulk, including mind control, elasticity, and the ability to split into four different versions of himself. Unus the Untouchable himself was hospitalized after the battle and unable to comment.

Despite differing descriptions of the encounter, in which the Hulk annihilated ground troops including giant manned robots, several consistent reports emerged.

The first was that the Hulk was apparently working side-by-side with the human terrorist organization Advanced Idea Mechanics, or AIM. Reported present in the battle were such noted renegades as "the Scorpion," her mother, AIM scientist Monica Rappaccini and cyber-mechanics expert Aaron Isaacs, whose son was apprehended. While the boy's current whereabouts is classified, sources claim that he has been airlifted to Sydney where the governor's elite guard will interrogate him.

The second report was that the Hulk was covered in what are believed to be Aboriginal tribal markings. This has led to speculation that either the Hulk or his alter ego, Banner, had taken up residence with an Aboriginal tribe. According to sources, the Mutant Forces attack route brought them through Aboriginal territory, and that might have brought the wrath of the Hulk down upon them.

The whereabouts of the Hulk and his AIM allies is unknown at the present time, but government forces were confident they would be located and arrested in short order. (Continued in Hulk #83-87)

A BRITISH BIRTHDAY BASH

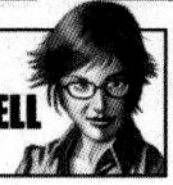
KAT
FARRELL

The British Royal Family decamped this morning from Buckingham Palace, London, to Braddock Manor, the ancestral family estate in the West of England, for a weekend of festival activities in celebration of the forthcoming birthday of Lord Magneto. The published guest list reads like an A-List "Who's Who" of both the Mutant and Baseline Society, headed by the Prime Minister and Mrs. Blair. The centerpiece of the scheduled events is a gala ball to be hosted by the Monarch himself and his consort, Her Royal Majesty, Queen Meggan. Initially, trial balloons had been floated about the possibility of Lord Magneto himself attending but it is now believed that he will be staying in his capital, Hammer Bay, Genosha.

The Monarch of course will be attending the actual birthday party itself in Genosha, along with the other Heads of State of the world's Great Powers.

One question making the rounds is the status of the Monarch's twin sister, Her Royal Highness Princess Elisabeth Gloriana. A self-described "rebel" from the start, she has always insisted on leading a wholly indepen-

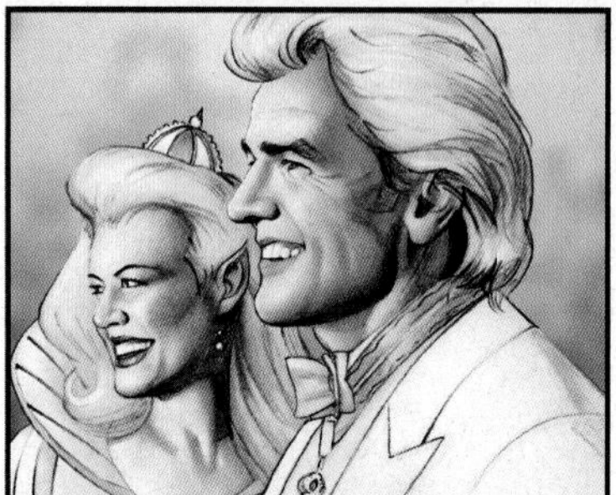

KING AND QUEEN TOGETHER - Brian and Meggan Braddock enjoy the day together.

dent life, passionately committing herself to a number of fringe causes, most notably the so-called "Human Rights Campaign," which claims that the Baseline Gene populace of the world is being oppressed by the dominant Mutant Humanity. Recently, her actions led to widespread reports–since refuted—of her death in Valencia, Spain at the hands of a Baseline terrorist, Vargas. Her current whereabouts, and plans, are unknown; most recent reports–little more than rumors, really–state that she is "traveling," along with her Lady-ir Waiting, Lady Rachel Grey. As has been polic from the start, there has been no commen from the Palace to repeated enquiries abou both; nor, according to Royal Spokesma Peter Wisdom, will there be.

Further complicating the planned celebra tions here in Great Britain are as yet uncon firmed reports of possible terrorist sighting within the Realm. A National Alert has bee issued for two unregistered aliens, one male two meters tall and wearing red armor, answe ing to the code-name "Juggernaut." Th other is female, of University age, describe as looking very much like a classical goblin with pointed "elf"-ears, indigo skin and hai Instead of the normal number of fingers an toes, she has two digits on her hands an feet and preternatural acrobatic abilities. Sh may also have a tail. The only name applie to her is "Nocturne."

Police and security forces are confident the pose no threat to the Monarch and soon expe to take the fugitives into custody. Further, a least one Sentinel has been deployed to stan in the Monarch's personal defense. (Continue in *Uncanny X-Men #462-465*)

KREE DELEGATION ARRIVES TO HOPEFUL RECEPTION

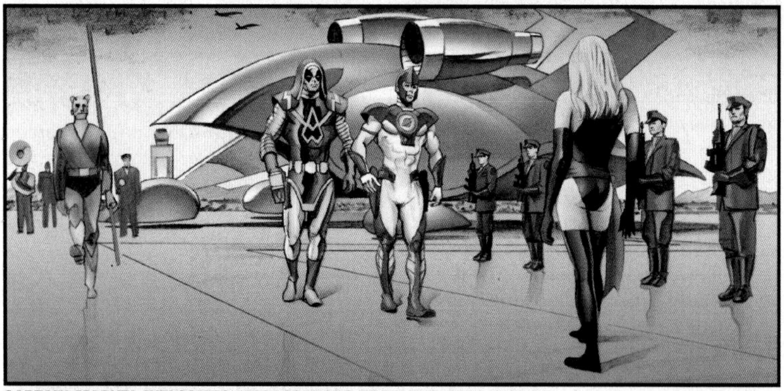

CAPTAIN MARVEL WELCOMES AMBASSADORS FROM THE KREE EMPIRE - Carol Danvers greets aliens from another world in unprecedented meeting.

McGuire Air Force Base, New Jersey – Amid secrecy, increased security and continued uncertainty, a delegation representing the interstellar Kree Empire arrived on Earth yesterday. Landing at 2:20 A.M. EST, the alien ship was met by the Chairman of the Joints Chiefs of Staff, Secretary of State Robert Kelly and the Kree-empowered superhuman known as Captain Marvel. The delegation arrived with the expectation of finalizing a treaty providing protection by the massive Kree Armada against interstellar aggressors. Earth's solar system, in recent years, has become a focal point in the shipping routes and wormhole transportation channels used by advanced alien races.

Captain Marvel, whose powers were created by Kree technology that had been hidden on Earth for centuries, welcomed the delegation, saying, "We greet the ambassadors representing the Kree Empire, and the delegate from the outpost on Titan's Moon, the son of my very dear, departed friend, Mar-Vell. We hope that you first step on Earth will be our first step togethe towards galactic peace and prosperity."

Although the delegates were not made availabl to the press, Chief Delegate Ronan issued statement claiming, "We have watched this worl grow in truly wondrous ways. Your evolution ha both surprised and intrigued us. We are here t see that your advancements continue free fron the threat of species jealousies and evolutionar reactionaries that permeate our galaxy."

The delegate from Titan referred to by Captai Marvel, Private Genis-Vell of the Kree Explorator Armada, was not made available for commen but he has been given clearance by the Unite Nations and the Unified Armed Forces of Eart to engage the planet and its people in a fac finding goodwill tour.

It is expected that while Ronan and th majority of the Kree delegation finalizes th parameters of the treaty at the United Nation starting today, Private Vell will make numerou public appearances. Vell is expected to tour t Magneto's "VICTORY" statue on the Great Law in Central Park on Friday, with controversia appearances at Cape Canaveral Space Cente and NORAD Control Center's Valhalla Bas planned for next week. (Continued in *Ne Thunderbolts #11*)

WORLD LEADERS GATHER FOR HISTORIC GENOSHA SUMMIT

MAGNETO, MOLE KING RIFT WIDENS AS TRADE TREATY STALLS

GENOSHA — Lord Magneto's "road map" to peace with renegade leader and longtime House of M opponent Mole King stalled yesterday as both sides failed to reach accord and the treaty was rejected. Joining the historic meeting with the leader of the rogue subterranean nation-ate of Molvia was Latverian ruler Victor Von Doom. The meeting, a bid to stem Moloid insurgent violence that has claimed more than 00 lives since September, took place in the capital of Genosha.

This summit, the first between Lord Magneto and Mole King, was originally hailed as a breakthrough in relations with mutant and Moloid people, and the first step toward legitimacy of the unrecognized Molvian nation state. However, the leaders were unable to reach an agreement, and sparred over matters of Molvian sovereignty. Also contested were mineral rights to vast uranium and vibranium deposits on disputed Molvian territory, and a trade proposal was also rejected.

In a brief press conference following the meeting, Lord Magneto said he was confident this is a first step on a path that will ultimately result in long and lasting peace between mutants, man and Moloids."

Mole King, however, was less optimistic, admitting "There are significant and fundamental philosophical differences between the Moloids and the House of M. If we are on a road to peace, it will be a long and difficult road indeed."

Latveria's temperamental leader Von Doom, who often refuses to participate in dialogue with Genosha's press corps altogether, offered a pessimistic assessment: The Mole King is a fool. He lacks respect, and an understanding of his true place in the world. This summit has been a farce, and a waste of Doom's time."

The summit, which was scheduled to last the remainder of the week, concluded prematurely, at Doom's insistence, when he is alleged to have smashed the conference table before angrily departing for Latveria. Magneto, however, remained upbeat. "The Mole King and I may not see eye-to-eye, but he is a passionate leader of his people and a wise man. I have no doubt we will eventually come to some sort of understanding."

Doom was unavailable for further comment. (Continued in *Fantastic Four: House of M # 1-3*)

LORD MAGNETO WITH LATVERIAN LEADER VON DOOM AND THE SUBTERRANEAN MONARCH MOLE KING: The summit's trade treaty discussions stall, creating a greater divide between nations

EMBASSY ATTACKED; SENTINEL STOLEN

KAT FARRELL

MEXICO CITY: Late Friday evening, an embassy building in Mexico City was the site of the latest bloody attack by non-mutant guerilla forces against the House of Magnus. Stolen during the attack was a Sentinel robot slated to be a gift to the Mexican government. The whereabouts of the Sentinel, as well as the details of the attack, remain largely unknown.

Sebastian Shaw, director of S.H.I.E.L.D., held a brief press conference in the hours following the attack. When asked if the elite Red Guard had been deployed, Shaw replied, "We believe that we already have one of our agents inside the organization."

Before leaving, Shaw was asked if the rumor that a S.H.I.E.L.D. agent had been killed during the attack was true. Shaw, smiling, replied, "This is a wild exaggeration. One of our agents was injured during the attack, but it was most assuredly not life-threatening. He'll be fine." (Continued in *Wolverine #33-35*)

S.H.I.E.L.D. DIRECTOR SEBASTIAN SHAW SPEAKS OUT AGAINST THE TERRORISTS. "They will be found. They will be caught. And they will be punished," he said.

FIFTIETH ANNIVERSARY OF CAPTAIN AMERICA'S WALK ON MOON CELEBRATED

By Ed "Scoop" Brubaker

It's hard to believe, with all the progress that manned space flight has made in the last generation, that it was only 50 years ago that the USA first landed on the moon. More memorable, of course, are the words of Astronaut Steve Rogers, who fought through World War Two as America's Super-soldier, Captain America; "One small step for man, one giant step for peace between man and mutantkind." For it was only through the joint work of Homo-Sapien and Homo-Superior scientists that America had reached the stars before the Russians, who were at that point still our enemy. And yet last night's celebration of the man's life and achievements in Manhattan was a sparsely attended affair, at best.

Among the attending, though, was the Sub-Mariner's son, Prince Wringor of Atlantis, who spoke at length about Rogers' heroism before the Senate Sub-Committee hearings on Mutant Activity in 1951. As you'll recall, Rogers resigned from his role as Captain America on live TV, on the Senate floor, during those hearings, after refusing to inform on his one-time teammate, Prince Namor, who the government at the time considered a dangerous mutant.

It was controversial for Rogers to be allowed into the Space Program after such a public incident, but it's believed some strings were pulled and arguments made behind closed doors about the proper use of Rogers' government-financed enhanced abilities. In any case, Rogers' statement at that time was literally a giant step forward in human/mutant relations, which were at the time, quite heated and dangerous. Historians now consider Rogers one of the key "bridge" figures who helped society move forward, helped move people beyond their prejudices and fears, and allowed Mutants to first be accepted as equals.

CAPTAIN STEVE ROGERS walks on the Moon 50 years ago.

Which is why Rogers' statements of warning about Magnus in the '70s, after his destruction of the Sentinel program, came as such a shock to many within the Mutant community. Rogers warned that Magnus's plans sounded suspiciously like the kind of tyranny he'd spent most of the '40s fighting against. Sources inside NASA claim he was forced into retirement shortly thereafter. This might explain the lack of any significant official Mutant presence at this event.

Rogers himself spoke for no more than a minute, in a careful and calm voice, yet one slightly tinged with sadness, thanking the men and mutants who'd fought and died beside him in the War, and those who'd sacrificed themselves in the Space Program. And then he was gone, leaving us with but a memory of a living legend, a man who walked among giants and among the stars. (Continued in *Captain America #10*)

S MUTANT MURDERER REALLY SAPIEN SCIENTIST?

DINBURGH, SCOTLAND — In recent onths, a string of ghastly murders originating in the Scottish capital have made eadlines around the world. Dubbed Mutant X" by the tabloid press, the as-yet-nidentified serial killer remains at large, nd authorities fear that he or she may xtend the murderous rampage beyond e borders of the United Kingdom. The nsational crimes first gained widespread otoriety owing to the fact that the vic-ms are exclusively mutants, and that each orpse was found in a hideous, emaciated ate, as if mummified. This telltale disfig-rement is Mutant X's calling card and eemingly clear evidence that the killer is a utant with the ability to somehow wither e victims' flesh. However, a theory recent-announced by Interpol throws a new spin n the Mutant X manhunt.

Detective Chief Inspector Roger Llewellyn, otland Yard's liaison to Interpol, revealed n Tuesday that the Mutant X Joint Task orce is now pursuing the theory that the llings may be the work of a fugitive Sapien

Surveillance photo of **DR. MOIRA MACTAGGERT,** courtesy of Interpol.

scientist with a well-established bias against Mutantkind. Scottish geneticist Moira MacTaggert was among the first scientists to recognize the ascendancy of mutants and rapid decline of the Sapien population. Rather than accept this natural step in human evolution, MacTaggert spoke at several international genetics symposiums

arguing the need for what she termed a "cure for the mutant condition." Of course, the mainstream scientific community rejected Doctor MacTaggert's work and all her funding was rescinded, but she continued seeking a way to curtail the spectacular rise in human mutation that characterized the past century. When Parliament passed legislation making her research illegal, MacTaggert fled her home and laboratory on Muir Isle and has remained a fugitive ever since. She is on Interpol's Most Wanted listings and Sentinel patrols across Europe have her features programmed into their active recognition systems. Still, MacTaggert eludes capture.

Interpol and Scotland Yard now fear that the emaciated corpses are not, as was previously believed, evidence of a flesh-wasting mutant ability. Rather, they speculate that the horrific deaths may be the result of MacTaggert's genetic "cure." Sadly, this dangerously misguided genius may have convinced herself that the only remedy for Sapien decline is the murder of innocent mutants. (Continued in *Exiles #69-71*)

THE SHALLOW END OF THE GENE POOL?

By Dr. Henry Pym—
Special to Scientific American

the world of biogenetics, Nathanial Essex both rock star and pariah. He is the rock ar whose years-long drug binge has left m a shell of the performer he once was, grudgingly respected, but with more than hint of regret. He is a pariah whose ever-calating theories on the acceleration and sultant gentrification of the Homo Mutatis ne pool has made him untouchable among ademic circles.

ttle is known about his whereabouts, less out his activities. For the first time in ten years, ssex has made a public entreaty, contacting is writer after he'd read my report in the ew England Journal of Medicine concerning e possibilities of cellular miniaturization as pertains to the agricultural fields, as well as pulation control and military applications.

ssex did not speak with me for very long, and e divulged little of what he had been doing for e last decade, but he did say that my theories ere proof of his long-held belief that Homo piens deserved "the opportunity of natural ogression as well as that of natural selection." ong derided for his convictions that Homo utatis proliferated across the planet at a r faster pace than natural evolution should ve allowed or would have preferred, Essex

DR. NATHANIAL ESSEX gives a lecture in Prague last September.

had been ostracized by the political pressure brought upon him by the mutant majority. He has made discreet congratulatory gestures to any humans he feels have "reached above and beyond their meager means."

I assume that, according to him, I made big strides with my theories on little things. In our brief conversation, I tried to get Essex to open up, talk about what he had been working on during his long isolation, but the most he would give me was a very cryptic, "The world will see in about eighteen years. Maturity and greatness can not be rushed. It must be

attained through age and experience."

With that, Essex hung up the phone, and before I called the editors of this publication to offer my experiences, I sat there for a few minutes, thinking about the fact that the biogenetics equivalent of Einstein had just made a call to me as casually as if he'd called for Domino's take-out. Underlying the thrill and uncertainty surrounding our brief conversation was also a nagging concern... a fear that had crawled down my spine with every one of Essex's whispered words.

I wondered what he had been doing for the last ten years, wondered why we would have to wait eighteen more years to find out. And I wondered if the greatness that man could achieve might not also quite possibly be a threat to all life on Earth. I feared that the madness of the rock star and the isolation of the pariah had turned Essex into something very different, something almost…sinister.

Whatever he had planned, I suspect the ego he wields and the rejection he obviously nurtures will lead Essex into trying to discover, or create, the next step in genetic evolution. Something greater than Homo Sapiens, beyond Homo Mutatis. Something new, some kind of link between the two, a lifeline, a cable leading to something…better? (Continued in *Cable and Deadpool #17*)

GREEN GOBLIN: SPIDEY'S 'A GOOD KID'

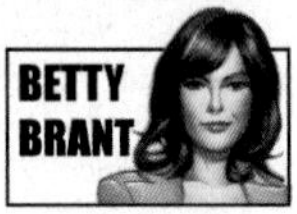
BETTY
BRANT

Joe "Crusher" Hogan remembers the night the skinny teenage boy hobbled into the Madison Square Garden wrestling ring. "He weighed about 10 pounds, and he was so uncoordinated I thought he'd trip over the ropes. Then there was his get-up; he had, like, a fishnet stocking on his face. The crowd laughed like crazy, and I couldn't help it, I laughed too. But I always felt bad about the whole 'Beat Crusher and win $300' contest. This kid especially, he looked like he really needed money, but all he'd get by wrestling me was a hospital bed."

Peter Parker, the Amazing Spider-Man, ended up with quite a lot of money. In the guise of the Green Goblin, Parker's favorite wrestling opponent, Hogan has done very well, too. But first "Crusher" had to undergo an astonishing public humiliation. "When he kicked my butt in the ring, nobody could believe it. How'd this little drink of water get so strong and so fast? I didn't know anything about mutants back then. But he sure taught me." Hogan returned the favor, training the rookie to compete professionally in the fledgling World Wrestling Alliance. "Best bet I ever made. He put the Alliance on the map, he put me on the map. And no matter how big he gets in Hollywood, or with his businesses, he never forgets us. He did a match with me just last month, and you know he doesn't have to, with all his money. He's just always been a good kid."

In giving Parker all of the credit for his success, Hogan glosses over his own talents. He was always a tough, athletic competitor, and his theatrical skills blossomed as Spider-Man's darkly villainous wrestling foe. "We were always a good fit. Spidey's so fun-loving with the wisecracks and all, and he encouraged me to go over the top with Goblin. Bad as I could be. Of course he designed the suit—he's good at that, you know, and he gave me the name and all. I'm just lucky. He walked into the ring that first night."

Has Spidey encouraged the Goblin to follow in his Hollywood footsteps? "Oh yeah, he's been great. He got me into that zombie picture a few years ago"—Hogan is referring to the straight-to-video Bloodbath of the Flesh-Eaters—"and I had a lot of trouble learning the lines, so they cut my part down a lot. Wrestling as the Goblin is acting, but there's not a lot of reading to it, you know? So it's better."

Of course, athletic careers don't last forever. When asked if he harbors any post-wrestling plans, Hogan's expression turns serious.

"I might run for governor." (Continued in *Spider-man: House of M #1-5*)

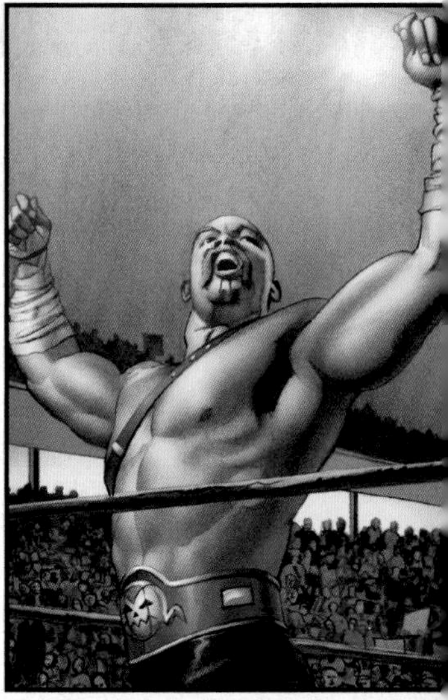

JOE "CRUSHER" HOGAN revels in victory after a matc

DRAGONS OVER CHI-TOWN AND STARK TRIUMPHANT
THE SAPIEN DEATH MATCH SEASON OPENER

By Flash Thompson

Season X of Sapien Death Match launched last night in Chicago with reigning champ and fan fave Tony Stark racking up another win, mangling MBC Productions' latest robo terror and pulverizing three challengers in the final round of one-on-one combat.

Fifteen armored gladiators entered the arena for the evening's first round of action. Within two minutes, the field had narrowed to seven. Clark, Benson, and Chang detonated land mines the instant they touched ground. At least they can tell the grandkids they set foot onto the arena of champions—just barely! Mendoza and Grierson succumbed to the usual volley of heat-seeking missiles while Takahashi and Ellison had the unfortunate luck to be standing behind Heavy-S when his suit's pulse cannon backfired.

Critics have long groused about the rapidity of the first round melee—with so much action so quickly in every corner of the field, it's hard to absorb and particularly disappointing for supporters of obscure up-and-comers who fall within seconds. But fans in the cheap seats love the grand sweep of those first few seconds of chaos. And you gotta love a sport which breaks it all down so fast, immediately culling the field of stragglers so that the true glory of great combat can shine—as it did last night in Round Two.

MBC Productions spent the off-season hyping the rumor mills about the mind-blowing new robos they'd be sending against this year's Sapien gladiators. I'll admit I was one of those who nodded cynically and said, "Yeah, another big tank, whatever." But this reporter's mouth literally fell open when the giant robo dragon descended from the skies at the top of Round Two.

Easily fifty feet long, the sinuous machine moved with the agility and speed of a flying cobra as it advanced on the gladiators. The stands rattled with chants of "Tony, Tony!" But Stark held back, observing as young Johnny Storm took the first shot against the beast. Developed in China by Triple F Industries, the dragon has been touted as the most advanced piece of large-scale robotics ever deployed outside of the military or aerospace industries. Maybe Tony was slipping into his day job as president of Stark Industries, taking notes on a competitor's product. Or maybe he's just smart. Because it was Johnny Storm who took the brunt of the dragon's surprise attack—gouts of fire from its mouth and nose, which dwarfed Storm's own flame-based weaponry and knocked the promising young gladiator out of the evening's fight.

While the dragon busied itself with dismantli O'Finley, Bates, and Habima, Stark formed a tempor battlefield alliance with Chin, F-Trane, and Skipper begin coordinated waves of attacks against the bea vulnerable joints, culminating in a blinding explosion, t glow from which Indiana residents report seeing on t horizon fifty miles away.

In the final round of individual combat, Stark quic trounced Chin and Skipper. F-Trane managed a handful interesting evasive moves and launched a surprise volley concussion grenades, but ran out of new tricks when Sta caught him by the scruff of the neck and put him out the night. (Continued in *Iron Man: House of M #1-3*)

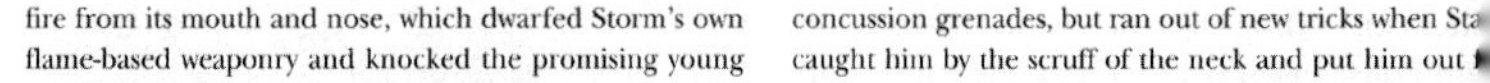
SHIELD

TONY STARK battles a bionic dragon in Sapien Death Match this season on MBC.

STORM CLOUDS OVER AFRICA

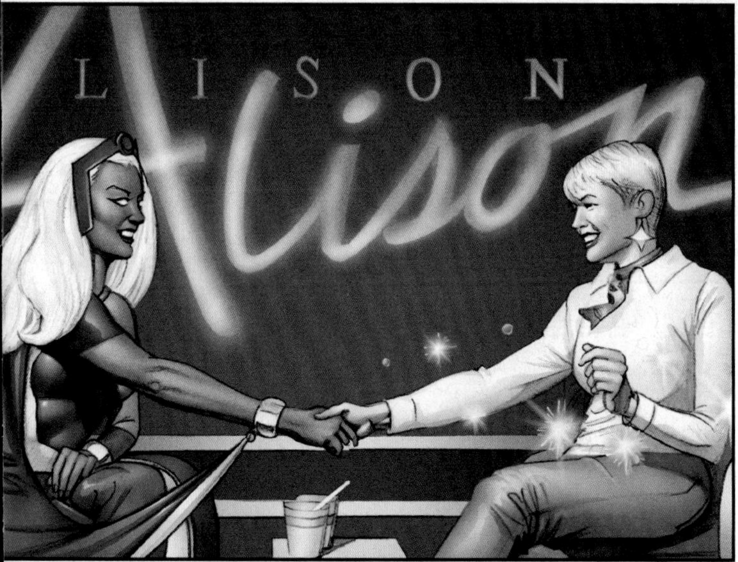
LISON
Alison

AZZLING STORM - Ororo Munroe visits the Alison Blaire show yesterday.

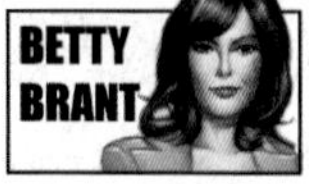
BETTY
BRANT

Of all the lands that have benefited from Magneto's reign, the continent of Africa has benefited the most. Under mutant control, poverty and pestilence have been replaced with abundance and a higher standard of living than ever before.

But on the popular ALISON show yesterday, Queen Ororo of Kenya hinted of political upheaval in the region's future. In an exchange that accused Magneto of racial bias, she seemed to ally herself with The Black Panther, the human leader of Wakanda, one of the last regions under human control.

The Black Panther has long been suspected of harboring human terrorists, but so far has upheld the terms of the non-aggression pact his father signed decades ago.

The question is, will Apocalypse, the Magneto loyalist who rules Northern Africa, be forced to intercede if weapons of mutant destruction are found on Wakandan soil? Weapons inspector Sabretooth is being dispatched today. His meeting with The Black Panther will decide whether a larger military intervention is necessary. (Continued in *Black Panther* #7)

FACE DOWN IN THE GUTTER

LL THE GOSSIP THAT'S UNFIT TO PRINT FROM DICK "IS THAT A PISTOL IN YOUR POCKET OR ARE YOU JUST GLAD TO- OH IT IS A PISTOL" JONSTON

'he hottest ticket in town this week had to be he premiere of "Let's Make Love — Again," he first of two back-to-back Marilyn Monroe emakes from the Kaufman Studio. So was he repeat experience a night to remember? Iore of an anti-climax, according to movie ritics, including our own Paul Cale who ommented acidly, "The face may be right ut behind the glamorous illusion, the acting as dead as the real Norma Jean. Frankly I'd refer a CGI Monroe with a voice-over."

But that won't stop the punters from ocking to multiplexes across the country, nd in the words of Daniel "Shaky" Kaufman: Butts on seats count for more than a bunch f awards from some cruddy Film Festival in lowheresville, France."

So once again, box-office gold for the self-nointed King of Hollywood and his fourth ife, Lara the Illusionist. Among the A-list elebs who flocked to the après film soirée t Kaufman's "Inferno" club were Tony "The on Man" Stark, recently voted most eligible apien Bachelor by our very own readers, ho arrived in the company of the wonderful Iary Jane Watson; Alison Blaire, dazzling the ssembled paparazzi in a revealing creation om Janet Van Dyne; Simon Williams whose mo arrived only minutes before Carol Danvers – a less than successful attempt to scotch rumors of a relationship. The two were spotted later by yours truly, canoodling in a most unplatonic fashion in a secluded corner of the club.

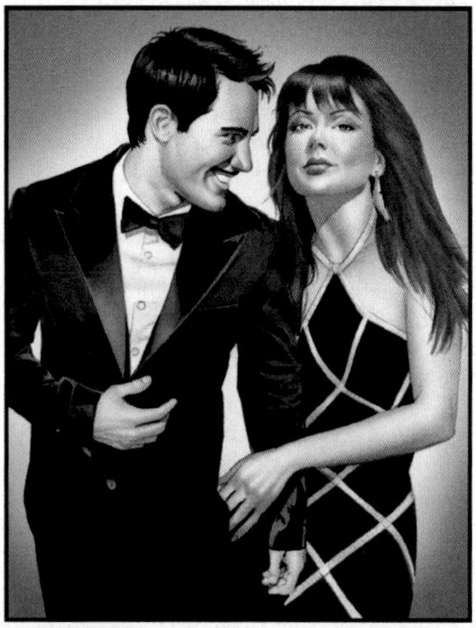

TONY STARK escorts MARY JANE WATSON down the red carpet.

A late arrival was Warren Worthington III, looking to these eyes, a little unsteady on his feet. WWIII received an unexpected champagne toast from the only real royalty present at the shindig, when Ororo Munroe upended her drink over the unfortunate Mr. Worthington. Was it something he said? Whatever happened between them, I'm reliably informed that Mr. Worthington was accompanied all the way home by his own private rain cloud.

And my own weather forecast for the week? More stormy weather ahead, when Jazz-E-Jazz hits town with a private performance to celebrate the climax of his "Kind of Blue" World Tour. The Jazzy One is planning to partaayy like it's 1999 all over again and the guest list is guaranteed to send the sparks flying. Shaky Kaufman and Filthy Frankie Zapruder in the same room? You heard it here first. The last time these two business rivals shared the same air, Shaky's personal bodyguard, Jimmy Damiano, known as "Mr. Punch," went down in a hail of bullets. Although charges were never pressed against Zapruder, Kaufman is thought to have sworn revenge for the death of his "best and most loyal friend." So what I'd like to know is—Where can I hire a bulletproof tux?

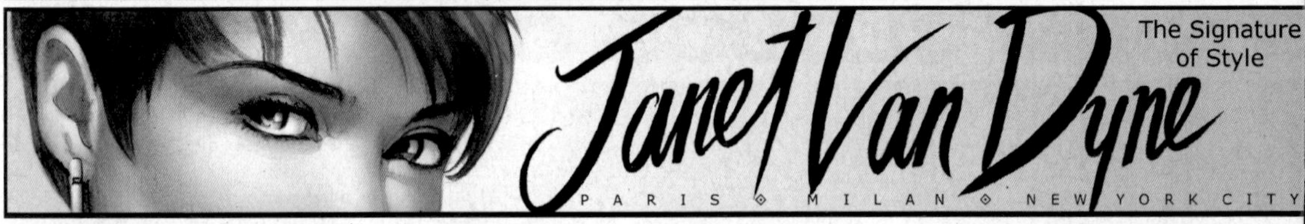
Janet Van Dyne
The Signature of Style
PARIS ◊ MILAN ◊ NEW YORK CITY

THREE PHASES TOWARDS SUCCESS: POPULAR PSYCHOLOGIST HAS TRADED A GOVERNMENT JOB FOR TEACHING GIG

One year ago, anyone watching the dealings of the House Of Magnus would have pegged Sean Garrison as the next Press Secretary for the world's ruling family. But one year ago, few people knew that Garrison had a higher priority: his daughter's education.

Dr. Garrison has written five best-selling novels on how to achieve your dreams. His term, "The Three Phases Towards Success," has entered the vernacular and become almost a cliché. His three steps are simple. First Phase: Decide what you really want to be. Second Phase: Eliminate obstacles towards your success. Third Phase: Become what you want to be. As anyone who's watched Garrison (or "Dr. Sean," as the faithful call him) on his television show knows, the trick is the First Phase. What do you want to be?

For Garrison, that seemed straightforward. A man known to the world as a trustworthy friend, his pheromone powers can put anyone at ease. Yet his ability to communicate was not just the product of his impressive mutant abilities. People feel strongly about Garrison watching him on TV, or reading his book–media that his pheromones could never affect. When Magneto needed a new spokesman, there seemed no better man for the job.

But Garrison is also a father. His fifteen-year-old daughter, Laurie, was invited to join the prestigious New Mutant Leadership Institute in New York, a training center for the next generation of mutant leaders. To be close with Laurie (who shares his mutant gifts), Garrison took a faculty position at the Institute, declining the job as Press Secretary.

When Dr. Garrison was young and newly famous, he became involved with a fan—a Sapien fan. She became pregnant with his child, and ran off. Gail Collins attempted to keep Garrison from knowing he was a father, and tried to raise Laurie as a baseline human.

The police tracked Ms. Collins down. The resulting standoff made the evening news for three nights running. Many feared Collins would take her own life, and perhaps Laurie's as well. But Garrison arrived on the scene, and, despite Collins' newfound immunity to his powers (the result of her pregnancy), talked her down. Collins went into a mental institution. And Garrison became a single father.

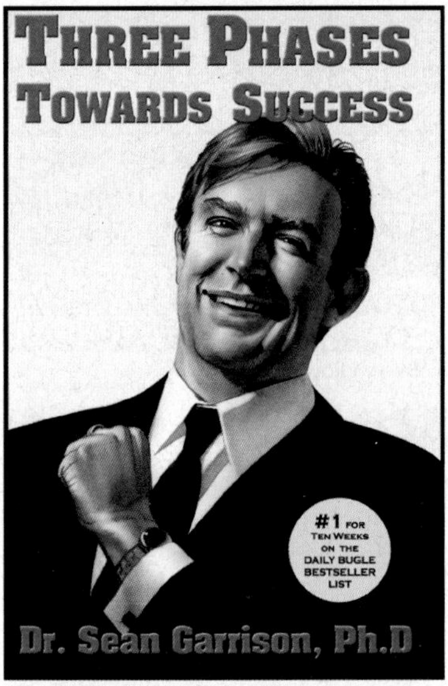
THREE PHASES
TOWARDS SUCCESS
#1 FOR TEN WEEKS ON THE DAILY BUGLE BESTSELLER LIST
Dr. Sean Garrison, Ph.D

DR. SEAN GARRISON'S latest bestselling book.

Despite her public coming-out, Laurie has been shielded from the spotlight. But the Institute trains leaders, so her father felt the time had come for Laurie to be the focus.

When asked if he regrets going to the Institute, Garrison is unequivocal. "Never. Laurie and I are close. We talk daily. I'm helping her to achieve her Three Phases. That, in turn, is the greatest success a man can ask for."

As for those who say a government job would better suit him, he has only this to say: "I still have friends in the government. When Laurie's dreams are achieved, it'll be my turn. You'll hear from me again." (Continued in *New X-Men #16-19*)

CAN YOU GUARANTEE THAT YOUR BABY WILL BE A MUTANT?

- HoM Scientists say that to increase chances of Mutant Birth, ambient temperature of the mother's home should remain at exactly 68 degrees.
- Stay away from organic vegetables. Produce treated with MGH encourages healthy gene stock.
- There is always a chance that a child will be born with the X-Gene, but that chance increases when one or more parents are Meta-Humans. (This means you, Wonder-Man and Captain Marvel!) ...and is almost guaranteed when one or both parents are Homo-Superior.

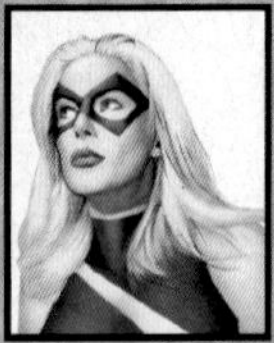

- Some happy mutant-mamas claim a daily prayer to the mythical Apocalypse can be a boon.
- If all else fails, pro-Sapien regimes like that of Latveria regularly put mutants up for international adoption.
- Don't filter your water—various environmental factors, while increasing the chance of bacteria and viruses, can also have positive effects on the human genome.
- While it is not strictly considered a mutation, exposing your children to: gamma radiation, cosmic rays, the power cosmic, vats of strange chemicals or the bite of an irradiated animal can make your child a meta-human, and as they say, "Metas better than Not-a!"
- House of M Sponsored Fertility clinics can, for a price, make use of the genetic donations of all types of mutants. Increase your chances of raising a Flyer!
- Although most likely unattainable by most of our readers, it has been said that a blessing from Lord Magnus himself, with his constant magnetic field, can act as the catalyst for children still in the womb.